Sämi Ludwig, Nicoleta Alexoae-Zagni (eds.)

The Legacy of Maxine Hong Kingston

Contributions to Asian American Literary Studies

edited by

Rocío G. Davis
and
Sämi Ludwig
(Université de Haute-Alsace Mulhouse)

Volume 7

LIT

The Legacy of Maxine Hong Kingston
The Mulhouse Book

edited by

Sämi Ludwig and Nicoleta Alexoae-Zagni

CONTRIBUTIONS TO
ASIAN AMERICAN
LITERARY STUDIES

LIT

Cover design: Rudolf Ammann

Photograph: courtesy of Random House Publishers

This book is printed on acid-free paper.

Bibliographic information published by the Deutsche Nationalbibliothek
The Deutsche Nationalbibliothek lists this publication in the Deutsche Nationalbibliografie; detailed bibliographic data are available in the Internet at http://dnb.d-nb.de.

ISBN 978-3-643-90299-3

A catalogue record for this book is available from the British Library

Klosbachstr. 107
CH-8032 Zürich
Tel. +41 (0) 44-251 75 05
Fax +41 (0) 44-251 75 06
E-Mail: zuerich@lit-verlag.ch
http://www.lit-verlag.ch

LIT VERLAG Dr. W. Hopf
Berlin 2014
Fresnostr. 2
D-48159 Münster
Tel. +49 (0) 2 51-62 03 20
Fax +49 (0) 2 51-23 19 72
E-Mail: lit@lit-verlag.de
http://www.lit-verlag.de

Distribution:
In Germany: LIT Verlag Fresnostr. 2, D-48159 Münster
Tel. +49 (0) 2 51-620 32 22, Fax +49 (0) 2 51-922 60 99, E-mail: vertrieb@lit-verlag.de

In Austria: Medienlogistik Pichler-ÖBZ, e-mail: mlo@medien-logistik.at
In the UK: Global Book Marketing, e-mail: mo@centralbooks.com
In North America: International Specialized Book Services, e-mail: orders@isbs.com
e-books are available at www.litwebshop.de

Acknowledgements

A warm thank-you goes to all the people who have made this project a success, starting from our generous peer reviewers, Rocío Davis, Helena Grice, and Pin-chia Feng, who have given their time and shared their insights with the editors. Among the volunteers and civil servants who helped organize the memorable event in Mulhouse, we merely mention Régine Margraff, who coordinated a wonderful team of student helpers, and the non-pareil Mme Souki of the faculty accounting office of the FLSH at the Université de Haute Alsace, who led us through the maze of French financial regulations and never lost her patience with the local Swiss organizer. We also received outstanding support from the Dean of the Faculté des Langues et Sciences Sociales, Yann Kerdiles, who even contributed a Breton poem to the conference, and from our Ecole Doctorale 520 Humanités and its director, Michel Faure. The most important practical support, however, came from Peter Schnyder. As president of ILLE EA 4363, the local research institute on European languages and literatures, he subsidized a big part of this event, including the publication you are holding in your hands, and helped us get in contact with all the crucial institutions which co-financed the rest: the Conseil Général du Haut-Rhin, the Conseil Régional d'Alsace, and the Conseil Scientifique of the UHA. We also received the predicate "Label EUCOR" and generous donations from the trinational confederation of the Upper Rhine Universities (i.e., Strasbourg, Freiburg/Br., Mulhouse, Basel), a solid contribution from the very supportive American Embassy in Paris, and some free books from Kingston's publisher, Random House.

Mulhouse and Paris, September 2013 Sämi Ludwig & Nicoleta Alexoae-Zagni

Table of Contents

Introduction: On the Excitement of Academic Gatherings 11
Sämi Ludwig and *Nicoleta Alexoae-Zagni*

Opening Speech 21
Maxine Hong Kingston

I. Revisiting the canonical texts,
The Woman Warrior and *China Men*

The Politics of Transnational Identity
in and of Maxine Hong Kingston's *The Woman Warrior* 33
Silvia Schultermandl

Critical Reception in the Cultural 'Homeland':
Maxine Hong Kingston's *The Woman Warrior* in China 45
Lan Dong

Maxine Hong Kingston's *Woman Warrior*
Beyond the Feminine and the Unfeminine:
Dismantling the Dualistic Perception of Gender and Ethnicity 61
Nelly Mok

Masks and Identity: Self-Fashioning in Chinese American
Children's and Young Adult Literature 77
Pin-chia Feng

Claiming America Through Land Empathy:
An Ecocritical Approach to Maxine Hong Kingston's *China Men* 95
Begoña Simal

On Maxine Hong Kingston's Manuscript Revisions
of *The Woman Warrior* and *China Men*: An Anecdotal Account 113
Cheng Lok Chua

Between Postmodernity and Taoist Beliefs: 125
Metamorphosis in "On Discovery" by Maxine Hong Kingston
Marie-Claude Perrin-Chenour

Born Among Ghosts: 133
Maxine Hong Kingston's *The Woman Warrior* as Asian American Gothic
Sean Mattio

Do Ghosts Grow Up? 147
Ghostliness in Maxine Hong Kingston's *The Woman Warrior*
and China Men
Janna Odabas

II. On less frequently discussed and recent texts

'I'll be a Skylark': 163
Maxine Hong Kingston's Confessional Poetics in *To Be the Poet*
Eulalia Piñero-Gil

Maxine Hong Kingston as Counterculture Writer 173
Agnieszka Soltysik Monnet

Maxine Hong Kingston's Peace Activism: Taking Stock 193
Christine Lorre-Johnston

The 'Engaged Aesthetics' of 207
Maxine Hong Kingston's *Fifth Book of Peace*
John Whalen-Bridge

Out of the 'Chinese' Box: 'Literary' Life Writing in 215
Maxine Hong Kingston's Tripmaster Monkey and The Fifth Book of Peace
Manuela Vastolo

"How does a writer write something true and permanent when events 225
are happening all over the place, and destruction is happening?":
Sanctuary in Hawai'i: a dramatic reading of three—plus Q&A
Maxine Hong Kingston, Earll Kingston, and *Buff Parry*

III. Parallel readings

… Because Violence Is Real: 239
Ishmael Reed, Maxine Kingston and the Case of Postmodern Referentiality
Sämi Ludwig

Surviving the Loss: Abjection and Hypochondria in 263
Maxine Hong Kingston's *The Woman Warrior* and Fae Myenne Ng's *Bone*
Anna Pehkoranta

Maxine Hong Kingston's *The Woman Warrior* in Fatima Mernissi's 277
Dreams of Trespass: A Legacy of Genre/Gender Transgression
Sihem Arfaoui Abidi

IV. Kingston's influence—between paying homage and experiencing an 'anxiety of influence'

Self-Referential Narrative and Creative Filiation in 297
Chinese American Writing: Maxine Hong Kingston and Shirley Geok-lin Lim
Nicoleta Alexoae-Zagni

Staying Alive: 313
Maxine Hong Kingston's *Woman Warrior* Afterlife and
Marilyn Chin's *Revenge of the Mooncake Vixen*
Sau-ling Cynthia Wong

Notes on Contributors 343

Introduction: On the Excitement of Academic Gatherings

Sämi Ludwig (UHA Mulhouse, France) and
Nicoleta Alexoae-Zagni (ISTOM and Université Paris Ouest, Nanterre, France)

At the beginning of this book is a Christmas letter, or rather, a response from Maxine Hong Kingston in the form of a card for the Chinese New Year, in which she offered to visit France again, after she had been invited by AFEA, the association of the French Americanists, to their annual meeting in Besançon and obviously had enjoyed that visit. She even suggested further contacts in France, which is how the two editors of this book met. We quickly decided that if we can have Maxine and Earll Kingston in town for a visit, we might as well tell our friends and organize a real conference. The response to our CFP was overwhelming. Everybody wanted to come to Mulhouse, that modest town in provincial southeastern France. Finally, we had a very healthy mix ranging from graduate student to senior professor, a forum where the debate, the shared knowledge and interest in Kingston's work were in the foreground, rather than academic stature.

They flew in from all corners of the world. Four continents and fifteen countries were represented: all of Europe, the U.S, Canada, Tunisia, far-east Asia. Last minute arrivals from Singapore and jet-lagged stragglers from Taiwan flew around the globe—just for a three-day conference at a cold time of the year in a grey, postindustrial town! The biggest surprise was when we received an email from one of Kingston's fictional characters, who offered to participate:

> Buff Parry <info@louisbuffparry.com>
> Symposium in honor of Maxine Hong Kingston
> 14. February 2011 22:57
>
> Dear Samuel Ludwig,
> I have only recently found in Maxine Hong Kingston's book, *The Fifth Book of Peace*, some 50 pages about me. She copyrighted this book in 2003. My account begins on page 194 of the 2004 First Vintage International Edition. She biographed something I did in late 1969, in this book. I am very interested in discussing this with her, particularly at the symposium in her honor March 18 - 20, 2011, at U of Mulhouse in Alsace, France. Could you do two things for me? First, forward this email to her so I can communicate with her directly; and second, send me info on the symposium. Since my life is detailed throughout over 15% of her book, I think it time for she and I to meet, wouldn't you say? My name, as she gave it in the book, is Louis D. Buffy

Perry. Today I am simply Buff Parry (she spelled my last name incorrectly). I know she will be pleased that I found her and wish to share more of the story. Thank you for your attention to these questions.
With the best,
Louis Buff Parry
Ph: 780-429-2378
email: info@louisbuffparry.com
Edmonton, Alberta, Canada
T5K 0Z4

Buff Parry added a postmodern dimension to our experience. Like others, he was picked up at Basel-Mulhouse Airport and joined the celebration. His dramatic reading of key sections from *The Fifth Book of Peace* together with Maxine and Earll Kingston turned out to be one of the highlights of the reunion. The three poems he contributed are printed in this volume.

It is in particular this performative part of the event that we also want to share with the photographs and video clips in our book's DVD. Conferences are personal. They make encounters possible. They associate prose (and even poetry) with people rather than reducing letters to the white page and formalist impersonal origins. Because we are unabashed supporters of this format, we go against the grain of most academic publishers nowadays, who look down on conference volumes. This is why we call it *The Mulhouse Book*. The chronotope is real. Time and place matter. They provide a particular intersection that can be very productive. Our book is the result of such an event. This does not mean that it is a comprehensive account of everything that was said there or some kind of mechanical recording of conference procedures. We pruned some of the oral statements. And we were selective with the material and submitted it to a set of peer-reviewers. As a result, we left out some submissions and we added others, by authors who have not been in Mulhouse, or who were unfortunately kept from coming (like Sau-ling Wong or Pin-chia Feng). And in some cases, we regret not having received a written version of the paper …

This book also testifies to a particular conference format because it focuses on a particular author. We were lucky to have Maxine Hong Kingston and her husband Earll among us and to get much information straight form the 'horse's mouth'. Both Maxine and Earll Kingston contributed some enlightening information on her oeuvre, the kind of source material that delights every Kingstonian. We think they enjoyed the contact and we are still grateful for the visit! But there is yet another point about this format: when a conference is well-focused and everybody knows the material well, the level of discussion will be much more intense. The dialogue may be about nitty-gritty details that everybody can relate to. Thus the attention always goes back from a theoretical angle to the original texts, which don't have to pay second fiddle to overarching conceptualizations or critical models that often appropriate academic debates when the variety of materials discussed is too big and/or merely topical, and the only point that the participants have in common is theory. In Mulhouse we got a taste of something real and we are glad that now we can share it.

Our collection opens with Maxine Kingston's opening speech, in with she announced that this was the first conference ever exclusively devoted to herself and her work … a surprising fact, considering that Kingston is the world's most taught living author at the university level. Her account is a compelling statement on the beginning of Asian American studies and her first contact with critics in Hawai'i: "All these words were brand new. There was no such thing as Asian American. It was all being invented." She elaborates on all kinds of debates ("a literary brawl, a fight") and focuses on orality and talk-story: "… when you take text you can examine it and it doesn't change, but talk-story changes. It changes from one speaker to another and from one listener to another." Kingston also discusses dialect, poetry, and her peace work. As for discoveries, don't forget to check out her memorable discussion of the Burlingame Treaty of 1868!

The critical essays start with a first section that revisits the two canonical texts *The Woman Warrior* and *China Men* and frequently discussed sections or themes through innovative theoretical perspectives. Silvia Schultermandl opens the debate with a discussion of "The Politics of Transnational Identity in and of *The Woman Warrior*," arguing that Kingston's first book "anticipates contemporary trends in the scholarship of the transnational" and "complicates the ways in which we regard identity in American literature." She argues that

> [f]or *The Woman Warrior*, transnationalism is thus an issue both on the level of the identity negotiations the protagonist claims for herself as well as for the identity negotiations global reading audiences assign to the protagonist / the text in general. It is not only the identity politics implied in Maxine's delineating of a transnational matrilineage which inform her own sense of self that make The Woman Warrior a transnational text […], but also the cultural conversations with their multiplicitous reading audiences.

Her piece is followed by Lan Dong's survey on the critical reception of *The Woman Warrior* in mainland China, which started fairly late compared with other discussions of Kingston outside of the United States in Europe or Taiwan, for example. She observes, however, that

> [d]uring the past decade or so, studies on Chinese American literature in general and on Kingston in particular have been fast growing in Chinese academia in the form of conferences, master's and doctoral theses, publication of journal articles, book chapters, and book-length manuscripts, adoption of related topics and texts in curricula, as well as the establishment and development of centers for Chinese American Studies at various universities.

Dong finds feminist perspectives, postcolonial perspectives, and, most interesting, comparative perspectives in which Kingston is compared with Chinese authors such as Lu Xun, Cao Yu or Anyi Wang!

Nelly Mok dismantles the dualistic perception of gender and ethnicity in *The Woman Warrior* "beyond the feminine and unfeminine" and explores "the ways Kingston questions the Western perception of the Asian woman and Asian femininity, upsetting the Orientalist stereotypes attributed to her sex and to her race." She points out the ways in which "the author succeeds in delineating a new, complex Chinese American female figure, without the boundaries of gender and race categories, thus providing the Chinese/Asian American community with a global imprint." In her thorough discussion, Mok focuses among other things on issues of Bhabha's distinction between 'imitation' and 'mimicry', which interestingly echo Butler's difference between 'performance' and 'performativity'. She finds that "Kingston clearly discards unfemininity as the locus for the Chinese American woman's emancipation from patriarchal stereotypes, rather pointing to the superficiality of gender role reversal," and concludes that "the author makes the anti-essentialist claim that the Chinese American woman's integrity lies in paradoxes and can be recovered only in her de-essentialized (self-) perception."

Pin-chia Feng provides an insightful analysis of self-fashioning in Chinese American children's and young adult literature. She observes a strategy of "some Chinese American writers [...] to reverse negative stereotyping by creating positive masks or personae of their choices in order to facilitate self-fashioning." Rather than being a simplistic evasion of problems, however, this strategic deployment of masking enables Chinese American writers "to revisit stereotypical representations of Chinese Americans and to construct an identity for the young protagonists with which readers can identify." Feng compares the child protagonist in *Woman Warrior* with young adult characters in Bette Bao and Laurence Yep through a timespan which covers seven decades and three generations of Chinese American lives. Beyond the rich cultural insights, she emphasizes the humanistic vision.

A new take on *China Men* is presented in Begoña Simal's ecocritical reading of Kingston's second novel. Observing that "her books have rarely been explored from an ecocritical point of view," Simal offers a whole series of convincing examples, noting that "an ecocritical reading of *China Men* arguably complicates and transforms the cultural nationalist paradigm known as the 'claiming of America.'" One important point in this new project is empathy. Tracing the experiences of the fathers and grandfathers in Kingston, Simal notes that "not only do we have to grasp our biotic interdependence intellectually, we also need to take it in at an emotional level: we must learn to feel an integral part of that biotic community, and the characters in *China Men* successfully do so by attributing human features and 'interiority' to the non-human Other." She concludes that "the characters in *China Men* eventually move away from proprietorial understandings of land and towards an egalitarian bond with the natural environment."

C. Lok Chua offers a very new perspective to Kingston criticism in his detailed analysis of revisions of key parts of *The Woman Warrior* and *China Men*, based on his consultation of Kingston's manuscript materials in the Bancroft Library at the University of California, Berkeley. He comments, not without irony: "One wonders about the losses to this field of scholarship now that writers are composing more frequently on computers." Not only does Chua find "sites of contestation between Kingston and her editors" that "provide revealing glimpses into Kingston's political, ethnic, and historical self-positioning," but he gives very insightful readings on the detailed revisions dealing with topics, vocabulary, and sentence structure applied to the ending of *The Woman Warrior* and the beginning of *China Men*: "[D]etails are being added during the revision process that render the sensory descriptions palpably more vivid; and the narrative mode of the episode also changes in the revisions, as do the narrative strategy and the narrative voice." Not surprisingly, Chua concludes that "Kingston is a meticulous crafter of words and a dedicated winnower of details—an exacting literary artist who chooses the most strategic turns of phrase to create a narrative persona and who sifts through to the most precise nuggets of imagery to make her readers experience the exquisite piercing of a body part or the ache of bending a bone in the foot."

Marie-Claude Perrin-Chenour also discusses "On Discovery." She looks at it as a liminal text between the two books and focuses on "the concept of metamorphosis, not only in the diegesis and the writing of the text, but also in the performative impact it can have on the reader," noticing that

> [g]ender-switching at the core of this story does not reinforce the narrative's ability to serve as a frame for self-aggrandizing values (such as courage, cunning or cleverness) as it does in the Fa Mulan warrior legend. Quite on the contrary, the reversal of roles acts as a distancing device whose purpose is to put into relief the constricting frames within which women find themselves entrapped willingly or unconsciously.

Triggering empathy, Tang Ao's experience is "equated to a process of degradation that could happen to anyone (of any gender) and which is particularly frightening because it is rapidly internalized by the people who are submitted to it, so that their final transformation is not only physical but also psychological." Thus "metamorphosis in 'On Discovery' has not the same positive impact on the character as Fa Mulan's cross-dressing and code-switching." Many of Perrin-Chenour's insights are based on the essays of François Cheng, the famous Chinese-French philosopher, essayist, novelist and poet.

The first section of this collection concludes with two discussions of Kingston's *ghosts*. First Sean Mattio gives a reading of *The Woman Warrior* that feeds into the field of the "Asian American Gothic." Starting from the work of Andrew Ng and his claim that "just as the Gothic has always been regarded as subsidiary to the dominant discourse, so is Asian American literature written against the prevailing ideology of the American literary catalog," Mattio claims that the "ghosts" of Kingston's subtitle "and the narrative's other Gothic features come to inform and express the anxieties of the Chinese-American woman, revealing the potential for a splintering of the self." He uses Freud's notion of the "Uncanny" and transgenerational trauma studies to make a case that "the transmission of narrative memory, or family stories, [...] reveal unresolved trauma," pointing out a "transgenerational legacy of repression [...] symptomatic of a patriarchal system." According to Mattio, Kingston's telling of the stories is a ritual that "transforms the dead from menacing ghosts to beneficent ancestral spirits, rendering them safely accessible."

Jana Odabas' take on the ghosts in Kingston is somewhat different: Asking the question "Do Ghosts Grow Up?," she provides a comparative reading that shows a poignant presence of spectral figures in *China Men* as well! If the narrator grows up, does the notion of ghosts change too? Focusing on "ghostly narration," Odabas finds in the stories of Kingston's fatherly ancestors, for example, a "collage [that] allows the narrator to position herself and her family in a history that emerges from the shadows of the past." But she is also interested in "reading 'against the grain' of Freud's unsuccessful attempt of defining the 'uncanny'" because "the depicted ghosts also promote a reading that troubles a classification into material reality and fantasy" and remain oscillating between the two spheres. After many examples, Odabas concludes that, "while China Men gives room to the stories of the past to create a family history, it constantly questions the reliability of any kind of representation." In that sense, as in *The Woman Warrior*, "ghostly narration" mainly functions "to question stable categories and to highlight troubling or silenced aspects."

After this long visit of the well-known Kingston classics, our collection provides a second section on less frequently discussed and very recent Kingston texts, which tellingly starts with the poetry. Eulalia Piñero Gil discusses Maxine Hong Kingston's confessional poetics in *To Be the Poet*, looking for a yet different autobiographical mode in which Kingston is trying to explore her private and her public life. Poetry offers a new freedom for this. As Piñero Gil states, it "entails for Kingston the opportunity of reinventing new literary ways of expressing her creativity which encompasses the inclusion of her own artwork in her new books. Thus, for the artist writing poetry entails a spontaneous and holistic self-expression that transforms the page into a sort of canvas." Piñero Gil demonstrates in her piece that "*To Be the Poet* is Kingston's mature opportunity for reinvention and liberation from the constraints of prose writing and from the heavy restraints of the narrative genre. She definitively removes the authorial mask of fiction in order to become the protagonist and the speaker of her poetry." It does in that sense mark a turning point in Kingston's career.

In contrast, Agniezska Soltysik is looking at popular culture and at Kingston as a counterculture writer "rooted in the values and vision of the radical movements of the 1960s that she experienced in Berkeley as a young woman." This is a useful "step towards breaking down the barriers within the discipline that keep 'ethnic writers' lumped together and critics focused only on their ethnic or gender identity." Soltysik offers a new angle that explains Kingston's "pacifism, as well as her signature aesthetic choices, including generic hybridity, informal tone, rhetorical playfulness and structural non-linearity." She even compares the experience of the drugged uncle I Fu in *China Men* with Timothy Leary and puts the *Tripmaster* into focus! Hence she suggests: "Kingston should be studied alongside Allen Ginsberg, Lawrence Ferlinghetti and Hunter S. Thompson. Precisely because the so-called hippie movement produced relatively little memorable literature, Kingston cannot be overlooked. Counterculture literature needs its female Chinese Beatnik as much as Asian-American literature needs its hippies and radicals."

Christine Lorre-Johnston picks up some of these vibes, taking stock of Kingston's peace activism, particularly in her last two works, *The Fifth Book of Peace* and *I Love a Broad Margin to My Life*. As she writes, these "later works can be read as books of maturity that celebrate and reflect on the author's lifelong quest for speech, origins and peace. They signal a significant shift in perspective." Lorre-Johnston emphasizes the connectedness of Kingston with American history. She focuses on family and sisterhood, on community and civil religion, and on America as utopia, and elaborates on the many dimensions of Kingston's work "as a teacher and peace activist."

John Whalen-Bridge complements this aspect of Kingston's work with a look at Kingston's engaged aesthetics in *The Fifth Book of Peace*, which he sees as a form of "Engaged Buddhism." He distinguishes this from other kinds of Buddhism by connecting it to literature and art: "Engaged Buddhism is a modern trend primarily known for the integration of political activism with the cultivation of mindfulness." Thus Whalen-Bridge finds "a literary correlative to Engaged Buddhism: the writer cannot settle for a tragic denouement but must keep writing until she finds a happy ending. To Kingston, the separation of fiction and non-fiction is itself a fiction." Or, as he quotes Thich Nhat Hanh, "Suffering is not enough."

Manuela Vastolo takes us back to art (which we haven't really left al all), in her discussion of "'Literary' Life Writing in Maxine Hong Kingston's *Tripmaster Monkey* and *The Fifth Book of Peace*." She investigates Kingston's "conscious use of the conventions of fictional narratives and her challenge to the conventional idea of a fictional plot as a well-built structure leading from a problem to a climax and then to a resolution and a happy ending, as well as the idea of character as a fully-fledged 'human being.'" Thus she takes us beyond formalism by showing that her peace work makes Kingston do nothing less than revise the conventional narratology of plotting and characterization!

This second section ends with a unique presentation done by Maxine and Earll Kingston together with Buff Parry, which started out as a dramatic reading of excerpts from *The Fifth Book of Peace* and ended in a lively discussion. The transcript provides new insights into Kingston's time in Hawaii and how she saw (and sees) herself as a woman writer and peace activist. We learn more about the identity of Wittman as her alter ego and about Kingston's work with the Vietnam veterans. The contribution also includes Buff Parry' observations on the sanctuary at the Church of the Crossroads and two poems which he composed for the occasion of the Mulhouse conference, making reference to the nuclear accident at the Fukushima powerplant and the Arab Spring—two events that were much discussed at the conference. As he states: "And by the way, this is exactly accurate. I mean I know the thing. The fiction stuff keeps coming up. And this is exactly what happened—it's on film."

The third section of this collection proceeds to juxtaposing Kingston's work to other writers that throw new light on specific themes and motifs. Sämi Ludwig finds some common concerns in the fictions of both Kingston and her Berkeley writer colleague Ishmael Reed that involve postmodern referentiality. Though both authors mix fiction and fact, Ludwig shows that there is an intentional target in their prose that is grounded in reality beyond fabulation. He finds in both writers "a more sophisticated kind of 'realism' that does not merely phenomenally collapse sign and thing, representation and object, but tries to navigate this tenuous relationship in more humane ways." Ludwig argues that "Reed and Kingston [...] have never lost sight of reality but instead fought for it. Though much of their discourse is powerfully 'fictional,' its intentional target has always been reality." It is rather the criticism that has celebrated irreverent nonreferentiality. Thus "the fictional nature of Kingston's prose is not its essence but an ancillary function used in order to elucidate a target of historical reality in the writing." Both writers have in common their struggle against violence, be it Reed's fight against racist representations or Kingston's peace work with war veterans.

A theoretically thorough contribution comes from Anna Pehkoranta, who looks at survival and loss in Kingston's *The Woman Warrior* and Fae Myenne Ng's *Bone*. She elaborates that "[l]oss is present in the lives of Kingston's and Ng's characters in numerous ways: as the loss of a love-object or a family member, as a sense of not belonging and as the lack of an integrated sense of self, and in the more abstract form of racial abjection, to name a few." In her detailed analysis, Pehkoranta argues that "these novels effectively challenge the Freudian conception of melancholia as a condition that [...] is characteristic of normative female subjectivity." She finds that the "Chinese American legacy of loss, then, is not simply a negative inheritance, but its expressions, such as

Kingston's and Ng's works, contain transformative power that actively seeks to point out some of the fractures and fissures within the national body that need to be addressed if healing is to be possible." Thus a "language defined by loss, abjection, and melancholia" is counteracted in a "narrative inclined toward self-reflection, active ethical agency, and a relentless quest for personal emancipation."

This is followed by Sihem Arfaoui Abidi, who finds a "legacy of genre/gender transgression" in Kingston that continues in the work the Moroccan writer Fatima Mernissi and her *Dreams of Trespass*. She "proposes a *shift from the dialogue between Kingston and her European/ethnic heritage to an emphasis on the legacy of Kingston in the context of so-called third world literature*, mainly North African Anglophone texts" (original italics). Trying to "re-orient the issue from the influences *on* Kingston to the influence *of* Kingston's literature," she finds a legacy of Kingston's work in "writers beyond the Western canon and/or outside the orbit of ethnically-oriented literatures." Via subtle analogies, Arfaoui demonstrates common concerns and stunning intertextual overlaps that may well testify to direct influence. The main concern is with "transgression in terms of deviating from artistic norms, space boundaries and social codes." Arfaoui finds in this comparison even "a religious tradition sowing the initial seeds of human rights."

In the last section of the book, Kingston's influence is at the same time paid homage to and extended to issues pertaining to the theme of the 'anxiety of influence.' First Nicoleta Alexoae-Zagni looks at the particular case of Shirley Geok-lin Lim and creative filiation in her memoir, in which Lim had to position herself beyond Kingston's influential role model. Referring to the diptych *The Woman Warrior: Memoirs of a Girlhood among Ghosts* (1976) / *China Men* (1980) by Maxine Hong Kingston, on the one hand, and *Among the White Moon Faces: An Asian-American Memoir of Homelands* by Shirley Geok-lin Lim (1996), on the other, Alexoae-Zagni relates filiation to attitudes toward cultural heritage. Tracing a principle of "interactive intertextuality" in the two texts, she comments on strategies of generic ambiguity and epistemological doubt. Analyzing peritexts and incipits, she outlines complex ways of enunciating the self in "a biographical focalization on other people or characters who are the inspiration and/or the skeletal structure of the *mise-en-scène* of one's own self." By looking at different facets of legacy and heritage, we find that "Lim is a genuine disciple of Kingston's" in the sense that "not only does she inherit from her, but equally takes her where she has not been or more precisely, where she will go much later."

Our collection ends on a powerful piece by Sau-ling Cynthia Wong that gives us not only a tour d'horizon of Kingston's literary influence but discovers beyond the craze and fashion of matrilinear stories a particularly stunning afterlife of her work in Marilyn Chin's *Revenge of the Mooncake Vixen*: "[T]he trickling down of feminist ideas into popular culture means that many new variations of the woman warrior figure from a variety of sources have appeared between the 1990s and today." Wong observes: "A young girl growing up today will have seen more iterations of the woman warrior than Kingston's early feminist supporters who came of age in the 1960s and 1970s, could ever have imagined." Asking herself whether *The Woman Warrior* will remain relevant, she looks at ways to rehistoricize the icon, posing "reanimating questions appropriate to the new times." Enjoy her analysis of parody: "In *Mooncake Vixen*, Chin's carefully executed combination of numerous borrowings from *The Woman Warrior* with rich contemporary contextualization has the effect of at once of *updating* it and *dating* it: maintaining the ground-breaking work's continued significance today, while exposing the distance Chinese American women have traveled in the decades since Kingston wrote it" (original italics). Analyzing rehistorization through repetition and difference, Wong looks at doubling, matrilinear legacies, and sexuality. Not surprisingly, we find that Chin "can be as unsparing toward minority-generated orthodoxies as toward hegemonic national myths."

Finally, we want to mention that this collection contains a DVD with videos and pictures from the conference in Mulhouse. It provides some fantastic footage of Maxine Hong Kingston presenting her case to an informed audience and it testifies to the performative value of our get-together in the spring of 2011. We owe this material to David Zagni, Nicoleta's husband, who knows how to handle a video camera and who provides us with documentary pictures that are too good to miss.

Finally, let's not end this introduction without mentioning that at our happy conference dinner, some enthusiasts cooked up a scheme to honor the Arab Spring and encouraged our participant from Tunisia, Sihem Arfaoui Abidi, to organize a follow-up conference on Indigenous Languages, celebrating the work of Noam Chomsky and Maxine Hong Kingston. Unfortunately, the honorees could not make it in person to the conference at the University of Jendouba because of health issues and terror warnings on the US foreign service web site … but the follow-up conference did take place in Tunisia, as "Science, Art, and Gender in the Global Rise of Indigenous Languages" (28th February to 2nd March 2012), in an impressive environment of North African hospitality that couldn't be beat, and with the enthusiastic participation of many local students, scholars from Tunisia and Algeria, and the odd North American or European in between, as the single Swiss participant can testify. The proceedings of the Tunisian follow-up conference should be published next year.

Opening Speech

Maxine Hong Kingston (University of California, Berkeley, USA)

I am so happy to see, oh so many friends that I haven't seen for so long, and also to make new friends. Welcome to an event that has never happened before, *never*! A conference on my writing—I am so thrilled! I am amazed and grateful, so very grateful for your attention to my life's work. This gathering is the very latest meeting of people who will be caring about Asian American and Pacific Islander writing. Just to begin, I want to go back to our history as people who are studying Asian American writing. In 1979, that would be how many ... 42 years ago? When I get excited, I can't subtract! [laughter. Voice in audience: "32 years"!] 32, oh, very good! We just gained ten years!

Well, 32 years ago, there was a second meeting of Asian American writing, and this was in Hawaii. And it was called the "Asian American and Hawai'i Writers' Conference." There was a first conference, and it was in San Francisco, maybe the year before, in 1978. All these words were brand new. There was no such thing as Asian American. It was all being invented. But what is amazing is that there were enough people who were writing, so that we could field a discipline. I had not published anything before that first conference. So people had it without me. And then the *Woman Warrior* came out—and the second conference in Hawaii. I actually wrote about that conference in *Hawai'i One Summer*. It is the only book that nobody has written a paper on. [laughter] Oh you did? [John Whalen-Bridge: "The Lew Welch one ..."]. Oh yes, you mentioned this book when you wrote your Lew Welch ... [Voice: "That was a play, actually."] Ah! Oh! Well, now.

I am going to read to you a little bit from *Hawai'i One Summer* in which I write about that second conference. What they called it was "Asian American and Hawai'i Writers Conference: Talk Story." They were using a term that is only used in Hawaii, which gave me a good translation for oral ... what do you call it? ... transmission. The Hawaiians called it "Talk Story: Asian American Hawai'i Writers Conference." I am going to read to you a paragraph, which just gives us the atmosphere of that conference:

> The opening party was at Washington Place, the Governor's mansion, where Queen Lili'uokalani stayed under house arrest in 1895. We ladies trailed our long skirts over the lawns and through the rooms of Victorian furniture to the lanai, where the band and the food and wine were. People blessed one another with leis and kisses, and the smell and the music of Hawai'i filled the air. The

> moon, full that very night, rolled out of the rushing clouds. I didn't get to the food because I was dazzled by meeting the people whom I had only imagined from their writings.
>
> The writers from the mainland, not used to Hawai'i, must have felt strange, having just come out of their solitary writing rooms. (*Hawai'i* 47)

Okay, so that was the beginning atmosphere! See how beautiful it was! And then right after that, as soon as we sat down at these conference tables, everybody started to fight. [laughter] Especially those activists from the mainland. They were not used to Aloha. They were used to argumentation, and rational discourse. Meanwhile the Hawaiians were moving and kissing and dancing. And so, so there was what … the newspapers covered our conference and they said what we got into was a literary brawl, a fight.

I want to let you know some of the issues that people argued over. There was Ozzie Bushnell, he was an elder in the Hawaiian literary community, and he said that "if us local kids do not write our stories, then the outsider, the haoles, will come in and take over." That was one of the big issues: what are *our* stories, and what stories are going to be expropriated by these people who are colonizing us.

And then there was a fight about the term "Asian American." I remember writers getting up and saying: "Don't call *me* an Asian American. I am not an Asian American. I'm an Oriental." And others: "I am a Hawaiian." "I'm an American." People of various minority groups: "But I am an American!" Terms such as Asian American had just been invented and not accepted at all. The Hawaiians had been colonized again and again, and here you are coming in and telling them that they are Asian American Pacific Islanders. It didn't go over!

But I myself was specifically attacked and so I will try to get over my hurt and explain to you some of the arrows that I was taking from many people. One of them was that I was writing autobiography, and autobiography is not an artistic form. It is like anthropology. All one has to do is write down what happens—there is no art involved. So it leaves this writing open to anthropological analysis, but not the honor of literary criticism. The people who were building the ethnic pride movement said that Chinese American literature is made up of only nine autobiographies, and seven of them by women. I was accused of being unfair to Chinese culture by criticizing Chinese culture as being sexist, and in all these autobiographies the women are talking about being oppressed and suffering from sexism. These critics were saying that it's not true that we have sexism in Chinese culture. That feminism and the feminist movement is not Asian and is not Chinese and we are being untrue to our culture.

There were lots of ideas about myth and the legends and old stories, and who do they belong to. They cannot belong to the haole. They cannot belong to a person who is even writing in English and expropriating, exploiting these stories, and putting them into a Western culture. And so I was accused of misusing the myths and … Okay, I am trying to explain it from that point of view: the myths belong to a culture. You can't fool around with them. You can't take them and change them. You can't have one myth blend into another. All these things I have done, and I was accused of messing with the myths … as if myth were fixed! Already writing them down fixes them and changes them. There is a big difference between the oral culture, where we hand down the stories by word of mouth. Then all of a sudden I write them down. Even that is doing something wrong with them. And then, you know, when you take text you can examine it and it doesn't change, but talk-story changes. It changes from one speaker to another and from one listener to another. And when you tell a story again, it changes. So there was this taboo that you must not change myth. I tried to defend myself by saying that a myth only stays alive if it changes, and it dies if it is fixed.

At the first conference in San Francisco—I wasn't there—the woman who took the brunt of criticism was Jade Snow Wong. She wrote *Fifth Chinese Daughter*, an autobiographical novel set around World War Two, a great patriotic work about America. In fact, she was sent as an ambassador all around the world to show the life of a minority person in America and how wonderful it was. She was attacked at that first conference for being too patriotic and also for being *exotic*. I believe that we all understand about that, about being exotic and pandering to the needs of the mainstream people for an exotic, romantic writing.

By the time of the second conference—she wasn't there—I took the brunt of accusations of being exotic and … oh, the way they put it, it's even worse: that you Chinese women, you are *in bed with the white publishing establishment*, and this is why you write the way you write, with all that exotic romance stuff, and publishers love it and they sell it to the mainstream. You are a sell-out. You sell out the race. Your work's popular not because you write well but because you are in bed with the white publishing establishment. Ok, that's the kind of stuff those early critics were writing. I think I sum it up kind of nicely in this essay:

> My feminist friends said we should have cheered for those seven women autobiographers. The newspaper said the 'brawl' was between the mainland Chinese Americans and the island Chinese Americans. But I think it was the men against the women—the men erecting Louis Chu, male novelist, as the father figure by knocking down the Jade Snow Wong mother figure. (*Hawai'i* 49)

I think this was all very Freudian, but unconscious. You know what this is? It's dualistic thinking.

What broke through dualistic thinking in my mind was the Hawaiians. They had only had written writing for a few hundred years… I mean, their culture was song and dance—not writing. The writing didn't come until the missionaries came, and then they had text. At the conference, the Hawaiians broke through words:

> The most wondrous presentations were two evenings given by the Hawaiians, who each gave his or her genealogy of teachers. They chanted and danced variations of the same mele, sometimes accompanied by gourd and sometimes by knee drums. They told how a new mele is written today, often first in English, then translated into Hawaiian by a teacher, who tells the poet what kind of a mele it is (an Entrance poem, a Call), and where it belongs in tradition.
>
> The panelists' families and students sat in the back of the auditorium, and after the program, the children walked up to the stage and sang for their teacher, John Kaha'i Topolinski. Some participants who had attended the two previous Asian American Writers' Conferences said that the Hawaiians were contributing the only new theory and scholarship. The Hawaiians also gave a vision of the artist, not as anchorite but as builder of community. (*Hawai'i* 49-50)

So I have given you part of the ancestry of the conference we are having here today!

I feel that my own contribution to literature is to show how to get from the oral to the written. I have a huge inheritance of talk-story from my ancestors, and my task has been to figure out how to work that into text.

I see that Eulalia Piñero Gil is the only writer here at this conference who is working on "How to Be a Poet." She is thinking about how stories and poems come to us first through the ears and then later, a more sophisticated stage, when we begin to read and write. I want to present the very first poem that I ever composed. This is before I knew how to write. This is my first language and my original language.

I had two grandfathers; they were my grandfather's brothers. They had a stagecoach drawn by two black horses. They converted the stagecoach to a vegetable wagon, and the horses pulled the vegetables into town. I remember my great-uncles sitting on top of the stagecoach with the reins, and the horses coming. When we heard them coming, my mother would take me upstairs and she'd hang me out the window and she'd say: "Sing to your grandfathers!" She would say: "Make them laugh!" She'd squeeze me and she'd squeeze the poem out of me.

> Sam Goong ah.
> Say Goong ah.
> Nay hoy nai,yah?
> Mah hai cup cup,
> Say ngyeuk, yow say ngyeuk,
> Nay hoi nai, yah? (*To Be the Poet* 4)

That translates like this:

> Hey, Third Grandfather.
> Hey, Fourth Grandfather.
> Where are you going?

Horse shoes clippety-clopping,
  four feet, then four feet,
Where are you going? (*To Be the Poet* 4)

I just wanted you to hear that language so that you can know how it affects the rhythms of what I do. And then the big challenge: How to get the living language which is spoken and heard, how to get that into text.

I know that many of you are writing on *The Woman Warrior* and that you are looking at that work concerning gender and genre and ghost. I think of those ghosts as hauntings. In *The Woman Warrior* I write about the No Name Woman, and how she haunts me to this day. Much of what comes to us are hauntings. How to make hauntings rational? One way is to write them down. I love your following the woman warrior through her incarnations. There she is in *The Woman Warrior,* and she appears again in the *Fifth Book of Peace* in a different form. In that book, she returns to her poetic form, closer to the chant, the war chant, the coming-home-from-war chant, that people sang a thousand years ago.

Since you're working on genre, one of the discoveries that I made was that the woman warrior was different when I wrote about her in prose than when I wrote about her in poetry. I made a lot of mistakes in *The Woman Warrior* and I hope that you critics have found them. One mistake is that I forgot to say that she's a weaver. I mean, I forgot! I don't see how I could forget something that's so very important! I forgot! I was so interested in her as a soldier that I forgot that she was actually Ulysses and Penelope in one. But I corrected that in *The Fifth Book of Peace*, where she chants "Jik, jik, jik." That's the way that poem actually begins. And "jik" means to heal. It means to knit; it means to weave.

Oh, another thing I did, but I hope somebody picks this up: in *The Woman Warrior* I call her Fa Mu Lan. And I never call her that again. Afterwards she is Fa Mook Lan. This is my original minor dialect, my Sayup dialect. When I wrote *The Woman Warrior*, like everyone else, I wanted to use the most elegant standard, the official best Mandarin Chinese. So I just kind of put away my Ebonics, and called her Fa Mu Lan. But as I wrote later, Ebonics became respectable. [Laughter] Ethnic pride became an important movement through these years, and so because of my ethnic pride I now use my dialect and call her Fa Mook Lan. I look forward to your reading *I Love a Broad Margin to My Life*, the new book. There I have the last story of Fa Mook Lan. She continues there and I tell you how she ends, but I won't say it today—you can find out for yourself. So her life has spanned three books.

For those of you writing about migration and travel, and *flânerie*, and tripping out, and crossing margins and borders … I want to read to you something very important in *China Men*, just a very short paragraph. I want to read this to you because we are all traveling and we all have our passports. You carry your passport, you know where it is, safe. I keep checking on mine and make sure I don't lose it! I'm going to read to you something called the

"Burlingame Treaty." This was a time when there was a vision of free travel, open borders. This treaty was made between the Emperor of China and the President of the United States. Notice we do not name the emperor and we do not name the president, because this is every emperor of China, every president of the United States, forever, we make this agreement:

> The United States of America and the Emperor of China cordially recognize the inherent and inalienable right of man to change his home and allegiance, and also the mutual advantage of the free migration and emigration of their citizens and subjects respectively for the one country to the other for the purposes of curiosity ... (*China Men* 152)

The right of curiosity! Why don't we have this right? We must bring this right back! We have to claim this right. We have a right of curiosity! "... for the purposes of curiosity, of trade, or as permanent residents." This is article 5 of the Burlingame Treaty, signed in Washington D.C., 28th July, 1868, and in Peking, 23rd November, 1869. I feel that we should all copy this paragraph, and cut it out and laminate it and keep it with our passport. If we get to a checkpoint or if you forget your passport, you just bring this out, show it to them: "Look! I have the right to my curiosity. And it also says 'residents': I can go and live anywhere I choose! The borders are open. Travel is free." I think that as writers and scholars we should always remember that we have the right to travel freely.

I am most grateful to you who are studying *The Fifth Book of Peace*. You are studying peace! Many papers on this ideal, this value. I am so gratified! And also someone is writing on *Veterans of War, Veterans of Peace*. Is that person here yet? Oh, you, Manuela, thank you for doing that! The *Veterans of War, Veterans of Peace* is this big book I edited. I didn't write this, I edited it! I gathered the writings—forty stories and forty poems from people who've come from many, many wars. I just want to read you one poem from that book. This man's name is Sandy Scull, and he is a veteran of the Vietnam War. He was a poet as a teenager and as a child—just like me, he was a poet. And then he was sent to Vietnam, where he went to Quang Tri. In Quang Tri he built an airstrip. When he came back from war, he lost his poetry. He lost his poetry for thirty years. Then he met this group that I started, in which we would have Buddhist meditation and writing-in-community. We would come home from war. Through our poetry and stories, we would write our way home. In this group Sandy started writing again. This poem is about coming out of isolation and silence. As you listen, think of him as a returning soldier with post-traumatic stress disorder; he's wounded, he's much traumatized, and he's numb. He cannot feel; he has lost feeling. And see how in the poem feelings come back. Listen to how writing connects him to community again:

Sea Salt

After the Vietnam War, I withdrew
to Nantucket: "faraway isle."
Hoping to glimpse the boy
before spirit fled the body.
Thirty-three miles of ocean exiling me
from a homeland offering little embrace.

Me and my dog Christopher. Christ-love
disguised as loyal canine. We combed beaches.
Working for the island newspaper connected me.
Tides soothed with ebb and flow.
A rhythm I could trust. Even eat by.
I fished the last three hours of the east tide.
Buried my toes in the sand, searching
for the texture of littleneck clam.

When water was warm, I sailed out solo.
Stripped then slid into the sound.
Looking up, toward the surface light.
Christopher's gaze wavering with wind
and water between us. Breath bubbles
rose, bursting under his nose.

My body now embraced,
a ritual purification in salt.
Dismembered dreams floated closer.
Something dissolved in a solution
that held me. Breathing easier,
I could imagine again. (Veterans 453-54)

That last line is very important! "Breathing easier, I could imagine again." Meditation—all it is learning to breath easier. He is talking about meditation. He learned to breathe again. And then he could imagine again. His imagination came back to him. Thirty years earlier, all he was allowed to imagine was an airstrip. And so he imagined that airstrip, and he built it. Okay. Thirty years later he could imagine again. And you know what he was imagining? He was imagining that life would be better; he was imagining peace; he was imagining that maybe we can do something to make Vietnam a better place. He was imagining that words, that poetry, stories, writing ... that writing has agency, that we could rebuild the world with our art, that his poetry has use. These veterans ... they didn't want to just write as therapy. They wrote their poems and stories, and they wanted to publish them. And so we gathered their poems and their stories, and we published this book, *Veterans of War, Veterans of*

Peace. And we did find a publisher. They were so happy; they said: "We're going to have royalties; we're gonna make money!" They kept talking about money, and I did not have the heart to tell them, "You are not going to make any money! [laughter] Poetry doesn't pay, you know!" I couldn't say it, I just couldn't say it! They were talking about how we are going to spend our royalties. [laughter] They had meetings, and they voted that they were giving the money to Code Pink, which is a peace organization. And then they were going to give it to East Meets West Foundation. And they were going to give it to the D.O.V.E. Fund, and the Friends of Vinh Son Orphanage. And sure enough—the book sold, and we made money! [laughter] We sent it to these organizations. And they built a school in Quang Tri. Do you understand the miracle of this? Sandy Scull built an airstrip and then he went back and built a school! And it was done through poetry! I mean this is just, ... I, ah, I think ... that just ... it's unbelievable! What I am trying to say is that our work is not abstract, that we effect and affect the real world! And that real life goes into our writing and real life comes out of the writing!

So, I was writing *The Fifth Book of Peace* and I was writing about a great hope for peace right in the middle of the Vietnam War in Hawai'i, which is the center of operations; all the planes and the bombs took off from there for Vietnam. In the middle of that war there was a miracle in this church, the Church of the Crossroads. Soldiers deserted and went AWOL, said, "No. We are going to make peace. Right here we will take a stand." They made Sanctuary at Church of the Crossroads. I wrote that story, but I wrote it as fiction. I was actually there but I did not see every part of Sanctuary. I wanted the point of view of an omniscient narrator instead of just me. So I have this omniscient narrator, which works very beautifully because the Church of the Crossroads was an amazing church. Its center was a courtyard. It was open to the sky, and I felt that the omniscient narrator was up here [she points up] looking down and could see everything. The people in Honolulu held the longest peace sanctuary in the United States, and I'd caught it in fiction.

And so many, many years go by, and I don't hear from anybody who was at that sanctuary. I think it was because it was a blue collar sanctuary; a lot of people were college dropouts and they didn't read. And then, here, today, at this conference, coming out of the books, in real life, comes a member of Sanctuary. And it's Buff Parry, in real life, there he is! So we can't say that that fiction is abstract or that writing is abstract. I feel that he is an embodiment of what I was writing and another miracle—just like that school that appeared in Quang Tri. And here is Buff Perry, right here among us! We are reading about him, writing about him, and he is real, here at our conference! Of course, I know he is his own person [laughter], but I do feel that my fictional character has come here to confront me [laugher. Buff Parry: "Blink your eyes and I may disappear!"] Oh, no, no, don't disappear! He's come with truth and reality. And I feel that I wrote about him and I evoked him. But I think that you also, you must have that same kind of feeling that I have when I meet Buff—but then the rest of you are meeting me, and I think that must be just as awful [laugther] because you've been writing about "Maxine Hong Kingston" [more laughter], but now here I am, and I am in the flesh and meeting you face to face. And so, oh my! So we'll see what happens as you tell me what you think about me and then I will also respond. I think there's never going to be a conference like this again, where people are popping out of text into real life. You're gonna know that the author's not dead! [laughter] Sure, the author is not dead! A text is not all.

So, I am going to begin this conference by ringing the bell of mindfulness. And when you hear it, all you need to do is breathe with awareness.

This reminds me: put down your pencils and your cameras and your books and your notes and your burdens. Put down your burdens! You can be at ease. You can breathe easily. [ding, ding—pause] I evoke Samantabhadra, bodhisattva of great action, bodhisattva of coming out of contemplation into action. [ding, ding, ding—pause] I evoke Avalokiteshvara, Buddha of compassionate listening. [ding, ding, ding—pause] Let the wild rumpus begin! [laughter, applause]

Works Cited

Kingston, Maxine Hong. *China Men*. New York: Knopf, 1980.

—. *The Fifth Book of Peace*. New York: Alfred A. Knopf, 2003.

—. *Hawai'i One Summer*. Illus. Deng Ming-Dao. San Francisco: Meadow P, 1987; Honolulu: U of Hawai'i P, 1998.

—. *To Be the Poet*. Cambridge, MA: Harvard UP, 2002.

—, ed. *Veterans of War, Veterans of Peace*. Kihei, Hawai'i: Koa Books, 2006.

I. Revisiting the canonical texts, *The Woman Warrior* and *China Men*

The Politics of Transnational Identity in and of Maxine Hong Kingston's *The Woman Warrior*

Silvia Schultermandl (University of Graz, Austria)

Nearly three decades before the onset of the "transnational turn" which Shelley Fisher Fishkin coined in her 2004 presidential address to the American Studies Association, Maxine Hong Kingston's *The Woman Warrior: Memoirs of a Girlhood Among Ghosts* (1976) set out to depict the cultural forces acting upon a person's attempt at self-definition, forces that are generated both within and outside the nation-state. In the case of Kingston's protagonist Maxine, these forces are circumstantial to the act of narrating the identity of a Chinese American girlhood to both American and global audiences. Although *The Woman Warrior* has been the subject of many different critical approaches over the decades which see in it a primary example of postcolonial and multiethnic literature within the American canon, the transnational framework in which Kingston's memoir has more recently been discussed complicates the ways in which we regard identity in American literature. This essay distinguishes between the transnational identity politics of *The Woman Warrior* details on the one hand and the ones it acquires through the global dissemination of Kingston's well-received debut work. The point I am making is that both on the intra-textual level, especially on the level of the book's narrative structure, as well as on the extra-textual level, through its world-wide circulation, its appearance in numerous translations, its inclusion into various literary canons and its position at a turning point in second wave feminism,[1] *The Woman Warrior* anticipates contemporary trends in the scholarship of the transnational.

The scholarship in Asian American Studies which Kingston in part generated shares the same challenges Fishkin postulates for the field of American studies, namely to "see the inside and outside, domestic and foreign, national and international, as interpenetrating" (21). Many scholars agree that "Asian American" as a concept is *sui generis* transnational. Inderpal Grewal's study *Transnational America* (2005), which discusses the highly animated and deeply political interactions between America and Asia on the level of popular culture and other commodities such as the Mattel Barbie doll, destabilizes the concept of American culture by exploring its transnational interpenetrations. The innately interdependent modes of cultural representation which Grewal sees

1. See, for example, Schueller, Wong ("Auobiography"), Cheung, Christie.

evidenced in the socio-economic structures underlying the circulation of pop culture commodities are also the focus of Lisa Lowe's study of the so-called "Intimacy of Four Continents." Lowe's analysis of the participation of Asian American indentured laborers in the global market of the early 19th century and the resulting interdependence of Europe, Africa, Asia and the Americas inscribes Asian American migratory history into the hemispheric and trans-hemispheric routes of global cultural exchanges. The aspect of transnationalism that Lowe and Grewal detail highlights the global interconnectedness of the idea of 'America' and the interpenetration of Asian histories with American histories.

As far as Asian American literature in particular is concerned, much of what has been published in the context of transnationalism addresses the case of texts which cannot be classified as an ethnic or multicultural American addendum to the great American canon of cultural pluralism. In the introduction to *Transnational Asian American Literatures: Sites and Transits* (2006), for instance, Shirley Lim et al. consider "the complex, dialogical national and transnational formulations of Asian American imaginations" (2). Lim and her co-editor's investigation of the current body of Asian American scholarship purports a definition of Asian American literature that "can no longer be viewed as merely a minor ethnic province of a domestic American canon" (22). Instead, *Transnational Asian American Literatures* emphasizes the multiple dynamics at play in Asian American cultural productions, dynamics that emerge due to

> the diasporic, mobile, transmigratory nature of Asian American experience, a history characterized by disparate migratory threads, unsettled and unsettling histories churned by multiple and different Asian ethnic immigrant groups each with a different language and cultural stock, different value and belief systems, and different notions of literary aesthetics, albeit most largely mediated through the English language. (1)

In this vein, all attempts at subsuming Asian American literature into the ethnocentric premises underlying the canon of American literature may fail in their emphasis on the nation state. Similarly, this transnational approach exposes the epistemic violence (Spivak) implied in the lines of inquiry pursued by Asian American nationalist discourses that sought to distinguish between "real" and "fake" Asian American literary productions based on a hegemonic mode of categorization (Chin vii).

These "diasporic, mobile and transmigratory" tendencies within Asian American literature are particularly interesting in *The Woman Warrior*, as the trajectories differ from the ones Asian American scholarship usually labels transnational. While the protagonist in *The Woman Warrior* is physically bound to place, rooted in the Stockton Chinatown of her childhood, her search for identity and storytelling takes her on a journey to new and unknown places, namely the China of her mother's stories and the lives of her Chinese ancestors.

This form of "displacement,"[2] albeit not physical but metaphorical, hinges equally on memory, speculation and imagination and leads Maxine into a realm of the unfamiliar and yet fully internalized as the stories she negotiates as an adult entail journeys into her childhood experiences. The transnationalism that Maxine experiences is a "philosophical transnationalism," one which "starts from the metaphysical assumption that social worlds and lives are inherently transnational" (Khagram and Levitt 2), but which nevertheless "can be conceived as a space of exchange and participation wherever processes of hybridization occur and where it is still possible for cultures to be produced and performed without necessary mediation by the center" (Lionnet and Shih 5). Although not a migrant *per se*, Maxine's cultural self-fashioning is shaped by this space of exchange and participation.[3] In this vein, Kingston's text explores the agency of a self-defined selfhood and delves into the challenges and opportunities to fashion identity on one's own terms through a highly original narrative act.

In five interlocking chapters, *The Woman Warriors* begins a negotiation of a childhood story Maxine grew up with and meanders along the streams of Chinese mythology and American culture in an attempt to formulate her personal identity. What Maxine realizes from the very first chapter onwards is that she can never feel complete unless she finds a means of reconciling her Chinese heritage with her American life. Through the act of remembering her childhood in the United States and the stories she heard about China during that time of her life, Maxine finds herself located in the midst of what Gloria Anzaldúa calls a "borderland" in which "two or more cultures edge each other [...] where the space between two individuals shrinks with intimacy" (19). From these "borderlands-within" (cf. Schultermandl, "'What am I, anyhow?'"), Kingston's text details the permeable boundaries between Chinese and American traditions and the ways in which their influences confuse identity concepts of the young protagonist. Maxine remembers:

> Night after night my mother would talk-story until we fell asleep. I couldn't tell where the stories left off and the dreams began, her voice the voice of the

---

2. I am referring here to Caren Kaplan's understanding of displacement in *Questions of Travel: Postmodern Discourses of Displacement* (1996).
3. Sociologist Peggy Levitt has pointed out the degree to which non-migrants experience transnationalism within their families in *The Transnational Villagers* (2001). Levitt also maintains that "[when] children grow up in households and participate in organizations in which people, goods, money, ideas and practices from their parents' countries of origin circulate in and out on a regular basis, they are not only socialized into the rules and institutions of the countries where they live, but also into those of the countries from whence their families come" ("Roots" 1226).

> heroines in my sleep. And on Sundays, from noon to midnight, we went to the movies at the Confucius Church. We saw swordswomen jump over houses from a standstill; they didn't even need a running start. (*Woman Warrior* 19)

This confusion between reality and imagination sets the tone at the beginning of her narrative and ends in a satisfactory resolution in the final chapter, where Chinese and American traditions merge in the form of a story which transgresses the cultural and psychological tensions between Maxine and her mother. That such a resolution is an imperative as well as a life-long process becomes clear through Maxine's emphasis: "Those of us in the first American generations have had to figure out how the invisible world the emigrants built around our childhoods fits in solid America" (5).

In the first chapter, "No Name Woman," Kingston raises one of the key questions in multi-ethnic American literatures, a question which resonates deeply within American literature and the quest for the individual. As though refusing an answer to the question who are you, a question that can imply an assumed difference and thus exclusion from an assumed norm, Maxine offers an elaborate rendition of the many parameters impacting Chinese American identity:

> Chinese-Americans, when you try to understand what things in you are Chinese, how do you separate what is peculiar to childhood, to poverty, insanities, one family, your mother who marked your growing with stories, from what is Chinese? What is Chinese tradition and what is the movies? (5-6)

This is also the context in which Maxine narrates her interest in her aunt whom her family has been "deliberately forgetting" (16) after she bore a child out of wedlock and brought shame to the family name. Throughout the chapter, this aunt is the object of Maxine's speculations about not only the personal circumstances that led to the aunt's fate but also the cultural significance implied in the aunt's life story that may impact Maxine's life. Carefully dissecting the multiple meanings contained within the story and applying them to her own life, Maxine sees in this aunt a figure of agency in whose exposure and transgression of social norms she recognizes the heroic women from her mother's storytelling. Despite the cultural differences between her aunt's life and her own, Maxine identifies with her aunt and successfully redeems her acts of deviance by making her the subject of her opening chapter, a chapter which, in part, can serve as a reading primer for the remaining chapters (cf. Schultermandl, "Teaching Kingston's 'No Name Woman'"). At the same time, Maxine acknowledges her own re-shaping of the aunt's story through a narrative act which is set in a transnational context. The chapter "No Name Woman" exemplifies Kingston's transnational perspective in approaching her family history. When Maxine concludes that she can only have a sense of her family history and thus a better understanding of her identity when she accepts that her aunt's life "branch[es]" into hers (8), she sees her two cultures as "interpenetrating" (Fishkin 21).

That her identity is the result of cultures which mutually inform each other brings about a sense of closure to Maxine's introspection and personal analysis. It is true that she positions herself at times into either one of her two cultural backgrounds, but never both at the same time, for instance in the chapter "White Tigers" through the use of the referents "we Chinese girls" (20) on the one hand and "[m]y American life" (45) on the other. But through the dialogic interconnectedness between the individual chapters, Maxine foregrounds the similarities between herself and her Chinese ancestors. As is the case with no name aunt, the mythological figure of Fa Mu Lan also provides Maxine with a model of female agency and activism. Kingston writes: "The Swordswoman and I are not so dissimilar. May my people understand the resemblance so that I can return to them" (53). Kingston's use of the term "return" emphasizes the notion of displacement. While return usually presupposes an act of leaving, and leaving presupposes a state of presence, Kingston envisions a return in the metaphoric sense, indicating identification and belonging in the same ways as the personal pronoun "my" does, even though her reference to "my people" remains obscure. It is this act of deliberately aligning herself with her culture(s) that characterizes the transnational politics of identity Kingston's text performs: "[W]hat we have in common are the words at our backs" (53), the swordswoman in the form of elaborate tattoos, Maxine through the narrative act, but both bearing witness to their personal investment into cultural agency.

Considering *The Woman Warrior* as a transnational text, however, not only offers a rich reading of Kingston's text; it also demands a shift in perspective as to how we think of the transnational as a category within Asian American literature. Like the texts that Lim et al.'s definition of transnational Asian American imaginations propose, Kingston's memoir deals not so much with literal but with metaphoric border crossings. The memoir represents these border crossings as primary modes of investigation for the protagonist's identity quest: the stories she inherits, the cultural traditions she examines, the different women in her family who offer potential role models—they all put Maxine into a transnational dialogue with her collective past. This dialogue emanates on the level of the memoir's narrative structure in the form of a polyvocal and trans-generational orchestra. The performance of Kingston's memoir, a text which transgresses many borders, including those of genre and canon (cf. Schultermandl, "Literary Ghetto" and "Writing Against the Grain"), highlights the degree to which the cultural encounters she depicts are already mediated through the literary form. The aspect of transnationalism in relation to the literary performances Kingston's memoir undertakes render the question obsolete as to how much of her use of myths and legends draws on real Chinese history and is thus the truth.[4] But more importantly, Kingston's text highlights the performative nature of narratives and thus resists classifications that rely on essentialist categories or reading practices which investigate mostly the social realities depicted in the text at the expense of a close look at the "literary gestures" (Davis and Lee) it employs.

These performances on the intra-textual level are seconded by performances on the extra-textual level, most notably the book's international reception. As an example of *The Woman Warrior* as performance in a global context, I would like to draw from a personal anecdote that involves my teaching of *The Woman Warrior* in several American Studies classes in Europe. In these classes, the focus is often on literary and cultural phenomena which are "typically American," which often means that they either confirm or deconstruct the notions of American-ness that my students bring to class. What Hans Robert Jauss terms a "horizon of expectations" (16) plays out twofold in this context: one refers to the act of reading and the communication between reader and text; the other one refers to the cultural dialogue in which the students enter when reading American literature. In the case of *The Woman Warrior*, a text which requires readers to enter into a very active "dialectic relationship between text, reader, and their interaction" (Iser x), students often confront the challenge of having to fill in gaps while feeling unsure about the cultural contents they see evidenced in the text. When I explain to my students why we read Kingston's memoir and in what way it will contribute to our explorations of American literature, I often get mixed responses: the very few students who have been taking classes in Chinese language are happy to see within the American Studies curriculum a text to which they think they can apply these language skills; on the same note, other students dismiss the text for the same reasons. Some even question the text's contribution to their interest in American Studies because they don't see this text as being representational of anything beyond a Chinese American subculture, or because they see it as being only that. Only when my students comprehend to what degree *The Woman Warrior* illustrates the dynamics of reception of what Rebecca L. Walkowitz has termed the "transnational book" do they begin to envision Kingston's text as a crossroads between the many cultural concepts they have internalized.

Walkowitz's concept of the "transnational book" exemplifies the myriad levels of migration and interaction *The Woman Warrior* undergoes; it also relates to my students' responses when they see *The Woman Warrior* on their reading lists. With the term "transnational book," Walkowitz refers to the multiple languages, locations, and trajectories that the global dissemination of books entails. This multiplicity is reflected both on the level of the actual literary

---

4. Lan Dong's study, *Mulan's Legend and Legacy in China and the United States* (2010), is more sensitive to the question of the origin of Kingston's use of mythology.

production, such as in the fact that many authors of British literature do not live in Britain, and on the level of the books' circulation, such as through the choice of publishing houses, the act of translation, and the books' international reception. At the same time, Walkowitz distinguishes between migrant literature and migrant writers, contending that one does not necessarily presuppose the other. Walkowitz deconstructs the image of the migrant writer as the primary agent of immigrant literature by suggesting that "[n]ot every book that travels is produced by a writer who travels" (532). Instead, Walkowitz argues that "the political and social processes of immigration shape the whole literary system, the relationships among all of the works in a literary culture, and not simply the part of that system that involves books generated by immigrant populations" (533). Walkowitz asserts that "the location of literature depends not only on the places where books are written but also in the places where they are classified and given social purpose" (527). In her assertion that migrant literature needs to be considered in terms of the migratory processes at play in its production and circulation and not only in terms of its physical trajectories of migration, including those determining the national and geographical location of the author, Walkowitz joins Susan Stanford Friedman's call for literary categorizations that privilege "transnational models emphasizing the global space of ongoing travel and transcontinental connection" (Friedman 906) over models that operate with the nation-state as their primary representational logic.

For *The Woman Warrior*, transnationalism is thus an issue both on the level of the identity negotiations the protagonist claims for herself as well as for the identity negotiations global reading audiences assign to the protagonist / the text in general. It is not only the identity politics implied in Maxine's delineating of a transnational matrilineage which inform her own sense of self that make *The Woman Warrior* a transnational text (cf. Schultermandl, *Transnational Matrilineage*), but also the cultural conversations with their multiplicitous reading audiences. In other words, there is a mutual dependence between the ways in which Kingston represents identity and the ways in which these representations emanate with her readers. As much as Maxine's identity is subject of inquiry, so too, is the identity of the reader in terms of the sensibility he or she brings to the text.

That such sensibilities are often missing in the reception of so-called minority texts is an issue Kingston has addressed on numerous occasions in her keynote lectures and her various speaking engagements as a public intellectual. One of her earliest comments to that effect appeared in her article "Cultural Mis-readings by American Reviewers," where Kingston takes issue with early receptions of *The Woman Warrior*. In a broader context, Sau-ling C. Wong's contestation that Asian American cultural criticism increasingly leads to a denationalization of the field caused an avid debate in the late 1990s for what critics saw as a too sanguine tendency towards a blending out of the nation-state as an organizational category in the history of Asian Americans. In particular,

Wong's concept of denationalization solicited an uneasy feeling among many scholars who study the everyday racism and discrimination Asian Americans experience. Wong's idea that Asian American literature is being given specific meanings by readers in various national contexts elicited strong resentment. While I understand both Wong's argument in favor of a denationalized move as well as the critical resistance to it, I wish to position my own reading of *The Woman Warrior* as a transnational book outside either of these lines of inquiry.

What I suggest, instead, is that Kingston's text, because it operates on the intra-textual level with a transnational politics of identity, animates readers to adopt a similar stance during the reading process. To the same degree as Maxine experiences transnationalism without actively participating in the mobility of the global era but through her negotiation of the cultural differences and similarities she perceives between herself and her Chinese ancestry, readers of Kingston's text also need to adopt a transnational framework through which to consider Maxine's narratives. In short, one possible way of avoiding cultural misreadings such as those produced in the attempt to label Kingston's text and place it into a category of identification is to apply to the text what I have called elsewhere a "transnational sensibility."

This notion of a transnational sensibility encompasses a form of identity politics that espouse transnationalism as a main referent without relying solely on the dynamics of migration and diaspora. It is a much more philosophical mode of inquiry, which

> begins by looking at life in and on borders, yet it goes beyond these inarguably contested subjects. It involves looking at the person who is looking, and can be fruitfully applied to hybridized subjects as well as to those whose identities are presumed to be fixed. As such, this transnational sensibility sees a lack of fixity as simultaneously inevitable and rich in possibility. A transnational sensibility is both a methodology and a mode of inquiry: a way of seeing and deliberately *not-knowing*, a way of living within the spaces between questions and answers. (Friedman and Schultermandl 5)

In the case of Kingston's text, this transnational sensibility extends into the realm of the relationship between reader and text, a relationship which Iser considers a definitive moment in the text's meaning. What limits, at times, the horizon of expectations is the question as to how to reconcile the literary performance of Kingston's memoir with the preconceived notions the readers hold of American literature. That Kingston's memoir transgresses these limitations by suggesting that both reader and text operate in the same transnational potential does not mean that Kingston eradicates the differences in power and knowledge that are present in every cultural interaction. On the contrary, the transnational politics of identity which emanate from Kingston's text enable reading practices which emphasize the performative qualities of a text.

Kingston even suggests a model for such a reading practice in the chapter "No Name Woman." The chapter starts with a mother's cautionary tale about premarital sex and the compartmentalization of female sexuality as a means of preserving the family's good standing within the community. As an adult narrator who revisits her past, Maxine dismantles the misogynist premises of the story her mother tells and envisions feminist alternative renditions of the aunt's sexual life. Maxine offers four alternative readings to her mother's version that all deal with the possible circumstances that led to her aunt's pregnancy out of wedlock. While the mother's narrative does not offer any further details beyond explaining, "[s]he could not have been pregnant, you see, because her husband was gone for years" (3), Maxine's versions of the story are more speculative and, at that, more sympathetic toward the aunt. In one version, she imagines her being the victim of sexual assault, the man who raped her "not much different from her husband. They both gave orders: she followed" (7). In another version, Maxine envisions her aunt as the lone romantic, who took a lover and "gave up everything for sex" after her husband left for the "Gold Mountain" (6). In the third version, Maxine imagines her aunt as a "wild woman" who "kept rollicking company" (8). In the forth finally, Maxine considers her aunt outside the traditional narratives of romantic love and imagines her as an independent girl who "combed individuality into her bob" (8) and used sex as a vehicle for social rebellion.

The ways in which Maxine deconstructs the story about her aunt and speculates about the alternative readings of her aunt's suicide take into consideration the possibly strategic omissions her mother made to the 'real' story. This quest for the truth also becomes evident from the narrative structure of "No Name Woman": the story about the aunt, as compelling as it is, is merely two to three pages long, whereas Maxine's speculations take up a good 12 to 13 pages.

The same mode that Kingston employs in "No Name Woman" to exemplify reading practices with a transnational sensibility also enables a reading of Kingston's text not merely as a "master narrative of generational conflict and filial relation" (Lowe, *Immigrant Acts* 26), but as an example of the multiple meanings of her narratives acquired in different global contexts. Kingston thus establishes a connection between her protagonist and her readers, no matter what their cultural background may be. There is something deeply universal in the ways she uses her texts as a meeting ground of her readers and protagonists.

In *De/Colonizing the Self: The Politics of Gender in Women's Autobiography* (1992), Sidonie Smith and Julia Watson remind us that the very genre of the autobiography is a Western literary form, one that, in the post-Enlightenment tradition, "sees its destiny in a teleological narrative enshrining the 'individual' and 'his' 'uniqueness'" (xvii). Smith and Watson argue that "autobiographical practices can be productive in that process as the subject, articulating problems of identity and identification, struggles against coercive calls to a 'universal humanity'" (xix). Kingston's memoir, because it solicits from the reader a transnational sensibility, is not necessarily a struggle against a universal humanity but an indication that such a universal humanity can be established through the reading process. Of course, this does not mean that there is such a thing as a universal global sisterhood at the basis of all women's experiences of gender, but that all attempts to subvert gender hegemonies always operate within specific cultural and political spaces. While Kingston's text does not gloss over these differences, it operates with what Caren Kaplan has called a "discourse of situation" (Kaplan, "Resisting Autobiography" 117). Such a discourse of situation is sensitive to the innate contradictions implied in the autobiographical project as a means of presenting a sense of selfhood, rather than as a project that performs, through a variety of textual performances the processes that shape identity-formation. Such a discourse enables a "literary imagination [which] can impact on de-transcendentalizing nationalism" (Spivak 20-21). It is in this sense that Kingston's memoir assigns to the protagonist and to the reader a transnational identity.

Works Cited

Anzaldúa, Gloria. *Borderlands/La Frontera: The New Mestiza*. 1987. 2nd Edition. San Francisco: Aunt Lute Press, 1999.

Cheung, King-kok. "'Don't Tell': Imposed Silences in *The Color Purple* and *The Woman Warrior*." *PLMA* 103.2 (1988): 162-74.

Chin, Frank, Jeffrey Paul Chan, Lawson Fusao Inada, and Shawn Wong, eds. *Aiiieeeee! An Anthology of Asian American Writers*. Washington, DC: Howard UP, 1974.

Christie, Stuart. "Centrifugal Tendencies around the Rim: Reading Maxine Hong Kingston's *The Woman Warrior* in the Hong Kong University Classroom." *English and Globalization: Perspectives from Hong Kong and Mainland China*. Eds. Kwok-kan Tam and Timothy Weiss. Hong Kong: Chinese UP, 2004. 85-99.

Davis, Rocío G., and Sue-Im Lee, eds. *Literary Gestures: The Aesthetic in Asian American Writing*. Philadelphia: Temple UP, 2006.

Dong, Lan. *Mulan's Legend and Legacy in China and the United States*. Philadelphia: Temple UP, 2010.

Fishkin, Shelley Fisher. "Crossroads of Cultures: The Transnational Turn in American Studies—Presidential Address to the American Studies Association, November 12, 2004." *American Quarterly* 57.1 (2005): 17-57.

Friedman, May, and Silvia Schultermandl. "Introduction." *Growing Up Transnational: Identity and Kinship in a Global Era*. Toronto: U of Toronto P, 2011. 3-18.

Friedman, Susan Stanford. "Migrations, Diasporas, and Borders." *Introduction to Scholarship in Modern Languages and Literatures*. Ed. David Nicholls. New York: MLA, 2006. 899–941.

Grewal, Inderpal. *Transnational America: Feminisms, Diasporas, Neoliberalisms*. Durham: Duke UP, 2005.

Iser, Wolfgang. *The Act of Reading: A Theory of Aesthetic Response*. Baltimore: The Johns Hopkins UP, 1978.

Jauss, Hans Robert. "Literary History as a Challenge to Literary Theory." Trans. Elizabeth Benzinger *New Literary History* 2.1 (1970): 7-37.

Kaplan, Caren. *Questions of Travel: Postmodern Discourses of Displacement*. Durham and London: Duke UP, 1996.

—. "Resisting Autobiography: Out-Law Genres and Transnational Feminist Subjects." *De/Colonizing the Subject: The Politics of Gender in Women's Autobiography*. Eds. Sidonie Smith and Julia Watson. Minneapolis: U of Minnesota P, 1992. 115-38.

Khagram, Sanjeev and Peggy Levitt. "Constructing Transnational Studies." *The Transnational Studies Reader: Intersections and Innovations*. Eds. Sanjeev Khagram and Peggy Levitt. New York: Routledge, 2008. 1-18.

Kingston, Maxine Hong. "Cultural Mis-readings by American Reviewers." *Asian and Western Writers in Dialogue: New Cultural Identities*. Ed. Guy Amirthanayagam. London: Macmillan, 1982. 55-65.

—. *The Woman Warrior: Memoirs of a Girlhood Among Ghosts*. 1976. New York: Vintage, 1989.

Levitt, Peggy. "Roots and Routes: Understanding the Lives of the Second Generation Transnationally." *Journal of Ethnic and Migration Studies* 35.7 (2009): 1225-42.

—. *The Transnational Villagers*. Berkeley: U of California P, 2001.

Lim, Shirley Geok-lim, John Blair Gamber, Stephen Hong Sohn, and Gina Valentino, eds. *Transnational Asian American Literature: Sites and Transits*. Philadelphia: Temple UP, 2006.

Lionnet, Françoise, and Shu-mei Shih, eds. *Minor Transnationalism*. Durham: Duke UP, 2005.

Lowe, Lisa. "The Intimacies of Four Continents." *Haunted By Empire: Geographies of Intimacy in North American History*. Durham: Duke UP, 2006. 192-212.

—. *Immigrant Acts: On Asian American Cultural Politics*. Durham: Duke UP, 1996.

Schueller, Malini Johar. "Questioning Race and Gender Definitions: Dialogic Subversions in *The Woman Warrior*." *Contemporary American Women Writers: Gender, Class, Ethnicity*. Ed. Lois Parkinson Zamora. London: Longman, 1998. 51-66.

Schultermandl, Silvia. "(Breaking out of) The 'Literary Ghetto': Where to Place Asian American Writers, Or De-Essentializing Canonicity." *Hungarian Journal of English and American Studies*, 2009. 287-302.

—. "Teaching Kingston's *No Name Woman* as a Primer for Reading Multi-Ethnic American Literature." *Exploring Spaces: Practices and Perspectives*. Eds. Dorothea Steiner and Sabine Danner. Vienna: LIT Verlag, 2009. 53-73.

—. *Transnational Matrilineage: Mother-Daughter Conflicts in Asian American Literature*. Vienna: LIT Verlag: 2009.

—. "Writing Against The Grain: The Cross-Over Genres of Maxine Hong Kingston's *The Woman Warrior, China Men,* and *The Fifth Book of Peace*." *Interactions* 16.2 (2007): 111-22.

—. "'What am I, anyhow?': Ethnic Consciousness and the Borderlands-Within in Maxine Hong Kingston's and Rebecca Walker's Autobiographies." *Close Encounters of An Other Kind: New Perspectives on Race, Ethnicity and American Studies*. Eds. Roy Goldblatt, Jopi Nyman, and John A. Stotesbury. Joensuu: Faculty of the Humanities, 2005. 3-17.

Spivak, Gayatri Chakravorti. *Nationalism and the Imagination*. London: Seagull Books, 2011.

Walkowitz, Rebecca L. "The Location of Literature: The Transnational Book and the Migrant Writer." *Contemporary Literature* 47.4 Special issue *Immigrant Fictions* (2006): 527-45.

Watson, Julia, and Sidonie Smith. "Introduction: Decolonization and the Politics of Discourse in Women's Autobiographical Practices." *De/Colonizing the Subject: The Politics of Gender in Women's Autobiography*. Minneapolis: U of Minnesota P, 1992. xiii-xxix.

Wong, Sau-ling C. "Autobiography as Guided Chinatown Tour?: Maxine Hong Kingston and the Chinese American Autobiographical Controversy." *Maxine Hong Kingston: A Casebook*. Ed. Sau-ling Cynthia Wong. New York: Oxford UP, 1999. 29-53.

—. "Denationalization Reconsidered: Asian American Cultural Criticism at a Theoretical Crossroads." *Amerasia Journal* 21.1 (1995): 1-27.

Critical Reception in the Cultural 'Homeland': Maxine Hong Kingston's *The Woman Warrior* in Mainland China

Lan Dong (University of Illinois, Springfield, USA)

> To American readers, *The Woman Warrior* is a very 'Chinese' book because of its poignant oriental sentiment; however, to Chinese readers, this is an 'American' book because its context of Californian life fills the text with strong foreign characteristics.
> —Zhichun Zhang (51)[1]

> Now we have enough writers of Chinese heritage writing, enough to have 'World Chinese Literature.' What a significant change this is!
> —Maxine Hong Kingston ("Common Ground" 550)

A call for denationalization within the field of Asian American literary studies was already in place in the 1990s among scholars in the United States (see Wong, "Denationalization Reconsidered"). During the subsequent two decades, Asian American scholars have continued to engage with critical issues in the field beyond the geo-political boundaries of the United States and beyond the hyphen (Ty; Ty and Goellnicht) and to reconfigure the cultural exchange between the United States and Asia as well as how such exchange influences Asian American literary production and criticism (Brada-Williams and Chow). The past twenty years also have witnessed scholarly examinations of Asian American texts within an international context along with the study of Asian American literature and culture from transnational, comparative, and global perspectives (Hune, Kim, Fugita, and Ling; Hu-DeHart; Wong, "When Asian American Literature Leaves 'Home'"; Lim, Gamber, Sohn, and Valentino; Wang).

Over the past two decades, European scholars have given close attention to Asian American cultural productions as well (see Davis, *Hitting the Critical Mass*; Schultermandl, *Interactions*; Unali; Davis and Ludwig; Boelhower, Davis, and Birkle). In Chinese-speaking regions, scholars in Taiwan have led the way in the study of Chinese American literature.[2] Te-hsing Shan provides an

1. Unless otherwise specified, all translation in this article is mine. All Chinese names are rendered according to Western tradition: that is, given name first followed by family name.
2. Te-hsing Shan compiled a bibliography of scholarly work on Chinese American literature published in Taiwan in the 1990s, including dozens of journal

overview of the study of Chinese American literature in Taiwan from the 1980s to the new millennium in his article, "Branching Out: Chinese American Literary Studies in Taiwan" (39-56).[3] According to Shan, studies on Chinese American literature in Taiwan can be traced back to the beginning of the 1980s. The first article, Joseph S. M. Lau's "The Albatross Exorcised: The Rime of Frank Chin," was written in English and published in the *Tamkang Review* in 1981. However, it was not until the end of the 1980s that the number of scholars and publications in this field became noticeable in Taiwan. Among influential Taiwanese scholars are Yu-Cheng Li, Wen-Ching Ho, and Te-hsing Shan (Shan, "Branching Out" 40). Shan's *Mingke yu zaixian: huayi meiguo wenxue yu wenhua lunji* (*Inscriptions and Representations: Chinese American Literary and Cultural Studies*, 2000) is the first monograph on Chinese American literature and culture written in Chinese and published in a Chinese-speaking region.[4] It not only examines classic Chinese American literary works by Maxine Hong Kingston and Frank Chin, but also discusses diaspora writers Geling Yan and Chin Yang Lee within a comparative framework while addressing the cultural and linguistic complexity and multiplicity in Chinese American literature. All these scholarly endeavors that analyze literary and cultural texts through a transnational and comparative lens have helped broaden the scope of Asian American studies.

Within this context of transnationalizing and internationalizing Asian American studies, this article examines the critical reception of Kingston's works in mainland China by focusing on her canonical work, *The Woman Warrior: Memoirs of a Girlhood among Ghosts* (1976), as a particular case in point.[5] During the past decade or so, studies on Chinese American literature in general and on Kingston in particular have been fast growing in Chinese academia in the form of conferences, master's and doctoral theses, publication of journal articles, book chapters, and book-length manuscripts, adoption of related topics and texts in curricula, as well as the establishment and development of centers for Chinese

---

articles and master's theses, some written in Chinese and others written in English (Shan and Ho 195-208). Later, Shan updated the bibliography and included more recent articles and theses (Ho and Shan 223-43; Shan, *Mingke yu zaixian* 365-87).

3. The article was published in Chinese. The English title cited here is Shan's.
4. Shan has since published a number of works on Chinese American literature and culture (see Shan, *Kaijiang*; *Gushi*; *Yu zhizhe weiwu*).
5. One of the most celebrated Asian American writers, Kingston has attracted much critical attention outside North America. For instance, many European scholars have presented refreshing perspectives and approaches to interpreting Kingston's works through multidirectional flows of ideas, imagery, and cultural modification (see Grice; Schultermandl; Ludwig; Bedingfield).

American Studies at various universities.[6] These studies have covered a broad scope of topics that range from historical overview to in-depth examination of specific authors and texts.[7] One of the most influential Chinese American writers, Kingston has produced works that—through their translation into Chinese (published in Hong Kong, Taiwan, and mainland China)—have kindled lively discussions among Chinese scholars. *The Woman Warrior* was translated into Chinese shortly after its publication. To date, there have been multiple Chinese translations published.[8] Almost all the books on Chinese American literature that have been published in China have a section on Kingston; moreover, the number of journal articles on her writing is notable. This rich field, however, has remained largely unexplored. Thus many unanswered questions regarding the reception of Kingston in the cultural "homeland" warrant a careful examination[9]: how have Chinese scholars and readers responded to the representation of China and Chineseness in Chinese American texts such as *The Woman Warrior*? What are their understanding and criticism of cultural authenticity as reflected in Kingston's works as well as in Asian American literary studies? In what dimensions have Chinese scholars examined identity politics, gender, and ethnicity in Kingston's writing in terms of overseas Chinese literature, Asian American literature, and world literature? What does their research have in common with or how does it differ from the investigations

---

6. According to Fanzi Rao, scholars in mainland China started their research on overseas Chinese literature in the late 1970s, initially focusing on writers from Taiwan, Hong Kong, Macau, and Southeast Asia. Rao's overview positions Chinese American literature within the broader field of overseas Chinese literature (29-38). Beginning in the 1990s, more and more scholarly attention has been paid to Chinese American literature materialized in conferences, journal and book publications, as well as theses and dissertations on related topics.
7. Yufeng Xue's *Meiguo huayi wenxue zhi wenhuayanjiu* (Cultural Studies of Chinese American Literature, 2007) is an example of the former; Yingguo Xu's *Kuawenhua shiye xia de meiguo huayi wenxue: Zhao Jianxiu zuopin yanjiu* (Cross-Cultural Study of Chinese American Literature: Frank Chin's Writing, 2007) is an example of the latter; Guicang Li's *Wenhua de zhongliang: jiedu dangdai huayi meiguo wenxue* (The Weight of Culture: Contemporary Chinese American Literature, 2006) is a combination of both. While most of the book-length monographs are written in Chinese, there are some publications in English (see Jing Zhang; Guan).
8. See Chang; Jing; Li and Lu.
9. Sämi Ludwig briefly addresses Chinese critics' reaction to *The Woman Warrior* and contends that Chinese readers commonly view this work a "hyphenated" text that gives them access to American culture ("Celebrating Ourselves" 38-39).

of scholars living in the United States? The discussion below examines three aspects of scholarship on Kingston in mainland China: feminist studies that focus on her representation of Chinese women, postcolonial studies that utilize Edward Said's Orientalism as their main theoretical approach, and comparative studies that examine Kingston side by side with Chinese writers. Chinese scholars in the first two groups rely heavily on studies on Chinese American literature in the United States while the comparative works in the third group make a unique contribution to Chinese American literary studies.

A (Chinese) American Woman Warrior: Feminist Perspective

Similar to their American counterparts, a number of Chinese scholars have closely examined the representation of Chineseness in *The Woman Warrior* in their studies, particularly the first two chapters entitled "No Name Woman" and "White Tigers." Some consider the character of No Name Woman (the narrator's paternal aunt who committed suicide after having an extramarital affair and an illegitimate baby in the early twentieth century) as an embodiment of the Oriental other while others interpret her character as a victim of feudalism. Attending to the representation of Chinese culture, tradition, and people in *The Woman Warrior*, Yan Hu and He Huang, for example, adopt Edward Said's theoretical approaches to reading Kingston's text and focus on its depiction of the remote, mysterious Orient from a Western perspective. Analyzing the story of No Name Woman as a case in point, they argue:

> Reading *The Woman Warrior* closely, [the reader] can see that Maxine Hong Kingston always takes the stance of a Western writer and looks at Chinese culture from the perspective of 'the other.' She portrays a large number of traditional Chinese cultural elements in *The Woman Warrior*: myth and legend, historical figures, [and] daily life and foodways, thus representing abundant Chinese images to Western readers. However, because of her environment, educational background, and identity, Kingston falls into the pitfall of orientalism during the process of [literary] expression, and coincides with the direction of 'the other culture' in the Sinology of mainstream American society. In her writing, Chinese society is portrayed as a place filled with feudal ethics, old customs, and backward habits, and Chinese people were depicted as mysterious, strange, ignorant, and superstitious. (Hu and Huang 14)

Such criticism of Kingston's American perspective and misrepresentation echoes that of Asian American critics such as Frank Chin, viewing her as an American writer who fails to do justice in representing Chinese culture. Likewise Lihua Li and Zhijuan Zhu contend that Chinese American women's writing, exemplified by Jade Snow Wong's *The Fifth Chinese Daughter* (1950), Kingston's *The Woman Warrior*, and Amy Tan's *The Joy Luck Club* (1989), essentially shows an assimilationist attitude. They argue that

> *The Woman Warrior* is made of several short stories, and all the protagonists are women. The Chinese American men in the stories are either tyrants who oppress women or irresponsible cowards: that is, obstacles for women's pursuit for independence and progression. Overall, through the fate of women [the book] denounces the oppression and harm that Chinese patriarchal culture has inflicted on women. (Li and Zhu 99)

These are only some examples of Chinese scholars' criticism of Orientalist stereotypes that they see represented in Kingston's writing.[10]

Addressing Kingston's *The Woman Warrior* as a feminist text grown out of the cultural gaps and emphasizing the cultural differences between the East and West, Lei Shi and Jianguang Wang interpret No Name Woman's story as a representation of Western feminism against Oriental patriarchy. They argue:

> The simple incident of a woman being seduced and raped in a remote Chinese village has become a miserable and longlasting chronic disease that affects the lives of the entire clan infinitely. This is the enormous power of the traditional Chinese patriarchal society. The everlasting evading, denouncing, and precautionary attitude that Maxine's relatives have toward this kind of family scandal seems natural within a context, in which a woman's chastity is more important than her life, a traditional Chinese culture in which male power controls everything and women are nothing but subsidiaries to the family. (Shi and Wang 87)

In their analysis, Shi and Wang use the scene in which No Name Woman gives birth after being attacked by the villagers and abandoned by her kin as a textual example to demonstrate how Western feminism deconstructs Oriental patriarchy by way of commemorating the intentionally erased record of No Name Woman and reinserting her into the family history (87). Their argument, despite its insights into feminist discourse, seems to suggest a problematic opposition of East versus West and patriarchy versus feminism, thus offering a limited understanding of Kingston's writing.

Adding another dimension to the discussion, feminist scholars in China frequently contextualize Kingston's works with other Asian American women's writings such as those of Sui Sin Far, Jade Snow Wong, and Amy Tan. They engage with feminist theory and critical works in Asian American studies such as those by Elaine Kim, King-kok Cheung, and Sau-ling Wong. Most scholars view *The Woman Warrior* as a feminist discourse that battles against male dominance. For example, while referring to Hélène Cixous, Simone de Beauvoir, and Virginia Woolf to structure her theoretical framework, Ye Hong considers the stories of No Name Woman and Moon Orchid (the narrator's maternal aunt who loses her sanity after coming to America) as representations of the silent, tragic Oriental woman. She contends that Kingston's work tells the reader that "marginalized women either die in silence or become insane in

---

10. Other examples include Ji 215; Gao and Shan 65-66.

silence; therefore, fighting against patriarchal society and mainstream culture and making their voice audible become particularly important" (Hong 1051). In a similar vein, applying the theoretical lens of feminist psychology, especially Elaine Showalter's work, Zhipeng Kang discusses the chapter on No Name Woman as a subversion of male-centered history through the act of writing (270-71). Kang views Kingston's vivid portrayal of No Name Woman and Moon Orchid's tragic lives—in sharp contrast to the resilient and heroic images of Fa Mu Lan and Brave Orchid (the narrator's mother)—as indications of a subversive narrative against the patriarchal social order.

A (Self-)Orientalized Rewriting: Postcolonial Perspective

Among Chinese scholars, criticism on Kingston's Orientalist writing does not stop with No Name Woman's story: the retelling of Fa Mu Lan's tale has been another focus of scholarly attention. Regarding Kingston's retelling of Fa Mu Lan, Chinese scholars have presented as many perspectives as have their American counterparts. Heeding the author's bicultural heritage, Hao Cheng views the character Fa Mu Lan in Kingston's work as a hybrid woman warrior who, as a product of cultural clashes between China and America, represents "individuality of the modern Western woman" with a strong rebellious spirit while still maintaining some "characteristics of the traditional Chinese woman" (54-55). Discussing historical representations in Kingston's work, Ruoqian Pu considers the characters Fa Mu Lan and Ts'ai Yen as capitalized "Mothers" (as opposed to Brave Orchid as the narrator's mother) who help connect the narrator with the female lineage in her family saga (11).

Besides discussions along thematic lines, Chinese scholars also have examined *The Woman Warrior* with a focus on symbolism and language.[11] What

---

11. For example, Xuehui Hu and Lixia Du examine symbolism in *The Woman Warrior*, in particular the bird, tiger, and dragon. In their interpretation, the bird symbolizes Brave Orchid who has supplied talk-stories as guidance to the narrator; the white tigers represent America while the dragon signifies China. They argue that "through creating symbolic items such as the guiding bird, dragon, white tigers, and a white horse the author reveals the influences she has received while growing up and indicates the complicated process of her cultural identification" (Hu and Du 24). Manyuan Hua, for instance, analyzes *The Woman Warrior* from a stylistic perspective, scrutinizing its narrative point of view, diction, and sentence structure. Pointing out a series of words beginning with an "s" in the story of No Name Woman: "saw," "slaughtering," "scream," "searchlights," "smeared," "swung," "slit," "splattering," "scattered," "swept," "sobbed," and "scolded," she concludes that these words are "uncomfortable" and their usage indicates "the author's

is worth noting is that a number of articles address in particular the debate—heralded by Kingston and Frank Chin in Asian American literary studies—surrounding *The Woman Warrior*'s adaptation of Fa Mu Lan's story.[12] In her discussion of this controversy, Ping Li refers to Asian American critical works by Elaine H. Kim, Sau-ling Cynthia Wong, and Frank Chin, and argues that Kingston's rewriting of traditional myth is an effective creative strategy (115-18). Xing Yu proposes that both Kingston and Chin, in their misreading of Chinese culture, are actually generating Chinese American myths and furthermore are representing China and Chineseness from a Chinese American perspective. Therefore, paradoxically, these debating authors ultimately achieve the same goal, though by different means: Kingston upholds feminism while Chin promotes heroism (Yu 61-64). Liang Chen, in a similar vein, argues that both Kingston and Chin—despite their divergent understandings of Chinese American literature—contribute to breaking Orientalist stereotypes as well as to establishing positive images of Chinese Americans in contemporary American literature (190-91). Whether praising Kingston's creative use of myth, legend, and storytelling or condemning her misrepresentation of Chinese culture, what these scholars seem to agree on is that the chapter "White Tigers" is a newly invented American myth and that the character Fa Mu Lan is not a Chinese heroine but rather a Chinese American woman warrior.

Using a first-person narrative to tell Fa Mu Lan's story, *The Woman Warrior* emphasizes the coexistence of womanhood and military prowess within her character, thus presenting an androgynous heroine. Fa Mu Lan starts out as a maiden combatant, transforms into a wife and mother in the middle of her military campaign, and then ends as a daughter-in-law returning to her husband's family. Regarding the female and male features represented by Fa Mu Lan, Zhichun Zhang considers the androgyny within this character to be an implication of the double chains imposed on women: they have to perform social roles like men and at the same time fulfill the traditional female role within the family. Under such a double burden, it becomes even harder for women to resist patriarchal rule (52). Conversely, other scholars praise Kingston for her groundbreaking rewriting of an androgynous heroine whose characteristics reflect a combination of Chinese tradition and American culture (see Tang; Zhang and Yang; Bai). For example, examining Fa Mu Lan's androgyny from an eco-feminist perspective, Yang Song discusses the character Fa Mu Lan in terms of the complimenting, compromising, and cooperating relationships between human and nature as well as between men and women (41-44).

As many readers and critics in the United States, Europe, and China have noted, the inspiration of Kingston's tattooed protagonist comes from the

---

sympathy for Chinese women and merciless criticism of conservative old fashion" (Hua 49).

12. See, for example, Xu 41-49, 89-103.

historical Chinese hero, Yue Fei (1103–1142). A skillful military leader and strategist, Yue Fei commanded his troops victoriously in combat on behalf of the Southern Song court and was executed due to a fabricated charge. In Chinese history, literary renditions, folk stories, and theater performances, Yue Fei is commonly known as a "national hero" and his character is celebrated for his unconditional loyalty to the imperial rule. Despite variations across many genres, one of the longlasting highlights of his story are the words carved on his back—"to serve one's country with complete loyalty"—a symbol of his utmost heroic patriotism. Thus, through the conflation of two characters from Chinese culture in the carving scene and through the marking of Fa Mu Lan's female body with "oaths and names" (*Woman Warrior* 34), Kingston consciously empowers the woman warrior. As Kingston herself has explained, "I take the power I need from whatever myth. Thus Fa Mu Lan has the words cut into her back; in the traditional story, it is the man, Ngak Fei the Patriot, whose parents cut vows on his back. I mean to take his power for women" ("Personal Statement" 24). Reading the carved words on Fa Mu Lan's back together with the last chapter of *The Woman Warrior* that adapts and transforms the historical poet Ts'ai Yen's story, the deconstruction and reconstruction of power through bodily writing become clear. Considering female bodily writing as a performance of virtue in premodern China, Daphne Lei, an American scholar of great expertise in Chinese and Chinese American opera performance, argues:

> It was mainly marginalized social and cultural groups that practiced tattooing, carving, mutilation, and other permanent bodily modifications in premodern China. However, the inclusion of text complicates the whole history of bodily reading and signifying. Literacy and reading are usually associated with male elite power; nothing reinforced more powerfully the ties between literary text and social and civil status than the tradition of the Imperial Examination. The combination of a lowly practice (tattooing) and elite power (text) thus creates an interesting phenomenon, turning the marking of the body into a virtuous performative act. Text prescribes meaning in bodily marking, while the visceral and barbaric associations of the act reinforce the power of the text. (101)

In this sense, the bodily writing in *The Woman Warrior* is a negotiation "between male bodily marking and female body ownership; it is also a hybridized performance of Chinese and Asian American ideologies. Ultimately, it is a negotiation between the critique of gender and the critique of culture" (Lei 120). Thus at the end of her book, Kingston conflates the characters of Fa Mu Lan and Ts'ai Yen to constitute "an evolving image of the woman warrior who surrenders her sword and takes up words as her chosen weapons" (Dong 95).

Forming World Chinese Literature: Comparative Perspective

In discussing Kingston, Chinese scholars not only have demonstrated strong interest in the primary texts and an awareness of their critical context in the United States, but they also made an effort to compare Kingston with modern Chinese writers, thus indicating the complex positionality of her writing at the crossing between Chinese literature and Chinese American literature. In analyzing the character of No Name Woman within the social context of early twentieth-century China, a number of Chinese scholars have addressed the connection between no name woman's story and its representation of feudal China, and have studied Kingston's writing in comparison with those of Chinese writers. Some of them have compared her work to that of Lu Xun (pen name of Shuren Zhou, 1881-1936), one of the most influential modern Chinese writers in the twentieth century who is particularly recognized for his sharp social criticism. Drawing on the parallels between a warrior and language, some Chinese scholars deliberately have referred to Lu Xun's work when discussing Chinese Americans' resistance to mainstream cultural domination reflected in *The Woman Warrior* (Cuijuan Li 14). Chen Luo and Man Luo titled their article on *The Woman Warrior* "A Warrior Calling for Arms," apparently alluding to one of Lu Xun's representative works *Na Han* (*Call for Arms*) (Luo and Luo 72, 75). A collection of fourteen short stories written between 1918 and 1922, *Call for Arms* established Lu Xun's fame in modern Chinese literature. His stories are well known for embedded social criticism of feudal ethics and a call for resistance and breaking from the restrictive old traditions. Luo and Luo conclude their article by stating that Kingston used her unique feminist perspective, adopted a non-traditional writing style, and published her debut "calling-for-arms" book. Thus there is strong evidence that Kingston herself is a woman warrior in the field of Chinese American literature whose writing calls for the reader's attention to the in-between position of Chinese Americans (Luo and Luo 75).

While these scholars have investigated Kingston and Lu Xun's criticism of the social environment at the macro level, Yueli Song shifts her focus to the micro level and discusses women characters in their families: the basic units of traditional Chinese social structure. Through her comparison of No Name Woman with Fan Yi, a character in the play *Lei Yu* (*The Thunderstorm*) by Cao Yu (pen name of Jiabao Wan, 1910-1996), Song examines women's role in the family in early twentieth-century China. In her view, No Name Woman's lack of education renders her unable to take charge of her fate, resist patriarchal oppression, nor flee from the feudal family and by extension from the village. Fan Yi, despite being educated and rebellious (for example, in the play she has an affair with her stepson), is not willing to leave home and pursue freedom, in her case because of economic restraints. Hence both characters face similar dilemmas in marriage and family life, although No Name Woman is an illiterate woman living in a remote village while Fan Yi has grown up in the city with wealth and education. From these two different perspectives, the tragic endings of their stories reveal the same ruthless subjugation of women who overstep the boundaries in a feudal society (Yueli Song 118-19).

In terms of challenging traditional generic boundaries and representing women's experience, Caihong Shen compares *The Woman Warrior* with contemporary Chinese writer Anyi Wang's autobiographical novel *Documentary and Fiction* (1992) through an examination of how both Kingston and Wang challenge the boundaries between fiction and nonfiction, how both main characters represent the isolation and alienation women experience in a modern society, and how both texts explore the pursuit of women characters' identity intertwined with marginalization, influence of the mother figure, love and marriage, as well as writing (11-13). Known for her portrayal of female characters and urban life, Wang's short stories, novellas, and novels have gained prominence nationally and internationally. Rocío G. Davis has argued that life writing can be "not only a potentially productive source for a nuanced reconstruction of the past, but also a valuable document for discerning processes of identity"; it is, moreover, "a privileged way to access personal and collective forms of subjectivity in changing contexts" (*Relative Histories* 4). Similar to *The Woman Warrior*, Wang's *Documentary and Fiction* reflects the complexity of the interrelated personal and collective subjectivity through a female narrative voice. Both texts pose a challenge to the reader and thus defy any singular generic categorization.

Kingston has pointed out that the "aesthetic freedom" embedded in "World Chinese Literature" not only refers to content creation, but also entails breaking generic boundaries between fiction and nonfiction as well as experimenting with new forms in literary production ("Common Ground" 553). During the past few decades, the genre of *The Woman Warrior* has incurred lively discussion among scholars. As Davis and Ludwig have pointed out, "Kingston's emblematic text not only opened the way for writers to engage the complexities of their ethnicity, but also signaled a narrative boldness and maturity regarding the appropriation and subversion of traditional genres" (9). Among Chinese scholars, the generic studies on Kingston have focused on the context of postmodern writing and genre crossing in contemporary women's works. For instance, Jian Qiu considers *The Woman Warrior* a typical postmodern text, emphasizing its "avant-garde style," "colorful collage," and "contradictory scattered narrative" (120-21). Min Shi also views Kingston as a postmodern writer (59-62). Diverging from their views, Na Liang argues that *The Woman Warrior* is not a postmodern text since its main goal is not to deconstruct but rather to reconstruct a Chinese American literary world (126-28).

One example of the increasing critical attention on Chinese American literature as part of "World Chinese Literature" is the international conference on Comparative and Transnational Studies in Chinese American Literature, hosted by the Research Center for World Chinese Literature at Fudan University in Shanghai in June 2005. This conference yielded a volume, *Querying the Genealogy: Comparative and Transnational Studies in Chinese American Literature*, that collects selected articles written in English and Chinese by American, European, and Chinese scholars. Kingston's keynote address, collected in this book, briefly addresses the idea of "World Chinese Literature" that loosely refers to texts written in various languages by people of Chinese heritage with different nationalities. According to Kingston, what these works share in common is the "aesthetic freedom" which is independent of the language a writer uses and the physical location within which he or she lives ("Common Ground" 550-51). Through such a lens, scholars can examine Chinese American literary productions as part of a larger entity as well as from a perspective that crosses linguistic and geographical boundaries.

This article has provided an array of evidence that Asian American literature offers a rich field of investigation by which the reader can "comprehend transcultural literary phenomena beyond geographic, national, ethnic, and even linguistic boundaries" (Davis and Ludwig 9). As early as 1991, Lisa Lowe already pointed out: "We might conceive of the making and practice of Asian American culture as nomadic, unsettled, taking place in the travel between cultural sites and in the multivocality of heterogeneous and conflicting positions" (39). I would further argue that the location of Kingston's body of work among "World Chinese Literature" adds another dimension to the nomadic, unsettled Asian American culture when viewed within a transnational context.

Works Cited

Bai, Li. "Tanxun *Nü yongshi* zhong de nüxing zhuyi (Exploring Feminism in *The Woman Warrior*)." *Yuwen xuekan* 3 (2010): 22-24.

Bedignfield, Agnieszka. "Trans-Memory and Diaspora: Memories of Europe and Asia in American Immigrant Narratives." Boelhower, Davis, and Birkle 333-46.

Boelhower, William, Rocío G. Davis, and Carmen Birkle, eds. *Sites of Ethnicity: Europe and the Americas*. Heidelberg: Winter, 2004.

Brada-Williams, Noelle, and Karen Chow, eds. *Crossing Oceans: Reconfiguring American Literary Studies in the Pacific Rim*. Hong Kong: Hong Kong UP, 2004.

Chang, Shih, trans. *Nü dou shi: guiying chongchong zhong de shaonü huiyi* (The Woman Warrior: Memoir of a Girlhood among Ghosts). Taipei: Huang Kuan, 1977.

Chen, Liang. "Toushi meiguo huayi zuojia Zhao Jianxiu he Tang Tingting de wenhua lunzhan (On the Cultural Debate between Chinese American Writers Frank Chin and Maxine Hong Kingston)." *Chongqing keji xueyuan xuebao* 12 (2009): 190-91.

Cheng, Hao. "Qianxi *Nü yongshi* xingxiang de zajiaoxing (Analyzing the Hybrid Image of *The Woman Warrior*)." *Xinxiang jiaoyuxueyuan xuebao* 22.1 (2009): 54-55.

Davis, Rocío G. *Relative Histories: Mediating History in Asian American Family Memoirs*. Honolulu: U of Hawai'i P, 2010.

—, ed. "European Perspectives on Asian American Literature." Special Issue of *Hitting Critical Mass* 4.1 (1996).

—, and Sämi Ludwig, eds. *Asian American Literature in the International Context: Readings on Fiction, Poetry, and Performance*. Münster and Hamburg: LIT Verlag, 2002.

Dong, Lan. *Mulan's Legend and Legacy in China and the United States*. Philadelphia: Temple UP, 2011.

Gao, Linjia, and Ronglin Shan. "Dui *Nü yongshi* zhong houzhiminzhuyi de jiedu (Postcolonialism in *The Woman Warrior*)." *Xinxiang jiaoyuxueyuan xuebao* 22.3 (2009): 65-66.

Grice, Helena. *Maxine Hong Kingston*. Manchester and New York: Manchester UP, 2006.

Guan, Hefeng. *Seeking Identity between Worlds: A Study of Chinese American Women's Literature*. Kaifeng: Henan daxue chubanshe, 2007.

Ho, Wen-Ching, and Te-hsing Shan, eds. *Zaixian zhengzhi yu huayi meiguo wenxue* (Politics of Representation and Chinese American Literature). Taipei: zhongyang yanjiuyuan oumei yanjiusuo, 1996.

Hong, Ye. "Cong chenmo, fasheng dao ronghe (From Silence, Voice to Reconciliation)." *Keji xinxi* 35 (2009): 1051-52.

Hu, Xuehui, and Lixia Du. "Zai xiangzheng shijie li jiangou wenhua shenfen (Constructing Cultural Identity in a Symbolic World)." *Gansu guangbodianshi daxue xuebao* 19.3 (2009): 24.

Hu, Yanm, and He Huang. "Tang Tingting xiaoshuo *Nü yongshi* de 'tazhe' jiedu (Reading 'The Other' in Maxing Hong Kingston's *The Woman Warrior*)." *Wenjiao ziliao* 4 (2009): 14.

Hu-DeHart, Evelyn, ed. *Across the Pacific: Asian Americans and Globalization*. Philadelphia: Temple UP, 1999.

Hua, Manyuan. "Cong wentixue kan *Nü yongshi* de zhutisixiang (A Stylistic Study of *The Woman Warrior*'s Theme)." *Gaodeng hanshou xuebao* 22.12 (2009): 49.

Hune, Shirley, Hyung-chan Kim, Stephen S. Fugita, and Amy Ling, eds. *Asian Americans: Comparative and Global Perspectives*. Pullman: Washington UP, 1991.

Ji, Weiwei. "Shixi Tang Tingting zuopin zhong de yiguo xingxiang (Analyzing the Image of the Other in Maxine Hong Kingston's Works)." *Keji zixun* 25 (2009): 215.

Jing, Xiang, trans., *Nü dou shi: zai guimei qun zhong de tongnian shenghuo huiyi* (The Woman Warrior: Memoir of a Girlhood among Ghosts). Taipei: Linbai, 1977.

Kang, Zhipeng. "Laisi fengyu, qusi weichen: cong nüxingzhuyi xinlixue fenxi Tang Tingting *Nü yongshi* zhi wuming nüren (Feminist Psychologist Reading of 'No Name Woman' in Kingston's *The Woman Warrior*)." *Guangxidaxue xuebao* 31 (2009): 270-71.

Kingston, Maxine Hong. "The Common Ground of World Chinese Literature: Address on International Working Women's Day at Fudan University." In Jennie Wang 550-54.

—. "Personal Statement." *Approaches to Teaching Kingston's* The Woman Warrior. Ed. Shirley Geok-lin Lim. New York: MLA, 1991. 23-25.

—. *The Woman Warrior: Memoirs of a Girlhood among Ghosts*. 1976. New York: Vintage, 1989.

Lei, Daphne P. "The Blood-Stained Text in Translation: Tattooing, Bodily Writing, and Performance of Chinese Virtue." *Anthropological Quarterly* 82.1 (2009): 99-128.

Li, Cuijuan. "Lun *Nüyongshi* zhong de wenhua kangzheng jingshen (Cultural Resistance in *The Woman Warrior*)." *Qingnian wenxue jia* 8 (2009): 14.

Li, Guicang. *Wenhua de zhongliang: jiedu dangdai huayi meiguo wenxue* (The Weight of Culture: Contemporary Chinese American Literature). Beijing: renmin wenxue chubanshe, 2006.

Li, Jianbo, and Chengyi Lu, trans. *Nü yongshi* (*The Woman Warrior*). Guilin: Lijiang chubanshe, 1998.

Li, Lihua, and Zhijuan Zhu. "Zhuixun yu chaoyue: huamei nüxingwenxue shenfenzhengzhi de suoqiu yu chuncuiyishu de tanxun (Pursuit and Beyond: Identity Politics and Exploration of Pure Art in Chinese American Women's Literature)." *Hainan shifan daxue xuebao* 22.2 (2009): 99.

Li, Ping. "Waiqu yihuo chuangzao?: *Nü yongshi* zhong lishi chuanshuo de zhenwei zhizheng (Misrepresentation or Creation?: Controversy of the True or False Historical Legend in *The Woman Warrior*)." *Yunnan nongyedaxue xuebao* 4.2 (2010): 115-18.

Liang, Na. "Lun Tang Tingting xiaoshuo de houxiandai xing (Postmodern Characteristics in Maxine Hong Kingston's Novels)." *Dalian haishidaxue xuebao* 7.2 (2008): 126-28.

Lim, Shirley Geok-Lin, John Blair Gamber, Stephen Hong Sohn, and Gina Valentino, eds. *Transnational Asian American Literature: Sites and Transits*. Philadelphia: Temple UP, 2006.

Lowe, Lisa. "Heterogeneity, Hybridity, Multiplicity: Marking Asian American Differences." *Diaspora* 1.1 (1991): 24-44.

Ludwig, Sämi. *CONCRETE LANGUAGE: Intercultural Communication in Maxine Hong Kingston's* The Woman Warrior *and Ishmael Reed's* Mumbo Jumbo. Frankfurt am Main: Peter Lang, 1996.

Luo, Chen, and Man Luo. "Nahan de yongshi: xi Tang Tingting de *Nü yongshi* (A Warrior Calling for Arms: Analyzing Kingston's *The Woman Warrior*)." *Heilongjiang shizhi* 20 (2009): 72, 75.

Pu, Ruoqian. "Huayi menguo zuojia bixia de lishi zaixian (Historical Representation in Chinese American Writing)." *Jinan daxue xuebao* 141.4 (2009): 11.

Qiu, Jian. "Lun meiguo huayi zuojia Tang Tingting *Nü yongshi* de xushi fengge (Narrative Style of Chinese American Writer Maxine Hong Kingston's *The Woman Warrior*)." *Zuojia zazhi* 3 (2010): 120-21.

Rao, Fanzi. "Zhongguo dalu haiwai huaren wenxue yangjiu gaiguan (Studies of Overseas Chinese Literature in Mainland China: An Overview)." Jennie Wang 29-38.

Schultermandl, Silvia. *Transnational Matrilineage: Mother-Daughter Conflicts in Asian American Literature*. Münster, Germany: LIT Verlag, 2009.

—, ed. "Asian American and Asian British Literature and Culture." Special Issue of *Interactions* 15.2 (2006).

Shan, Te-hsing. "Branching Out: Chinese American Literary Studies in Taiwan." Jennie Wang 39-56.

—. *Gushi yu xsheng: huamei wenxue yu wenhua yanjiu* (Story and New Life: A Study of Chinese American Literature and Culture). Tianjin: Nankai daxue chubanshe, 2009.

—. *Kaijiang yu pitu: meiguo huayi wenxue yu wenhua* (Breaking New Ground: Chinese American Literature and Culture). Tianjin: Nankai daxue chubanshe, 2006.

—. *Mingke yu zaixian: huayi meiguo wenxue yu wenhua lunji* (Inscriptions and Representations: Chinese American Literary and Cultural Studies). Taipei: Maitian chuban gufen youxian gongsi, 2000.

—. *Yu zhizhe weiwu: yanmei wenxue yu wenhua mingjia fangtanlu* (In the Company of the Wise: Conversations with Asian American Writers and Critics). Taipei: yunchen wenhua shiye gufen youxian gongsi, 2009.

—, and Wen-Ching Ho, eds. *Wenhua shuxing yu huayi meiguo wenxue* (Cultural Heritage and Chinese American Literature). Taipei: zhongyang yanjiuyuan oumei yanjiusuo, 1994.

Shen, Caihong. "Xunqiu ziwo renting de nü yongshi: Tang Tingting *Nü yongshi* yu Wang Anyi *Jishi yu xugou* zhi bijiao yanjiu (A Woman Warrior Seeking Self-Realization: A Comparative Study of Maxine Hong Kingston's *The Woman Warrior* and Anyi Wang's *Documentary and Fiction*)." *Jingmen zhiyejishu xueyuan xuebao* 24.3 (2009): 11-13.

Shi, Lei, and Jianguang Wang. "Shilun *Nü yongshi* zhong dongxifang wenhua de jiaocuo (Intersection of Oriental and Western Cultures in *The Woman Warrior*)." *Zuojia zazhi* 6 (2009): 87.

Shi, Min. "Meiguo houxiandai nüzuojia de xiezuo tezhi chutan (Characteristics of American Postmodern Women's Writing)." *Guangdong gongyedaxue xuebao* 8.1 (2008): 59-62.

Song, Yang. "Shengtai nüxing zhuyi shiye zhong de *Nü yongshi*" (*The Woman Warrior* from Eco-feminist Perspective). *Xichang xueyuan xuebao* 20.2 (2008): 41-44.

Song, Yueli. "Butong de xingge, xiangtong de mingyun: Fan Yi he wuming guma de beiju mingyun jiexi (Different Characteristics, Same Fate: Analyzing the Tragic Lives of Fan Yi and No Name Aunt)." *Shanhua* 11 (2009): 118-19.

Tang, Jie. "Dianfu yu chongsu: Tang Tingting xiaoshuo renwu wenhuashenfen de tanxun yu jiangou (Subversion and Reconstruction: Exploration and Identity Construction in Maxine Hong Kingston's Novels)." *Huaihua xueyuan xuebao* 28.4 (2009): 68-70.

Ty, Eleanor. "Rethinking the Hyphen: Asian North American and European Ethnic Texts as Global Narratives." *Canadian Review of American Studies* 32.3 (2002): 239-52.

—, and Donald C. Goellnicht, eds. *Beyond the Hyphen: Asian North American Identities*. Bloomington: Indiana UP, 2004.

Unali, Lina, ed. *Story in Chinatown and Away: Essays on Chinese American Literature and on U.S.-China Relationships*. Rome: Sun Moon Lake, 1998.

Wang, Jennie, ed. *Querying the Genealogy: Comparative and Transnational Studies in Chinese American Literature*. Shanghai: Shanghai yiwen chubanshe, 2006.

Wong, Sau-ling Cynthia. "Denationalization Reconsidered: Asian American Cultural Criticism at a Theoretical Crossroads." *Amerasia Journal* 21.1&2 (1995): 1-27.

—. "When Asian American Literature Leaves 'Home': On Internationalizing Asian American Literary Studies." Brada-Williams and Chow 29-40.

Xu, Yingguo. *Kuawenhua shiye xia de meiguo huayiwenxue: Zhao Jianxiu zuopin yanjiu* (Cross-Cultural Study of Chinese American Literature: Frank Chin's Writing). Tianjin: Nankai daxue chubanshe, 2007.

Xue, Yufeng. *Meiguo huayi wenxue zhi wenhuayanjiu* (Cultural Studies of Chinese American Literature). Beijing: renmin wenxue chubanshe, 2007.

Yu, Xing. "Guangong bubi zhan Mulan: toushi meiguo huayi zuojia de Zhao Tang lunzhan (Unnecessary Battle between Guangong and Mulan: On the Cultural Debate between Chinese American Writers Frank Chin and Maxine Hong Kingston)." *Ningde shizhuan xuebao* 88.1 (2009): 61-64.

Zhang, Jing. *The Representation of Chineseness in Chinese English Literature*. Jinan: Shandong daxue chubanshe, 2008.

Zhang, Xihua, and Zhemei Yang. "Zhongxi Mulan xingxiang duibi (A Comparison of Mulan in China and the West)." *Zhongguo wenhua yanjiu* 3 (2009): 168-72.

Zhang, Zhichun. "*Nü yongshi*: fanying huayi nüxingyishi juexing de shijie xiaoshuo (*The Woman Warrior*: A Global Novel Reflecting Chinese American Feminist Awareness)." *Yan'an zhiyejishu xueyuan xuebao* 23.5 (2009): 51.

Maxine Hong Kingston's *Woman Warrior* Beyond the Feminine and the Unfeminine: Dismantling the Dualistic Perception of Gender and Ethnicity

Nelly Mok (Bordeaux 3, France)

In Maxine Hong Kingston's autobiographical novel, *The Woman Warrior* (1976), the narrator, who speaks on behalf of Kingston herself, recalls her childhood as a Chinese American girl while fantasizing her life in China as a woman warrior and musing over the family tales she grew up with; she reports and/or imagines the story of her Chinese aunt—her father's sister—whom she paradoxically names No Name Woman, as well as the Chinese American experiences of her mother, Brave Orchid, and of her mother's sister, her aunt Moon Orchid.

In this paper, I will explore the ways Kingston questions the Western perception of the Asian woman and Asian femininity, upsetting the Orientalist stereotypes attributed to her sex and to her race. I will underline the ways the author succeeds in delineating a new, complex Chinese American female figure, without the boundaries of gender and race categories, thus providing the Chinese/Asian American community with a global imprint.

"Performing" American femininity to be assimilated

In the last section of the book, the narrator recalls her teenage years in the Chinese school she used to attend after class at the American school. She describes one of her classmates, a girl who is singled out in the Chinese class because of her mutism. The Chinese girl's silence and her clean, orderly, yet immutable, almost dehumanized physical appearance make her look like a doll:

> She was so neat. Her neatness bothered me. [...]. I hated her clothes—the blue pastel cardigan, the white blouse with the collar that lay *flat* over the cardigan, the homemade *flat*, cotton skirts she wore... I hated pastels; I would wear black always. [...]. She wiped her eyes with her *papery* fingers. The skin on her hands and arms seemed powdery-dry, like tracing *paper*, onion skin. I hated her fingers. I could snap them like breadsticks. (177, my emphasis)

Her flawless appearance, her flat and shapeless outfit, as well as the "papery" look of her skin, convey her one-dimensionality: the girl stands out as the living version of the flat paper dolls her aunt Moon Orchid has brought from Hong-

Kong (120): "I hated her for her China doll hair cut" (173). The narrator's loath for such a colorless, invisible and inaudible girl signals her rejection of the Western stereotype of the silent, passive China Doll, which Renee Tajima points out as one of the main Western Orientalist stock images imposed on Asian American women. The China Doll is a variation on the demure, meek, self-sacrificing Oriental Flower/Lotus Blossom Baby figure, which Tajima defines as "utterly feminine, delicate" (309), sharply contrasting with their self-confident, extroverted American female peers. Like the narrator's schoolmate, Brave Orchid's sister, Moon Orchid, and the latter's daughter, both stand out as the embodiment of the "dainty" (127)—a word used by Brave Orchid—passive Oriental Flower: "Brave Orchid thought that her niece was like her mother, the lovely, useless type" (128).

These stereotypes, to which Asian American women have been confined, function as synecdoches of what Edward Said identifies as the Occident's ideological and rhetorical construction of the "Orient," that is, the Western representation of a weak, submissive East. "Orientalism" names the discursive process through which the East turns into the West's fantasized Orient, shedding its actual referentiality to become the mere token of the Occident's socio-cultural, political, economic, intellectual and moral superiority:

> The West became more western, the East more eastern, the West rational, mature and normal, the East irrational, backward, depraved. Orientalism as a political doctrine could be 'willed over the Orient because the Orient was weaker than the West, which elided the Orient's difference with its weakness' [...] and therefore presumably with its alleged inferiority. (MacKenzie 9)

Reflecting on Said's *Orientalism*, MacKenzie underlines the phallocentric nature of the Western imperialist discourse on the East, focusing on "[Said's] identification of a monolithic and predominantly male-originated discourse" (11). The "Orient" refers to the feminized Western representation of the East, therefore vouching for the Occident's resolutely masculine supremacy.

Critics like Elaine Kim and Yen le Espiritu privilege a gender-b(i)ased reading of the dissymmetric, unbalanced East-West relationship that is ingrained in both the occidental and the oriental collective imaginary. Espiritu points out "the [Western] gendering of ethnicity—the process whereby white ideology assigns selected gender characteristics to various 'ethnic' others" (88); in other words, the critic highlights the Western genderization of the Asian American community—that is its emasculation and/or feminization. Kim's remarks complement Espiritu's statement, by emphasizing sexuality as the medium for such a genderizing construction of Asian Americans. She notes that both men and women are marginalized as sexual oddities, for men are seen as effeminate or feminized, whereas women are viewed as overfeminine. Men are anomalies while women are excesses, therefore enhancing white sexual supremacy. Yet, the stereotypes attributed to Asian women testify to the double—racist and patriarchal—stigmata they have to bear, both as Asians, and as women: "[B]oth sexism and racism have been blended together to produce the sexualization of white racism" (Kim qtd. in Espiritu 93). Thus, the demeaning of Asian women—through their reifying hypersexualized, overfeminine image—is the locus of white men's matchless sexuality.

The hope for assimilation, for Americanization, for the second-generation narrator and the first-generation women of her family, therefore lies in the secret of American femininity. Brave Orchid constantly urges her sister Moon Orchid to disguise herself so that she can claim her Americanized, re-married husband back: "'I brought my wig,' said Brave Orchid. 'Why don't you disguise yourself as a beautiful lady? I brought lipstick and powder too. And at some dramatic point, you pull off the wig and say, 'I am Moon Orchid'" (145). Being feminine, pretty and desirable in America means playing another part, impersonating a one-dimensional Hollywood poster icon: "Do you want him to see you with your eyes and nose swollen when that young so-called wife wears lipstick and nail polish like a movie star?" (151).

Brave Orchid's pressing her sister to disguise herself—she offers her a wig and makeup—actually formulates the Euro-American injunction to what Homi Bhabha calls "mimicry" as the sole condition for a successful assimilation. The critic defines "colonial mimicry" as a rhetorical strategy used by colonial powers to control colonized subjects: the colonized is impelled to put on "white masks"—Bhabha explicitly refers to Frantz Fanon's analysis of black people's relationship to the dominant ideal of "whiteness"—to imitate the colonizer by acquiring and internalizing his/her socio-cultural norms, traits and codes, so as to achieve complete assimilation. Faced with model images that present "whiteness" as the primary condition for their integration into the dominant society, ethnic subjects are torn between their identificatory desire for "whiteness" and their anxious awareness of their invariable non-whiteness: "Colonial mimicry is the desire for a reformed, recognizable Other, as a subject of difference that is almost the same, but not quite" (Bhabha 86). According to Bhabha, such a gap between the copy and its original both signals the colonizer's unquestionable superiority and reminds the colonized of their irremediable deficiency.

In *The Woman Warrior*, American and Americanized women are erected into inaccessible models which have to be imitated. Yet, Moon Orchid's assimilation is doomed to failure right from her arrival in America as she is unable to inflect her feminine attributes. Integrating American society does not merely mean making oneself "American-feminine," to quote the narrator. It implies maiming one's Asian features: slit eyes and straight hair have to become Caucasian-like. Anne Anlin Cheng emphasizes that the process of assimilation necessarily implies symbolical amputation and faking: "The notion that cultural assimilation always requires certain acts of personal relinquishment and even disguise is a common one, easily and conventionally understood as the price of 'fitting in'"

(106). Far from endowing her with dimensionality and substance, mimicry lures the Asian American woman with the prospect of identity recovery only through her impersonation of an American version of herself.

Relying on John Langshaw Austin's distinction between descriptive, declaratory and performative statements, Judith Butler applies the concept of "performativity" to the notion of gender in her 1990 essay *Gender Trouble*. Like a performative statement which allows the speaker to perform an act by wording it, gender should be viewed as both the object of the dominant (phallocentric) discourse—the body is defined as male or female—and a socio-cultural construct, namely a sexual identity determined by a set of practices, rites, discourses and behaviors that condition a human being's femininity or masculinity. Thus, the notion of gender depends on its constant reassertion and reenactment: by acting "as a woman" or "as a man," individuals see themselves as innately gendered beings while they actually perform femininity or masculinity according to norms devised by the socio-cultural sphere they belong to. Cheng underscores the relevance of Butler's concept of gender performativity to ethnic identity issues: confronted with the hegemonic imperative to fit the standards of Euro-American femininity, Asian American women are likely to indulge in the constrained and unaware re-enactment of a set of codes or standards, expectations and assumptions which are socially, culturally, politically and historically pre-established and defined, therefore exposing themselves to the danger of ethnic self-alienation (57). Bhabha's distinction between "imitation" and "mimicry" interestingly echoes Butler's difference between "performance" and "performativity." Both conceptual pairs are based on the tenuous frontier between the subject's *conscious* identification with the model he/she is striving to imitate and his/her *alienating* sense of identity through impersonation.[1]

Brave Orchid's insistently pushing her sister Moon Orchid to disguise herself as a proper "American-feminine" wife who could arouse her husband's admiration and measure up to the latter's English-speaking, fully-assimilated young Chinese American wife, has led the old woman to self-alienation. America's call for Americanized femininity and for identity usurpation has

1. Butler stresses the subject's illusory sense of authenticity while performing his/her gendered identity since he/she remains unaware of the socio-political foundations of his/her acts and speech as a man or a woman: "Performativity is [...] not a singular 'act,' for it is always a reiteration of a norm or a set of norms [...]. This act is not primarily theatrical [...]. Its apparent theatricality is produced to the extent that its historicity remains dissimulated (and, conversely, its theatricality gains a certain inevitability given the impossibility of a full disclosure of its historicity) [...]. Indeed, could it be that the production of the subject as originator of his/her effects is precisely a consequence of this dissimulated citationality?" (Butler, *Bodies* 12-13).

eventually driven her crazy. Persuaded that she is chased by Mexicans who want to kill her and her family, she suffers from paranoia. When Moon Orchid visits Brave Orchid, her sister does not recognize her anymore: "Her sister's skin hung loose, like a hollowed frog's, as if she had shrunken inside it. Her clothes bagged, not fitting sharply anymore. 'I'm in disguise,' she said" (155). The disguise she has to wear in America does not fit her. Moon Orchid is the victim of performativity: overwhelmed by America's demand to perform Americanness, the Chinese woman is trapped within self-estrangement and is bound to flee from codes she does not recognize.

Gender role reversal in *The Woman Warrior*: Kingston's anti-assimilationist stance?

Kingston's woman warrior therefore stands out as the female avenger determined to free the Asian American woman from the ideological strangleholds to which she is confined in the imperialist Western perception. She embodies the Chinese American author's and her own community's will to question the hegemonic representations of Asians. This is emphasized by Lisa Lowe: "Although orientalism seeks to consolidate the coherence of the West as subject precisely through the representation of 'oriental' objects as homogenous, fixed, and stable, contradictions in the production of Asians and in the noncorrespondence between the orientalist object and the Asian American subject ultimately express the limits of such fictions" (67). By emphasizing the discrepancy between Western perceptions of Asians and the expression of Asian Americans' actual inner turmoil, Asian American men and women invalidate Western stereotyped representations of the community and denounce them as erroneous fantasies. Such a contestation in Kingston's novel apparently lies in what could be perceived as a counterhegemonic masculinization of her female characters,[2] as they are portrayed as strong, rebellious women, who refuse to cater to Western and Chinese patriarchy's "sex-role stereotyping" (see Millet).

---

2. To Antonio Gramsci, the stereotyping of a minority is both the tool and the symptom of the "hegemony" of the dominant culture within a country. He defines hegemony as the processes through which the political, cultural and ideological supremacy of a dominant group is not only imposed, identified and acknowledged but also contested, resisted and endangered by budding and evolving minor groups. So hegemony necessarily engenders and comprehends its own hemlock, "counterhegemony." Lisa Lowe explains Gramsci's concepts as such: "We might say that hegemony is not only the political process by which a particular group constitutes itself as 'the one' or 'the majority' in relation to which 'minorities' are defined and know themselves to be 'other,' but is equally the process by which various and incommensurable positions of otherness may ally and constitute a new majority, a "counterhe-

Hence some American reviewers' confusion when the book was released in 1976. Michael Malloy, of the *National Observer*, was puzzled by Kingston's Chinese female characters, some of them being hostile, others being meek; thus he concluded that these confusions were "especially hard for a non-Chinese" and that *that* was "the troubling aspect of the book" (qtd. in Kim xvii). The reviewer's response to Kingston's autobiographical novel exemplifies Western reluctance to perceive the Chinese/Asian woman as an ambivalent individual, likely to oscillate between subservience and subversion, to be either a martyr or a warrior. Besides, Malloy's puzzlement points out Kingston's achievement in upsetting the Western representation of a docile Chinese woman. For example, the narrator's mother, Brave Orchid, is far from being characterized by the Western-assumed "feminine" qualities of Chinese women. Contrary to her sister Moon Orchid, who embodies the Western conception of Chinese femininity, Brave Orchid is neither submissive nor weak or passive. She indeed sharply contrasts with her sister and her niece whom she sees as burdens. Believing it is her duty to "toughen up these two" (128), she stands out as a "brave" negative countering the specter of the Lotus Blossom.

The first-generation Chinese American mother displays what Kate Millet identifies as Western masculine "active," "instrumental" traits, possessing "rationality" and "power," to use the feminist writer's terms in her 1970 essay *Sexual Politics* (qtd. in Eisenstein 5).[3] In the light of Evelyn Fox Keller's remarks about the traditional Western association of science with masculinity, Brave Orchid's scientific knowledge and achievements at the To Keung School as well as her outstanding skills as a doctor subversively appear unfeminine. In her 1978 analysis "Gender and Science," Keller examines Western assumptions

---

gemony" (69). Western cultural and ideological imperialism is paradoxically dependent on the existence and empowerment of its foes. "Minorities" which do not conform to the rules and to the discourse of the "majority" are marginalized and erected into a vital foil. Still, these alien groups are likely to unite and form a countermajority. Thus, the Asian American community—which encompasses Chinese Americans, Japanese Americans, Filipino Americans, and so on—stands out as a cultural and political alliance challenging Western domination.

3. Kate Millet distinguishes Western-feminine traits from Western-masculine traits: "Millet demonstrated that for female, 'normal' meant passive, while for male, it meant active. Men had instrumental traits: they were tenacious, aggressive, curious, ambitious, planful, responsible, original, and competitive. Women had expressive traits: they were affectionate, obedient, responsive to sympathy and approval, cheerful, kind, and friendly. Social pressure kept women conforming to the expressive role expected of them, a role that dictated conformity and obedience, while men occupied the instrumental role of rationality and power" (qtd. in Eisenstein 5).

of science as essentially masculine: "The characterization of both the scientific mind and its modes of access to knowledge as masculine is significant. Masculine here connotes, as it so often does, autonomy, separation, and distance" (qtd. in Eisenstein 99). She accounts for this connection by arguing that science requires cognitive skills and abilities, such as "objectivity" and analytical distance, which are traditionally attributed to men. Significantly, Brave Orchid's American daughters view science as a means to ensure intellectual equality with men and to resist male abuse. Having witnessed Moon Orchid's breakdown after her humiliating failure to compete with her husband's American wife, the old woman's nieces decide to find immunity in science: "Brave Orchid's daughters decided fiercely that they would never let men be unfaithful to them. All her children made up their minds to major in science or mathematics" (160). In choosing to study science, they both parallel their mother's "masculine" doctoring training and symbolically pit their wits against their uncle with equal skills—Moon Orchid's husband working as a neurosurgeon.

However, Kingston's narrative should not be hastily categorized as a sameness feminist discourse, built on the belief in women's androgyny, in women's mixture of feminine and masculine traits as a way to demystify the so-called natural gender gap, and to minimize the overestimated differences between men and women (Cusset 159). Feminist Hester Eisenstein stresses the deceptive nature of mere role-reversal between men and women (xiii). Far from being a long-term subversive strategy, superficial role-reversal is a carnivalesque game, the token of patriarchy's magnanimous self-derision: instead of dismantling patriarchal machinery, it ensures its permanency by occasionally mocking sexist rules and customs without ever questioning them.

Kingston is aware that true contestation does not lie in the mere masculinization of her heroines. In her fantasized life as a woman warrior, the narrator complies with Chinese patriarchy once she has beheaded the emperor and executed the baron who enslaved the villagers. She returns to her husband and her in-laws, relinquishes her armor and her helmet to her son and devotes herself to the duties she is expected to perform as a Chinese woman:

> I went home to my parents-in-law and husband and son. My son stared, very impressed by the general he had seen in the parade, but his father said, 'It's your mother. Go to your mother.' My son was delighted that the shiny general was his mother too. She gave him her helmet to wear and her swords to hold.
>
> Wearing my black embroidered wedding coat, I knelt at my parents-in-law's feet, as I would have done as a bride. 'Now my public duties are finished,' I said, 'I will stay with you, doing farmwork and housework, and giving you more sons.' (45)

In taking off her armor and in putting on her wedding coat, she signifies the unquestionable status of patriarchy. Her masculinization is legitimized only by her patriotic intents, her heroic efforts—her "public duties"—to maintain patriarchal tradition. And yet her disguise as a man has to remain secret: "I never told [my soldiers] the truth. Chinese executed women who disguised themselves as soldiers or students, no matter how bravely they fought or how high they scored on the examinations" (39). Cross-dressing cannot hamper the functioning of patriarchy.

Likewise, in America, the narrator's shy attempts to defeat her 'opponents' at work are to no avail. When her tyrannical, exploiting boss fires her after she tried to stand up to him, she allows herself to be a warrior and to display masculine, warlike aggressiveness to him *only* in her imagination:

> 'I refuse to type these invitations,' I whispered, voice unreliable.
>
> He leaned back in his leather chair, his bossy stomach opulent. He picked up his calendar, and slowly circled a date. 'You will be paid up to here,' he said. 'We'll mail you the check.'
>
> If I took the sword, which my hate must surely have forged out of the air, and gutted him, I would put color and wrinkles into his shirt. (49)

The soldier in her is contained within Kingston's hypothetical sentence and does not punish this American "baron."

Subversion through mere "role-reversal" remains sterile as long as genderization is countered by genderization: the threat of self-misperception still hovers in ideological retaliation. The paper dolls merely take on other shapes and testify to the community's internalization of an oppression it enacts in its turn. Significantly, the teenage narrator's aggressiveness and brutality toward the mute girl at the Chinese school conveys the Asian American female subject's feelings of self-alienation and self-repulsion in the process of assimilation as she bullies the China Doll she no longer wants to embody in the Western gaze (176-78). Yet, by assaulting her own hated double and alter ego, she attacks herself, and eventually harms herself, as after the incident, she catches a serious illness that compels her to stay in bed for a year and a half (181-82).

The strong and vindictive nature of Kingston's female characters, and the author's criticism of Chinese patriarchy, have fuelled nationalist criticisms of the "assimilationist" quality of *The Woman Warrior*; Chinese American critics like Frank Chin denounced the novel's "anti-male" and "anti-nationalist" stance (qtd. in Lowe 76). Even the remarks of the Asian American feminist Lynn Lu take on a nationalist tone when alluding to renowned Asian American women writers like Kingston and Amy Tan: "We now have our own Woman Warrior, our own Joy Luck Club, our own successful role models in Hollywood, on Capitol Hill, in the Fortune 500, and on the evening news. But proving that some Asian women can succeed on the terms of the dominant culture fails to question the injustices that remain in place" (19). According to Lu, the works of these women writers have produced assimilationist stereotypes. The Woman Warrior now typifies an Asian American woman who has successfully integrated in America by making its signifiers and expectations her own.

Kingston's work has indeed been accused of depicting Chinese American women's assimilation as a masculinizing process, often at the cost of Chinese men's emasculation. For instance, Brave Orchid is ready to act as a bodyguard for her sister whom she forces to go and claim her Americanized husband back: "'I'll hit *him*. I'll protect you. I'll hit him back. The two of us will knock him down and make him listen.' Brave Orchid chuckled as if she were looking forward to a fight" (145). She insists on their ability to physically overpower him. Also, earlier in the text, Brave Orchid describes her adaptation to the United States as a masculinizing process: "'In China I never even had to hang up my own clothes. I shouldn't have left, but your father couldn't have supported you without me. I'm the one with the big muscles. [...]. I didn't need muscles in China. I was small in China.' She was. The silk dresses she gave me are tiny. You would not think the same person wore them" (104). Yet, her masculinization has been a way for her to make up for her husband's physical inferiority. Similarly, the woman warrior's husband mirrors Brave Orchid's husband's emasculation since he also stands as a foil to his wife. Though admired by his spouse as a "good fighter," he is never pictured fighting and cries when he sees the family names carved on her back: "He *wept* when he took off my shirt and saw the scar-words on my back" (39, my emphasis). He is thus weeping for his wife who, unlike him, did not allow herself to let out her pain during the carving: "It hurt terribly—the cuts sharp [...]—pain so various. I gripped my knees. I released them. Neither tension nor relaxation helped. I wanted to cry" (35).

Nevertheless, Kingston clearly discards unfemininity as the locus for the Chinese American woman's emancipation from patriarchal stereotypes, rather pointing to the superficiality of gender role reversal. As a young girl, she constantly fears she might be sold by her parents to some Chinese husband. Thus she strives to make herself an undesirable, unmarriageable tomboy, showing meticulous disrespect for Chinese patriarchal codes and dreaming of becoming a boy: "I refused to cook. When I had to wash dishes, I would crack one or two. 'Bad girl,' my mother yelled, and sometimes that made me gloat rather than cry. Isn't a bad girl almost a boy?" (47). She comically foresees herself as "[a] lumberjack in Oregon," valuing virility and masculine physical strength as the tokens of her American identity. Yet, only to the naive teenage narrator can radical masculinization be envisaged as the sole means to escape the bonds of Chinese patriarchy and to become Americanized. Kingston's irony pervades the passage here, as the narrator readily trades one stereotype for another, willing to turn the China Doll into the so-called all-American lumberjack so as to sabotage her parents' marital plans for her, and to achieve assimilation.

Questioning gender and race categories: the Chinese American woman beyond androgyny and the unfeminine

Kingston also avoids indulging in an essentialist feminist point of view, namely a "woman-centered perspective" on the world and on gender hierarchy, nurtured by a belief in women's "intrinsic moral superiority" (Eisenstein 140-41). If patriarchy is challenged in *The Woman Warrior*, matriarchy is equally questioned. For instance, the Chinese women whom the woman warrior frees and who become amazons are not described as offering a viable and tangible alternative. They are criminals, killing men and boys, and the narrator is not willing to assert their existence, even in her imagination: "I myself never encountered such women and could not vouch for their reality" (45). Generally acclaimed as "a work that challenges and redefines boundaries of culture, gender, and genre by transgressing them" (Van Spanckeren 44), *The Woman Warrior* strives to offer gender, and particularly the feminine, a delineation that goes beyond social and political assumption; Kingston's work can therefore be related to anti-essentialist feminism, which values the deconstruction of any gender hierarchy through the "de-essentialization" of genders and the invalidation of the socially constructed "eternal feminine" (Cusset 135).

Kingston subtly manages to deconstruct her female characters' apparent androgyny, never confining the depictions of her women in femininity or masculinity. She thus dismantles the patriarchal perception of femininity as either intrinsically weak or lacking masculinity. Despite their being depicted as warriors, the narrator and her mother's femininity are never denied. If femininity is a flaw in patriarchal society, it actually empowers them. Brave Orchid, a skillful doctor and a powerful shaman, is also acknowledged as a graceful woman: "She stayed awake keeping watch nightly in an epidemic and chanted during air raids. She yanked bones straight that had been crooked for years while relatives held the cripples down, and she did all this never dressed less elegantly than when she stepped out of the sedan chair" (77). Though these women are warriors as strong as men, they are never depicted as "weremen" and "werewomen." To the Chinese baron she is about to kill, the woman warrior proudly announces, "I am a female avenger" (43). Moreover, when she is finally ready to go to war, dressed like a soldier, what is most respected and admired by the villagers is her femininity and beauty: "I put on my men's clothes and armor and tied my hair in a man's fashion. 'How beautiful you look,' the people said. 'How beautiful *she* looks'" (36, my emphasis). She is admired as a strong, charismatic woman warrior, not as a convincing, true-to-life imitation of masculinity.

Kingston's portrayal of her female characters sheds light on the deceitfulness of femininity and masculinity as patriarchal constructions. Maurine Devine's analysis of Margaret Atwood's *Surfacing* (1979) may also apply to *The Woman Warrior*: "For Atwood, androgyny is not a meaningful concept, but neither is feminine nor masculine. [...]. In going beyond the concepts of the feminine and masculine as social constructs, Atwood 'deconstructs' the basis of androgyny" (152). In Kingston's perspective, gender is no longer discriminating, for it rejects any socially conceived hierarchy between the feminine and the masculine.

The author manages to deconstruct the racial and ethnic "homogenization" and "essentialization" of her community by emphasizing paradox as the Asian figure's intrinsic nature. Western critics' puzzlement in the face of the Chinese woman's ambivalence in *The Woman Warrior*—either docile (and feminine) or aggressive (and masculine)—actually reveals Western readers' difficulty to depart from genderization when dealing with Asian people. Yet the critics' reaction also proves Kingston's successful upsetting of the genderized perception of Asian women who cannot be contained within the boundaries of typification. In redefining femininity, Kingston enlarges the representation of Asian women, depicting them in a way that goes beyond superfemininity and masculinization, thus efficiently responding to both Western ideological oppression and Asian American criticisms of the apparent assimilationist quality of her book.

A multi-faceted Chinese (Asian) American female figure

Kingston is careful to portray the Asian American woman as a multiple yet consistent figure. The way Kingston's autobiographical narrative is composed contributes to the construction of the Asian American woman's complexity. *The Woman Warrior* consists of five chapters, each focusing on different women; yet the latter's stories are mediated through the narrator's perspective. Thus the patriarchal martyr, the fearless dutiful warrior, the powerful shaman, the defeated meek empress, as well as the aggressive daughter and anti-patriarchal storyteller are one and the same Chinese American woman who comes to take on depth.

The recurrent motifs which the reader encounters throughout the chapters are also part of the construction: they connect the diverging narratives, encouraging the reader's dialogic involvement in the text, and erect each woman and each experience into one facet of the multi-dimensional Asian American female figure.[4] For example, the allusion to the woman warrior's breast milk—"It was

4. Referring to Mikhail Bahktin's theory on dialogism, Wolfgang Iser in *The Act of Reading*, defines reading as a "dynamic happening," the product of a "dyadic interaction" between the text and the reader. According to him, the reader must get involved in the text, so as to contribute to the creation of meaning through an active reading. Iser encourages the reader to search for thematic correspondences in the text, so as to create a dynamic relationship

during this lonely time, when any high cry made the milk spill from my breasts, that I got careless" (41)—echoes the description of No Name Woman with her newborn child: "Full of milk, the little ghost slept. When it awoke, she hardened her breasts against the milk that crying loosens." (15)

Moreover, the "satin triangle" sewn in Brave Orchid's quilt, "a red heart to protect [her] at the neck" (68) recalls the one her daughter, imagining herself as a woman warrior, sews on the sling carrying her baby inside her armor: "We made a sling for the baby inside my big armor [...]. At the back of the sling I had sewn a tiny quilted triangle, red at its center against two shades of green; it marked the baby's nape for luck" (40).

Also, Cheng Lok Chua notes that the title of the second chapter "White Tigers" can be paralleled with the title of the fourth chapter "At the Western Palace." Indeed, on the one hand, the "White Tiger" is one of the four mythic beasts standing for geomantic power, each of them reigning over a quadrant of the Chinese compass (147). Insofar as the White Tiger traditionally dominates the West, cardinal points turn out to be the motifs that connect "White Tigers" to "At the Western Palace," the woman warrior's story to Moon Orchid's experience, so that even the meek old Chinese woman is erected into a warlike empress and a savior:

> 'A long time ago,' began Brave Orchid, 'the emperors had four wives, one at each point of the compass, and they lived in four palaces. The Empress of the West would connive for power, but the Empress of the East was good and kind and full of light. You are the Empress of the East, and the Empress of the West has imprisoned the Earth's Emperor in the Western Palace. And you, the good Empress of the East, come out of the dawn to invade her land and free the Emperor. You must break the strong spell she has cast on him that has lost him the East.' (143)

The new Asian American female figure is literally constructed in the minute "collage" of Kingston's different portrayals (Kim 200).

Mythopoesis as a medium for Kingston's "womanist" perception of the Asian American woman

Trinh T. Minh-Ha highlights the importance of inscribing Asian American collective subjectivity into a communal heritage: she urges Asian Americans "to cut across ethnic allegiances while assuming a specific and contingent legacy" (qtd. in Dariotis 180). And Mitsuye Yamada stresses the "need [for Asian American women] to affirm [their] own culture while working within it to change it" (73). She thus words the necessity for them to re-appropriate and re-

---

between apparently contradictory speeches, thus nurturing and enriching the meaning of the text.

create their Asian culture in the light of their American experiences. And this is what Kingston undertakes to do: "Kingston's method of composition in *The Woman Warrior* is a mythopoeic synthesis of Asian and American cultures, producing a unique identity and imagination that throws an Asian slant of light on American realities" (Chua 150). By fusing her cultural resources, the Asian American woman writer manages to create a personal mythology that encompasses genders and races.[5] The "mythopoeic synthesis" Kingston performs refers to what Alicia Ostriker calls "revisionist mythmaking" in her study of women poets' use of language, "The Thieves of Language": "Whenever a poet employs a figure or story previously accepted and defined by a culture, the poet is using myth, and the potential is always present that the use will be revisionist: that is, the figure or tale will be appropriated for altered ends, the old vessel filled with new wine, initially satisfying the thirst of the individual poet but ultimately making cultural change possible" (317). To Ostriker, the artist engages in the process of cultural revision by appropriating his/her cultural collective legacy and by modifying it at will to answer his/her personal questions and to relate individual experiences.

In re-telling the Chinese myth of Fa Mu Lan, the woman writer conceives the Asian American myth of a heroine whose training, ordeals, battles and empowerment are meant to be easily transferred from China to America. Kingston gets down to mythologizing the Asian American self beyond gender and race, within the larger confines of humanity. At fourteen, the woman warrior decides to take an initiation test in the Chinese wilderness. During her journey, she attends a "cosmic dance" staging the keys for identity achievement and existence:

> I saw two people made of gold dancing the earth's dances. They turned so perfectly that together they were the axis of the earth's turning. They were light; they were molten, changing gold—Chinese lion dancers, African lion dancers in midstep. I heard high Javanese bells deepen in midring to Indian bells, Hindu Indian, American Indian. [.... O]ne of the dancers is always a man and the other a woman. (27)

The dance is characteristically cross-cultural, and encompasses both the feminine and the masculine not as socially fixed gender categories but as complementary principles, as is underscored by Cheng Lok Chua: "This universal dance, suggesting the destroying and creating dance of the Hindu Siva or the agon of the dying and resurrecting Christ, also recalls the taoist rhythm of yin-yang, female-male, light-dark" (149). Noting the different cultural resources—both Western and Asian—by which this scene has been inspired, the

---

5. Kingston herself underlines that she is "telling [the old Chinese myths] in a new American way," by "integrat[ing them] into the Chinese American's life" (qtd. in Chua 146).

critic emphasizes complementarity—destruction-creation, life-death, female-male, Asian-Western—as the thematic pivot of Kingston's mythopoesis.

In the writer's revised version of Fa Mu Lan's training, the woman warrior is given to understand self-perception and identity achievement as the results of a 'universal' process encompassing all differences. In fact, her power is the writer's power, namely the faculty to see and represent people and herself beyond the confines of race and gender. In her enlightened perception, differences and contradictions form a coherent universal whole:

> I learned to make my mind large, as the universe is large, so that there is room for paradoxes. Pearls are bone marrow; pearls come from oysters. The dragon lives in the sky, ocean, marshes, and mountains; and the mountains are also its cranium. Its voice thunders and jingles like copper pans. It breathes fire and water; and sometimes the dragon is one, sometimes many. (29)

Thus she ends up embodying humanity: "I learned to move my fingers, hands, feet, head, and entire body in circles. I walked putting heel down first, toes pointing outward thirty to forty degrees, making the ideograph 'eight,' making the ideograph 'human'" (23).

Kingston highlights fantasy and imagination as the thematic and artistic breeding ground for multiplicity. At the narrative level, it is in the world of possibilities and cognitive openness that the narrator and her warlike double can see themselves as fundamentally human. At the artistic level, fantasy is where the writer is able to mythologize the multiple nature of the Asian American self.

Through Kingston's mythopoesis, *The Woman Warrior* takes on a "womanist" quality, fitting Alice Walker's definition in *In Search of Our Mother's Gardens* (1983): "*Womanist*: [...]. Committed to survival and wholeness of entire people, male *and* female. Not a separatist, except periodically for health. Traditionally universalist, as in: 'Mama, why are we brown, pink and yellow, and our cousins are white, beige and black?' Ans.: 'Well you know the colored race is just like a flower garden with every color flower represented'" (qtd. in Razak 167). In the light of Walker's metaphor, the narrator's words—"'We belong to the planet now, Mama.' [...]. Will American flowers smell good too now?" (107)—underline the womanist stance of the novel.

Kingston's concluding her book with the story of the Chinese poetess Ts'ai Yen (born about AD 177), abducted by Barbarians and then returned to her people, stresses the writer's plea for a universalist representation and perception of Asian Americans: "She brought her songs back from the savage lands, and one of the three that has been passed down to us is 'Eighteen stanzas for a Barbarian Reed Pipe,' a song that Chinese sing to their own instruments. It translated well" (209). Interestingly, at the conference at the UHA Mulhouse, the Chinese American author underlined "the transnational sensibility [of her work]," locating it without geographical and cultural boundaries.

To conclude, Chinese and Chinese American female characters in *The Woman Warrior* testify to both Kingston's awareness and contestation of the white imperialist perception of the Asian woman. Refraining from resorting to any illusory gender-biased role reversal as a valid retaliatory process, the author makes the anti-essentialist claim that the Chinese American woman's integrity lies in paradoxes and can be recovered only in her de-essentialized (self-) perception. She thus offers her readers her own revised version of Chinese philosophy and legends, skillfully wielding mythopoesis to question the solely race-based, culture-based delimitation of the Chinese/Asian community.

Works Cited

Bhabha, Homi K. *The Location of Culture*. New York: Routledge, 1994.

Butler, Judith. *Bodies that Matter: On the Discursive Limits of "Sex."* New York: Routledge, 1993.

—. *Gender Trouble: Feminism and the Subversion of Identity*. New York: Routledge, 1990.

Cheng, Anne Anlin. *The Melancholy of Race: Psychoanalysis, Assimilation, and Hidden Grief*. New York: Oxford UP, 2001.

Chua, Cheng Lok. "Mythopoesis East and West in *The Woman Warrior*." *Approaches to Teaching Kingston's* The Woman Warrior. Ed. Shirley Geok-lin Lim. New York: The Modern Language Association of America, 1991. 146-50.

Cusset, François. *French Theory: Foucault, Derrida, Deleuze & Cie et les mutations de la vie intellectuelle aux États-Unis*. Paris : Éditions La Découverte/Poche, 2005.

Dariotis, Wei Ming. "Developing a Kin-aesthetic." *Mixed Race Literature*. Ed. Jonathan Brennan. Stanford, California: Stanford UP, 2002. 177-99.

Devine, Maureen. *Woman and Nature: Literary Reconceptualizations*. Metuchen, NJ: The Sacrecrow Press Ltd., 1992.

Eisenstein, Hester. *Contemporary Feminist Thought*. London: Unwin Paperbacks, 1984.

Espiritu, Yen Le. *Asian American Women and Men: Labor, Laws, and Love*. Thousand Oaks, California: Sage Press, 1997.

Iser, Wolfgang. *The Act of Reading: A Theory of Aesthetic Response*. Baltimore, MD: The Johns Hopkins UP, 1978.

Kim, Elaine H. *Asian American Literature: An Introduction to the Writings and their Social Context*. Philadelphia, PA: Temple UP, 1982.

Kingston, Maxine Hong. "Asian American Literature and the Legacy of Maxine Hong Kingston." UHA Mulhouse, France. 17-20 March 2011. Presentation.

—. *The Woman Warrior: Memoirs of a Girlhood Among Ghosts*. New York: Knopf, 1975.

Lowe, Lisa. *Immigrant Acts: On Asian American Cultural Politics*. Durham, NC: Duke UP, 1996.

Lu, Lynn. "Critical Visions: The Representation and Resistance of Asian Women." *Dragon Ladies: Asian American Feminists Breathe Fire*. Ed. Sonia Shah. Boston, MA: South End Press, 1997. 17-28.

MacKenzie, John. *Orientalism: History, Theory, and the Arts*. New York: Manchester UP, 1995.

Millet, Kate. *Sexual Politics*. London: Virago, 1989.

Ostriker, Alicia. "The Thieves of Language: Women Poets and Revisionist Mythmaking." *The New Feminist Criticism: Essays on Women, Literature and Theory*. Ed. Elaine Showalter. London: Virago Press, 1993. 315-38.

Razak, Arisika. "Toward a Womanist Analysis of Birth." *Reweaving the World: The Emergence of Ecofeminism*. Eds. Irene Diamond and Gloria Feman Orenstein. San Francisco, California: Sierra Club Books, 1990. 165-72.

Tajima, Renee E. "Lotus Blossoms Don't Bleed: Images of Asian Women." *Making Waves: An Anthology of Writings By and About Asian American Women*. Ed. Asian Women United of California. Boston, MA: Beacon Press, 1989. 308-17.

Van Spanckeren, Kathryn. "The Asian Literary Background of *The Woman Warrior*." *Approaches to Teaching Kingston's* The Woman Warrior. Ed. Shirley Geok-lin Lim. New York: The Modern Language Association of America, 1991. 44-51.

Yamada, Mitsuye. "Asian Pacific American Women and Feminism." *This Bridge Called my Back: Writings by Radical Women of Color*. Eds. Cherríe Moraga and Gloria Anzaldúa. New York: Women of Color Press, 1981. 71-75.

Masks and Identity: Self-Fashioning in Chinese American Children's and Young Adult Literature

Pin-chia Feng (National Chiao Tung University and Institute of European and American Studies, Academia Sinica, Taiwan)

> If I want to think of myself as a Chinese American, it would be like looking in a mirror and seeing only a mask; and if I took off that mask, all I would see would be no face underneath that mask. And the mask would be out of a Hollywood prop room: I would be a Chinese laundryman; I could be a Chinese houseboy or any kind of stereotype that comes out of the movies.
> —Laurence Yep, *Duggins* (102-3)

In an interview with James Duggins, Laurence Yep describes his nightmarish experience of confronting his Chinese American identity. The dark rendition of the Lacanian mirror stage in Yep's confessional statement bespeaks the difficult passage that must be transversed for a member of an ethnic minority, like Yep, to arrive at a positive self-image. The mask with "no face underneath" alludes to the imposition of negative stereotypes upon Chinese Americans in the media and literature. Like most Chinese American writers, Yep dedicates his creative energy to exorcising the nightmare of stereotyping and creating a self with a real "face."[1] As Amy Ling points out, Chinese Americans, like many other ethnic minority groups, are entrapped in a troubling double-bind of visible difference and social invisibility, and a feeling of existing "between worlds" (20). The quest for a genuine identity, however, is complicated by the fact that these writers struggle not only with stereotypes produced in mainstream culture, but also by constraints from within their own ethnic culture. Furthermore, self-conscious Chinese American writers often need to tackle their readers' lack of information about the Chinese American culture that they are trying to reclaim.

1. Frank Chin satirically categorizes this kind of cultural stereotyping as writing "science fiction" (24). Ruthanne Lum McCunn justly points out that if "all that Children see of Chinese and Chinese Americans is stereotype, that stereotype will become reality" (51). Elaine Aoki also voices for all Asian Americans that even now Asian Americans are still viewed as exotic foreigners. She therefore demands that both publishers and educators cooperate to present "a multitude of viewpoints of Asian American experiences" for all children to share together (383-84).

There is yet another problem with writing about Chinese American experiences for young readers: the authors have to get their audiences interested in and comprehend these complicated emotions and possible political conflicts. The comparative scarcity of Chinese American children's and young adult writings evidences these multiple barriers.

One strategy that some Chinese American writers develop to cope with these difficulties is to reverse negative stereotyping by creating positive masks or personae of their choices in order to facilitate self-fashioning. Here the deployment of masking is the very opposite of the mainstream stereotyping, being used not to disguise one's true identity, but rather to construct a persona that effectively embodies the elusive "Chinese American identity" so as to resist marginalizing invisibility and thereby create a channel for expression and communication. Through this strategic deployment of masking, Chinese American writers are able to revisit stereotypical representations of Chinese Americans and to construct an identity for the young protagonists with which readers can identify.

In this paper I analyze the search for, and construction of, identity through creative and positive masking in five texts by three Chinese American writers: Laurence Yep's *Dragonwings* (1975), Maxine Hong Kingston's *The Woman Warrior* (1975), Bette Bao Lord's *In the Year of the Boar and Jackie Robinson* (1984), and two more books from Yep's Gold Mountain Chronicles, *Child of the Owl* (1965) and *Sea Glass* (1979).[2] "The project of writing the ethnic presence in America and the evolution of cultural identity has a special resonance in children's literature," as Dolores de Manuel and Rocío G. Davis observe, "with its tendency to focus on issues of selfhood in the context of family, peers, and community while experiencing rejection and discovering the ways of society" (vii). The thematic thrusts of the five texts exemplify exactly these struggles to construct selfhood. Together, they insert stories of Chinese American "children

2. There are nine novels included in the Gold Mountain Chronicles. In a way, the San Francisco Chinatown in this series is Yep's own version of William Faulkner's Yoknapatawpha County. According to Yep, when he was writing *Dragonwings* he was also working on his dissertation about Faulkner's early novels. Yep felt strongly sympathized with Faulkner's impulse of transforming a realistic locale into an imaginary space. As Yep confesses, "I sympathized with that impulse because I wanted to do the same with the San Francisco Chinatown.... *Dragonwings* and the eight other novels became the Gold Mountain Chronicles which tells the adventures of seven generations of a Chinese family and their friends through 150 years of American history" ("Dragon I Have Known and Loved" 389). As Rocío G. Davis points out, an underlying message introduced by the series of historical novels "is empowerment of children in keeping with the operation and function of their own culture—that of the children and ethnicity—within American history" (393).

of immigration" from various origins and generations, into the American literary and cultural landscape.[3]

Another objective of this paper is to construct a quasi-historical framework to accommodate the identity quest of five Chinese American child and adolescent protagonists. The time frames of these five books spans seven decades and covers three generations of Chinese American lives, reflecting the construction of Chinese American identity from the beginning of the twentieth century up to the early 1970s. The specific temporal framework chosen is intended to allow for a look into the individual and historical experiences of three generations of Chinese Americans before the 1965 "new immigration" wave,[4] and to ensure that we can read each text in its proper historical context, thereby gaining a relatively comprehensive perspective of Chinese American childhood and adolescence in this era.

I. Welcome to the Land of the Demon: Laurence Yep's *Dragonwings* and the First-Generation Chinese Americans

> For one moment I glimpsed howling, sweating, red-and-white faces, distorted into hideous masks of hatred and cruelty, a sea of demon heads that bobbed restlessly outside our store. I could not understand the words they were growling out, but their intention was plain. They wanted to burn and loot and hurt. Looking into that huge mass of faces was like looking into the ugliest depths of the human soul.
> —Laurence Yep, *Dragonwings* (29-30)

The above quote describes Moon Shadow's first night in San Francisco, 1903. Moon Shadow Lee is an eight-year old Chinese boy who has immigrated to America to live with his father, Windrider, who left China before Moon Shadow was born. Prior to his transpacific journey to America, Moon Shadow had two contradictory ideas of San Francisco. On the one hand it is the land of the Golden Mountain where "all a man has to do is wait until the sun warms the mountain and then scoop the gold into big buckets," as Grandmother's fairy tale

---

3. According to Carola and Marcelo M. Suárez-Orozco, children of immigrants—both American- and foreign-born—made up twenty percent of the youth population in the United States at the end of the twentieth century (1). The Suárez-Orozcos argue in their monograph *Children of Immigration* (2001) that while many immigrant children arrive with positive social attitudes, "their developing psyches are susceptible to the negative 'social mirroring' that many experience in the new land" (2). The reference to mirroring echoes Laurence Yep's dark description of a Chinese American's encounter with his social "mirror stage."
4. The "new immigration" refers to the wave of immigration that began in the 1960s with the 1965 Hart-Cellar Act and intensified in the 1990s (Suárez-Orozco and Suárez-Orozco 55).

goes (6). On the other hand it is the land of "the American devil" who would beat up the Tang people, or the Chinese, for no good reason. What Moon Shadow discovers upon landing in America is that the fairy-tale mountain of gold does not exist, but the harmful "demons" do. Moon Shadow experiences the nightmare that haunts many first-generation Chinese in the United States—the ruthless, racist violence directed against Chinese immigrants who helped build the Central Pacific Railroad and the California economy alongside European immigrants. These overseas Chinese had to endure discrimination, brutal treatment, and loneliness to survive in this foreign land. Due to the 1882 Exclusion Law, Chinese immigrants were forbidden to bring their wives and children with them, and therefore formed societies of bachelors—the company with which the Lees live is one such example. Moon Shadow is lucky to be united with his father, but the challenges posed by living in the "demon land" and with a father who is a stranger prove simply overwhelming.

Moon Shadow is helped to face these challenges by his father's dragon story. In an inserted narrative, Windrider tells a story of his meeting with the Dragon King: the Chinese god of the sea. In this fantasy, Windrider is a dragon that has degenerated into human form, losing his innate nobility in the process. To return to his "dragon self," the Dragon King advises Windrider "to watch for the tests and hold to the dragon-ness within that softskin body" (44). His final test, Windrider believes, is to fly an aeroplane—a new invention at that time. Here the choice of the dragon figure is rich with Yep's personal investment, for Yep once talked about how he first learned from his maternal grandmother of the benevolent Chinese dragons "who brought the rains and helped make crops grown" ("Dragon I Have Known and Loved" 386). The evil dragons he encounters in his sci-fi and fantasy readings, were the exact opposite. Yep observes, "dragon made me aware that my Chinese culture may not be in sync with my American culture—that instead, they might clash" (387). These conflicting conceptions of dragons embody Yep's feeling of being an "Outsider" in American society, while Windrider's sense of loss and alienation, suggested by his dream, mirrors the author's own sense of otherness.

In this dragon story, Yep combines elements of Chinese mythology with historical facts to craft a new, Chinese American myth. In a sense, his creation of a personal dragon legend is a practice of Alicia Ostriker's "revisionist mythmaking." For Ostriker, in such a revisionist practice "the figure or tale will be appropriated for altered ends, the old vessel filled with new wine, initially satisfying the thirst of the individual poet but ultimately making cultural change possible" (317).[5] To Frank Chin, the dragon myth in *Dragonwings* is "an Asian

5. The uses of revisionist myth making, Ostriker points out, are making corrections, representing what the women find divine and demonic in themselves, retrieving images of what women have collectively and historically suffered, and giving instructions for survival (318). Ostriker's theory is of course

American myth that will someday be as deeply rooted in American folklore as Paul Bunyan and Johnny Appleseed" (25). Although this celebration seems overly optimistic, Chin correctly argues for the need of "a body of Asian American myth to form and express what we value in ourselves and our history" and to counteract "the myth of white supremacy and yellow decency" (25). The symbolic temporal setting of Windrider's dream, the day when he first arrived in San Francisco, indicates that his lost dragon form is, in fact, the Chinese identity that he left behind in China. By encouraging Windrider to preserve and keep the "dragon-ness" alive, Yep provides both father and son with a dragon mask to hold unto.

Moon Shadow's belief in the dragon mask helps him break the invisible barrier between himself and the "demons" as well. For instance, he is fascinated by Miss Whitlaw's stained glass window, on which is illustrated the story of St. George slaying an evil dragon. Moon Shadow then attempts to "educate" his landlady about the "true" dragon—that is, the good dragon of the Chinese. In this way, he wins the friendship of Miss Whitlaw and her niece, Robin, and has an opportunity to learn English, as Moon Shadow later admits: "While I had set out to reeducate the demons about dragons, she was educating me in the demonic language" (129). Through his friendship with these two white people, Moon Shadow is able to discover his own version of the Gold Mountain: "I had found my mountain of gold, after all, and it had not been nuggets but people who had made it up: people like the Company and the Whitlaws" (210). Following this discovery, Moon Shadow recognizes anew the beauty of life, despite its pettiness, and rediscovers the courage needed to live in this strange land.

In *Dragonwings,* Yep successfully reconstructs Chinatown before the San Francisco Earthquake, and the story of the first Chinese American pilot, Fuey Joe Guey, who flew a biplane in 1909 near Oakland. Through Moon Shadow's first-person narrative, Yep recreates a distinct dragon mask for the "dull, faceless mass" of the first-generation Chinese immigrants. The dragon mask is useful not only for Yep's child protagonist, but also for himself. As Yep states, "Growing up as I myself did without form or shape, I felt as ghostly as the spirits of the dead and so by giving them form, I was also giving form to myself" ("Writing *Dragonwings*" 163). Years later, he also confesses: "Wearing a dragon skin allowed me to start discovering the shape of my face if not its exact features" ("Dragons I have Known and Loved" 388). Moreover, by framing historical fact within the context of a fantasy story, Yep is able to appeal to the imaginations of both Chinese American and general child readers, and contribute significantly to Chinese American children's literature.

---

about feminist appropriation of poetic language, but I would submit that it is also useful in analyzing Yep's attempt to create a different myth from that of the mainstream Western tradition.

II. Growing Up A Warrior Woman: Maxine Hong Kingston's *The Woman Warrior* and the Second Generation Chinese American Girlhood

> At last I saw that I too had been in the presence of great power, my mother talking-story. After I grew up, I heard the chant of Fa Mu Lan, the girl who took her father's place in battle. Instantly I remembered that as a child I had followed my mother about the house, the two of us singing about how Fa Mu Lan fought gloriously and returned alive from war to settle in the village. I had forgotten this chant that was once mine, given me by my mother, who may not have known its power to remind. She said I would grow up a wife and a slave, but she taught me the song of the warrior woman, Fa Mu Lan. I would have to grow up a warrior woman.
> —Maxine Hong Kingston, *Woman Warrior* (19-20)

For Maxine, the narrator of *The Woman Warrior: Memoirs of a Girlhood among Ghosts*, the recollected story of the legendary warrior woman Fa Mu Lan is a source of empowerment that allows her to go beyond the limit of patriarchal mandates. As a second-generation Chinese American woman, Kingston herself also needs this transforming power to "translate" her experience as a descendant of Chinese immigrants in America, the land of "ghosts," into English—a language she only started to learn at the age of seven. The source of her "translation" is Mother's "talk-story"—a repertoire of myths, legends and sayings communicated through the oral traditions of the old China.[6] In translating Mother's talk-story, Kingston simultaneously situates herself within her Chinese American community and constructs an articulating selfhood. Although as a part of the literary canon and one of the most important Asian American literary texts, *The Woman Warrior* can hardly be read as young adult literature, the intimate delineation of the growing pains of the young Maxine, I would argue, still best exemplifies a cultural- and gender-specific experience of a second-generation Chinese American young women.

In *The Woman Warrior,* we witness the same practice of revisionist mythmaking as in *Dragonwings*. As Kingston argues, "Mythology dies if it's not useful to present-day people. It's useful only if it changes—only if it (Chinese myth) becomes an American story as well as Chinese" (Castagonzzi 7). Hence,

---

6. Orality in general is very important to Kingston's writing. In an interview with Shirley Geok-lin Lim, Kingston stresses the importance of orality with the theory of DNA: "Karen Yamashita talked about the DNA; there are the stories that are in your DNA. I think there are the sounds that are in our DNA. We hear words—the Word—words—and they come into our bodies, into our ears, and then we find a way to transmit it into the written word" (162).

by revising the legend of Fa Mu Lan, Kingston creatively invents a Chinese American myth for herself and the other women in her community.[7] And she goes on to assume the positive role of a powerful warrior woman to fight and exorcise the many "ghosts"—both Chinese and Western—that haunt her girlhood. By masquerading as the legendary folk heroine, much praised for her filial piety and courage, Kingston imaginatively constructs a self-image possessing both physical and spiritual prowess.[8]

Kingston's version of Fa Mu Lan is a hybrid construction of the various swordswomen in Chinese tradition. Her power to control mental swords and her training with the ageless and sexless couple, for example, are derived from the tradition of Taoist swordswomen. Yet Kingston's Mu Lan also has roots in silver screen melodramas. She describes a childhood routine of going with her mother to the Sunday movies at the Confucius Church and seeing swordswomen who "jump over houses from a standstill" (20). The primary missions of those swordswomen in the movies, Lily Tom tells us, are to right wrongs and to be champions of the oppressed and helpless (28). Thus, the swordswomen often appear as avengers who fight against injustice. The theme of revenge is reiterated throughout the "White Tigers" chapter, in which Maxine imagines herself as the warrior woman. The warrior woman's revenge is both physical and linguistic: she not only kills those who were oppressing her family, but also reports the crime. The warrior woman slashes the baron to revenge herself for taking away her childhood (43). Here, she is referring to Maxine's pain and anxiety as she grows up a silent child living between cultures. The feudal tyrant represents both Chinese patriarchy and oppressive American society. Unlike the melodramatic image of reticent swordswomen, the woman avenger in "White Tigers" has special linguistic power: she is a storyteller. The old couple praise her for skillfully telling the story of her adventures while training in the mountains of the white tigers (28). The warrior woman is also a singer of "glorious songs" (37), like the Han poetess T'sai Yen we encounter in the final

7. "Seeking the legacy of the warrior women," Siew Hwa Beh points out, "contributes to the creation and re-creation of a positive female mythology" (125).
8. According to Sämi Ludwig, in the "White Tigers" section Maxine "explores the limits of her imagination, which border on unreliable fantasy" (79). In a "fantasy of omnipotence," for instance, the hut of the old couple is created like a "dollhouse" in which there is a "fusion of reality and meta-reality" (92). Still, Ludwig recognizes the power of Kingston's writing and the value of the narrator's fantasies: "[T]he fantasies of her youth define the metaphorical basis on which she has built her identity. Thus, however mixed, concocted and confused they are, they are hers, and, having been experienced, they are real. However childish the vision, Kingston defends her own point of departure as the center of her book" (101).

chapter. Hence, the transformed Fa Mu Lan is an amalgam of artist and warrior. When Maxine realizes the impossibility of physical revenge within American reality, she turns to language. Thus, in a way *The Woman Warrior* as a text embodies the familial and personal revenge for Maxine.

Kingston also appropriates masculine heroic legends to embellish her woman warrior mask. For example, in the episode in which the parents tattoo the back of the warrior woman, the inscription may be regarded as a case of patriarchal violence scarring the female body; but an understanding of the original version of the tattooing scene can help the reader better understand the revisionist power of the story. Kingston appropriates the legend of the historical hero Yueh Fei. In the original Chinese legend, Yueh Fei's mother carved four Chinese characters meaning—"Report Loyalty to the Country"—on his back before he joined the fight against an invading barbarian tribe. Later, Yueh Fei is imprisoned and sentenced to death by the Chinese emperor due to slanders and political intrigues; only the characters on his back testify to his patriotism. Those four characters, in a sense, become the report of crime against this national hero. By inscribing the report of crimes against her family on the back of her warrior woman, Kingston places her heroine on the same level of the historical hero. Another subtle revision occurs when the content of the script is changed from that of a patriotic motto to a text declaring family grievances. The warrior woman is thus free to confront even the emperor, and effectively build a new dynasty on her own. Most importantly, the script on her back embodies a family acknowledgement. Through the warrior woman, Maxine vicariously satisfies her urgent need for family recognition. Thus she thanks her parents for they "had carved their names and address on me, and I would come back" (37). She would never be a homeless ghost like Maxine's no-name aunt in the first chapter.

Another revision of the patriarchal myth takes place in the episode when the warrior woman kills the snake on her way to fight the wicked emperor (38). A similar story of the legendary feat of Liu Bang, the founder of Han dynasty, is recorded in Chinese history. Liu also killed a snake on his way to fight a tyrannical emperor and start a dynasty of his own. It is, in fact, a habitual strategy of Chinese royal families to mythologize and glorify the origins of their ancestors, and Kingston appropriates mythmaking as a political maneuver to glorify her woman warrior.

The warrior woman is invested with Asian religious connotations, as well. During her survival test in the wilderness, a white rabbit jumps into the fire to feed the starving warrior woman in training (26)—an adaptation of a Buddhist sutra in which the queen rabbit—as a previous incarnation of Sakyamuni or Lord Buddha—and her son commit sacrificial self-immolation in order to feed a Brahman who later is reincarnated as Maitreya, the Buddha of the Future.[9]

---

9. In the original sutra, the Brahman was deeply touched by the sacrifice of the rabbits and also jumped into the fire. The central message contains a plea to

Hence, Kingston includes not only historical legends but also religious tales in her re-sourcing of the creative performance of the warrior woman. The medley of sources for Maxine's warrior mask bespeak the hybrid nature of this persona and the difficult task of self-fashioning for this second-generation Chinese American girl.

At the end of *The Woman Warrior,* Kingston further embellishes and expands on the warrior mask by revising and retelling the story of Ts'ai Yen, the Han poetess who was abducted and held by barbarians for twelve years. In Kingston's version, the poetess is also a warrior, and unlike the helpless, star-crossed woman of history, whose body was been treated as either booty or a reproductive vessel by two tribes, in *The Woman Warrior,* Ts'ai Yen can fight and "cut down anyone in her path during the madness of close combat" (208). Moreover, Ts'ai Yen became a prototype of a cultural translator capable of transforming her painful experience in a foreign territory through poetic articulation. One of the three songs Ts'ai Yen crafted and brought back from the barbarian land, "Eighteen Stanzas for a Barbarian Reed Pipe," can be sung to a Chinese instrument; and as the narrator explains, it is "translated well" (209). Wearing the warrior mask, the narrator, like the outlaw knot-maker, artfully "twisted" her mother's stories and stepped into her role as a cultural translator. In so doing, she succeeds in writing women into Chinese American community and inserting Chinese Americans into American life through literature. Just as Maxine Hong Kingston is an important inspiration for Chinese American women writers and the development of Asian American literature, the narrator Maxine has also become a positive role model for Chinese American young women.

III. China's Little Ambassador: Bette Bao Lord's *In the Year of the Boar and Jackie Robinson* and Chinese American Immigrants in the 1940s

> Always be worthy, my daughter, of your good fortune. Born to an illustrious clan family from the ancient civilization of China, you now live in the land of plenty and opportunity. By your conduct show that you deserve to enjoy the best of both worlds.
> —Bette Bao Lord, *Year of the Boar* (58)

Mother's advice to Shirley Temple Wong in the above quote stresses the sense of helplessness surrounding this new Chinese immigrant in the year 1947. Earlier, Mother called Shirley "China's little ambassador" upon whom "rests the

---

demonstrate the sacrificial and loving spirit of Lord Buddha, and to refrain from killing. Ludwig reads the image of the white rabbit as a combination of "Otherness (WHITENESS)" and "familiarity (RABBIT)": "The traditional Chinese meanings of death and mourning are challenged by a soft, white 'hug-me' rabbit, who seems to come straight out of Lewis Carroll" (81).

reputation of all Chinese" (43-44). The fifth grader starts with great enthusiasm about immigrating to "*Mei Guo*, Beautiful Country." Her chosen name—taken from the American silver screen sweetheart Shirley Temple—speaks to her hopeful anticipation. At the juncture of Mother's admonition, however, Shirley is painfully aware of her alienation from her white peers. In her own words, Shirley watches the other children play, "like a hungry ghost," left out, alone, in the playground (55). Apparently she suffers from maladjustment, being caught between "the best of both worlds."

Bette Bao Lord's autobiographical fiction, *In the Year of the Boar and Jackie Robinson,* represents another kind of Chinese American experience—one that differs from those of Moon Shadow and Maxine Kingston. Shirley's family does not come from southern China, as did earlier immigrants. Nor do they come to the United States because of poverty. Rather, they immigrate to pursue individual advancement and fulfillment. For example, Shirley's father immigrates to the United States to pursue a career in engineering, and has high expectations for his daughter as well. As Shirley later explains, her father's intention in coming to America was also to raise his daughter in a manner different from the demands of Chinese traditionalism and patriarchy: "Here, she did not have to wait for gray hair to be considered wise. Here, she could speak up, question even the conduct of the President. Here Shirley Temple Wong was somebody" (93). All such new hopes, however, were placed on hold until Shirley solved her immediate problem—learning a new language and culture so that she could merge into the life of her new home and learn to get along with her peers.

Shirley's solution is to identify wholeheartedly with a model ethnic hero: Jackie Robinson, the first African American baseball player in American Major League Baseball. By adopting her "Jackie Robinson mask," and with the help of her new friend Mabel, Shirley is finally able to join her peers in baseball games. More importantly, Shirley becomes aware of the democratic underpinnings of the United States. In school, Shirley's teacher combines sport with civic education while introducing Jackie Robinson:

> [E]ach player is a member of a team, but when he comes to bat, he stands alone. One man. Many opportunities. For no matter how far behind, how late in the game, he, by himself, can make a difference. [...]. In the life of our nation, each man is a citizen of the United States, but he has the right to pursue his own happiness. For no matter what his race, religion, or creed, be he pauper or president, he has the right to speak his mind, to live as he wishes within the law. (92)

Whole-heartedly accepting this grandiloquent, idealistic combination of American individualism and nationalism, Shirley embraces this newly discovered American Dream and decides to make a difference, just like Jackie Robinson.

Nonetheless, Shirley's problems are complicated by her Chinese heritage. After merging successfully with her peers, Shirley is anxious about losing her Chinese past. Here, Lord employs a Chinese legend to reveal and resolve Shirley's internal conflict. The story of the Chinese girl who was divided by her filial responsibilities and her love for a fisherman, and then is reintegrated into one person wearing two garments signifies Shirley's reluctance to give up either her Chinese cultural heritage or her hard-earned integration into American society. Through this sartorial story, Shirley not only freely expresses her unspeakable anxiety but also lays claim to her ancestral inheritance as the tale was a gift from her grandfather. Thus, through storytelling, Shirley is able to release her anxiety and perform another act of integration.

In the Year of the Boar and Jackie Robinson starts with Chinese New Year—the major Chinese festival—in China, and ends with Christmas—the major Western holiday—in the United States. The geographical and temporal framing of the text is symbolically indicative of Shirley's integration into Western culture. Even the title combines Western and Chinese traditions in its mixing of a Western name and a Chinese zodiac sign. The condensation of four years into twelve chapters, presented in the form of a single year, is an example of what Roni Natov calls a "fairy-tale style" that foreshadows a happy ending (39). Exorcising the anxiety of transcontinental relocation with an embrace of cultural integration, Bette Bao Lord's success story embodies yet another fulfillment of the American Dream. Despite this emphasis on acculturation and fairy-tale wish-fulfillment, which appears to be overly simplistic and in danger of conforming to the model minority discourse promoted by mainstream political ideology, what Lord offers her young readers is the courage to face up to the challenges of transcultural migrations. In 1985, once "China's little ambassador" has matured and returned to China as the wife of the American ambassador, a year after her autobiographical fiction was published, Bette Bao Lord's fairy-tale success story has indeed come full circle.[10]

IV. Inside the Invisible Walls: Laurence Yep's *Child of the Owl* and the Third-Generation Chinese American Experience

> It was like we'd gone through an invisible wall into another world. [... The American buildings] were pushing all the sunshine and all the buildings of Chinatown together. [...]. But it was the people that got me. I don't think I'd ever seen so many Chinese in my life before. [...]. I noticed that my hand on the window handle was colored a

10. Bette Bao Lord is noted for her devotion to the pursuit of democracy. When her husband's ambassadorship ended in April of 1989, Bette Bao Lord stayed behind to serve as an interpreter for CBS News to report on the student democratic demonstration. She did not leave Beijing until June 3rd, the day before the Tiananmen Massacre.

> honey kind of tan like some of the people outside. [... T]hey couldn't be my hands. [... M]aybe it was because I thought of myself as an American and all Americans were supposed to be white like on TV or in books or in movies; but I felt like some mad scientist had switched bodies on me like in all those monster movies, so that I had woken up in the wrong one.
> —Laurence Yep, *Child of the Owl* (25-27)

Thus goes Casey Young's first impression of San Francisco's Chinatown and her first awareness of being different from white Americans. Casey represents the third-generation of Chinese Americans who grew up in an environment "with little or no Chinese spoken and Chinese myths and legends were looked upon as a source of embarrassment" (Yep, "Writing 'Dragonwings'" 360). Moreover, Casey is raised by her gambler father outside of Chinatown until 1964, when she turned twelve. As such, her culture shock and feeling of displacement inside of Chinatown are only natural. Moreover, she was sent to Chinatown by her uncle as punishment for having a bad attitude, and made to live with Paw-Paw, her maternal grandmother who is a total stranger to her, and who always embarrasses the family by telling Chinese legends. Hence, the narrative structure of *Child of the Owl* reflects the two phases of Casey's life: her pre-Chinatown phase as an "American" girl, and her Chinatown phase as a Chinese American, which is full of the rhetoric of anxiety, alienation, and imprisonment. Bridging these divides is a great challenge to Casey, whose mother is dead and whose father cannot take proper care of her. Casey feels acutely her identity crisis, and desperately tries to convince herself that "There had to be something good to being Chinese" (44).

Casey does find a positive cultural role model with which she can identify in Paw-Paw's owl story. Here, as in *Dragonwings*, Yep inserts a revised Chinese fairy tale, that is, another Chinese American myth. The story of the Owl Spirit, who sacrifices her freedom and is transformed into an earth-bound woman, provides Casey with an owl mask to express herself affectively. As Casey admits, "if I pretended I was an owl, I suddenly had a way of telling my feelings" (81). The Owl spirit, as the legendary foremother of Casey's family, is trapped inside a human form, just as Casey feels she has been placed within a monstrous body. Instead of feeling alienated, through her owl mask, Casey can name her anxiety and attempt to resolve it. As Celestine Woo contends, this tale "both instances and instigates an allegorized representation of Asian American identity formation" (180).[11] In addition, by virtue of believing in Paw-Paw's owl

---

11. Woo reads the novel as an example of Asian American fantasy that is bicultural and hybridized: "Structurally, the owl tale functions in a bicultural and Asian American manner, for it is a Chinese tale deployed to help Casey the American survive and establish an identity in her foreign new Chinese environment; moreover, the values affirmed in the tale included the typically American ones of independence and the pursuit of individual fulfillment

story, Casey wins the trust of the elderly woman, and is therefore able to share in her cultural insights.

The nature of Chinatown changes once Casey sees it through her owl mask, too. Before assuming the owl persona, Casey felt trapped and imprisoned, but later she began to see something positive in living inside of the "invisible walls" of Chinatown. "I realized that it all depended on how I looked around myself," Casey acknowledges, "if there were invisible walls around Chinatown for Paw-Paw, they were like the walls of a turtle, walls behind which you could remain warm and alive" (91). Casey's vision of Chinatown expands from being a prison, to a place offering protection. More significantly, Casey knows that she can break out of the walls once she feels fully grown.

However, her opinion of Chinatown again changes when she is rejected and cheated by her fellow Chinese Americans because she cannot speak Chinese. There are some people, Casey realizes, who are trapped inside of Chinatown, who cannot pull themselves out. Although, at this time, Casey still feels like an outsider among her own people, she takes a step to better understand her Chinese identity. For the first time, Casey learns how to use chopsticks, and gets to know her Chinese name, Spring Taste. Casey's exclamation—"My first name. My real name. My true name" (143)—indicates that this an important moment in her developing Chinese connections. Like Shirley Temple Wong, Casey has found her "second garment." Working through her owl mask, Casey is capable of transforming her cognitive crisis inside Chinatown into a maturing process. Here in Chinatown she finally finds her "roots" after years of wandering (195).

Maxine Hong Kingston insightfully observes that in *Child of the Owl* there are scenes which "will make every Chinese-American child gasp with recognition" ("Middle Kingdom to Middle America" E1). I would add that there are scenes, throughout the book, with which all child readers can identify. Although *Child of the Owl* is specifically about the identity problem of American-born Chinese teenagers, Yep expresses a universal sympathy with young people who feel out of place in their environments. The process of growth—from resentment to understanding—is hence a model for youths of all races.

V. Outside the Invisible Walls: Laurence Yep's *Sea Glass* and the Third-Generation Chinese American Experience

> 'We're moving in with Western people, you know.' *Western people* was a Chinese term Dad and Mom politely used for white Americans. '... You got to get out and prove you're just as good as one of

---

apart from family, as well as characteristically Chinese values such as fierce familial loyalty and a long memory" (180).

> them.... [Y]ou got to remember one thing, Craig: A Chinese has to try twice as hard as any *Western person*.'
> —Laurence Yep, *Sea Glass* (4)

This is Father's lecture to the eighth-grader Craig Chin, delivered while moving out of San Francisco's Chinatown to a small seaside town, Concepion, in 1970. *Sea Glass* portrays the problems of third-generation Chinese Americans during approximately the same time period as *Child of the Owl*. Unlike Casey, Craig's has a problem confronting his identity crisis outside of Chinatown. In Concepion, Craig faces taunting from his peers, the pressure of Father's high expectations, the contempt of first-generation Chinese immigrants, and the coldness of his all-American cousins. Unlike Casey, who has felt out of place in Chinatown, Craig feels isolated without the protection of those same invisible walls: "I wanted a Chinatown, where I fit in so well," Craig exclaims (37). The Chinatown that Craig longs for is not only a physical place, but also a symbolic space in which he finds a sense of belonging.

However, what assists Craig to solve his problem are not the protective walls of a Chinatown, but a sea mask and an awareness of being himself. Through the metaphors of the sea and sea creatures Craig is able to better understand the people around him. For instance, Craig has tried to communicate with his father, who according to Craig has shut the door to his unhappy past like a sea anemone. After his failure, Craig understands that "maybe it hurts to be all closed up like an anemone. But [...] it sometimes hurt even worse to open up to other people" (105). The title of the book—*Sea Glass*—symbolizes a catharsis through sea change. The term sea glass actually refers to the metamorphosis of a piece of junk, a broken piece of the Coke bottle, into the likeness of a precious stone, after being washed and polished by the sea over time. It is significant is that Craig knows how to appreciate and treasure this piece of sea glass as it is now.

In fact, in *Sea Glass* Yep gives his protagonist more than a mask that aids in articulation; he also gives Craig a vision of being truthful to oneself. Through patience, Craig is able to reconcile the traumatic memory of Uncle Quail, the first-generation Chinese immigrant who could not forgive his violent treatment at the hands of white people of the past. It is Uncle Quail who tells Craig the story of the dragon mother, who can see things as they really are, but it is Craig who teaches Uncle to look beyond painful experiences and appreciate the merits of others, be they Chinese or otherwise. Craig's patience and understanding also wins over Kenyon, a white American girl and an outcast like Craig, and builds their friendship. Most importantly, Craig is able, finally, to be reconciled with his father, who has projected his failed all-American dreams into his son. Yet Craig fails both in school and sports, two areas in which his father expects him to excel. It is difficult for Craig to face his father's disappointment alone, and to resolve all the problems around him. However, in his lonely struggle, Craig serves as a figure with which all young adults can identify. Donald Kao insightfully points out that in this novel Yep focuses on people's potential to offer something special once they have acknowledged who they really are. Kao goes on to contend that Craig "becomes a pivotal point around which the characters either deal with their own identities or assume some facade" (16) — first through the help of a sea mask, and then with his true self.

Significantly, in his previous two installments of the Gold Mountain Chronicles, Yep relied much upon the use of mythological frameworks and fantasies, but in *Sea Glass* he takes a more realistic approach to resolving the problem of identity. This departure from heavy reliance upon mythical masks for achieving self-realization, I submit, shows a hopeful note for the future development of Chinese American young people.

The five texts by three authors examined in this paper represent aspects of the formation of selfhood for Chinese American children and young adults in many similar ways. First of all, they are all heavily invested with autobiographical elements. Laurence Yep's Chinatown stories, which explore Chinese American identity from three different perspectives, are actually rooted in his own concerns and experiences of being a Chinese American. Maxine Hong Kingston and Bette Bao Lord each articulate their personal hopes and frustrations in confronting a dual heritage as well. The pressing sense of anxiety and alienation in these texts actually originate in the fictionalized personal experiences of the writers themselves. Secondly, all the young protagonists are more or less struggling with their ethnic identity on their own. Moon Shadow's father is too preoccupied with his flying dream to help Moon Shadow with his identity crisis while his mother is thousands of miles away. Maxine constantly engages in soul searching and imaginative fantasies in her personal struggle with her between-world dilemma. Shirley, Casey, and Craig each fight lonely battles on different fronts. As Lowell Chun-Hoon points out, one of the greatest ironies of the Asian American experience is that it is the young, and those least secure, who are forced to shoulder the greatest responsibility for preserving their heritage (134). What underpins the five narratives of development is a plea for parental attention and support to guide their children through the labyrinth of cultural differences and ethnic marginality.

Finally, although these five texts represent different ways to fashion Chinese American selfhood—Moon Shadow with his dragon mask, Maxine with her warrior mask, Shirley with her Jackie Robinson and storyteller mask, Casey with her owl mask, and Craig with his sea mask and self-recognition—the experiences of these young protagonists are nonetheless universal. Laurence Yep phrases his belief in the universality of good writing as such: "[I]f a book is good, it ought to be read by anybody from any culture, because it is going to be about people basically" (Duggins 104). *Dragonwings*, *The Woman Warrior*, *In the Year of the Boar and Jackie Robinson*, *Child of the Owl*, and *Sea Glass*, with their expressions of intimate feelings, personal insights and sympathy with children, are such wonderful literary works that they present their readers not only with cultural insight but also with humanistic vision.

Works Cited

Aoki, Elaine M. "'Are you Chinese? Are you Japanese? Or are you just a mixed-up kid?': Using Asian American Children's Literature." *The Reading Teacher* 34.4 (1981): 382-85.

Beh, Siew Hwa. "Growing Up with Legends of the Chinese Swordswomen." *The Poetics of Women's Spirituality: Essays on the Rise of Spiritual Power within the Feminist Movement*. Ed. Charlene Spretnak. New York: Anchor, 1982. 121-26.

Castagonzzi, Mary. "Maxine Hong Kingston Discussed Her Writing." *East/West* May 13 1981. 7.

Chin, Frank. "Where I'm Coming From." *Interracial Books for Children Bulletin* 7.2&3 (1976): 24-25.

Davis, Rocío G. "Reinscribing (Asian) American History in Laurence Yep's *Dragonwings*." *The Lion and the Unicorn* 28.3 (September 2004): 390-407.

de Manuel, Dolores, and Rocío G. Davis. "Editor's Introduction: Critical Perspectives on Asian American Children's Literature." *The Lion and the Unicorn* 30 (2006): v-xv.

Duggins, James. "Laurence Yep." *From Writers to Students: The Pleasure and Pains of Writing*. Ed. M. Jerry Weiss. Delaware: International Reading Association, 1979. 98-106.

Kao, Donald. "Rev. of *Sea Glass*, by Laurence Yep." *Interracial Books for Children Bulletin* 11.6 (1980): 16.

Kingston, Maxine Hong. "Middle Kingdom to Middle America." *The Washington Post* 1 May 1977: El, E8.

—. *The Woman Warrior: Memoirs of a Girlhood among Ghosts*. 1975. New York: Vintage, 1989.

Lim, Shirley Geok-lin. "Reading Back, Looking Forward: A Retrospective Interview with Maxine Hong Kingston." *MELUS* 33.1 (Spring 2008): 157-70.

Ling, Amy. *Between Worlds: Women Writers of Chinese Ancestry. New York: Pergamon*, 1990.

Lord, Bette Bao. *In the Year of the Boar and Jackie Robinson*. Illus. Marc Simont. New York: Harper & Row, 1984.

Lowell, Chun-Hoon. "Jade Snow Wong and the Fate of Chinese-American Identity." *Asian-Americans: Psychological Perspectives*. Ed. Stanley Sue, and Nathaniel N. Wagner. California: Science and Behavior, 1973. 125-35.

Ludwig, Sämi. *Concrete Language: Intercultural Communication in Maxine Hong Kingston's* The Woman Warrior *and Ishmael Reed's* Mumbo Jumbo. Frankfurt am Main: Peter Lang, 1996.

McCunn, Ruthanne Lum. "Chinese Americans: A Personal View." *School Library Journal* 34 (June/July 1988): 50-51.

Natov, Roni. "Living in Two Cultures: Bette Bao Lord's Stories of Chinese-American Experience." *The Lion and the Unicorn* 11.1 (1987): 38-46.

Ostriker, Alicia. "The Thieves of Language: Women Poets and Revisionist Mythmaking." *The New Feminist Criticism: Essays on Women. Literature, and Theory*. Ed. Elaine Showalter. New York: Pantheon, 1985. 314-38.

Suárez-Orozco, Carola and Marcelo M. Suárez-Orozco. *Children of Immigration*. Massachusetts: Harvard UP, 2001.

Tom, Lily. "Swashbuckling Swordswomen of the Silver Screen." *Ms*. 1(1973): 28-32.

Woo, Celestine. "Bicultural World Creation: Laurence Yep, Cynthia Kadohata, and Asian American Fantasy." *Literary Gestures: The Aesthetic in Asian American Writing*. Ed. Rocío G. Davis, and Sue-Im Lee. Philadelphia: Temple UP, 2006. 173-86.

Yep, Laurence. *Child of the Owl*. 1965. New York: Harper & Row, 1977.

—. "Dragon I Have Known and Loved." *Journal of the Fantastic in the Arts* 21.3 (2010): 386-93.

—. *Dragonwings*. New York: Harper & Row, 1975.

—. *Sea Glass*. New York: Harper & Row, 1979.

—. "Writing 'Dragonwings'." *The Reading Teacher* 30.4 (1977): 359-63.

Claiming America through Land Empathy: An Ecocritical Approach to Maxine Hong Kingston's *China Men*

Begoña Simal (Universidade da Coruña, Spain)

Maxine Hong Kingston's works, especially her seminal first books, *The Woman Warrior* and *China Men*, have been approached from many perspectives: as part of an emergent Asian American literary canon, as a powerful indictment of sexist discrimination, as a compelling postmodern commentary on (ethnic / racial / gender) identity formation, and as a subversive answer to the very notion of genre, to name just a few examples. However, her books have rarely been explored from an ecocritical point of view.[1] Even when critics started to pay attention to environmental justice issues and their reflection in literature, they bypassed Asian American texts that did not feature or only indirectly tackled "environmental racism and inequity" (Hayashi 61), like Kingston's *China Men*.

From the very outset, ecocriticism has explored "the relationship between human and non-human life as represented in literary texts," while at the same time discussing "the place of literature in the struggle against environmental destruction" (Coupe 302), an agenda later supplemented, as mentioned above, by environmental justice concerns. Although ecocriticism initially focused on nature writing, in the last decade relevant critics have emphasized the need for environmental criticism to go beyond traditional nature-focused narratives and widen their scope in order to include other texts.[2] According to Lawrence Buell, all literary texts encode a certain type of environmentality, consciously or unconsciously (*Writing* 18-27), and Kingston's *China Men* is no exception. What makes Kingston's book particularly interesting is the way in which its

---

1. One obvious exception to such scarcity of scholarly work is Hayashi's "Beyond Walden Pond" (2007), which discusses Kingston's *China Men* in its last sections (65-70).
2. This need to go beyond our obsession with nature writing, and especially with wilderness narratives, has been pointed out by Karla Armbruster and Kathleen R. Wallace (3-4), Lawrence Buell, Hayashi (58, 60, 65) or Timothy Morton (5). As Hayashi cogently puts it, the emphasis on "pristine" nature and the "privileging of wilderness not only hides the nearly ubiquitous connection between human labor and the natural environment; it also silences the views of those who most impact the environment through their work" (65).

obvious nationalist master-narrative coexists with, and is partially subverted by, the environmental subtext.

The conjoining of environmental awareness and nationalism / regionalism is by no means a new phenomenon (e.g., bioregionalist movements), but recent studies by Ursula Heise and other ecocritics seem to move away from that traditional localist focus and instead announce a new stage in environmental criticism, variously described as the "transnational turn" (Heise, "Ecocriticism") or the "global shift" (Simal, "Junkyard"). In the last few years, in an attempt to broaden the field of study, ecocritics have been concerned with developing "environmental allegiances that reach beyond the local and the national" (Heise, *Sense* 21). And yet, traditional ecocritics like Patrick Murphy still emphasize the relevance of "localism" for ecocritical theory:

> To achieve its goals and remain honest to the literature it seeks to study, ecocriticism should remain pivotal, rather than foundational, and localist, rather than global, in its grounding orientation. [...]. While there are issues requiring a global perspective and there are phenomena truly global in scope, the local and the particular can never be forgotten or ignored. (1)

Following Murphy and other ecocritics, then, we cannot deny the continuing investment of environmental awareness and activism in local / national / allonational paradigms, even if, as Heise has amply demonstrated, such a position proves more and more problematic in an increasingly globalized world. Historically, though, localist / nationalist paradigms have proved helpful—at least temporarily—when used by disenfranchised people, as seen, for instance, in the ethnic minorities' involvement with the territory they inhabited and their concomitant fight for rights, either as "natives" of the land or as "co-builders" of the new nation. One way in which environmentalism has been successfully coupled with the nationalist impulse can be traced back to those early Asian American texts that "claimed America," to use the often quoted phrase coined by Kingston herself.[3] Asian American works such as Shawn Wong's *Homebase* or Kingston's *China Men* claimed America by inscribing Asian Americanness into the American landscape. Although such inscription in official history and in the land itself is present in *China Men,* Kingston's book also traces the development of a new relationship with the land, more akin to "land empathy"

---

3. The phrase is used by Kingston in Timothy Pfaff's "Talk with Mrs. Kingston" (1). According to Shirley Lim, the very term "'claim' brings to mind a claim as a piece of land especially for mining purposes, recalling that the first groups of Chinese American came to the United States to work in the gold-fields of California. Kingston's statement asserts an identity right and an empirical history of mining and land claims that became gradually disallowed through state and federal laws barring Chinese from land ownership and U.S. citizenship" (299).

than to previous colonialist attitudes of dominion. Such an ecocritical reading of *China Men* arguably complicates and transforms the cultural nationalist paradigm known as the "claiming of America." Before we delve into the text itself, however, we need to explore the social and historical context in which it was produced.

Asian Americans and the American Land: an Ambivalent and Fragile Connection

If, as Sulaiman Madhi argues, "land sovereignty" constitutes the core of the environmental justice movement (qtd. in Smith 190), the case of Asian Americans becomes the most paradigmatic and salient example of the impossibility of "land sovereignty" in multiethnic America. Throughout their history in the US, spanning almost two centuries, Asian Americans have experienced a peculiar relationship with the American land. Unlike Native Americans, who had inhabited North American landscapes for many centuries before the first Europeans arrived, nineteenth and twentieth century immigrants apparently had a more fragile connection with the land. Even though their presence in continental America could be traced back to the mid-nineteenth century, Asian Americans only came to claim America as "rightfully theirs" late in the twentieth century. Until the 1970s, when Asian American cultural nationalism emerged, most Americans of Asian descent were routinely perceived as not belonging in that land, on American soil. While the slaves uprooted from Africa had been forced to sever all ties with their countries / continent of origin, many Chinese, Japanese, Korean and Filipino Americans, to name just a few national communities, continued to have contact with their countries of origin and, in some cases, to travel back and forth.[4] For most of the nineteenth and twentieth century, Asian Americans were perceived not only as homogeneous—all of them "yellow" or "Mongoloid," in the racist terminology of the time—, but also as homogeneously *alien*: "strangers from a different shore," to echo Ronald Takaki's book.

The conspicuous presence of homesick characters in *China Men*, together with the more general sense of displacement that pervades this and other Asian American narratives of the twentieth century, would seem to support the claim that the lack of "property ownership and citizenship rights" effectively prevents

4. With the possible exception of Japanese Americans, who became the obvious target of racist hatred and "scapegoating" during the 1940s, WW2 effectively put an end to the immigration (and travel) restrictions set by the Asian Exclusion Act (1924), and earlier by the Chinese Exclusion Act (1882, repealed in 1943). However, it was not until the passing of the 1965 Immigration Act that the normalization of international mobility for Asians was finally confirmed.

disempowered communities from establishing "an emotional bond to the land," an argument that can be found in much African American environmental discourse; if such a connection with the land was taken for granted among "white" Americans, in the case of ethnic minorities and the foreign-born "it had to be consciously created and fought for" (Smith 88, 89).[5] The tortured relationship with the land that they contributed to shape (physically and figuratively), but could not legally own, affected the life of several generations of Asian Americans and has accordingly haunted their literature. We must not forget that, well into the twentieth century, Asians were the only immigrants whose access to both property and citizenship was consistently denied, not only *de facto*, but also *de iure*, a point that Kingston emphasizes in "The Laws" chapter of *China Men*: "Though the Chinese were filling and leveeing the San Joaquin Delta for thirteen cents a square yard, building the richest agricultural land in the world, they were prohibited from owning land or real estate" (374). Deprived of the possibility of legally possessing the land where they lived and toiled, first-generation Asian Americans—most notably the Chinese in the late nineteenth century and the Japanese in the first half of the twentieth century—could only create a bond with the land they helped to shape, clear and cultivate on a temporary basis. In addition, the particular exploitative conditions under which most Asian immigrants worked decisively shaped the manner in which they viewed and experienced the new land. In *African American Environmental Thought* (2007), Kimberly Smith convincingly argues that exploitative labor generally "make[s] the workers less careful," but also fosters in those agricultural laborers certain "ambivalence toward the land: a sense of alienation from the land and community coupled with a desire (and perhaps strategies) to come into a more meaningful and creative relationship with the natural world" (93). Although no system of indenture can be compared to the "peculiar institution" of slavery, the Asian Americans' indentured labor first and hard working conditions later fostered an ambivalent attitude towards the land among these workers, in some respects like "the slave system that forced slaves into an intimacy with the natural environment but also tended to alienate them from it" (Smith 10; cf. Yang 75). Such ambivalence would be textualized in different and significant ways in Asian American literature.

In attempting to trace the environmental aspects of Kingston's *China Men*, with special attention to the characters' ambivalent relationship with the land, we soon discover that there is more to the Chinese immigration story than meets the eye. These immigrants have been generally construed as "conquering pioneers" of the new land, an interpretation that seems to transpire from the text itself (Yang 77, 80), and which would be in keeping with a utilitarian,

---

5. It goes without saying that not all white citizens were landowners, but no law denied them the right to own land, as indeed was the case for many African Americans and Asian Americans.

anthropocentric worldview of the natural environment. In fact, the characters in *China Men* exhibit a special closeness to the land or a penchant for cultivating it, or both, a common trait that problematizes the traditional reading of the text.[6] At one point in the narrative one of the Chinese immigrants asks himself: "Who really owns the land? ... The man who farms it with his sweat and piss or the man whose name is on the paper" (416). In other words, who is an American, a person with citizenship papers or the one who has toiled, sweated and hurt in that land?[7] Both history and fiction attest to the fact that Asian Americans, like other "pioneers" before them, literally changed the shape of the American land(scape) by building the railroad, planting seeds and harvesting fields. This is precisely the subtext in *China Men* and, as such, it has been studied and construed as contributing to cultural nationalist efforts to claim America, to claim visibility and a sense of belonging for Asian Americans. However, this nationalist agenda should be questioned and rewritten from an ecocritical perspective. In particular, I would like to argue that Kingston's book explores the tension that Aldo Leopold situates in the following dichotomies: "man the conqueror *versus* man the biotic citizen; [...] land the slave and servant *versus* land the collective organism" (223). Ultimately, a detailed ecocritical reading of *China Men* subverts the canonical appraisal of the text as claiming the land in "conquering" and "servile" terms. Instead, as the following analysis will illustrate, the narrative focalization emphasizes the deep connection with the non-human biozens, what I will call "land empathy."

---

6. Because of space constraints I cannot explore all of these issues in detail, but will concentrate on the interaction of these pioneers with "wild nature" and uncultivated land. Although the book has abundant "descriptions of waste land, literally territory that is unclaimed and unclaimable" (Lim 304), together with the impressive mountains and similar "pristine" natural landscapes, *China Men* includes images of nature that come closer to the literary *topos* of the *locus amoenus* (cf. 253, 233, 292, 313, 317, 486), or else scenes that explore "middle-landscapes," such as the passage devoted to BaBa's gardening efforts (483).
7. The narrator espouses this vision when she points out that "[e]ven if Ah Goong had not spent half his gold on Citizenship Papers, he was *an American for having built the railroad*" (366). Crazy Ah Goong finally becomes a *pariah* and has to be brought "home," back to China, or he dies in San Francisco, we never know for sure: "The family called him Fleaman. They did not understand his accomplishments as an American ancestor, a holding, homing ancestor of this place" (372).

Land Ethics and Land Empathy

The Asian American cultural nationalist discourse that "claimed America" in the 1970s implicitly or explicitly approached the land as a commodified object which could be sold and bought. The land was, above all, property to which one was (or was not) entitled. As such, the land itself had no agency or rights, but was passively owned by an active subject, a citizen with land-owning rights. Asian American nationalists sought to be recognized as figuratively *belonging within* the American territory / land and to attain property rights, that is, to have that land *belong to* them. When such rights were finally gained by birth or legal amendment, the subject / object dialectic was not substantially altered. Simply, Asian Americans were finally allowed to enter into the category of subjects who could possess, own, control the object: the land. Important though the recognition of civil and property rights was, it is no less true that the relationship to the land apparently remained unaltered. The affective bond between land and human beings was conceived as non-existent or, at most, was pushed to a secondary position. The (human) property rights superseded the (non-human) land rights, and obscured the fact that social ethics has to be supplemented by ecological ethics, which situates the human interaction with the land, with the planet, beyond the utilitarian, anthropocentric paradigm.

In *A Sand County Almanac* (1949), Aldo Leopold advocated such a revolution in our understanding of the world, and called for a new ethics. In the chapter aptly titled "The Land Ethic," Leopold sketches the ideal progression that this ethical development should take, from individual, to collective, to ecological ethics, although his own ethical hierarchy at times proves problematic.[8] Inspired by Leopold's extended notion of ethics and by other theorists, Greta Gaard and Patrick Murphy further denounce the human tendency to see non-human elements in terms of self-interest, that is, as "things-for-us," instead of "things-in-themselves" (5-6). Against this utilitarian view of the non-human members of the biotic community, what Leopold calls "the land," ecocritics, including ecofeminists such as Gaard and Murphy urge us to consider them "things-in-themselves," thus endowing them with an intrinsic value, a value more typically associated with human beings in the Western, Judeo-Christian tradition.

8. Curiously enough, Leopold's chosen analogy in the July entry of his *Sand County Almanac* constitutes a conspicuous example of ethnocentrism and non-empathy concerning Chinese people: "The erasure of a human subspecies is largely painless—to us—if we know little enough about it. A dead Chinaman is of little import to us whose awareness of things Chinese is bounded by an occasional dish of chow mein. We grieve only for what we know" (48).

If Leopold's "land ethic" was still a utopian desire in the 1940s, it is still far from widespread in the western world. True enough, much has been done in the way of environmental education and consciousness-raising, and we human beings are starting to assume, voluntarily or involuntarily, our dependence *on* the planet. Our interdependence *with* the planet is a different issue, though: while most of us are well aware that we are part of a social, human community, it is less clear whether we all extend "the boundaries of the community to include soils, waters, plants, and animals," what Leopold summarizes in the concept of "the land" (204). Leopold's insight that we cannot broaden those collective boundaries without learning about and learning to love that new, extended biotic community leads us to consider the concept of "land empathy." Although Leopold does not use the phrase explicitly, it can be surmised that this is what he is aiming at when he declares the following: "We can be ethical only in relation to something we can see, feel, understand, love, or otherwise have faith in" (214). For a land ethic to exist, therefore, there must be "an ecological conscience," which "in turn reflects a conviction of individual responsibility for the health of the land" (221). After all, as Leopold suggests, developing a land ethic involves "an intellectual as well an emotional process" (225). In other words, not only do we have to grasp our biotic interdependence *intellectually*, we also need to take it in at an *emotional* level: we must *learn to feel* an integral part of that biotic community, and the characters in *China Men* successfully do so by attributing human features and "interiority" to the non-human Other.[9]

Claiming America through Land Empathy

In the second half of the nineteenth century, a sizable number of Chinese people, most of them men, emigrated to Hawai'i (Sandalwood Mountains) and mainland US (Gold Mountain). As the narrator in *China Men* puts it, Cantonese villagers, like ocean people, had itchy feet, and, in their restlessness, they traveled to the Sandalwood Mountains and the Gold Mountain: "[T]he ocean and hunger and some other urge made Cantonese people explorers and American" (306). The narrator's father, BaBa, was no exception to that collective drive. Yet, that apparent mobility was not without its social restraints. When leaving, Chinese men vowed to their wives and mothers that they were mere "tourists," sojourners, birds of passage, in other words, they promised "to come back, not settle in America with new wives" (257). Wives or no wives, the narrator's

9. See "From Phallic Binary to Cognitive Wager: Empathy and Interiority in Lois-Ann Yamanaka's *Wild Meat and the Bully Burgers*," where Sämi Ludwig convincingly argues that Yamanaka's novel deconstructs the "phallic binary" precisely through the empathic attribution of interiority to animals such as Bully the cow.

ancestors finally left for America and, in many cases, they eventually settled there.

However, until the "Brother in Vietnam" finally secures a Q Clearance, "certifying that the family was really American, not precariously American but super American" (257), the status of the narrator's family in the US is doubtful, and she often wavers between "legal" and "illegal" versions of her ancestors, most notably her father. In the legal version of BaBa's life, "The American Father," the narrator emphasizes BaBa's power of "making places belong to him": small, specific places marked by "father smells," but also, implicitly, larger places like America (463). Similarly, in one of the "illegal" versions of the father's coming to the US, the narrator tells how BaBa had hidden in a box, a stowaway on a ship bound for America, "coming to claim the Gold mountain, *his own country*" (266, emphasis added).

In another version of the story, BaBa comes in a ship full of Chinese emigrants. As soon as they arrive at San Francisco Bay, they are taken to the Immigration Station at Angel Island. During the long stay there, waiting to be examined and in constant fear of deportation, these immigrants often despair and write their anguish on the walls of the detention building—writings/carvings later known as the Angel Island poems. At times, the fog prevents these sojourners from seeing the city opposite the island: "The fog horns mourned. San Francisco might have been a figment of Gold Mountain dreams" (270). After all, as the narrator warns us, America, the Gold Mountain, was nothing but a Chinese *invention*, the Cantonese being "people with fabulous imaginations" (302). Despite the lingering nature of that doubt, San Francisco turns out not to be a mirage after all. Fellow detainees not only remind BaBa of the solidity of America, but also of their belonging in that territory even before setting foot or landing on it: "Let me land. Let me out. Let me land. I want to come *home*" (270). Significantly enough, when the "legal father" finally "passes" the Immigration interview, he feels he has "won America," thus confirming the initial conception of the land as "conquerable" (274).

If the claiming of America is a leitmotif linking every version of BaBa's journey, it becomes even more conspicuous and recurrent in the narratives of the grandfathers and great-grandfathers who first travel to the distant "mountains": the Sandalwood Mountains or the Gold Mountain. Two of those ancestors become pivotal characters in *China Men*: Bak Goong, the great-grandfather of the Sandalwood Mountains, and Ah Goong, the "crazy" Chinese grandfather of the Sierra Nevada Mountains. Significantly, the narrator's ancestors will not only claim American territory in figurative terms, but will also re-claim that land in technical terms, either by turning it into agricultural land (Bak Goong's land reclamation in Hawai'i) or by making room for the new railway road (Ah Goong in the Sierra Nevada Mountains).

In China, Ah Goong, like other farmers in a predominantly agricultural peasant society, had "plowed fields hour after hour alone, inching along between earth and sky," but in America he would have to carve the very land and shape it anew (226). From the outset this character reveals a strangely intimate connection with the earth: while still in China, he is able to hear the planet move, "the gears on its axis snap" (346). It is precisely by following a faraway sound resembling the fireworks during a New Year holiday that Ah Goong finally reaches "the blasting in the Sierras" in the American continent (346). In other words, the narrator's grandfather, like many other Chinese "sojourners," arrives in America just as the transcontinental railroad is being built, in 1863.

Once in America, Ah Goong, the grandfather of the Sierra Nevada mountains, and the other Chinese laborers, "men like ants changing the face of the world" (351), start to reconfigure the land in a literal manner, by blowing their way through mountains and by clearing valleys. In so doing, many Chinese workers risk their lives and their dead bodies join the rocks and debris below, thus literally becoming part of the land. Ah Goong is first told to clear the lands by felling trees. As a consequence, he engages in some "bloody" battles with trees that not only seem to resist being cut or uprooted, but, more importantly, take on human or animal characteristics:

> He axed for almost a day [...]. The tree swayed and slowly dived to earth, creaking and *screeching like a green animal*. He was so awed, he forgot what he was supposed to yell. Hardly any branches broke; the tree sprang, bounced, pushed at the ground *with its arms*. The limbs did not wilt and fold; they were a small forest, which he chopped. The trunk lay like *a long red torso; sap ran from its cuts like crying blind eyes*. At last it stopped fighting. (346-47, emphasis added)

Already in this early task, the character-focalizer Ah Goong endows trees with sentient animal / human characteristics (*arms, torso*, "crying blind eyes," "screeching like a green animal"). The tree he has to cut is not a passive object, but is explicitly given agency, to the point that its fierce struggle overwhelms Ah Goong. The new lumberjack is "awed" and "humbly aware that with each stroke [of the axe] he is writing his signature on the face of the land" (Leopold 68).

Next, the ant-like workers try to work their way through the impressive granite mountains and their initial failure emphasizes the insignificance of human beings before those mountains: "After tunneling into granite for about three years, Ah Goong understood the immovability of the earth. Men change, men die, weather changes, but a mountain is the same as permanence and time. This mountain would have taken no new shape for centuries, then thousand centuries, the world a still, still place, time unmoving" (354). When dynamite replaces gunpowder, granite is finally subdued, but the cost is high: "Human bodies skipped through the air like puppets and made Ah Goong laugh crazily as if the arms and legs would come together again. *The smell of burned flesh remained in rocks*" (356, emphasis added). Not only does sweat make those mountains part of the pioneers and *vice versa*, but these men literally "impregnate" the land with their blood, when they die or get wounded, or, symbolically, with their urine and semen. The powerful image of Ah Goong's peculiar way to "claim" the land deserves being quoted at length:

> The mountainface reshaped, they drove supports for a bridge. Since hammering was less dangerous than the blowing up, the men played a little; they rode the baskets swooping in wide arcs; they twisted the ropes and let them unwind like tops. 'Look at me,' said Ah Goong, pulled open his pants, and pissed overboard, the wind scattering the drops. *'I'm a waterfall,'* he said. He had seen a part of himself hurtling. On rare windless days he watched his piss fall in *a continuous stream from himself almost to the bottom of the valley*. (351-52, emphasis added)

Smith has argued that hard work, "particularly agricultural labor [...] can make creative, sensitive response to the land difficult, if not impossible" (11), and yet, the quotation above demonstrates that, playful as always, Ah Goong manages to engage creatively with the land to the extent that he metaphorically emerges as a continuation of the surrounding environment, a peculiar "waterfall" that, as it were, "completes" the picture. Much the same can be said of the other fluid that literally connects him with the land:

> One beautiful day, dangling in the sun above a new valley, not the desire to urinate but sexual desire clutched him so hard he bent over in the basket. He curled up, overcome by beauty and fear, which shot to his penis. He tried to rub himself calm. Suddenly he stood up tall and squirted out into space. '*I am fucking the world*,' he said. *The world's vagina was big, big as the sky, big as a valley*. He grew a habit: whenever he was lowered in the basket, his blood rushed to his penis, and he fucked the world. (352, emphasis added)

This scene has been read as indicative of Ah Goong's literal and metaphorical impotence, a metonymic reference to the symbolic castration of the early Chinese American community (Hayashi 66).[10] It has also been interpreted as "a triumph for the body" if not for the whole person, "a moment of transcendence" for an otherwise alienated worker (Yang 77). In addition, from an ecofeminist perspective, the passage could also be construed as a metaphorical "rape" of the land. However, the fact that the fear-induced scene is told in a celebratory, even triumphant tone points at another interpretation: the narrative shows Ah Goong joyfully bonding not only with that specific place, the Sierra Nevada mountains and valleys, but also with the planet.

---

10. It is true that, when the Chinese workers finally reach granite mountains, their sledgehammers prove useless and Ah Goong feels powerless: "The mountain that was millions of years old was locked against them and was not to be broken into. The men teased him, 'Let's see you fuck the world now.' 'Let's see you fuck the Gold Mountain now.' But he no longer felt like it" (353).

This metaphorical, sexual entering of the land becomes literal on the frequent occasions when Chinese laborers die and their bones cannot be rescued and sent back to China, as tradition dictates: their bodies are eventually left there to nurture the American land. When bodies are recovered, there is talk of burial ceremonies in American land, much to the suspicious resistance of most sojourners: "The men who died slowly enough to say last words said, 'Don't leave me frozen under the snow. Send my body home. [...]. Aiya. To be buried here, nowhere'" (357-58). To this, however, visionary pioneers like Ah Goong answer in a positive vein: "But this is somewhere. [...]. This is the Gold Mountain. *We're marking the land* now. The track sections are numbered, and your family will know where we leave you" (358, emphasis added). Once more, the literal marking of the railway track is enhanced by a figurative reading of Ah Goong's words as reminiscent of an animal marking territory, an action that, even though it constitutes a "naturally-sanctioned" phenomenon, still has negative-possessive connotations.

Ah Goong's feeling of belonging in the new land, his attempt to claim America, reappears in Bak Goong, the great-grandfather of the Sandalwood Mountains (323). There, in Hawai'i, Bak Goong works long days at the sugar cane plantations and, on his "day offu" (323), he joins his fellow countrymen and goes to Honolulu: "They dressed for town in their black silk suits and yellow straw boaters with the black band and forked streamers; their braids hung between the swallowtails. 'I'm going to town,' Bak Goong sang and sang *town* as if Honolulu were *his own village*" (324, italics in the original).

If Ah Goong had symbolically impregnated the Sierra Nevada mountains, Bak Goong also leaves some seed in the Sandalwood Mountains: after sowing the field Bak Goong "pats the pregnant earth," in a more pastoral and paternalistic fashion than "crazy" Ah Goong. Bak Goong ultimately goes back to China and thus fulfills his promise to his wife before leaving (321). However, in one of his feverish nightmares he dreams that he returns to China, penniless and physically wasted, and he is scolded by his wife, who reminds him of the new belonging and allegiance: "Moneyless and bodiless, you better go back to the Sandalwood Mountains. Go back and pick up your money and your body. *Go back where you belong*. Go now" (334, emphasis added). It is there, in those islands known as the Sandalwood Mountains, where the narrator's great-grandfather seems to belong now.

If Ah Goong had shaped the land in continental America, in Hawai'i Bak Goong also reconfigures the islands by clearing the land for the sugar-cane plantation. Chinese workers like Bak Goong cut down thickets and move rocks, while the Hawaiians, more reluctant to interfere with their ancestral land, "quit rather than help pull the boulders out of the earth" (320).[11] It is back-breaking

11. For a critical analysis of how the book portrays, or rather, fails to portray Native Hawaiians, as well as women workers, see Yang 74-76.

work, but Bak Goong eventually manages to clear the land for cultivation, following an obviously masculinist (fairy-tale) script: "One day, like a knight rescuing a princess, Bak Goong broke clear through the thicket," and the bullocks "yanked out" the last stumps (320). Gradually, though, land reclamation is replaced with land empathy. Like the trees in the American Sierras, which fell "with a tearing of veins and muscles" when cut down or uprooted with gunpowder, the very soil of the Sandalwood Mountains metamorphoses into a suffering being, bleeding like an animal or a person (347). Thus, while the Chinese pioneers have the sad honor of becoming "the first human beings to dig into this part of the island and *see the meat and bones of the red earth. After rain, the mud ran like blood*" (320, emphasis added), the narrator demonstrates that these workers are conscious of the land's sacrifice. This moment signals the emergence of some sort of incipient land empathy among those Chinese American pioneers. Having chosen these male ancestors as the main focalizers—if not the narrative voice—of the text, Kingston links up those humanizing metaphors with these men's own feelings and worldview. The choice of words reveals the intense empathy those "China men" feel *with / for* the land.[12] In feeling *with / for* the trees, the animals or the rocks, these pioneers embody the ethical broadening that Leopold advocated, "the extension of the social conscience from people to land" (209). These men learn to value the other members of the biotic community as "things-in-themselves," in Murphy and Gaard's terminology, not just as "things-for-us."

Home, Homelessness and Belonging

Two other grandfathers / great uncles, now turned into oldtimers living in California, appear in the book. Their presence is linked by the narrator to that of the two horses which she had found so fascinating as a toddler and young girl. Against the backdrop of silence and omission in the official history, these "China men" and their relatives start to create an alternative oral narrative, in which they inscribe themselves not only as Gold Mountain pioneers, but also as real Californians / Americans. After many years in California, Kau Goong, the Great Uncle who looked like a giant to the young narrator, ponders whether to go back to China, where the Great Aunt awaits him, but he finally opts for staying in America: "'California. This is my home. I belong here.' He turned and, looking at us, roared, '*We* belong here'" (407). Thus, when Kau Goong

12. And not only the soil: the hundred-year-old man in the homonymous story really becomes a Chinese American everyman, the first to arrive in Hawaii in 1885; significantly, he brings "with him pigs in cages, and chives and onions growing in cans" and chooses to share "his ration of fresh water with the pigs, the chives, and the onions" (538)—an apt metaphor for the empathic coexistence of human beings with animals and plants.

dies, the other oldtimers tell the people attending the funeral how Kau Goong had chosen to stay in the Gold Mountain: "He was a Gold Mountain Man. They said 'Gold Mountain' a lot, 'Gum Sahn' many times. 'Long time Califoon,' they said in English" (409).

Not only the oldtimers, but also the narrator's extended family collaborates in this claiming of the land. When pointing at the places the ancestors used to inhabit (and haunt), their relatives join in the rites of claiming America:

> When their descendants came across the country to visit us, we took them to the place where two of our four grandfathers had had their house, stable, and garden. [...]. They took pictures with a *delayed*-shutter camera, everyone standing together where the house had been. The relatives kept saying, 'This is *the ancestral ground*,' their eyes filling with tears over a vacant lot in Stockton. (391, emphasis added)

Their presence in official history may have been erased, but these grandfathers are now re-imagined as silently claiming America by claiming the land.[13] "Delayed" in time, this recognition arrives in the guise of the sacralization of "minor" spaces standing synecdochically for the larger ones. Thus, the "vacant lot in Stockton," California, stands for the "apparently" vacant land which Maxine's ancestors have worked through and / or cultivated, a foreign space that they turn into their home, into "the ancestral ground" where their memory (if not their bones) can finally rest.

Although the great-grandfather of the Sandalwood Mountains, Bak Goong, the grandfather of the Sierra Nevada Mountains, Ah Goong, and other ancestors like Bak Sook Goong eventually go back to China, their sojourn in America has awakened a new sense of land empathy and gradually consolidates a deep bond with those places they have inhabited for years. Bak Goong, as we have just seen, embraces Honolulu as "his own village" and the Sandalwood Mountains as his "home." And yet, the same Bak Goong often feels homesick and longs to go back to China. Like the king in the prince-kitten story, he cannot keep the secret any longer, so he transgresses all the silence norms in the plantation and shouts it out (335-36). Following the traditional prince-kitten story, the homesick Chinese sojourners dig "a wide hole" and they all slump down, lying there "with their faces over the edge of the hole and their legs like wheel spokes" and shouting into the big hole. What Bak Goong, Bak Sook Goong and the other pioneers had done, in symbolic terms, was to dig "an ear into the world" in order to tell "the earth their secrets": "'I want home,' Bak Goong yelled, pressed the soil, and smelling the earth. 'I want my home,' the men yelled together. 'I want home. Home. Home. Home. Home.' / Talked out, they buried their words,

13. For an analysis of Kingston's *China Men* as an intervention in and rewriting of official history, see Sledge's and Cheung's articles.

planted them ..." (337). A close analysis of the text reveals how the men's intentions are thwarted in several ways. First, the earth seems to contradict their desires, because the echo of their shouts, both bouncing back and trapped within that hole, keeps reminding those who yell that *home* may be there, precisely where they are.[14] The words have been "buried," "planted" in that alien land, thus leaving some of the speakers' own selves behind. Second, even in those moments of nostalgia, when the great-grandfather concedes that he wishes he were back in China, he also acknowledges his foundational attachment to the new land: "That wasn't a custom [in that island ...]. We made it up. We can make up customs because we're the *founding ancestors of this place*" (337). Finally, just as in the traditional story, where the earth had not been able to hold the king's secret for too long, here in Hawai'i the landscape would also tell of these China Men's lives and longings: "Soon the new green shoots would rise, and when in two years the cane grew gold tassels, what stories the wind would tell" (338).[15]

The episode of the shouting hole becomes even more significant because it is presented after the narrator describes her visit to the Hawaiian island known as Chinaman's Hat, so called because of its shape and, as such, a "tribute to the pioneers" (305). Here, in this island, the process of claiming the land becomes especially poignant, since the autodiegetic narrator at last participates in that pioneering ritual. When she first arrives in Hawai'i with the explicit desire to discover and claim the Chinese legacy in those islands, the narrator does not seem able to distinguish the pioneers' singing voice (303). It is only when she plunges into the ocean and swims towards the island, that is, when she literally enters the very space she needs to claim that she manages to hear some humming noise:

> ... a howling like wolves, like singing, came rising out of the island. 'Birds,' somebody said. 'The wind,' said someone else. But the air was still, and the high, clear sound wound through the trees. It continued until we departed. It was, I know it, the island, the voice of the island singing, the sirens Odysseus heard.

---

14. Alternatively, the scene can be construed as a plea for understanding that the entire planet is your real home, since the echo in the hole, which keeps repeating "home, home, home" can also be read as the very voice of the earth, the planet speaking and shouting back that we all belong together. From sense of place to sense of planet, to echo Heise's title.

15. Alternatively, the scene can be construed as a plea for understanding that the entire planet is your real home, since the echo in the hole, which keeps repeating "home, home, home" can also be read as the very voice of the earth, the planet speaking and shouting back that we all belong together. From sense of place to sense of planet, to echo Heise's title.

> The Navy continues to bomb Kaho'olawe and the Army blasts *the green skin* of the red mountains of O'ahu. But *the land sings*. We heard something. (305, emphasis added)

Significantly, the narrative voice and the focalizer are one and the same here: the autodiegetic narrator. At this particular moment, she finally hears the land singing: she bears witness to her ancestors' stories "by listening in the cane" (305). According to Patricia Linton, the whole scene constitutes "a complex and powerful metaphor that demonstrates how people appropriate the land, making it so completely their own that the land itself tells their story" (42). I would argue, however, that there is another underlying narrative that supplements the paradigm of claiming America: by letting the land itself a "sing / speak" as a subject, nature is no longer imagined as a passive object, but rather an active agent in a nationalist project that may have been originally anthropocentric, but which has broadened and incorporated a new ecological sensibility.

Conclusion

From the discussion above we can conclude that Kingston's *China Men* "claims America" in subtly different ways from those in which it has traditionally been read. True to the cultural nationalist agenda, the narrator, by textualizing the visible imprint of bones, blood and other bodily fluids that Chinese Americans have left on the very territory they are claiming as rightfully theirs, makes a powerful statement: America belongs to these pioneers because they have physically become the territory they are claiming. At the same time, beyond this anthropocentric paradigm of dominion and possession, Kingston's book offers a glimpse into a new relationship with the land. *China Men* combines the awareness of nature's agency, of its "sentient" features, on the one hand, with the characters' incipient sense of "land empathy," implicit in Leopold's land ethics, on the other. If, as Leopold maintained, "a land ethic changes the role of *Homo sapiens* from conqueror of the land-community to plain member and citizen of it," thus entailing "respect for his [her] fellow-members, and also respect for the community as such" (204), the characters in *China Men* eventually move away from proprietorial understandings of land and towards an egalitarian bond with the natural environment. Contrary to what we would expect in such alienating conditions, the pioneer China men, who first meet the land as a hostile element they have to struggle with, finally learn to feel *with* and *for* the land. Not only does the text offer us a glimpse of Nature's "feelings," but we eventually hear it "speak." *Natura sentiens, natura loquens*. In this new dialogue between human and non-human, the old "claiming of America" is dismantled and built anew.

Works Cited

Armbruster, Karla, and Kathleen R. Wallace, eds. *Beyond Nature Writing: Expanding the Boundaries of Ecocriticism*, Charlottesville: UP of Virginia, 2001.

Buell, Lawrence. *Writing for an Endangered World: Literature, Culture, and Environment in the United States and Beyond*. Cambridge, MA: Harvard UP, 2001.

Chang, Sucheng. *Asian Americans: An Interpretive History*. Boston: Twayne Publishers, 1991.

Cheung, King-kok. "The Woman Warrior versus The Chinaman Pacific: Must a Chinese American Critic Choose between Feminism and Heroism?" *Conflicts in Feminism*. Eds. Marianne Hirsch and Evelyn Fox Keller. New York: Routledge, 1990. 234-51.

Coupe, Laurence, ed. *The Green Studies Reader: From Romanticism to Ecocriticism*. London and New York: Routledge, 2000.

Gaard, Greta, and Patrick Murphy. "Introduction." *Ecofeminist Literary Criticism: Theory, Interpretation, Pedagogy*. Urbana and Chicago: U of Illinois P, 1998. 1-13.

Glotfelty, Cheryll. "Introduction: Literary Studies in an Age of Environmental Crisis." *The Ecocriticism Reader: Landmarks in Literary Ecology*. Eds. Cheryll Glotfelty and Harold Fromm. Athens, GA: U of Georgia P, 1996. xv-xxxvii.

Hayashi, Robert T. "Beyond Walden Pond: Asian American Literature and the Limits of Ecocriticism." *Coming into Contact: Explorations in Ecocritical Theory and Practice*. Eds. Annie Merrill Ingram, Ian Marshall, Daniel J. Philippon, and Adam W. Sweeting. Athens, GA: U of Georgia P, 2007. 58-75.

Heise, Ursula K. "Ecocriticism and the Transnational Turn in American Studies." *American Literary History* 20.1–2 (2008): 381–404.

—. *Sense of Place, Sense of Planet: The Environmental Imagination of the Global*. New York: Oxford UP, 2008.

Kingston, Maxine Hong. 1976; 1980. *The Woman Warrior; China Men*. New York: Everyman's Library, 2005.

Leopold, Aldo. *A Sand County Almanac*. Oxford: Oxford UP, 1949.

Lim, Shirley Geok-lin. "The Native and the Diasporic: Owning America in Native American and Asian American Literatures." *Women's Studies Quarterly* 34.1/2 (2006): 295-308.

Linton, Patricia. "'What Stories the Wind Would Tell': Representation and Appropriation in Maxine Hong Kingston's *China Men*." *MELUS* 19.4 (1994): 37-48.

Ludwig, Sämi. "From Phallic Binary to Cognitive Wager: Empathy and Interiority in Lois-Ann Yamanaka's *Wild Meat and the Bully Burgers*." *Writing American Women: Text, Gender, Performance*. Eds. Thomas Austenfeld and Agnieszka Soltysik. *SPELL* (*Swiss Publications on English Literature and Language*), 2009. 205-21.

Morton, Timothy. *Ecology without Nature: Rethinking Environmental Aesthetics*. Cambridge: Harvard UP, 2007.

Murphy, Patrick. *Ecocritical Explorations in Literary and Cultural Studies: Fences, Boundaries, and Fields*. Lanham, Maryland: Lexington Books, 2009.

Pfaff, Timothy. "Talk with Mrs. Kingston." *The New York Times Book Review* (June 15, 1980): 1, 24-26.

Sledge, Linda Ching. "Maxine Kingston's *China Men*: The Family Historian as Epic Poet." *MELUS* 7.4 (1980): 3-22.

Smith, Kimberly K. *African American Environmental Thought: Foundations*. Lawrence: UP of Kansas, 2007.

Takaki, Ronald. *Strangers from a Different Shore: A History of Asian Americans*. 1989. Boston: Little, Brown, 1998.

Tsai, Shih-shan Henry. *The Chinese Experience in America*. Bloomington: Indiana UP, 1986.

Yang, Caroline H. "Indispensable Labor: The Worker as a Category of Critique in *China Men*." *MFS: Modern Fiction Studies* 56.1 (2010): 63-89.

On Maxine Hong Kingston's Manuscript Revisions of *The Woman Warrior* and *China Men*: an anecdotal account

C. Lok Chua (California State University, Fresno, CA, USA)

Maxine Hong Kingston is one of the most frequently assigned authors in American college courses, and her nonfiction as well as her fiction titles appear with regularity in anthologies and syllabi intended for classes in writing, composition, and literary analysis alike. Indeed, as one scholar reported in 1991, "according to the Modern Language Association of America, *The Woman Warrior* has become the most widely taught book by a living author in U.S. colleges and universities" (Chun 85). For example, at the University of California, Berkeley, alone, it had been adopted by instructors "in some twelve departments, ranging from Comparative Literature, [...] Rhetoric History, [...] to Ethnic Studies" (85). As such, the compositional process of Kingston's literary creation would be a matter of pedagogical and scholarly interest. Fortunately, Kingston has deposited several of her manuscript materials, especially those pertinent to *The Woman Warrior* and *China Men* in the Bancroft Library at the University of California, Berkeley.[1] There one may delve into her manuscript revisions which, after all, are a kind of archeological record of the evolution of any higher form of written art. (One wonders about the losses to this field of scholarship now that writers are composing more frequently on computers.)

As one leafs through Kingston's manuscript pages, one readily notices the many improvements made to her descriptive passages. Often, details are added that render the imagery considerably more vivid in the published version. A case in point is this added visual and kinetic image describing Fa Mu Lan during her warrior training: "Knees bent, I would swing into the slow, measured 'square step,' the powerful walk into battle"—this and several other details describing Mu Lan's training are not in Kingston's typewritten manuscript. Added details can also heighten the verisimilitude of a scene, as is effected by the details about dollar amounts (originally absent from the typescript) when Maxine quizzes Brave Orchid about her purchasing a slave girl:

1. The author wishes to acknowledge the generosity of the Bancroft Library of the University of California, Berkeley, for permission to reproduce photocopies of Maxine Hong Kingston's manuscripts.

"How much money did you pay to buy her?"
"One hundred and eighty dollars."
"How much money did you pay the doctor and the hospital when I was born?"
"Two hundred dollars." *(Woman Warrior* 83)

On the other hand, images are sometimes excised from the manuscript, such as this passage originally included to describe Mu Lan's entering into the imaginary world where she is to receive her training: "It would be like skin-diving in Hawaii when you swim through a dark part of the ocean and can't tell how deep the ocean floor is, perhaps so close the moray eels can nibble at your belly, perhaps so far away you can't touch bottom, and you're heading out to sea where rainbow fish bend to the current." One must agree that, were it to be left in place, this marine image would not have sorted well with the mountain scene into which Mu Lan is being drawn (cf. *Woman Warrior* 20).

Frequently, too, one is struck by the lapidarian care which Kingston accords to her word choice. For instance, when her editor wants her to change the word "bunds" (*Woman Warrior 4*) to the more familiar "dikes" in describing No Name Woman's family rice field, Kingston stoutly resists the change, arguing the politico-cultural resonance of "bund" (the word is, of course, famously associated with Shanghai) and even invoking its etymology: "I'd rather use 'bund' because it is from Hind[i] and specifically refers to Japan, China, India, whereas 'dike' is Anglo-Saxon [...] in origin." Such sites of contestation between Kingston and her editors can provide revealing glimpses into Kingston's political, ethnic, and historical self-positioning.

However, in order to cast some light upon the writerly process by which Kingston makes decisions about tone, voice, and ultimately, the content that is included or excluded, I propose to focus on two sites of Kingston's composition which I found especially intriguing when I first came upon her manuscripts. Both manuscript sites are from her early nonfiction works, one being the ending of *The Woman Warrior*, and the other the beginning of *China Men*.

In both manuscript form and in published final form, the ending of *Woman Warrior* is a classic tale imported into the personal narrative of the Maxine persona to constitute a highly significant and allegorical coda to the whole book. Each tale is of Chinese provenance. There the resemblance ends: they are radically different from each other in narrative content and thematic meaning. The final published ending is a historical legend. The rejected manuscript ending is a fable. Why did Maxine Hong Kingston choose one tale over the other? What can we surmise from this about her compositional decisions as a writer of nonfiction prose?

The manuscript ending of *Woman Warrior* is a retelling of a Chinese version of King Midas. In Ovid's *Metamorphoses,* Book XI, King Midas' ears were changed into those of an ass when he judged Apollo's music to be inferior to Pan's. Midas took to wearing turbans, and only his barber/hairdresser knew of this, but he was sworn to secrecy or else ... However, the barber could not contain himself, so he dug a hole in a wheat field and shouted King Midas' secret into it. When the grain ripened, all the ears of wheat sang the secret out to the winds, and hence throughout the kingdom. Thus Ovid's Latin version (pages 263-65). In Kingston's Chinese version (orally transmitted through Kingston's mother), it is a King's son who is born with cat's ears. In the photocopy of the manuscript pages reproduced below (see appendix A), the story begins with the phrase, "A long time ago in China ... "; its equivalent moment in the published *Woman Warrior* is located on page 207: "I like to think that at some of those performances, they heard the songs of Ts'ai Yen ..."

Most writers and readers will agree that the ending of any book is a crucial textual site. Consequently, when I chanced upon this manuscript version of the ending of *Woman Warrior*, I was very curious about it. At that time I was auditing a course taught by Maxine Hong Kingston at the University of California, Berkeley, and unable to harbor my secret, I asked her during one class discussion why she had changed the original ending of *Woman Warrior*. On the spur of the moment, she had no clue what I was talking about, not even when I summarized the passage for her. But some months later, at a reception in San Francisco, she remembered my question, though she still could think of no explanation; instead she bemoaned her loss of a talisman-like framed photocopy of the unpublished manuscript ending of Hemingway's *Islands in the Stream* which she had hung in the study of her then fire-gutted house in Oakland.

Finding my hoped-for informant to be so unhelpful and digressive, I began to speculate on my own. Why would she have used the cat's ears story in the first place? Actually, a strong case could be made for its placement there. Thematically, it is absolutely germane to the book because it deals with the subject of keeping secrets versus speaking out, of silence versus assertion. If one recalls the opening sentence of the published *Woman Warrior*, one will see that it is her mother's injunction to Maxine to keep a familial and communal secret: "You must not tell anyone [...] what I am about to tell you." But it is precisely this secret which Kingston immediately spills out in the first chapter. In fact, for some readers, the whole of *Woman Warrior* is a sometimes overly generous and tendentious revealing of too many secrets about the unfairness of growing up female in Asian America and the ugliness of being Asian in America (Chan). As a defiant coda to such a revealing book, the cat's ears fable would reassert the belief that such injunctions to silence, such taboos against telling unpleasant truths about individuals and communities, are ultimately impossible to keep or to enforce. The fable reasserts to the reader that such truths are by nature irrepressible and, like murder, will out.

On the other hand, the final published ending of *Woman Warrior* retells the story of Ts'ai Yen, the legendary Chinese woman poet of the third century who was kidnapped and married to a Hun chieftain, forced into bearing him two children, and then after twelve years, she was ransomed and repatriated into China in order to marry a Chinese man so as to provide descendants for her famous and well-connected father whose only child she was (Liu and Lo 36-39, 538). Obviously, the fabric of the Ts'ai Yen legend contains more thematic strands relevant to *Woman Warrior* than does the cat's ears story. One such thematic strand would be that of woman as writer and creator of aesthetic beauty out of ugliness and unfairness (for Ts'ai Yen was one of the earliest if not the first named Chinese woman poet). A second theme would concern woman's autonomy or lack thereof in a patriarchal society (for Ts'ai Yen was abducted to be married to one man and then ransomed to be married to another man without being consulted). And a third thematic strand would be immigration / emigration and cultural hybridity (for like many Chinese Americans as for the Hong family, Ts'ai Yen had emotional, familial, and cultural ties both in China and in a non-Chinese culture).[2]

Furthermore, beyond the comparatively richer thematic multiplicity of the *Woman Warrior*'s published ending, this final version's use of the Ts'ai Yen legend strikes a different tone from the cat's ears story. The cat's ears story has a whimsical and ironical tone, and Kingston even puns good-humoredly with "years" / ears (when describing the barber's yells). Its tone is more in keeping with a chapter like "At the Western Palace" (*Woman Warrior* 113ff). If *Woman Warrior* had ended on that note, it would have left the reader with a smile on the lips. By contrast, the final published ending of *Woman Warrior* is an excruciatingly painful and thought-provoking story of a woman creating, procreating, and enduring in incredibly difficult conditions. It is a legend that celebrates and asserts the resilience of the human spirit in the face of cruel circumstances and the imperious ways of powerful men towards their hapless women. Of Maxine Hong Kingston's two possible endings, the manuscript one would have been a witty and elegantly rounded closure of the theme of silence in the book. The final published ending is a more somber, complex, and profound one, chosen, one feels, in order to resonate in the reader's mind and heart long after the book is closed. In my view, Maxine Hong Kingston chose carefully and chose well.

As a coda to this, I should report that, during a subsequent conversation I had with Maxine Hong Kingston in her childhood hometown of Stockton later on (5 April 1997), she seemed to have a better recall of this manuscript ending,

---

2. It is interesting to note that Kingston again alludes to the Ts'ai Yen story near the end of her *I Love a Broad Margin to My Life* (218-20). There she writes about her wish to translate her father's unpublished poems, and provides a sample of one such poem which she calls "his 19th song for a barbarian reed pipe" (218). Clearly Kingston sees this poem of her father's as continuing the tradition of Ts'ai Yen, whose surviving poems number 18, and which are called "song[s] for a barbarian reed pipe" in Kingston's *Woman Warrior* (163 ff). See also Liu Shang's handsomely illustrated handscroll copy of Ts'ai Yen's *Eighteen Songs of a Nomad Flute*.

especially after I pointed out to her that she had actually used the cat's ears story in the middle of *China Men* (116-17). "See," I recall her saying, "I didn't waste it!" And after a moment's thought, she added: "I must have wanted the Ts'ai Yen story in *Woman Warrior* because it was a woman's story, and it fitted better into a book about women. And the other story was about men, and so fitted better into *China Men*."

It is a truth universally acknowledged that the beginning of a story is a moment of critical importance to the whole. Therefore, the other manuscript site I would like to highlight is the beginning episode of *China Men* (3-4), entitled "On Discovery."[3] It is one of the most heavily revised sites of Maxine Hong Kingston's manuscripts (see appendix B). Although the episode's main narrative strand and subject remain constant (it is, to put it boldly, the story of a sex change from male to female), details are being added during the revision process that render the sensory descriptions palpably more vivid; and the narrative mode of the episode also changes in the revisions, as do the narrative strategy and the narrative voice. It should be further noted that in between the composition of the manuscript version (appendix B) and its final publication in *China Men* in 1980, Kingston had published an intermediate version of this episode in *Hawaii Review* in Fall 1977 (pages 43-44) entitling it there as "On Understanding Men" and explaining that it was "meant to serve as a transition between *The Woman Warrior* and *Gold Mountain Man,* a work in progress." ("Gold Mountain Man" or "Gold Mountain Heroes" were the working titles of the manuscript that was eventually published as *China Men*).[4]

In the manuscript version (see appendix B), one may readily observe several instances where Kingston added details to heighten verisimilitude and to make her narrative and description more vivid and more immediate. For instance, when Tang Ao is being divested of his armor, the manuscript contains a rather straightforward description: "...one of the guards helped him off with his armor..." But in the intermediate *Hawaii Review* version and in the final *China Men* version, Kingston eliminates the straightforward description and enlivens the moment by adding a snippet of disarming dialogue: "'Let me help you off with your armor and boots,' said the women" (*Hawaii Review* 43, *China Men 3*);

---

3. Dr. Helena Grice, who is familiar with the *China Men* manuscript at the Bancroft Library, does not comment on this episode but focuses instead on Kingston's "Statement of Plans" for *China Men* (see Grice 42-49).
4. Professor Diane Simmons has commented on "On Understanding Men," though not in terms of Kingston's revision process but in terms of what it indicates about Kingston's thematic intention for *China Men*: "Kingston suggests that, to understand the pain of women, men must imaginatively *become* them" (110). Professor Simmons also discusses the modifications that Kingston made to the original Tang Ao of the Li Ju-chen novel *Flowers in the Mirror* (109-11).

also, a titillating hint of flirtatiousness is added when Kingston changes the gender-neutral "guards" of the manuscript into the "women" of the later versions. Similarly, the description of Tang Ao's footbinding is vividly elaborated by the addition of familiarizing images of sight and smell when Kingston includes the following: "They [the women] forced him to wash his used bandages, which were embroidered with flowers and smelled of rot and cheese. He hung the bandages up to dry, streamers that drooped and draped wall to wall. He was embarrassed; the wrappings were like underwear, and they were his" (*China Men* 4)—the *Hawaii Review*'s version (44) is very close to this, though it still lacks the image of "embroidered [...] flowers" which contrasts so piquantly with rotten cheese and which was added by Kingston only in her final revision.

In addition to increasing the vividness of imagery and verisimilitude of narrative by such manuscript revisions, Kingston is also refining her narrative strategy and fine-tuning her narrative voice. In the manuscript version that we have before us, it is apparent that Kingston wishes to adopt the same narrative voice and narrative frame that she used to begin *Woman Warrior*, that of a narrator re-telling a story heard from her mother while the narrator was a child. *Woman Warrior* had begun with the sentence: "'You must not tell anyone,' my mother said, 'what I am about to tell you.'" Our manuscript version of the beginning of *China Men* reads: "*My mother tells a story first told by Li Ju-Chen*: During the reign of the Empress Wu (A.D. 684-705), Tang Ao traveled to the Land of Women ..." (my italics signify Kingston's handwritten words); the *Hawaii Review* version further identifies Li Ju-Chen as a writer "who lived just after Jonathan Swift" [43], as if to mollify any reader incredulous of Tang Ao's fantastical sex change by a reminder of Gulliver's equally incredible Lilliputians and Brobdingnagians. Also, at the end of the manuscript version, in a passage that is crossed out but still legible, Kingston alludes again to the maternal oral provenance and then seems to be weighing whether to adopt a mock scholarly narrator's voice in which she cites historical data, as if feeling a need to validate her tale: "Having first heard this story by word of mouth, I have since discovered that it was written by Li Ju-chen, a man who lived from 1763 to 1830."

In the final published version, Kingston retitles this episode "On Discovery" and launches into her narrative confidently and forthrightly, without feeling the need to mention sources or provenance or to seek aid in suspending disbelief by pointing to literary precedence: "Once upon a time, a man named Tang Ao, looking for the Gold Mountain, crossed an ocean, and came upon the Land of Women" (*China Men 3*). In its final published version, therefore, Kingston's narrative voice takes on the timbre of a secure and autonomous teller of tales and maker of myths, depending neither on the umbilical connection with maternal oral authority, nor on the props of scholarly sources, nor on analogies with famous writers of the past: it is the voice of a narrator independently empowering herself as an agent of mythopoesis who is revealing an enigma. (I use the word "mythopoesis" advisedly, for Kingston uses the term "myth" in her marginal notes on the page proofs: she pleaded unavailingly with her publisher to have all the short episodes of *China Men* set in italics or in "a different type face [to] make the myths stand out.") Only after the narrative proper has ended in this published version does Kingston mention in a footnote-like paragraph a historical prop for her myth, Empress Wu, accompanied by some disputable dates and a sly gesture at a dream of a country, a tax-free, war-free, North America.[5]

To conclude, I hope that even this cursory glance at these mere four pages of Maxine Hong Kingston's manuscripts has shown us that Kingston is a meticulous crafter of words and a dedicated winnower of details—an exacting literary artist who chooses the most strategic turns of phrase to create a narrative persona and who sifts through to the most precise nuggets of imagery to make her readers experience the exquisite piercing of a body part or the ache of bending a bone in the foot. I daresay that much more may be gleaned about Kingston's literary artistry and her constative intentions from further study of her manuscripts and what they record of her writing process. In any case, I hope that this brief presentation has demonstrated a few of the many ways in which Maxine Hong Kingston may indeed be considered a consummate and painstaking artist of twentieth-century American nonfiction prose, an eminently worthwhile model for writers, readers, and their teachers alike.

Works Cited

Chan, Jeffrey Paul. "Jeff Chan, Chairman of SF State Asian American Studies, Attacks Review." *San Francisco Journal* 4 May 1966: 6.

Chun, Gloria. "The High Note of the Barbarian Reed Pipe: Maxine Hong Kingston." *Journal of Ethnic Studies* 19 (Fall 1991): 85-89.

Goellnicht, Donald C. "Tang Ao in America: Male Subject Positions in *China Men*." *Reading the Literatures of Asian America*. Eds. Shirley Lim and Amy Ling. Philadelphia: Temple UP, 1992. 191-212.

Grice, Helena. *Maxine Hong Kingston*. Manchester: Manchester UP, 2006.

Kingston, Maxine Hong. *China Men*. New York: Knopf, 1980.

—. *I Love a Broad Margin to My Life*. New York: Knopf, 2011.

—. "On Understanding Men." *Hawaii Review* 7 (Fall 1977): 43-44.

—. *The Woman Warrior: Memoirs of a Girlhood Among Ghosts*. New York: Knopf, 1976.

5. Professor Donald C. Goellnicht has ably explored the significations of this imaginary continent in his article "Tang Ao in America ..."

Liu, Wu-chi and Irving Yucheng Lo, eds. *Sunflower Splendor: Three Thousand Years of Chinese Poetry*. Bloomington: Indiana UP, 1990. (A translation of Ts'ai Yen's poem can be found on pages 36-39.)

Liu, Shang. *Eighteen Songs of a Nomad Flute: The Story of Lady Wen-chi* [Ts'ai Yen]: A Fourteenth-Century Handscroll in the Metropolitan Museum of Art. Trans. and ed. Robert A. Rorex and Wen Fong. New York: Metropolitan Museum of Art, 1974.

Ovid. *Metamorphoses*. Trans. Rolfe Humphries. Bloomington: Indiana UP, 1961.

Simmons, Diane. *Maxine Hong Kingston*. New York: Twayne, 1999.

Appendix A

Or do they really pay only 2% tax and keep the rest? It would be good if the Communists were taking care of themselves, then I could buy a color t.v.

Here is another story that - with imperfect listening - I've heard my mother tell:

A long time ago in China, a king waited for a son to be born, but when it came, his wife and the midwives hesitated to show him the new prince. The infant seemed healthy enough, but the king almost dropped him when he saw that on either side of his bald head, he had little pointed furry ears like a kitten. "Oh, no," said the king. "Order the midwives not to talk. We must never tell anyone that the prince has cat ears. We will keep it our secret. The people must not know."

So the years went by; the prince grew into royal perfection except for the ears, and the king said not one word about them. The queen combed the prince's long hair over the ears, and the subjects exclaimed over his beauty. The king said nothing, but the secret grew large within him.

One day when he could not hold it in anymore, he walked alone to a winter field, and dug a hole. He lay upon the earth and shouted into the hole, "The king's son has cat ears!" He yelled as loudly as he pleased, years loud. "The king's son

Hong Kingston - 286 1

has cat ears!" He shouted until he felt the secret gone from his chest, and, satisfied, he pushed the dirt back into the hole and stamped it down.

But in the spring, grass grew tall in that field, and when the wind blew through it, the people heard words. They grew louder through the summer until the people knew for sure what the grass and the wind said again and again, "The king's son has cat ears! The king's son has cat ears!" and it grew into a song. "The king's son has cat ears!"

It made the people laugh to hear it.

THE END

Appendix B

"Sped Mtn Heroes"

I: 5 (3rd & 4-16 Sheets)

During the reign of the Empress Wu (A.D. 684-705), ~~Lin Chih-yang~~ a man travelled to the Land of Women, where he was immediately captured because he looked so different from the inhabitants. ~~He was~~ they easily caught him, not on guard against lovely women. They merely asked him to come along with them, and he did; if he had had companions, he would have winked over his shoulder. "We have to prepare you to meet the Queen," his guards said. "Of course," he said. They brought him to a caparisoned room, where they asked him to take off his boots and armor. The apartment was obviously a woman's, pots of make-up in front of the mirror, closets filled with a woman's clothes. As one of the guards helped him off with his armor, she clamped his wrists together into handcuffs. The guards who had kneeled to take off his boots chained his ankles together. A door slowly opened, and he expected to meet his match, but it was only some old women with sewing boxes in their hands. "The less you struggle, the less it will hurt," said the old women, as they threaded their needles squinting bright black eyes. One of the jailers sat on him while another held his head down. He felt an old woman's dry fingers trace his ear, the long nail on her little finger scraping his neck. "What are you doing?" he said. "Sewing your lips together," she said, and the ones sitting on him bouncing with laughter. But they did not sew his lips together. Old women on either side of his face pulled his earlobes taut and jabbed the needles through them. They had to poke and stab again and again before the needles broke through the layers of skin, it being especially hard to line up the holes in the front of the lobe with the one ~~on~~ in the ~~bottom~~ back, the layers of skin slipping ~~around~~ about so. They ~~pulled~~ worked the needles all the way through - a last jerk for the eye. Then they pulled the string through the raw flesh; he could feel the fibers.

Then the women turned around and bent his toes so far backwards that his arched foot cracked. They ~~also~~ squeezed his feet + broke many little bones along the sides ~~of his feet too~~. They gatherered the toes together, toes over and under one another, and ~~they would~~ bandanged ~~tight enough to break off circulation~~ them ~~tightly~~ against the foot - Tang ao wept w/ pain.

For a week they fed him on women's food, chrysanthemum tea for the cold winds in his body, chicken wings ~~beautiful hair~~ to make his hair grow black & shiny, vinegar soup. They ~~pulled the string~~ drew the string loops ~~back and forth through their holes to break~~ through the holes in his ankles to stimulate his Yin womb (if he had one) the scabs and any flesh that was growing ~~back together~~. + They put in gold hoops. They unbound his feet regularly every night + pushed the bones closer, and tied the bandages tighter. When blood rushed back into his veins, ~~He went with the pain~~ cried to have the bandages put back on,

One day they strapped his feet to little shoes shaped like round bridges. They changed his gold hoops to emerald studs. They powdered his face, plucked out each facial hair on his face, painted his eyebrows like moth's wings, painted his cheeks and lips red. Walking on ~~broken feet~~ his dainty feet, he served a meal at court, his body swaying in his hips + shoulders to keep his balance. "She's pretty, don't you think?" the diners said as he put dishes ~~in front of~~ before them, smacking their lips at the food + his swaying hips.

~~Having first heard this story by word of mouth, I have since discovered that it was written by Li Ju-chen, a man who lived from 1763 to 1830.~~ What torture might Li Ju-Chen have ideated for a woman who would understand men? +

Between Postmodernity and Taoist Beliefs: Metamorphosis in "On Discovery" by Maxine Hong Kingston

Marie-Claude Perrin-Chenour (Université Paris Ouest, Nanterre, France)

"On Discovery" is a short text placed at the beginning of Maxine Hong Kingston's second novel, *China Men*. Given its mythic quality, it seems at first disconnected from the rest of the narrative. It could thus function as a paratext, or perhaps should we say as a transition between Kingston's previous novel, *The Woman Warrior,* entirely devoted to women and the second book intent on exploring the experience of the men in the author's life and their "discovery" of America. Because of its liminal position between the two books, it seems isolated and self-contained, though we shall see that it actually partakes of both narratives. Critics have analyzed it as either a postmodern text rewriting and parodying older Chinese stories or legends, or as an allegory for the real wrongs and sufferings that Chinese men 'discovered' when they emigrated to the United States in the 19th or 20th centuries, a situation contemporary male critics have described as the 'feminization' (or emasculation) of 'China men' in America.

In other words, the first approach emphasizes the aesthetics of the text, while the second one lays the stress on its ethic dimension. Though both approaches are equally valid, this article aims at demonstrating that these two critical stands can also be combined to challenge the very concept of aesthetics and the language used to socially construct acceptable standards of 'beauty.' It will then contend that the blending of ethics and aesthetics is in fact deeply ingrained in Chinese art and philosophy, and finally it will focus on the concept of metamorphosis, not only in the diegesis and the writing of the text, but also in the performative impact it can have on the reader.

A challenge to the concept of aesthetics

"On Discovery" can be viewed as the counterpart and mirror image of the story of Fa Mulan in the previous novel, the story of "thc girl who took her father's place in battle" (*Woman Warrior* 10). It is also a tale of transformation, metamorphosis and cross-gendering. Yet there are fundamental differences between the two narratives. Though the girl in the rewriting of the Fa Mulan legend disguises as a man and a soldier, she retains her feminine attributes. She even marries and has a child that she carries with her in battle, hidden inside her armor. And at the end, she returns to her 'woman's place': "I knelt at my parents-in-law's feet, as I would have done as a bride. 'Now my public duties are finished,' I said. 'I will stay with you, doing farmwork and housework, and giving you more sons'" (45). Yet, during her pregnancy, she had become somehow androgynous: "When I was naked, I was a strange human being indeed—words carved on my back and the baby large in front" (40). On her body were inscribed together the signs of the Imaginary Order (the baby in her womb) and the marks of the Symbolic Order (the written words carved on her back). But this association of the two realms in one person does not last. First it is characterized as "strange" and relinquished as soon as the character's duties are accomplished. Moreover, this story, which can be read as an allegory of feminine empowerment, an assertion of strength and a plea for equality ("So for a time I had a partner—my husband and I, soldiers together just as when we were little soldiers playing in the village. We rode side by side into battle" [39]), does not go as far as shattering the barriers and boundaries between genders. When fighting, the girl is only a woman in disguise, and all along, she knows that what people are seeing is not her "real" identity: "I never told them the truth. Chinese executed women who disguised themselves as soldiers or students" (39). So there is a rock bottom truth to her self, and her experience of doubleness and androgyny—when it does take place—is highly polarized on two fixed and antagonistic characteristics (the word and the womb) that never completely blend and never permanently alter her consciousness of herself or her representation of her body.

In this text, the concept of beauty is not really challenged by the heroine's experience as a warrior. For instance, when she is reunited with her husband, his first remark is, "you are beautiful," but later he is shocked by the sight of the words written on her back: "[H]e wept when he took off my shirt and saw the scarwords on my back. He loosened my hair and covered the words with it" (39). In other words, the feminine beauty epitomized by her hair is incompatible with symbolic expression through the written word. Besides, the list of grievances carved on her back has been inscribed by her parents. It is programmatic and meant to map out her destiny. So not only doesn't she master her own life but she does not even become the author of her own legend in the end: "From the words on my back, and how they were fulfilled, the villagers would make a legend about my perfect filiality" (45). Furthermore the written text through which the reader discovers the story of the woman warrior does not on the whole undermine the conventions of masculine epic narratives. From a stylistic point of view, it essentially functions on a reversal of roles, placing at its center a female character who conducts an army of liberation rather than an army of conquest, but without upsetting the usual pattern of heroism found in such tales extolling the figure of an outstanding character performing extraordinary deeds.

As for the introductory story to the novel *China Men*, it is also a rewriting of a famous Chinese text, a 19th century novel by Li Ru-Zhen entitled *Flowers in the Mirror*, itself borrowing elements from a very ancient book of mythology whose English title is *The Classic of Mountains and Seas*. This article does not intend to compare the original stories with Maxine Hong Kingston's version—this has already been done by other critics. It will rather concentrate on Kingston's own thematic and stylistic choices.

First, from a generic point of view, the story of Tang Ao, who left China looking for the Gold Mountain and came upon "the Land Women," where he was made a prisoner before being transformed into a woman who must serve food at the queen's court, appears as a counter-epic story. It starts with the usual adventurous hero, clad in armor and boots and ready for conquest, but this representation of him does not extend beyond the first paragraph. Besides, the narrative is cast in the frame of a fairy tale (the first words are "once upon a time"), which is a Western form of oral, then written, folklore. As opposed to Chinese epic stories based on war and martial arts, fairy tales are usually considered a feminine form of expression. Most of the time their central figures are girls since fairy tales are also cautionary tales serving a didactic purpose to warn pre-sexual young women of the dangers of the world. As Cristina Bacchilega explains in *Postmodern Fairy Tales: Gender and Narrative Strategies*, they always contain a voice informing the girl of society's expectations (for instance, the mother in "Little Red Riding Hood" warning her daughter against the wolf, or the mirror in Snow White, which, she says, frames social norms of conduct and defines standards of beauty). Here the voice could be that of the old women who inform Tang Ao that the "less [he] struggle[s], the less it'll hurt" (*China Men* 3) when they pierce his ears for earrings. It is a lesson in passivity, quite in keeping with the usual message of fairy tales. If it sounds shocking in Kingston's text, it is simply because the central character has been replaced by a man who was first construed as the typical hero of an epic narrative. If the central character of the fairy tale had been a girl, not only would the story fail to surprise the reader, but its ending, in which she becomes an attendant at the queen's court, could even be envisioned as a positive case of social upward mobility. Gender-switching at the core of this story does not reinforce the narrative's ability to serve as a frame for self-aggrandizing values (such as courage, cunning or cleverness) as it does in the Fa Mulan warrior legend. Quite on the contrary, the reversal of roles acts as a distancing device whose purpose is to put into relief the constricting frames within which women find themselves entrapped willingly or unconsciously. "On Discovery" can thus be read not so much as a story of revenge, as some critics have claimed, but as a story which lays bare the mechanisms of oppression perpetrated by society and often reproduced by women themselves in the referential world as well as within the confines of certain narrative genres conveying and perpetuating this oppression.

Here displacement serves to enhance the self-reflexivity of the text and, together with the mock historical reference at the end, to re-contextualize its definition of beauty. By saying that, according to scholars, the story could take place either in ancient China or in North America, the ending does not simply destroy the myth of the discovery of America by Christopher Columbus, it also de-exoticizes the aesthetic values conveyed in the fairy tale. As a matter of fact, the only typically Chinese transformation inflicted on the hero's body in this story is the footbinding practice. Ear-piercing, hair-plucking, and make-up are common beauty practices everywhere. But if the Western reader is encouraged to locate the story in America, and if, as is likely, he does not find bound feet aesthetically appealing, particularly when toes are described as "a knot of ginger root" (*China Men* 4), he may realize that the concept of beauty is a lure, a social construct which, in all cultures throughout history, has always been targeted at satisfying the needs of a dominant group by reinforcing, if not creating, the powerlessness of the dominated. Bound feet prevent women from walking without help and make them dependent on others for survival. The enforcement of this beauty standard emphasizes their secondary position in society and facilitates all forms of control over them—like, for that matter, all other extraordinary standards of beauty, such as the long necks of giraffe women in Africa, as much as the extremely slender waists of 19th century western women tight-laced in corsets which prevented them from breathing normally. The fact that aesthetic criteria are instruments of power is underlined in the text by its location in "the land of Women," where those who are in control (the women in a position of authority) do not seem to be submitted to the same constricting rules as the people (men or women) whom they dominate; power relations thus are not a matter of gender: women's bodies are not fashioned according to culturally constructed canons of beauty because they are weak. But what we see here through the transformation of a man into a woman is that the gendering of the body is a strategy practiced in most societies to keep some of its members in a weaker or secondary position.

The metamorphosis of Tang Ao's body is usually read as a metaphor of the way Chinese immigrants have been 'emasculated' or 'feminized' in America by their relegation to 'women's jobs' (like washing or cooking—represented in the text by Tang Ao having to wash his own bandages or to wait at table at the Queen's Court). But why should feminization be considered an insult by China men or by modern critics? Probably because being female simply means giving up hope at first-rate citizenship, at the male-bonding that Tang Ao was familiar with before his capture and which was predicated on easy control over women's bodies (Tang Ao is captured because he is not "on guard against ladies"; so he follows them and "if he had had male companions, he would've winked over his shoulder" [*China Men* 3]). It is the assumed knowledge of the power he shares with other men that makes him careless. Yet here the gender roles are not polarized as they are in the rewriting of the Fa Mulan story.

Instead feminization is equated to a process of degradation that could happen to anyone (of any gender) and which is particularly frightening because it is rapidly internalized by the people who are submitted to it, so that their final transformation is not only physical but also psychological. For instance, when Tang Ao is made a prisoner, he first tries to understand and questions what is happening to him. "What are you going to do?" he asks the old woman who has come to pierce his ears. "Sewing your lips together," she answers as a joke (4). She will not sew his lips together in the end, and yet he will be efficiently silenced, muted. In the rest of the story there are no more questions asked by him, he only moans, weeps, and begs. And the final question mentioned in the text is not uttered by him, but by the diners at the court: "She's pretty, don't you agree?" (5). At this point, the 'hero' turned feminine or 'anti-hero' no longer talks; he is not even talked to, he is only talked about. Paradoxically, he is both noticed (as "pretty") and totally ignored. His presence as a human being is not acknowledged; he is silenced and objectified. People talking about him address one another, they bond together (as he used to do with his male companions in the past) while his "pretty" new self is left out in the margin. Thus metamorphosis in "On Discovery" has not the same positive impact on the character as Fa Mulan's cross-dressing and code-switching. It is essentially a staging of power relations, a performance in devaluation of the individual under the guise of collectively accepted aesthetic values. And yet it is also possible to contend that the story contains its own regenerative power located in the very concept of "discovery" that opens up the narrative.

Tang Ao's first reaction when he meets the ladies against whom he is not "on guard" suggests that no one ever discovers anything without first transposing former clichés, preconceived ideas and codes upon the new situation. At the end of the story, the diners do the same thing with Tang Ao whom they look at but do not really see. But it is also possible to imagine that the former hero who came in search of adventures has had his whole worldview shattered by this experience and that he finally understands that claiming his virility, as he did in the first place, meant participating in an act of destruction of which he has now an inside knowledge. This would give another, more positive meaning to the notion of 'transformation'. All the more so as "discovery" refers to a process, an encounter with new possibilities and unsettling situations, rather than a belief in fixed entities and identities; it emphasizes in-betweenness, instability and flux. It is the recognition that no truth can lie in stasis or in stable and immutable positions. Which is, as we shall now try to demonstrate, one of the basic tenets of Taoist philosophy.

Metamorphosis as a Taoist concept in *The Woman Warrior* and in "On Discovery"

In this part of the article, all references to Taoist beliefs will be derived from François Cheng's essays. Cheng is a Chinese-French philosopher, essayist, novelist and poet who won national recognition when he was elected a permanent member of the French Academy of Arts and Letters. If his work is of particular relevance to our subject, it is because of the way he links philosophical concepts to artistic expression and creation, whether it be poetry, music, drama or painting, as, for instance, in his book entitled *Vide et plein. Le langage pictural chinois*. In this study, he explains that Chinese art does not aim at producing a simple aesthetic object; through the representation of a microcosm, it tries to capture a sense of the whole. Its purpose is not to reproduce the external appearance of things but to catch their inner shape and the relation they entertain with each other behind the surface, since a Taoist representation of the world is an organic one in which everything is interrelated. This idea relies on the concept of a world in constant movement, a universe never construed as stable but forever reshaping, rearranging, reformulating itself. What are commonly perceived as fixed entities are in fact deeply interpenetrating units in an endless process of mutual transformation. And what makes this transformation possible is the presence of a void, a vacuum, an empty space in between where disintegrating elements can recombine in a new shape and produce new solid forms which, in their turn, will undergo a process of dissolution and metamorphosis. In landscape painting, and more specifically, in the category known as "mountain-water" ink-washes, the presence of a vacuum or a void is highly codified. It can sometimes occupy three quarters of the surface of the canvas. 'Occupy' is actually an apt word to describe it, since emptiness is not envisioned as an absence, a loss or a lack (as in Western culture), but as the very matrix where an interrelation between material objects can take place, so that emptiness is never conceived without its opposite of fullness, completeness and fulfillment (the perfect balance between earth and sky, between man and the cosmos) that all human beings and also the whole universe itself are aiming at.

At first this conception of a fluxional world seems antithetic to the gender divisions of the Fa Mulan story in *The Woman Warrior*, based as it is on clear-cut oppositions of fixed entities that can be juxtaposed (as in the phrase the "woman warrior") but always seem in the end to retain their essentialist quality. And yet we shall see that these polarities are undercut by the very aesthetics used to frame the story of the woman warrior. For instance, when the girl climbs the mountain to undergo her initiation to a superior form of physical and mental control, the story is treated like a Chinese painting of the "mountain-water" type:

> The call would come from a bird that flew over our roof. In the brush drawings it looks like the ideograph for 'human', two black wings. The bird would cross the sun and lift into the mountains (which look like the ideograph 'mountain'), there parting the mist briefly that swirled opaque again. I would be a little girl of seven the day I followed the bird away into the mountains [...]. At the height where the bird used to disappear, the clouds would grey the world like an ink wash.

> Even when I got used to that grey, I would only see peaks as if shaded in pencil, rocks like charcoal rubbings, everything so murky. There would be just two black strokes—the bird. (*Woman Warrior* 20)

The writing actually oscillates between a linear narrative and an ink brush. The first two sentences suggest a static painting. The only element of movement is the bird, but its image is immediately fixed on the page through its representation as the Chinese character meaning "human." The reference to the ideograph is an interesting shortcut that allows for instant assimilation of the girl (trying to transcend the laws of gravity) to the bird, which the English language could not have done as efficiently. The following sentence returns to the usual narrative mode by reintroducing movement through verbs, but again the parentheses stall the progression, introducing calligraphy—the mountains "which look like the ideograph 'mountain'"—showing thus that painting and writing overlap as two facets of the same activity. In the rest of the paragraph, the girl resumes her movement forward until the last words ("like an ink wash") bring it again at a standstill. The modal form "would," which at first expresses the girl's dreams and wishes of becoming a powerful warrior, becomes an iterative form ("when I got used to that grey, I would only see peaks as if shaded in pencil, rocks like charcoal rubbings"). Now the picture is complete; the narrator has become the heroine of the legend; she has entered the painting. But we could as well say that, thanks to her, the painting has become dynamic and animated.

By oscillating between motion and stasis, but also by blending two forms of art, writing and painting, and two cultures, one Western and one Oriental, the text finally *does* transcend boundaries and offers, if not thematic, at least *aesthetic* possibilities of solving irreconcilable contradictions. The concept of passage and relation is metaphorically conveyed by the bird that moves from one element of the painting to another, using the empty space which both separates and binds seemingly fixed entities.

Similarly, "On Discovery" is based on alternative modes of representation. In the first sentence, the reference to "the Gold Mountain" and to the ocean introduces the basic elements of a "mountain-water" painting. Except that their meaning here is transformed and distorted. The Gold Mountain, as a metaphor for America at the time of the Gold Rush, bears no resemblance to the landscapes which Chinese artists hoped to invest with spiritual meaning. The story, in spite of its mythic quality, remains down to earth. As for the ending of the text, which introduces a different narrative form—historical analysis—it is undermined by the uncertainty of its data and references. Yet, beyond mere postmodern playfulness, the two components of this text (the fairy tale and the essay) may be said to introduce some kind of textual truth: the two parts function in relation to each other and are eventually transformed one into the other. For, if historical facts cannot always shed light on the meaning of experience, fiction may sometimes offer a glimpse at an understanding of it. In other words, in the diegesis of the fairy tale, there is no absolute certainty that Tang Ao will draw a positive lesson from his ordeal, but there is a very good chance that the reader of this myth of transformation will.

Furthermore, the two forms of narratives, the tale and the historical reference, are not simply juxtaposed on the page. They are also separated by an empty space. Thanks to this blank, this vacuum, Kingston introduces breathing in her text. In like manner, the almost self-contained chapters of the novel, often presented with a blank page between each other, allow for the reader to circulate among the various stories, inventing his/her own links, letting the void and the silence act upon him/her to create new meaning. Emptiness thus paves the way for a possible transformation or metamorphosis of the reader's worldview and sense of aesthetics, and as such it offers a perfect example of what Edouard Glissant, a writer from yet another entirely different culture, has defined as "a poetics of relation."

To sum up, we shall say that the use of myth allows Kingston to challenge standards of beauty and aesthetic rules meant to create gender divisions and/or social hierarchies. Yet she makes use of aesthetics to repair these divisions in her turn, to reestablish a sense of wholeness and to recreate a unity that is never frozen and stultified, based as it is on a constant dynamic recombination of multiple cultural influences.

Works Cited

Bacchilega, Cristina. *Postmodern Fairy Tales, Gender and Narrative Strategies.* Philadelphia: U of Pennsylvania P, 1997.

Cheng, François. *Vide et plein. Le langage pictural chinois.* Paris: Editions du Seuil, 1991.

Glissant, Edouard. *Poétique de la relation.* Paris: Gallimard, 1990.

Kingston, Maxine Hong. *China Men.* 1980. New York: Vintage International, 1989.

—. *The Woman Warrior: Memoirs of a Girlhood Among Ghosts.* 1976. New York: Vintage International, 1989.

Born Among Ghosts: Maxine Hong Kingston's *The Woman Warrior* as Asian American Gothic

Sean Mattio (University of North Carolina at Chapel Hill, USA)

When the modifier American is appended to the literary term Gothic, the latter seems to lose many of its referents—such eighteenth century British authors as Walpole, Radcliffe, Lewis, and Mary Shelley. According to Theresa Goddu, this is because, as a critical category, the American Gothic lacks the "self-evident validity" of its British counterpart (3). Unlike its European cousin, the American Gothic is not easily specified in terms of a particular time frame or group of authors; even when writers such as Edgar Allen Poe or periods such as the twentieth-century Southern Renaissance are associated with the genre, they reveal the difficulty in defining the American Gothic in national terms. Though it is often identified with the South, the genre generally comes to serve as the repository for everything from which the nation wishes to dissociate itself.[1] Whereas the British Gothic has a direct past to deal with, the American Gothic, as critic Andrew Ng observes, comes to be characterized by a simultaneous nostalgia for an "old world continuity and the repudiation of that self-same heritage" (34), as is the case with the works of the dark romanticist Nathaniel Hawthorne, who grappled with a Puritan legacy that he felt continued to haunt the newly-formed national conscious.

With slavery, however, the American Gothic was provided with the necessary opportunity to divorce itself from its English legacy, though this also troubled America's national myth of new-world innocence by voicing the cultural contradictions that undermined the nation's claim to goodness and equality (Goddu 10). As such, the American Gothic takes on an interrogative nature that questions national formation of identity, one which necessitates the repression of historical horrors. In her *Playing in the Dark,* Toni Morrison remarks on how "troubled, how frightened and haunted our early and founding literature truly is," before insisting that issues of race haunt American literature

1. According to Anne Williams, the Gothic is not necessarily a genre, but a "language that signals a revolution within the established system" (66). Accordingly, the Gothic offers a rich and varied vocabulary which proves particularly useful (if not surprisingly apt) when speaking of transgressive ethnic American narratives, such as Kingston's, which in their turn reveal a kind of "fault line" in the national imagination.

(35). Morrison's slave narratives seek to resurrect what the nation's history has tried to repress, disrupting the dream world of national myth with the nightmares of the past, disclosing the instability of America's self-representations (Goddu 10). Her Gothic tales thus write within an oppressive culture without somehow supporting that same culture, one which relegates the writer to the status of Other by defining her as the lack of something within the status quo. Ng maintains that as the voice of those marginalized figures that refuse to be subordinated by the official canon, also Asian American literature shares many similarities with the Gothic. He makes the case that, just as the Gothic has always been regarded as subsidiary to the dominant discourse, so is Asian American literature written against the prevailing ideology of the American literary catalog. If a canon serves the nationalistic agenda to "unify aesthetic culture as a domain in which material stratification and differences are reconciled," then Asian American literature defies this effort, as any attempt at homogenizing this writing is futile since its authors hail from various national, cultural, and generational backgrounds (Ng 37). The more complicated moniker *Asian* American Gothic demonstrates then an ability to look squarely at the cultural anxieties which confront it, and in doing so, develops a penetrating analysis of the forces of oppression within its society.

As in Morrison's work of African American—and therefore firmly American—Gothic, *Beloved,* the Asian American Gothic, in disturbing the seamless authentication of the national narrative by the irruption of a peripheral history, finds its definitive archetype in the intersectional narrative of the minority American female. Maxine Hong Kingston's *The Woman Warrior: Memoirs of a Girlhood Among Ghosts* functions as one such American Gothic tale, articulating themes of fragmented intersectional identity, trauma, and silence. As the subtitle of the novel[2] suggests, the work is replete with ghostly

---

2. Much has been made about the generic classification of Kingston's book. Though I have, throughout this paper, used the term "novel" in describing Kingston's work, *Woman Warrior* remains a collection of Kingston's childhood memories which merge the fantastic productions of an active imagination with the banalities of everyday life. Though the novel's subtitle is indeed *Memoir of a Girlhood Among Ghosts*, the notion of the autobiography is not an unproblematic one, and Carol Mejia-LaPerle argues for the genre's ambiguity, especially with regards to Kingston's narrative. After all, if *Woman Warrior* marks the convergence of many voices (many hauntings and ghostly returns), of which the narrator's voice is just a medium, then can Kingston's work be rightfully called a memoir? For more on the debate surrounding Kingston's novel as a "work of fiction passing for autobiography," see Sau-ling Cynthia Wong's "Autobiography as Guided Chinatown Tour? Maxine Hong Kingston's *The Woman Warrior* and the Chinese-American Autobiographical Controversy."

forms and histories that come to haunt the narrator as the returned elements of cultural repression, both Chinese and Chinese American. These ghosts and the narrative's other Gothic features come to inform and express the anxieties of the Chinese-American woman, revealing the potential for a splintering of the self. Ghosts in *Woman Warrior* come to function in two capacities: as recollections of a Chinese past and its horrors, but also as a means of Othering—expressing a hyphenated Chinese-American hybridity. In short, the character Maxine is haunted by America's legacy of racial trauma, the specter of race in the United State, as much as she is by the ghosts of her Chinese ancestry. Kingston's work is thus placed solidly in conversation with American Gothic conventions as well as the racial haunting which Morrison so clearly articulates. There is a challenge implicit in this notion: what if one were to view Kingston not as an Asian American author in this sense, but as an American author of Asian descent writing in the Gothic mode? It is in this way that the construct of the Asian American Gothic presents its most direct challenge to prevailing notions of literary canon.

In examining the role of trauma and repression in Kingston's novel, I predicate much of my analysis on Sigmund Freud's 1919 essay, "The Uncanny," which I draw upon here as an intertext and which has been so instrumental in discussing the many themes found in the Gothic mode. Freud seeks to distinguish the uncanny within the field of the frightening, declaring in advance that his own investigations led him to the singular conclusion that the uncanny is "that species of the frightening that goes back to what was once well known and had long been familiar" (124). Over the course of *Woman Warrior*, Maxine is haunted by the returned ghosts of her family's Chinese past as well as those which remind her of her attempts at assimilation into (white) American society. While the former functions as a literal return of the repressed, the latter serves as a making strange of what was once familiar, a fixation on the internal alien. Similarly, Freud calls attention to the semantic ties between the German words *heim* (home) and *unheimlich* (uncanny), specifically locating this tension at the female body, that is, "the *unheimlich* place [...] the entrance to the former *Heim* of all human beings, to the place where each of us lived once upon a time and in the beginning" (151). In *Woman Warrior*, the gendered and racialized female body becomes involved in a change of narrative reproduction, from that which inscribes the body with the mark of trauma, to an experimental testimony that attempts to release the body from the collective anxiety projected onto it (Griffiths 354). This recovery, in breaking from traumatic repetition, involves a renewed connection between body and voice, a bringing to light of "everything that was meant to remain secret and hidden" (Freud 132) through the expression of post-traumatic experience and the uncanny figures of female sexuality inherited through patriarchal cultures. These uncanny and spectral figures materialize over the course of Kingston's novel—the No Name Aunt, Fa Mu Lan, the Silent Girl, Ts'ai Yin—only to fade away again, but not without leaving their mark upon the narrator. In fact, these female bodies come to serve as doubles for Maxine, or in Freud's language, doppelgangers, persons with whom one might identify and in doing so "become unsure of [one's] true self" (141). There occurs, across and through successive generations, the recurrence of the same facial features, the same destinies, the same names, even the same misdeeds (142). Essentially, *Woman Warrior* posits that the Gothic Asian American female body and its doubles may come to serve as a means by which to communicate what remains outside conventional American national narrative. Maxine's assertion of voice, her telling of stories both personal and ancestral, functions as an intentional return or disclosure of the repressed elements of cultural anxiety which seem, in fact, inseparable from gendered anxiety. Kingston's Gothic mode and these elements of oppression are distinctly intersectional, raced and gendered as the *Asian* American *female* Gothic.

According to Jennifer Griffiths, a specialist in Trauma Studies, "[f]rom transgenerational transmission [of trauma] described in the oral and written traditions of several cultures, it appears that experiences that occur with intensity—positive or negative—are imprinted on the parent or family in such a way that they emerge in subsequent generations" (354). In this way, subsequent generations pass on the experience through the transmission of narrative memory, or family stories, that reveal unresolved trauma. *Woman Warrior* begins with an injunction to silence by Brave Orchid, Maxine's mother:

> You must not tell anyone [...] what I am about to tell you. In China your father had a sister who killed herself. She jumped into the family well. We say that your father has all brothers because it is as if she had never been born [...]. Don't let your father know that I told you. He denies her. Now that you have started to menstruate, what happened to her could happen to you. Don't humiliate us. You wouldn't like to be forgotten as if you had never been born. (3-5)

In her use of second-person pronouns like "we," "us," and "you," Brave Orchid not only makes apparent her complicity in this forgetting but also seeks to induct Maxine into a legacy of transgenerational repression. Furthermore, this command originates with Maxine's father; it is symptomatic of a patriarchal system that dictates what is to be discussed, what is to be kept quiet, wherein menstruation becomes a time of potential danger. This forgotten aunt, devoid of name, comes to stand as the first body of trauma introduced to the narrator just as she enters womanhood, and, as the first story in Kingston's memoir, subversively serves as the basis for the author's construction of ancestry. No Name Woman, impregnated outside of marriage—likely through rape—during a time of famine in her Chinese village, operates as a complex figure of cultural anxiety, communal repression, and the effects of the dominant patriarchal narrative. The aunt is exorcised by her village and driven to suicide. As Carol Mejia-LaPerle notes, "the object of sexual trafficking while alive and the subject of erasure in her death" (117), she is erased in the family history because her sexualized body represents a curse. Condemned to die even as she is considered the harbinger of ruin, she is admonished: "Aiaa, we're going to die. Death is coming. Death is coming. Look what you've done. You've killed us" (Kingston 13-14). The aunt's body, by dint of its very femaleness and all it is assumed to entail—its inability to perform effective manual labor, the potential for unwanted pregnancy—takes on a valence of communal peril. Stories of their reproductive lives reinforce women's status as threatening figures, aligning them with the un- (or even super-) natural, such that female sexuality becomes, in Freudian terms, the familiar made strange. As Maxine observes: "To be a woman, to have a daughter in starvation time was a waste enough. [...]. Adultery, perhaps only a mistake during good times, became a crime when the village needed food" (6, 13). No Name Woman's pregnancy—be it the product of assault or otherwise—is understood as an act of extravagance, a flaunting of the community's mores and interests.[3] She becomes the relative of Hester Prynne, ostracized from her own Puritan community for her brazen sexuality and emblazoned with the scarlet token of her ignominy. This is certainly not an uncommon tradition in the American Gothic (of which Kingston's work is, again, firmly a part) which has always looked at female sexuality as monstrous, as that which should be repressed. However, instead of merely branding her with her crime, the village and Maxine's family seek to expunge No Name Woman completely.

As Griffiths observes, the community—and Maxine's immediate family—perpetuate a "pedagogy of shame reinforced by story and experience" (358), by the command to remain silent. Maxine herself acknowledges that in the village, "No one talked sex, ever" (7). The aunt's body signifies the anxiety and the violence that the family must contain either through secrecy or denial, silence or repression. And yet, in telling her aunt's story and defying her mother's order to remain silent, Maxine seeks to undo this "erasure of female corporeality" (Mejia-LaPerle 117). She imagines the ghost of her drowned aunt and her dead infant returning from the family well to seek vengeance, to reassert their existences, the return of the repressed. Kingston narrates the process of gaining access to this secret familial and communal memory, which is itself ghostlike—elusive and hidden. In this telling, the drinking well inhabited by No Name Woman's spirit becomes the autobiographer's inkwell. The traumatized female

3. For more on this necessity/extravagance binary, see Sau-ling Cynthia Wong's *Reading Asian American Literature: From Necessity to Extravagance*. These terms, Wong explains, signify two contrasting modes of existence and operation: one contained, survival-driven and conservation-minded, the other attracted to freedom, excess, and emotional expressiveness. Wong's book argues that this dichotomy and its derivative work/play binarism, are major themes throughout Kingston's work.

body emerges as the decipherable text from the scene of the traumatic event, silenced in its own moment but resonating in the passed-down narrative. Maxine acknowledges: "My aunt haunts me—her ghost drawn to me because now, after fifty years of neglect, I alone devote pages of paper to her, though not origamied into houses or clothes" (Kingston 16). The pages of Kingston's memoir become the means to entitle her aunt to her rightful place in the family heritage, a filial act of readmission and rebellious ancestor worship, resisting the oppressions of a patriarchal system. In creating this female ancestry, Maxine violates the paternal edict to repression; in claiming the aunt as her "forerunner," Maxine supplants patrilineage with matrilineage (8).

In so doing, Maxine challenges her mother's version of No Name Woman's story, one in which women's bodies, because of their reproductive power, must remain under tight social control. She recasts her aunt as a spectral female body, an alternative to the corporeal form that binds and traps women in the roles of mother, daughter, wife. In her defiant historical revision, Maxine imagines that her aunt was punished for "acting as if she could have a private life, secret and apart from [the villagers]" (9). She conjures a new narrative for the aunt, not necessarily one in which she was raped, forced into silence by the laws of patriarchal obedience, but one in which she was a woman free to love:

> She looked at a man because she liked the way that hair was tucked behind his ears, or she liked the question-mark line of a long torso curving at the shoulder and straight at the hip. For warm eyes or a soft voice or a slow walk—that's all—a few hairs, a line, a brightness, a sound, a space, she gave up family. [...]. To sustain her being in love, she often worked at herself in the mirror, guessing at the colors and shapes that would interest him, changing them frequently in order to hit on the right combination. She wanted him to look back. (9)

Maxine pictures her aunt living in a society free from the constraints of patriarchy, free from filial obligation, free to chose whom she loved, free to indulge in fantasies of courtship and romance. The aunt is comfortable with her body and her sexuality, taking care of her appearance in the hopes that the man will return her gaze, the ability to look upon a man with feelings of desire itself a marker of liberty. In this way, the No Name Woman enriches the culture that banishes her, living a life of extravagance, luxury, and passion. Her transgression transforms her into a mother, the nurturer of an American generation of woman warriors, Maxine included. The narrator tells her story in writing, "appropriating a textual privilege that has been predominantly male," and in English, not her mother's Chinese tongue, thus heralding a new Chinese-American tradition (Cheung 85), a breaking free of the cycle of transgenerational transmission of cultural repression. This act in and of itself may be considered Gothic in effect: an attempt to utter the unspeakable, a linguistic transgression. Maxine's exposition of her aunt's story is an exorcism of her ghost, a chance for the woman to change from a rape victim into a nonconformist, a supernatural body which forces a revision of the communal and familial pedagogy of shame.

Carol Mejia-LaPerle insists that Kingston's novel reminds us that "to create a subversive female lineage, and to base one's identity on this ghostly manifestation, is to allow the hauntings of the past to affect the present." In her analysis, Mejia-LaPerle focuses on the presence of ghosts in *Woman Warrior* and their role in autobiography. She contends that these ghosts represent not just the unknown and unrepresentable in the world, but also the unrepresentable in the self, expressed through the reappropriation of a repressed personal history (118-19). Hence in Brave Orchid's experiences in China the ghosts embody and release the internal anxieties that generally haunt the women of Kingston's narrative. The story presented in the "Shaman" section of *Woman Warrior* is that of Maxine's mother prior to her immigration to America during her time at a medical academy for women, the To Keung School. Brave Orchid recounts her confrontation with a "Sitting Ghost," a supernatural manifestation that comes to represent anxieties both internal and external regarding the vulnerability of the women's social situation as practitioners of a predominantly male profession as well as fears toward a society that would see their professionalism as a threat to a system of gender inequality. As Brave Orchid recalls: "She did not know whether she had fallen asleep or not when she heard a rushing coming out from under the bed. Cringes of fear seized her soles as something alive, rumbling, climbed the foot of the bed, it rolled over her and landed bodily on her chest. There it sat." The ghost comes in the dead of night while the woman is alone and vulnerable. It pins her down, "pressing her, sapping her," making her resistance ineffectual (68-69). The ghost is described only in fragments—heavy, eyeless, furry, which adds to its surreality. Nevertheless, Mejia-LaPerle argues that this does not take away from the immediate threat of the ghost, and in fact, the story resembles a rape narrative in its troubling depiction of a woman's sense of safety and autonomy stripped by physical force (111). The Sitting Ghost is the literal specter of the patriarchal structure of Chinese society that Brave Orchid worries will not afford her the proper freedom and respect as a female doctor, but instead consider her a threat and seek to sap her of her strength and force her into submission. By citing these examples of Chinese patriarchal oppression, Kingston draws a parallel to the kind of oppression—threatened with unemployment when she seeks to challenge the (white male) authority of her boss—that continues to haunt her as an Asian American woman (48-49).

When Brave Orchid migrates from China to America, her ghosts come back to haunt not her, but her daughter, Maxine, for they are part of a generational legacy of oppression. And yet, these are not Chinese ghosts per se, but the specter of race in America; there is a double nature to Kingston's Gothic elements, for living as an Asian American woman in the US *is* a kind of haunting for Maxine. After hearing stories of her mother's work as a midwife "to whatever spewed forth" (85), Maxine is plagued by "nightmare babies" that shrink and slip between her fingers. She is woken at night by "an infant's grunting and weeping," or dreams of bathing her child but accidently "scalding the baby until its skin tautens and its face becomes nothing but a red hole of a scream." She recalls a particular story of her mother's: "The midwife or a relative would take the back of a baby girl's head in her hand and turn her face into the ashes [...]. It was very easy" (86-87). Though Brave Orchid never admits to killing babies, the narrator still comes into an understanding of Chineseness that is deeply rooted in the Gothic and the grotesque, an inheritance of guilt and the return of the repressed in the form of such cultural horrors. Maxine is plagued by the thought of her real or imagined dead siblings. She confronts her mother—"Is it true then that Oldest Daughter and Oldest son died in China?"—only to have her question dismissed—"You must have been making up stories. You are all the children there are" (103). Whether or not Brave Orchid is to be believed, it becomes clear that being Chinese-*American* has a primacy of existence—those wholly Chinese relatives are, for all intents and purposes, dead, either literally so (No Name Woman) or because they are separated by distance. Thus for Maxine, memories and the people of China are always figured in terms of a spectral, Gothic presence, one that haunts her negotiation of identity as a Chinese American woman.

In *Cultural Haunting*, Kathleen Brogan argues that the presence of ghosts in ethnic American literature serves to illuminate the more shadowy aspects of characters, externalizing their state of mind or inadequately repressed feelings (3). Just as Hawthorne borrowed from the Gothic to serve his interest in Old World memory and inheritance, so too does Kingston turn to the supernatural to examine the troubled transmission of immigrant culture. As such, Kingston's text is as much a part of an American Gothic as an Asian American Gothic. Brogan posits the ghost in ethnic literature as a go-between, an "enigmatic transitional figure moving between past and present, death and life, one culture and another" (6). Certainly Maxine's dreams of her mother's dead children are symptomatic of a struggle with the transition from China to America. What parts, if any, of the native culture are to be left behind, and how does one assimilate into American society those Chinese ghosts that refuse to be forgotten? How does one construct a coherent identity from the daily routine of present life and the resurgent fragments of a spectral past? At the start of *Woman Warrior*, Maxine remarks: "Those of us in the first American generations have had to figure out how the invisible world the emigrants built around our childhoods fits in solid America" (5). Her confusion stems from an inability either to parse out what is Chinese from American, or to integrate the two into a unified self.

What results from Maxine's struggle with her Chinese ancestry and American acculturation is a questioning of the idealized category of both, creating a fragmented and hybrid Chinese American identity. The narrative incoherence of the ghosts in Kingston's novel exposes the anxieties of the racialized immigrants and their hyphenated experience, pertinent to those Chinese who encounter cultural exclusions that frustrate their participation in American self-representation and disrupt their attempts at cultural authenticity within an American assimilation (Mejia-LaPerle 113). The ghosts in Kingston's narrative, rather than exoticize and commodify her Chinese heritage for the fascination and consumption of the dominant white culture, as critics have accused her of doing, actually functions to personify the cracks in American identity. Maxine is alienated from both cultural frameworks, her Americanness being no less problematic or ghostly than the *Asian* which persistently qualifies the former self. Kingston's text forces readers to consider the intersection of various oppressions in a transnational context; her work engages with tropes of the American Gothic and its racial haunting as much as with Chinese patriarchal traditions. And as an Asian American woman, Kingston is forced to negotiate both. The resulting fragmentation pervades the author's life from childhood: she appears to the dominant culture as a minority, and yet her mother insists that she is already too much like the inhabitants of the ghost country. Maxine remembers: "We had been born among ghosts, were taught by ghosts, and were ourselves ghost-like. [Our parents] called us a kind of ghost" (Kingston 183).

Obviously the ghosts referred to here by the narrator's relatives are of a different sort: American[4] ghosts. As Maxine herself observes, "America has been full of machines and ghosts—Taxi Ghosts, Bus Ghosts, Police Ghosts, Fire Ghosts, Meter Reader Ghosts, Tree Trimming Ghosts, Five-and-Dime Ghosts. [...] I could hardly walk, limping my way around the White Ghosts and their cars" (97). These ghosts are far more monotonous. They are not the return of the repressed, but a manifestation of the struggle for identity of Maxine's Chinese family in America. These ghosts express the nature of diasporic displacement by giving a name to the invisible cultural boundaries that mark the family's interaction within the American cultural experience (Mejia-LaPerle 114). America becomes a land of Newsboy Ghosts, Milk Ghosts, and Mail Ghosts, all of which regularly visit Maxine's home, or become unavoidable in the daily routines of life. They seem to display a comical menace, a kind of mundane threat to the Chineseness that Brave Orchid wishes to instill and preserve in her children:

> Staying off the streets did no good. They came nosing at windows—Social Worker Ghosts; Public Health Nurse Ghosts; Factory Ghosts recruiting workers during the war [...] two Jesus Ghosts who had formerly worked in China. We hid directly under the windows, pressed against the baseboard until the ghost, calling us in the ghost language so that we'd almost answer to stop

4. The implication here is that "American" refers almost exclusively to *white* Americans, as the child Maxine seems to differentiate between Mexican and Black ghosts.

> its voice, gave up. [...]. It seemed as if ghosts could not hear or see very well. (98)

These ghosts become objects of entertainment and light-hearted fright for Maxine and her siblings. They seem quaint and bumbling, oblivious in their dull routines, their useful chores performed for whatever ghostly purpose. Their visitations, unlike those of their Chinese counterparts, do not substantially threaten to break down the demarcation between the home (*heim*) and the unhomely (*unheimlich*): they may knock, peep, or even trespass on the premises, but their existence is always exterior, their actions a "banal carrying out of professional roles rather than a genuine lapsing of natural limits and boundaries" (Kong 126). As much as Chinese ghosts belong to an order of metaphysical otherness and cultural ancestry, so do American ghosts inhabit the temporal present and the cultural everyday. These ghosts do not necessarily paint America as an uncanny, potentially hostile setting, but nevertheless articulate the anxieties of diasporic displacement. As Mejia-LaPerle points out, the ultimate irony here is that, within the context of American assimilation, it is the Chinese who have remained ghosts, whose status is rendered ephemeral. But in speaking of Americans as ghostly, Brave Orchid resists a hegemonic culture that treats *her* like a ghost (Kong 115). By referring to the white majority and other people of color in America as "ghosts," the Chinese immigrants attempt to claim their legitimate status and to some extent, debase the existence of the others. Calling whites "ghosts" quite simply becomes a process of Othering non-Chinese. The metaphoric invisibility of racial minorityzation finds its fullest expression in the vocabulary of ghostliness that pervades Kingston's tales of life in America. In this case, it is not the uncanniness of ghosts that is their most relevant quality, but the feeling of otherness inherent in every interaction: the persistent reminder of the family's marginalized existence in America. Once again, Morrison's words ring true: the specter of race haunts the America Gothic landscape.

By employing these ghosts to comment on her American experience, Kingston problematizes the claimed hybridity of American Gothic criticism: *Woman Warrior* underscores that excluded in this criticism is an account of the migrant traumas and fragmented self-construction of the Asian American (Mejia-LaPerle 116). Ng continues to reiterate in his *Intersecting Interstices* that a Gothic perspective on Asian American writings dealing with problems of assimilation and the crisis of the liminal self will reveal the troubled space of the hyphenated identity (38). In Kingston's novel, Brave Orchid and the older Chinese immigrants not only refer to Americans as ghosts but even their own Chinese American children. The word they come to use to refer to their hybrid children is *ho chi kuei*, a problematic term to translate into English. In an attempt to understand the meaning of the word, Maxine attempts to look it up:

> So far I have the following translations for *ho* and/or *chi*: 'centipede,' 'grub,' 'bastard carp,' 'chirping insect,' 'jujube tree,' 'pied wagtail,' 'grain sieve,'

> 'casket sacrifice,' 'water lily,' 'good frying,' 'non-eater,' 'dustpan-and-broom.' Or perhaps I've romanized the spelling wrong and it is *hao* chi kuei, which could mean they are calling us 'Good Foundation Ghosts.' (204)

Maxine's struggle to define this phrase – she comes up with thirteen useless translations—is indicative of her struggle to define herself as a Chinese-American. Even if she is *ho chi kuei*, she still has no idea what that means, either within the context of her Chineseness or her Americanness. All she knows is that she is *kuei*: a ghost. It seems that by her exposure to American culture, the children are turning into the Other that their mother ambivalently critiques yet dismisses as inevitable. At the root of this appellation lies the question of insubstantiality; the implication is that the children's foreign experience, the act of living in an inferior land, has somehow deprived them of things needed to make one whole. Both of Maxine's cultural identities are compromised by the simultaneous anxious preservation of her Chinese culture by her parents and the stereotypes manifested in an American representation of that culture. Thus Maxine, as a ghost, comes to inhabit "the invisible borderlands between China and America, the geography of the immigrant nation, the country of diasporic people" (Mejia-LaPerle 114). She faces the charge of being too ghost-like (American) by her mother, yet she experiences America as an ethnic minority, also as a ghost, but one that is too Chinese. Straddling her parental Chinese culture and the dominant American one, *ho chi kuei* is neither/nor as well as both/and, and at the same time, occupies the "in-between" space. And yet, in writing and retelling her stories—those of China and America, her ancestor's and her own—Kingston translates a cross-cultural experience and transforms the supposedly derogatory meaning of *ho chi kuei* into a more positive, hybrid identity. Grown up, the narrator visits her mother and tells that she has found "some places in this country that are ghost-free. And I think I belong there" (108). More importantly, Kingston has actually *created* a narrative space for herself inhabited by these very ghosts—she is creating an Asian American Gothic to reflect her hybrid identity, her negotiation of the racial specter that continues to haunt her. In her attempts at navigating this self, Maxine chooses to expose rather than repress these spirits; she utilizes her ghosts to confer significance to the most troubled parts of her intersectional identity construction.

For Kingston, this telling-as-exorcism is "the transformation of haunting as deathly possession into a haunting that enlarges self within the *selective* integration of family history" (Brogan 9). Gayle K. Fujita Sato, a researcher in psychoanalytic theory and Asian American literature, asserts that the very ghosts that drive the narrator of *Woman Warrior* from China also bring her back, for she realizes that "banishing them all means banishing all poetry and magic too," including those cultural legends such as Fa Mu Lan, the novel's titular heroine (Sato 40). This is an exorcism without banishment or repression, but an exorcism that entails a bringing to light, a saying and revealing. Maxine's own ghosthood, in that it reconciles her to a hyphenated self, becomes a willingly embraced, rewarding experience of alienation. This ghosthood—the positive affirmation of *ho chi kuei*—still means a loss of identity through separation from one's family, but such a loss yields a renewed sense of affiliation, as is the case with Brave Orchid's encounter with and defeat of the Sitting Ghost. Maxine confronts her own spectral adversaries, including No Name Woman. She fights through words by "unghosting" or telling about the suicide aunt; by writing her extravagant presence back into family history the narrator asserts her own life of extravagance as a writer (Sato 142). Reinterpreted as an empowering isolation, this ghosthood becomes a means of overcoming insecurity while renewing self-confidence—as with Brave Orchid at To Keung—and of reconstructing needed ties to family and tradition—as Kingston does in invoking her aunt's ghost. The Asian American Gothic which Kingston creates is her answer back to both the American Gothic tradition and her Chinese ghosts; it is a way of telling which demonstrates her identity and location as a Chinese American woman writer.

The final story included in the text, "A Song for Barbarian Reed Pipe," is Kingston's retelling of the Chinese legend of Ts'ai Yen—a poet held captive among barbarians—though Kingston subverts its original moral. She focuses not on Ts'ai Yen's eventual return to her native people but on the interethnic harmony forged through an integration of disparate art forms—the music of the barbarians and Ts'ai Yen's singing. Maxine starts the tale: "Here is a story my mother told me, not when I was young, but recently, when I told her I also talk story. The beginning is hers, the ending, mine" (206). Instead of struggling against her two cultures, like Ts'ai Yen, Kingston seeks to unify the two (and her identity) through her art, her storytelling. *Woman Warrior* begins with Brave Orchid's command not to speak, the idea of enforced silence, but it ends with triumphant song. The journey is from speechlessness to voice, the forced silence of No Name Woman to the lyrical ballads of Ts'ai Yen. Kingston ends her work in speech and song, as this Asian American Gothic is a negotiation of traditions both Chinese and American, the intersection of race and gender that can haunt but may also be exorcised through words. In this tale of Asian American Gothic, the return of the repressed is what Kathleen Brogan refers to as a "secondary burial" wherein the dead—one's ghosts—are exhumed after an initial burial to then be reinterred properly and finally (22). The ritual, Kingston's telling, transforms the dead from menacing ghosts to beneficent ancestral spirits, rendering them safely accessible.

To view not just *Woman Warrior* but other works of Asian American literature through a Gothic lens opens up new critical insights into these writings. Themes of trauma, repression, fragmented identity, violence, and even the supernatural are present in the cultures of Asian peoples, though these "unspeakable" issues are often themselves marginalized or muted given the tendency of contemporary Asian American literary theory toward the historical or sociological (Ng 11).[5] In such narratives of diaspora and displacement, the Gothic aesthetics of loss and transgression—implicit in the return of the repressed—become almost unavoidable. Andrew Ng combats the argument that such a project "rehearses a 'colonial imposition' of a Western literary and critical heritage onto an array of [...] Asian American narratives" by maintaining that such works do not necessarily constitute Gothic literature, but that they contain many thematic and philosophical elements which become critically manifested under the scrutiny of Gothic criticism (26). To claim an Asian American Gothic is not necessarily an attempt to expand the Gothic canon, but an effort to illuminate and complement both literatures, for a work of Asian American Gothic *is* a work of American Gothic. To implement a perspective of Asian American Gothic is to further question the national formation of identity that imposes a certain degree of silence and repression, a marginalization and exclusion from the dominant discourse. This genre truly exposes the artificial foundations of American identity, revealing what haunts the nation's narratives and working to exorcise those lingering ghosts.

Works Cited

Brogan, Kathleen. "Haunted Tales of Heirs and Ethnographers." *Cultural Haunting: Ghosts and Ethnicity in Recent American Literature*. Charlottesville: U of Virginia P, 1998.

Cheung, King-Kok. *Articulate Silences: Hisaye Yamamoto, Maxine Hong Kingston, Joy Kogawa*. Ithaca: Cornell UP, 1993.

Freud, Sigmund. "The Uncanny." *The Uncanny*. Trans. David McLintock. Ed. Adam Phillips. New York: Penguin, 2003.

Goddu, Teresa A. *Gothic America: Narrative, History, and Nation*. New York: Columbia UP, 1997.

Griffiths, Jennifer. "Uncanny Spaces: Trauma, Cultural Memory, and the Female Body in Gayl Jones's *Corregidora* and Maxine Hong Kingston's *The Woman Warrior*." *Studies in the Novel* 38.3 (2006): 353-70.

Hunsaker, Steven V. *Autobiography and National Identity in the Americas*. Charlottesville: UP of Virginia, 1999.

Kingston, Maxine Hong. *The Woman Warrior: Memoirs of a Girlhood Among Ghosts*. 1976. New York: Vintage International, 1989.

5. For more on developments in Asian American psychoanalytic literary criticism, see Ann Cheng's *The Melancholy of Race* and David Eng's *Racial Castration*. See also Sau-ling Cynthia Wong's *Reading Asian American Literature*, wherein she deploys the Freudian trope of the doppelganger as a means of elucidating thematic concerns in Kingston's text, especially in regard to the 'racial shadow' which haunts both Americans and Asians.

Kong, Belinda. "The Asian-American Hyphen Goes Gothic: Ghosts and Doubles in Maxine Hong Kingston and lê thi diem thúy." *Asian Gothic: Essays on Literature, Film and Anime*. Ed. Ng, Andrew Hock Soon. Jefferson, NC: McFarland & Company, 2008. 123-29.

Lee, Ken-fang. "Cultural Translation and the Exorcist: A Reading of Kingston's and Tan's Ghost Stories." *MELUS* 29.2 (2004): 105-26.

Mejia-LaPerle, Carol. "The Ghostly Rhetoric of Autobiography: Maxine Hong Kingston's *The Woman Warrior* as American Gothic Narrative." *Asian Gothic: Essays on Literature, Film and Anime*. Ed. Ng, Andrew Hock Soon. Jefferson, NC: McFarland & Company, 2008. 108-22.

Ng, Andrew Hock Soon. *Interrogating Interstices: Gothic Aesthetics in Postcolonial Asian and Asian American Literature*. Oxford: Peter Lang, 2007.

Rusk, Lauren. "The Hard-Won Harmonics of Selfhood." *The Life Writing of Otherness: Woolf, Baldwin, Kingston, and Winterson*. Ed. William E. Cain. New York: Routledge, 2002. 55-104.

Sato, Gayle K. Fujita. "*The Woman Warrior* as a Search for Ghosts." *Approaches to Teaching Kingston's* The Woman Warrior. Ed. Shirley Lim. New York: Modern Language Association of America, 1991. 138-45.

Wong, Sau-ling Cynthia. "Autobiography as Guided Chinatown Tour? Maxine Hong Kingston's *The Woman Warrior* and the Chinese-American Autobiographical Controversy." *Multicultural Autobiography: American Lives*. Ed. James R. Payne. Knoxville: UP of Tennessee, 1992. 248-79.

—. *Reading Asian American Literature: From Necessity to Extravagance*. Princeton, NJ: Princeton UP, 1993.

Do Ghosts Grow Up?
Ghostliness in Maxine Hong Kingston's *The Woman Warrior* and *China Men*

Janna Odabas (GSNAS, JFK Institut, FU Berlin, Germany)

The subtitle of Maxine Hong Kingston's *The Woman Warrior,* namely, *Memoirs of a Girlhood Among Ghosts,* already emphasizes the significance of the 'ghosts' for this text. Kingston introduces the puzzling combination of the genre memoir with supernatural existences. Although *The Woman Warrior* has sparked an academic engagement with its ghosts, *China Men* has been largely ignored with respect to this aspect. My interconnected reading of the striking presence of spectral figures in both works is a first attempt to close this gap. I observe what happens to the ghosts in *China Men*, when—as Kingston has stated in an interview—the narrator "grows up" (Hoy 57). Do they also change and grow up? In order to answer this question I first take a look at the content level of the stories to analyze the ghostly figures that haunt these works. In a second step I consider the level of narration: I argue that both texts employ a way of telling their stories that I call a 'ghostly narration.' Taken together, these two steps reveal insights into the function of ghostliness in *The Woman Warrior* and *China Men* and allow a comparative reading that emphasizes both differences and similarities.

Following Sigmund Freud's seminal essay "The Uncanny," ghosts are generally considered as a return of something repressed. Ghosts, in other words, are something that is secretly familiar and that recurs to haunt a person (Freud 241). This reading is still highly relevant for a consideration of ghosts. However, it needs to be complemented with other ones: for example, Renée Bergland argues that ghosts need to be considered in their positive as well as their negative functions. Drawing on Jacques Derrida's *Specters of Marx*, she argues that ghosts are always linked to power relations and hierarchies: "[H]egemonic power [...] is structured around ghosts" since both are made from the same things—such as history, memory, fear, and desire—and both concepts are somehow imaginary, yet structure reality nonetheless (Bergland 6). Accordingly, "[b]ecause the politics of the national, the racial, the classed, and the gendered are the politics of memory and false memory, they are also, necessarily, the politics of spectrality" (6). Carol Mejia-LaPerle productively connects these two thoughts, when she argues that ghosts represent "repressed communal and personal anxieties" (110). As such, ghosts link the personal and the communal, the private and the political. In doing so, they link the past and the present: they allow for a reflection and reworking of the past in order to serve the present (Brogan 29).[1] One striking feature of ghostliness is the oscillation between different binary oppositions such as dead versus alive or reality versus fantasy. In Jacques Derrida's words, "it would be necessary to learn spirits," to "learn to live *with* ghosts," "[e]ven and especially if this, which is neither substance, nor essence, nor existence, *is never present as such*" (xviii, emphasis in the original). The ghosts' status as simultaneously absent and present and their oscillation between these concepts, demands an engagement that differs from the ordinary neat classifications of everyday life. Thus, as figures that are in-between, ghosts challenge dualistic readings.

In an insightful essay on ghosts as transpacific and transatlantic figures, Nicole Waller argues that the ghosts in *The Woman Warrior* need to be recognized as figures that belong to the reality of the narrator's world (267). Significantly, the memoir offers no separation between the ghost as metaphor and the ghost as ghost—it uses both (273). So, to use Avery Gordon's words, the ghost needs to be recognized as "a social figure" (8). Among others, Mejia-LaPerle reads the ghosts as figures that "reveal the anxiety, and the potentiality" of the narrator's status in between the two worlds: China and America (109). In other words, the ghosts stand for the narrator's troubled identity and her lack of belonging to either world; they scare, haunt, and torture her. Yet, the ghosts also present a way of forming a 'cultural memory' or tradition that allows the narrator to reconcile her two backgrounds by accepting ambiguity. Belinda Kong argues in her article "The Asian-American Hyphen Goes Gothic" that in Kingston's memoir "ghosts function as figures of cultural singularity" in that they are either Chinese or American but never both at once (124). I am going to demonstrate the simultaneous threat and enrichment that the ghosts present for the narrator's development as a Chinese American woman in giving a few examples from *The Woman Warrior*. Moreover, I question Kong's proposition of a dual and mutually exclusive reading of Chinese and American ghosts.

The Woman Warrior opens with a chapter on the ghost of "No Name Woman," the narrator's aunt who bore a child out of wedlock, killed her baby and committed suicide by drowning herself in the family well. As this aunt is punished by being erased from the family history, the narrator does neither know about the circumstances of the pregnancy nor even her aunt's name, and refers to her as 'no name woman.' The narrator is frightened by this ghost:

My aunt haunts me—her ghost drawn to me because now, after fifty years of neglect, I alone devote pages of paper to her. [...]. I do not think she always

---

1. In her insightful *Cultural Haunting* Kathleen Brogan reads ghosts as a pan-ethnic phenomenon. She emphasizes the connection between ethnic identity and ghostliness as a process that allows a reworking of the past to fit into the present.

means me well. I am telling on her, and she was a spite suicide [...]. The Chinese are very frightened of the drowned one, whose weeping ghost, wet hair hanging and skin bloated, waits silently by the water to pull down a substitute. (*Warrior* 22)

This ghost is clearly a threat to the narrator. Although doubly dislocated—by space and time as this story has happened in China even before the narrator was born in America—this ghost haunts her in the present and calls for an engagement with the past. The ghost forces the narrator to deal with this repressed past, as the narrator states in the memoir: "Unless I see her life branching into mine, she gives me no ancestral help" (16). It is exactly this 'branching' that reveals the mentioned 'anxiety and potentiality' of the ghosts as the narrator's "forerunner[s]" (15): they present both a threat to her identity as well as an enrichment by connecting her to a family history. As such, the ghosts in general and the aunt's ghost in particular are "the very materials from which [the narrator] confirms and celebrates a personal ancestry, at the risk of acknowledging the fragility of her epistemological ground" (Mejia-LaPerle 118).

The white American ghosts that the narrator encounters in America stand in stark contrast to this Chinese ancestral ghost. They are figures of everyday life: "America has been full of machines and ghosts—Taxi Ghosts, Bus Ghosts, Police Ghosts, Fire Ghosts, Meter Reader Ghosts, Tree Trimming Ghosts, Five-and-Dime Ghosts" (*Warrior* 90). In this context, ghostliness is used as an ethnic marker to create distance between insiders and outsiders: although the Chinese are a minority in America, they categorize the white Americans as 'foreigners' by calling them ghosts. As Robert Lee explains, these ghosts become "reduced to their immediate function [...] all without memory or culture" (60). Although the narrator struggles with these American ghosts, stating that "[o]nce upon a time the world was so thick with ghosts, I could hardly breathe; I could hardly walk, limping my way around the White Ghosts and their cars" (*Warrior* 90-91), she also does not want to return to China "where the ghosts took shapes nothing like our own" (93). Here, the narrator shows her trouble: to her, the boundaries of inside and outside are blurred. Being born in America, she feels less threatened by the American ghosts that resemble her more than the Chinese ones. Belinda Kong sees these white ghosts as "American spooks" and "mock-Gothic" (126). In other words, these ghosts are only metaphorical references to the disorientation of the immigrants. While these ghosts might appear less threatening than the Chinese ghosts, like the haunting no name aunt's ghost, they still are disturbing presences for the narrator and her family. One example of a scary American ghost is the encounter with the 'Garbage ghost':

> 'Come see the Garbage Ghost get its food,' we children called. 'The Garbage Ghost,' we told each other, nodding our heads. The ghost looked directly at us. Steadying the load on his back with one hand, the Garbage Ghost walked up to the window. He had cavernous nostrils with yellow and brown hair.

> Slowly, he opened his red mouth. 'The ... Gar...bage... Ghost,' he said, copying human language. [...]. We ran, screaming to our mother, who efficiently shut the window. (*Warrior* 92)

Although the beginning appears to be only a playful engagement between some children and a white American worker, the atmosphere shifts towards the end of the quote. The scary features of the ghost, the 'cavernous nostrils' and the 'red mouth,' are already indicating a nightmarish turn to the play. The most gruesome aspect, though, is the seeming knowledge of the Chinese language that the ghost's repetition of the Chinese words implies: to the children, this is the transgression that triggers horror because the ghost invades their (linguistic) space. Moreover, the mother's reaction heightens their fear: instead of telling the children that this is not a ghost but an American human being, she simply shuts the window without explanation or reassurance. Significantly, in the context of the story this horror is never resolved. The window is closed, but the haunting effect still lingers with the children long after this event.

While Kong's analysis of the cultural singularity of the ghosts seems so far confirmed by the Chinese 'no name woman' and the white American ghosts, I argue that the memoir already challenges such a simplified reading. The narrator is called "Ho Chi Kuei" by her mother (*Warrior* 182): "[W]e had been born among ghosts, were taught by ghosts, and were ourselves half ghosts. They called us a kind of ghost. Ghosts are noisy and full of air; they talk during meals. They talk about anything" (165). What makes the narrator ghostly here in the eyes of her mother is her lack of understanding Chinese traditions. If this half-ghostly status is read from a Freudian return of the repressed, then it supports the idea of a troubled identity. The narrator represses her features that are considered 'other'—in her mother's eyes her lack of understanding of Chinese traditions, in the eyes of the white Americans her Chineseness—in order to fit in. Yet, these aspects of her identity recur as ghostly features that continue to haunt her. The narrator has to leave her family for a while in order to figure out a way to include both traditions into her evolving identity. According to Ruth Jenkins, the result is a woven, not homogenized, Chinese American identity (68), and therefore ultimately challenges Kong's dualistic reading. The narrator thus needs to question stable concepts, definitions, and categories, for, as a half-ghost, she embodies the supernatural and cannot separate it from daily existence (Blinde 64, 69). Indeed, these references to the narrator's ghostly status are neither explained as mere metaphorical ornamentation nor as an actual presence of a ghost. Instead, they remain startling figures in this memoir that challenge essentialist assumptions.

Since Belinda Kong's findings apply to *The Woman Warrior* partially—at least if we consider the actual ghosts that are described, I want to look at the ghostly figures that appear in *China Men* in order to see whether these ghosts also follow the 'cultural singularity' pattern. Are they different from the ghosts in her first book? Have they developed? Have they 'grown up'?

In Maxine Hong Kingston's second autobiographical work, we also encounter various ghosts. I read *China Men* as a ghostly history, as a family history, and as a ghostly story. As such a (hi)story, it is both fictive and factual: it constructs both a story and a history. A ghostly history reveals and transports 'cultural memory' on a personal as well as on a collective level. The ghosts that the narrator faces in *China Men* serve as a means to unearth secrets in order to recover such lost (hi)stories. As Gayle Fujita Sato argues, "[b]oth works reclaim ancestors from oblivion and misinterpretation, but they use 'ghost' differently to represent these unidentified ancestors" (143). She claims that in *The Woman Warrior* the ghosts are more metaphorical because the 'ghost text' of Chinese American woman warriorhood needs to be invented to a great extent. The ghosts in *China Men*, instead, are more sociohistorical as their stories can be recovered (143). However, the narrator's strategy in the first book is similar to that in the second: in Mary Slowik's words, the narrator also needs to "start with the X, the erasing, the silences of her fathers" and to "push the ghosts [...] towards meaning" (80-81). These traces of the lost histories lead the narrator to the times of her great grandfathers, whom she re-writes as the 'founding ancestors' in Hawaii, to the times of her grandfathers, who she imagines as the 'binding and building ancestors' of the railroad in the United States, and her father's and finally her own time. The collage of these stories allows the narrator to position herself and her family in a history that emerges from the shadows of the past. The ghostly traces that the narrator follows are inscribed into her surroundings: "I have heard the land sing. I have seen the bright blue streaks of spirits whisking through the air. I again search for my American ancestors by listening in the cane" (*China Men* 90). And the narrator does so; she acknowledges the spirits and listens to the traces and then tells her family history. As she explains to her father: "I'll tell you what I suppose from your silences" (15). While ghostly presences serve to unearth lost histories, they simultaneously—as bodiless and shifting creatures—represent anything that is in-between and unresolved. Thus, the ghostly traces that run through the text and from which the text was initially created, highlight the ambiguities of such (hi)stories. This plural is central to the question of whether the ghosts grow up: while *The Woman Warrior* addresses the question of memory and identity on a rather personal level, *China Men* represents a communal process of coming to terms with the ghosts of the past and the present.[2] The focus in the first memoir is clearly on the narrator's personal coming of age. In contrast, in Yan Gao's words, in *China Men*, Kingston's "thematic focus expands from the concept of

2. I want to clarify here that I see *The Woman Warrior* also as a 'relational' autobiography—Rocío Davis applies John Paul Eakin's term to indicate that the women's lives branch into each other (44).

self to that of *home*, and her desire for recognition and search for identity shifts from the personal and domestic level to the historical and communal level" (76). Seen this way, the ghosts do 'grow up' in the sense that they start to shift their focus from the personal to the social, indicating a coming of age. But let us take a look at the actual ghosts that haunt the narrator in *China Men*.

The reader also encounters the white "demons" and meets traditional Chinese ghosts in folktales. Then, there is the same figure of "Ho Chi Kuei," of the half-ghost who belongs to neither China nor America. The narrator's brother, for example, fights in the Vietnam War. He joins the navy as a pacifist and remains true to his resolution to kill no one. Diane Simmons interprets this brother as the embodiment of a solved identity conflict (139). Let me clarify why I disagree with this reading. The brother is constantly haunted by images of the war that appear in his nightmares. In these, he participates in killing and gruesomely slicing up Asians. When he wakes up, he notices that, in his dream, he has killed some of his own kin for he recognizes "his own family, Chinese faces, Chinese eyes, noses, and cheekbones" (*China Men* 291). This last aspect points to the problem of identity: as a Chinese American, the brother does not see himself in a binary opposition of 'us' versus 'them.' Instead, he identifies also with the Asians, and when he tries to repress this feeling, it recurs in ghostly figures in his dreams. Following King-kok Cheung's argumentation, the brother, as half-ghost, highlights the positive effects of questioning the simplified oppositions in any war (120). Thus, the ghost has grown up in so far that it is not merely concerned with its own personal struggle, but rather represents a communal and political questioning of, on the one hand, identity conflicts of Asian Americans during the Vietnam War, and on the other hand, warfare in general with its reasoning that rests on binary oppositions.

Although I argue that the figure of the half-ghost is not merely metaphorical, I want to support my questioning of Belinda Kong's claim that the ghosts are either Chinese or American but never both at once by looking at one actual ghost that holds a rather prominent position in *China Men*: Say Goong's ghost. Say Goong is one of the narrator's grandfathers. He lives with his brother Sahm Goong close to the narrator's home in America. After Say Goong's death, his ghost returns to his brother: he "was still there, no shimmering, no wavering, just as solid and real as ever before" (*China Men* 170). This ghost—the narration implies—is not part of a creepy, fictionalized ghost story, but it is part of the real world. Sahm Goong is advised to scold the ghost 'home.' While to him it seems out of question that this ghost needs to 'return' to the 'home' China, the very presence of this ghost in America points to another reading. According to Mejia-LaPerle, Say Goong's ghost expresses the "nature of the diasporic displacement by giving name to the invisible cultural boundaries that mark the family's interaction within an American cultural experience" (114). Having spent his life in America, Say Goong's ghost is suddenly not so sure about his place of belonging. Even if Say Goong's ghost is read as a return of Sahm Goong's repressed feelings of loss between the two 'homes,' this ghost still raises questions about the communal place of belonging for Asian Americans in general. Thus, it troubles the neat definition of Kong's dualistic reading: it is an Asian American ghost that embodies the displacement of the Chinese Americans. Throughout *China Men*, the narrator introduces other ghosts like this one, for example, the ghost of Mad Sao's mother. Therefore the ghosts in Kingston's second autobiographical novel clearly show a resistance to obey binary oppositions and neat categorizations. Not only do they reject a separation into Chinese and American ghosts, but they moreover create spheres that challenge dichotomies on a personal as well as communal level.

As a second step to my argument, I want to suggest a significant correlation between the way Kingston narrates her memories in both *The Woman Warrior* and *China Men* and the spectral figures she depicts: I call this strategy a 'ghostly narration.' In her playful transgression of genre boundaries, Kingston weaves fact and fiction into her story and—similar to a ghost's status between life and death—defies categorization. In relation to the oppositional pair of fact vs. fiction, Maxine Hong Kingston said in an interview with Eric Schroeder that

> having two categories—fiction and nonfiction—is too small. I picture a border between fiction and nonfiction, and I am making that border very wide; fiction is a narrow place on one side, nonfiction is a narrow place on another side, and there's this big border in the middle, in which real life is taking place and also fantasies and dreams and visions. (Schroeder 216)

Writing on the borders of existing categories, Kingston blurs Western concepts of reality: she argues that the space in-between fact and fiction is where 'real life is taking place' and that reality consists also of 'fantasies and dreams and visions.' In other words, the narration mirrors or reinforces the same questioning of binaries as the ghosts on the content level do: it rejects a clear separation of fact and fiction and instead oscillates between fiction and reality, never favoring one over the other and often keeping the reader in doubt about the 'truth-value' of the narration.

So far I have used Freudian thought in a classical sense. For the remainder of this article, however, I am rather interested in a reading 'against the grain' of Freud's unsuccessful attempt of defining the 'uncanny.' While he identifies certain features and also seems to invoke a feeling of closure, the whole set-up of his essay points to another reading. He does not arrive at a conclusive answer to the question as to what makes the 'uncanny' uncanny. Instead, his article is very much a reminiscing about uncanny experiences in reality and in fiction. And exactly this differentiation that he emphasizes, is—as I argue—already undermined by his article itself because the way that he narrates his definitional attempts rather foregrounds his inability to differentiate between fact and fiction. Take, for example, the footnote towards the end of his essay, in which he relates an incident from his own experience of mistaking his own reflection to be a stranger. Freud starts his anecdote with the words: "I can report a similar adventure" (248) and ends it with a questioning of his own emotional reaction to the event, implying a doubting of his own reliability as a narrator and as a psychological observer, stressing the fictionality of human experience. This passage reflects the oscillation between fiction and fact that runs through the whole essay. Connecting this issue to *The Woman Warrior* and *China Men*, we can say that the depicted ghosts also promote a reading that troubles a classification into material reality and fantasy. Therefore, the definition of 'ghostly narration' in this article is based on the oscillation of the texts, its figures, and the narration between the spheres of material reality and fantasy, of life and death. In my reading, I follow Mejia-LaPerle in her argumentation that ghosts create "narrative incoherence" (112).

In *The Woman Warrior* this 'ghostly narration' appears in various forms. In the following paragraphs I will consider the function of talk-stories and myths. In general, as Patricia Lin Blinde argues, the "transgeneric mode Kingston uses appears to be eccentric in its vacillations between accounts of her own life told in the straightforward reportage of autobiography and the imagined situations the writer encounters rendered in fictive terms while assuming the persona of some imagined heroine" (63). One example of this combination is the story of Fa Mu Lan, in which the narrator imagines herself to be a heroine who took revenge on a racist and misogynist baron. Although it is based on a classical Chinese myth, Kingston's version includes various changes from the original (see Blinde 66) and is clearly marked as an imagined story. The introduction to the myth shows the influence of fiction upon the narrator's life and highlights the shift from the realm of autobiographical telling to the fictional account:

> I had forgotten this chant that was once mine, given me by my mother, who may not have known its power to remind. She said I would grow up a wife and slave, but she taught me the song of the warrior woman, Fa Mu Lan. I would grow up a warrior woman.
>
> The call would come from a bird that flew over our roof. (*Warrior* 26)

Blinde argues that "this retelling represents a throwing off of impositions and the subsequent freedom to choose the fictions by which one wishes to live" (66). Even though I agree with this reading that problematizes the influence of fiction upon realities, I would take the argument one step further. I think that *The Woman Warrior* is most transgressive in its playing with genres whenever the distinctions between reality and fiction are not as clearly marked as in this example—particularly these are the instances that I term 'ghostly narration.'

One example of such a 'ghostly narration' is the depiction of the above-mentioned no name woman. When the narrator is entering puberty, her mother tells her the story of the no name aunt "to grow up on" (*Warrior* 13). She tells only the necessary facts to bring her message across, to warn her daughter about the risks of life. Yet, after the telling and the imposition not to tell this story to anyone, the narrator begins to imagine the life of her aunt and her reasons and motives. On the one hand, the aunt is shown as a victim of rape, with a neighbor from the village demanding sex of her who "was not, after all, much different from her husband. They both gave orders: she followed" (14). On the other hand, she is imagined as a more powerful woman in charge of her life, who breaks with traditions by symbolically "comb[ing] individuality into her bob" (16) in order to attract a certain man (Wong 8). Although the narration implies that these parts are imagined with the inclusions of "maybe" or "perhaps" before any one account of this woman's life, all of these are left standing next to each other without any favoring of one over the other. This creates the uncanny effect of a ghostly, repressed history that needs to be reworked in order to gain meaning for the present. Furthermore, it reflects the indecision of an uncanny account, as the above reading of Freud's oscillations between reality and fiction has also shown. While I agree with Robert Lee's reading of this reworking as a subtle resistance to the authoritative interpretation of history (58), I want to emphasize the ghostliness of the narration here. This account is ghostly in its indecision, in its oscillation between imagination and reality, in its breaking up of such a binary distinction after all. In Ruth Jenkin's words, the "supernatural, then, provides women writers a means to challenge monolithic histories, narrative styles, evaluative standards, and scripts that dictate what experience is worthy of record and how that experience is to be articulated" (70). Although I hesitate to agree with all of Jenkin's argumentation in her article,[3] I do think that she has a point in this general tendency of a 'ghostly narration' to provide opportunities for writing and reading against the grain, and thus, for a rethinking of history. At least in *The Woman Warrior*, the ghostly narration has this effect.

In *China Men* the narrator also explicitly mixes different narrative styles. For the purpose of this article I want to look at two distinct ways of creating a 'ghostly narration': firstly, Kingston's use of 'real' sources such as the exclusion laws and secondly her inclusion of unreliable memories. In closely analyzing these narrative forms, I question the truth value of seemingly factual sources and suggest the 'reality' of fictional accounts.

Probably the most striking chapter in-between the longer ones that deal with the narrator's family history is the one that is called "The Laws." This chapter gives seven pages of pure facts: it lists the anti-Chinese laws from 1868 up to the 1960s (*China Men* 152–59). "The Laws" introduces a historical reality that is

3. I think that Jenkins provides an inspiring feminist-based reading of ghosts in her essay, yet, I do not agree with her conclusion that "ghosts and spirits provide authority for articulation and identity" (68). This oversimplified reading focuses too much on the positive aspect of the ghostly presences and ignores the possible negative reading of a ghosting process as doing away with an obligation to react to injustice. For a thorough analysis of ghosting as both a silencing and an empowering process, see Bergland.

largely forgotten by mainstream American historical recording or repressed by the Chinese American victims of these laws (Li 491–92). The centric position of this factual account—precisely in the middle of this book that is otherwise so creatively built on imagination—calls for an analysis. This chapter is meaningfully non-fictive; the narrator is similarly absent and leaves it without further comments; its style is highly fact-oriented and scholarly; it remains separate from the rest of the book, yet constitutes its very center. These aspects set the chapter apart. However, the laws are the very reason why *China Men* is written the way that it is written and that the characters are the way they are: it gives reasons for the silences that appear throughout the ghostly family memoir. Thus, the chapter can be read as background information for readers who lack this knowledge. Or it can be seen as a final documentation of an often neglected chapter of the American past, as suggested above. Moreover, "The Laws" creates a subtle ironic undertone: "[B]y imitating the monological voice of authorizing History—the history imposed by the dominant culture that made the laws—this section uncovers both the dullness of this voice and its deafness to other, competing voices" (Goellnicht 233). As a result, the fictional history that surrounds this most factual account seems more "truthful than the official version" and illustrates the power of the margins (233). Although I hesitate to reduce *China Men* to an attempted 'authentic' historical documentation from the margins, Goellnicht's reading still allows for a re-thinking of existing categories of fact versus fiction. The subtle irony that he names is certainly given. Thus, even though there is no oscillation in this chapter between fact and fiction, what creates the 'ghostly narration' is its link to the rest of the book: its questioning of a factual account as a truthful representation of history. This way, the oscillation happens on the larger level, namely in between its chapters.

Yet, *China Men* also includes a ghostly narration within its chapters. One example of this is the inclusion of what I call 'ghostly memories.' Following Mejia-LaPerle's argument that the telling of memory is connected to the ghostly shapes that haunt this attempt (108), I emphasize the fragmented and evasive quality that memories possess in this autobiographical novel. For example, the narrator's father is depressed after he lost his job, sitting in his chair unmoving until the children "irked him" so much that suddenly he chased after the narrator's sister,

> who locked herself in a bedroom. 'Come out,' he shouted. But, of course, she wouldn't, he having a coat hanger in hand and angry. I watched him kick the door; the round mirror fell off the wall and crashed. The door broke open, and he beat her. Only, my sister remembers that it was she who watched my father's shoe against the door and the mirror outside fall, and I who was beaten. But I know I saw the mirror in crazy pieces; I was standing by the table with the blue linoleum top, which was outside the door. I saw his brown shoe against the door and his knee flex and the other brothers and sisters watching from the outside of the door, and hear MaMa saying, 'Seven years

> bad luck.' My sister claims that same memory. Neither of us has a recollection of curling up inside that room, whether behind the pounding door or under the bed or in the closet. (*China Men* 253)

Significantly, the conflicting memories of the sisters are not resolved. This passage is left standing as a demonstration of the unreliability of memory, with both sisters claiming vivid memories of the other sister being chased. Most prominent are the details that the sisters remember: the father's 'brown shoe,' the falling mirror, then the mirror 'in crazy pieces,' the other siblings outside the door. Both sisters 'claim that same memory.' And neither remembers being frightened behind the door, yet one of them must have been. This quote deliberately emphasizes the obvious limitations of memory (Neubauer 18). Thus, it is a 'ghostly memory' in that it oscillates between different possibilities and also breaches upon the imaginary. For, if no one remembers being inside the room, maybe this whole episode never took place? Consequently, while *China Men* gives room to the stories of the past to create a family history, it constantly questions the reliability of any kind of representation.

In fictionalizing history in both *The Woman Warrior* and *China Men*, the narrator transcends generic boundaries: she does not write either fact or fiction, but combines the two artistically. Thus, she depicts her experience of reality (Nishime 266) that is interwoven with half-truths, fictions, and ghostly presences. To conclude, the 'ghostly narration' that Kingston employs in both texts, creates an unresolved oscillation between different genres. This narration mirrors the puzzling presence of the ghosts on the content level and the inability to ascribe neat functions to their existence. Both texts include white American ghosts, Chinese ghosts like the no name woman's, and—maybe most strikingly—ghostly figures that transgress this distinction: the siblings' status as half-ghosts or Say Goong's Asian American ghost. Thus, Belinda Kong's proposition of the ghosts' "cultural singularity" has been challenged both with reference to *The Woman Warrior* and especially to *China Men*. But what about the ghosts' development? I argue that the ghosts appear in both works as figures that are in-between: neither dead nor alive, they cannot be easily categorized or labeled. Borrowing Robert Lee's words, in both works, they "insist that the social—past, fixed, and articulated—be confronted by the personal—present, flexible, and felt, that history be opened up by memory" (63). Yet, although the ghosts in *China Men* seem to have a broader reference to the Chinese American history at large and as a communal story than those of *The Woman Warrior*, they have neither changed in their function to question stable categories and to highlight troubling or silenced aspects, nor has the way of narrating this (hi)story changed because both texts rely on a 'ghostly narration.' As such, the ghosts reinforce a narration that is highly ambiguous, but powerfully moving. In Maxine Hong Kingston's own words:

> I have learned that writing does not make ghosts go away. I wanted to record, to find the words for, the 'ghosts,' which are only visions. They are not concrete; they are beautiful, and powerful. But they don't have a solidity that we can pass around from one to another. I wanted to give them a substance that goes beyond me. (Rabinowitz 67-68)

Thus, the ghosts in both *The Woman Warrior* and *China Men* are an attempt to reveal and transport the ambiguous experience of the narrator with the ghosts around her. While they are not solid facts to be accounted for, they still demand an engagement. Accordingly, talking about the Chinese culture, in yet another interview, Kingston notes that "the mythic is real" (Hoy 61).

Works Cited

Bergland, Renée L. *The National Uncanny. Indian Ghosts and American Subjects*. Hanover and London: UP of New England, 2000.

Blinde, Patricia Lin. "The Icicle in the Desert: Perspective and Form in the Works of Two Chinese-American Women Writers." *MELUS* 6.3 (Autumn, 1979): 51–71.

Brogan, Kathleen. *Cultural Haunting: Ghosts and Ethnicity in Recent American Literature*. Charlottesville: UP of Virginia, 1998.

Davis, Rocío G. "The Self in the Text versus the Self as Text: Asian American Autobiographical Strategies." *Asian American Literary Studies*. Ed. Guiyou Huang. Edinburgh: Edinburgh UP, 2005. 41-63.

Cheung, King-kok. *Articulate Silences: Hisaye Yamamoto, Maxine Hong Kingston, Joy Kogawa*. Ithaca: Cornell UP, 1995.

Derrida, Jacques. *Specters of Marx. The State of the Debt, the Work of Mourning, and the New International*. Trans. Peggy Kamuf. New York and London: Routledge, 1994.

Eakin, John Paul. *How Our Lives Become Stories: Making Selves*. Ithaca: Cornell UP, 1999.

Freud, Sigmund. "The Uncanny." 1919. *The Standard Edition of the Complete Psychological Works of Sigmund Freud*. Ed. James Strachey. London: Vintage, 2001. 218–52.

Gao, Yan. "A Metaphorical Strategy: An Interpretation of Maxine Hong Kingston's 'Ghost Stories'." Microfilm. A Dissertation submitted to the Faculty of the Graduate School of Emory University, Department of English. 1993.

Goellnicht, Donald C. "Tang Ao in America: Male Subject Positions in *China Men*." *Critical Essays on Maxine Hong Kingston*. Ed. Laura E. Skandera-Trombley. New York: Hall, 1998. 229–45.

Gordon, Avery F. *Ghostly Matters: Haunting and the Sociological Imagination*. Minneapolis: U of Minnesota P, 2004.

Hoy, Jody. "To Be Able to See the Tao." *Conversations with Maxine Hong Kingston*. Eds. Paul Skenazy, Tera Martin. Jackson: UP of Mississippi, 1998. 47–66.

Jenkins, Ruth Y. "Authorizing Female Voice and Experience: Ghosts and Spirits in Kingston's *The Woman Warrior* and Allende's *The House of the Spirits*." *MELUS* 19.3 (Autumn, 1994): 61–73.

Kingston, Maxine Hong. *China Men*. 1980. New York: Vintage, 1989.

—. *The Woman Warrior: Memoirs of a Girlhood Among Ghosts*. 1976. New York: Picador, 1981.

Kong, Belinda. "The Asian-American Hyphen Goes Gothic: Ghosts and Doubles in Maxine Hong Kingston and lê thi diem thúy." *Asian Gothic: Essays on Literature, Film and Anime*. Ed. Andrew Hock Soon Ng. Jefferson, North Carolina and London: McFarland & Company, 2008. 123–39.

Lee, Robert G. "*The Woman Warrior* as an Intervention in Asian American Historiography." *Approaches to Teaching Kingston's* The Woman Warrior. Ed. Shirley Geok-lin Lim. New York: The Modern Language Association of America, 1991. 52-63.

Li, David Leiwei. "China Men: Maxine Hong Kingston and the American Canon." *American Literary History* 2.3 (Autumn, 1990): 482–502.

Mejia-LaPerle, Carol. "The Ghostly Rhetoric of Autobiography: Maxine Hong Kingston's *The Woman Warrior* as American Gothic Narrative." *Asian Gothic: Essays on Literature, Film and Anime*. Ed. Andrew Hock Soon Ng. Jefferson, North Carolina and London: McFarland & Company, 2008. 108–22.

Neubauer, Carol E. "Developing Ties to the Past: Photography and Other Sources of Information in Maxine Hong Kingston's *China Men*." *MELUS* 10.4 (Winter, 1983): 17–36.

Nishime, Leilani. "Engendering Genre: Gender and Nationalism in *China Men* and *The Woman Warrior*." *Critical Essays on Maxine Hong Kingston*. Ed. Laura E. Skandera-Trombley. New York: Hall, 1998. 261–75.

Rabinowitz, Paula. "Eccentric Memories: A Conversation with Maxine Hong Kingston." *Conversations with Maxine Hong Kingston*. Eds. Paul Skenazy, Tera Martin. Jackson: UP of Mississippi, 1998. 67-76.

Sato, Gayle K. Fujita. "*The Woman Warrior* as a Search for Ghosts." *Approaches to Teaching Kingston's* The Woman Warrior. Ed. Shirley Geok-lin Lim. New York: The Modern Language Association of America, 1991. 138-45.

Schroeder, Eric J. "As Truthful as Possible: An Interview with Maxine Hong Kingston." *Conversations with Maxine Hong Kingston*. Eds. Paul Skenazy, Tera Martin. Jackson: UP of Mississippi, 1998. 215–28.

Simmons, Diane. *Maxine Hong Kingston*. New York: Twayne Publishers, 1999.

Slowik, Mary. "When the Ghosts Speak: Oral and Written Narrative Forms in Maxine Hong Kingston's *China Men*." *MELUS* 19.1 (Spring, 1994): 73–88.

Waller, Nicole. "Transpazifische und transatlantische Gespenster in Maxine Hong Kingston's *The Woman Warrior* und Toni Morrison's *Beloved*." *Gespenster. Erscheinungen, Medien, Theorien*. Eds. Moritz Baßler, Bettina Gruber, Martina Wagner-Egelhaaf. Würzburg: Königshausen and Neumann, 2005. 267-78.

Wong, Sau-Ling Cynthia. "Necessity and Extravagance in Maxine Hong Kingston's *The Woman Warrior*: Art and the Ethnic Experience." *MELUS* 15.1 (Spring, 1988): 3-26.

II. On less frequently discussed and recent texts

"I'll be a Skylark": Maxine Hong Kingston's Confessional Poetics in *To Be the Poet*[1]

Eulalia Piñero Gil (Universidad Autónoma de Madrid, Spain)

> I am making a broad margin
> to my life. The margin will be broader when we part,
> and I am alone.
> —Maxine Hong Kingston, *I Love a Broad Margin to My Life* (10)

Maxine Hong Kingston's *To Be the Poet* (2002) is a collection of lectures she delivered at Harvard University.[2] Its three parts describe, in a rather confessional way, Kingston's decision to commit herself to poetry, to look for the muses that provide for the necessary inspiration and to explore in an autobiographical mode her private and public experiences. In this self-descriptive journey, the writer depicts her creative processes and the poet's complex life. Moreover, throughout her metapoetic explorations she discovers "the easiness of poetry, the brevity of the poem, and the happiness and freedom of poets" (3).

It is beyond doubt that Kingston has become among the most widely read of classic American fiction authors. This fact is the result, among other reasons, of her tireless commitment to decades of persevering and successful fiction writing that have obviously contributed to a solid career in the intricate world of the American publishing industry. For Kingston it was about time to look for other literary genres that could channel her changing vital interests. In her own words: "I'll be free to live. I won't be a workhorse anymore; I'll be a skylark. Free of obligations. I am sixty years old; I have enough reputation and fame and money" (3). This sensitive, passionate and inspiring poetic metamorphosis implies a deep transformation, a new creative life based on experimentation, "truth, grace and beauty" (3). Moreover, poetry entails for Kingston the opportunity of reinventing new literary ways of expressing her creativity which encompasses the inclusion of her own artwork in her new books. Thus, for the artist writing

---

1. The author of this essay gratefully acknowledges financial support from the Spanish Ministry of Science and Innovation (Project FFI2008-04355-E: "Written on the Female Body": VIOWOBODY).

2. I would like to thank Maxine Hong Kingston's insightful and illuminating commentaries and suggestions on this paper which was presented at the "Maxine Hong Kingston Symposium, 18-20 March 2011" at the UHA Mulhouse, France.

poetry entails a spontaneous and holistic self-expression that transforms the page into a sort of canvas. Related to this, she even mentions how some poets from the Beat generation such as Ferlinghetti and Ginsberg could sell their notebooks for millions dollars, and "I prosateur, am giving away my papers, scratch paper for free. Theirs are sheaves of handwritten poems, calligraphy, artwork" (34).

To Be the Poet is Kingston's mature opportunity for reinvention and liberation from the constraints of prose writing and from the heavy restraints of the narrative genre. She definitively removes the authorial mask of fiction in order to become the protagonist and the speaker of her poetry. This transcendental decision is probably a consequence of the twelve years Kingston worked intensively on her last novel, *The Fifth Book of Peace* (2004).

According to the Chinese American poet Li-Young Lee, "poetry is a 24-hour-a day job" (Milstead 613). It seems that Kingston's approach to her new life as a poet is very similar to Lee's, as in *To Be the Poet* she applies the daily discipline of a diary in which she tries to unveil the invisible nature of her daily routine. Throughout this process, the poet shares with the reader very deep and insightful feelings with a confessional tone such as the lines, "Strange, I hardly cry anymore except for political events, such as genocides, executions, wars" (37). Kingston's autobiographical mode of verse reveals her compromise with the socio-political context as well as her personal experiences. I call this poetic approach confessional in the way that she uses the personal or autobiographical with a "distinctive sense that depends on the candid examination of what were at the time of writing virtually unmentionable kinds of private distress" (Baldick 43). Therefore, I find many parallelisms between Kingston's poetics and the literary movement that was given the label 'confessional.' But for the author of *The Woman Warrior* the private has always public dimensions; or, in other words, the personal is political and social. And this is precisely what distinguishes Kingston's poetic imagination from other poetic discourses: the clear connections with her social and political contexts and her desire to create a lyric public voice.

In this light, Juliana Chang points out that "the poetic, narrowly conceived, is generally considered lyric and therefore the realm of the private, as opposed to the public or social" (85). The opposition mentioned by the critic does not apply to Kingston's poetry, as her personal conflicts are never isolated from the community. On the contrary, "the individual is seen as receiving value and dignity in relationship to some worthy others: conflict submits to familial and community integrity" (Lim 56). From my perspective, in Kingston's poetry the private sphere always has a public dimension that connects not only with the Asian American community but with the society in general. This is really what makes her poetry universal because she departs from the communal identities and transforms them in all-embracing ties that make meaning of the poet's world.

In the first section of the book, "I Choose the Poet's Life," the voice describes the beginning of her journey and how it is clearly connected to her California childhood as the daughter of Chinese immigrants. This biographical period is the origin of her poetic mind in a bilingual context. Likewise, she remembers her ancestors as well as the pristine innocence of that lifetime: "Let me have poetry to be like that once again, and I shall die happy" (5). Her inspiring poetic explorations echo William Wordsworth's "Ode: Intimations of Immortality from Recollections of Early Childhood" in the permanent emphasis on the primal sympathy and candid innocence of childhood that frees her from the demands of prose. In the same way, she idealizes the early poetry of her childhood when her father, a Chinese poet, played with sounds and she also felt how poetry flew like a free migratory skylark with the pleasant family word games:

> Hey, Third Grandfather.
> Hey, Fourth Grandfather.
> Where are you going?
> Horse shoes clippity-clopping
> Four feet, then four feet,
> Where are you going? (5)

Kingston vindicates the freedom of poets as her voice is driven into spontaneous extravagance and wilderness by the anxiety of poetic influence. She has also moments of great visionary insight in her quest for a poetic voice. However, her personal poetry is too divergent to be easily classified and summarized. In my view, the seeds of Kingston's poetic imagination developed much earlier in time; we can see this in the poems she published in anthologies such as Garret Hongo's *The Open Boat* (1993) and in her poetic novel *The Woman Warrior* (1976). The Asian American poetry anthology includes Kingston's intriguing poem "Absorption of Rock," which is the poet's meditation about the difficulties of translating culture, and the Asian diaspora associated with a deep sense of displacement and uprootedness:

> We search out facts to defend a Vietnamese,
> Who has allegedly shot to death a Lao
> In Stockton, outside a bar. It was in fear,
> we hear him say, of a cantaloupe or rock
> that the Lao man had caused to appear
> insidc him. Onc anthropologist tcstifics
> that Vietnamese driving in the highlands
> rolled up the windows against the H'mong air.
> The H'mong in Fairfield were not indicted for
> their try at family suicide; there was a question
> of a Lao curse or want of a telephone.
> Three translators have run away—this fourth
> does not say enough words. (138)

In this early poem, Kingston shows her commitment to the representation of the complexities of multiracial coexistence within the Asian community. The poem ends with the evidence that language sometimes is not enough to represent cross-cultural experiences. At the same time, she foregrounds the consequences of ghettoization and discrimination among the different Asian ethnic groups. We can infer from the previous poem that one of Kingston's main tasks in her creative process is to understand, tell the truth, and help others tell the truth about their experiences. Related to this, her fictionalized autobiography, *The Woman Warrior*, is a clear paradigm of this vital quest which brilliantly combines a metaphorical poetic prose style that deepens into the complexities of the Chinese and the Western cultural experiences. In the extended descriptions of the narrator, the beginnings of her poetic imagination may be discovered and appreciated:

> I learned to make my mind large, as the universe is large, so that there is room for paradoxes. Pearls are bone marrow; pearls come from oysters. The dragon lives in the sky, ocean, marshes, and mountains; and the mountains are also its cranium. Its voice thunders and jingles like copper pans. It breathes fire and water; and sometimes the dragon is one, sometimes many. (35)

It goes without saying that the narrative voice explores her inner self through the assumption of qualities or features that seem to conflict with one another in a rather Whitmanesque way that clearly echoes "Song of Myself": "Do I contradict myself, / Very well then I contradict myself, / (I'm large I contain multitudes)" (Whitman 88).

In the second section of *To Be the Poet*, "I Call on the Muses of Poetry, and Here's What I Get," Kingston's confessional and autobiographical poetic voice emerges again stronger in her beliefs as an antiwar activist, in her defense of the oral tradition, her quest for peace, her reflections on poetic subjectivity, in the difficulties of translating culture and in the importance of dreams and myths. In this part of the book memory becomes the poet's muse, replacing invention as she focuses on the Vietnam war: "Our war was Viet Nam. Earll and I talked about the veterans we know, their delicacy, their courtesy" (55). Furthermore, Kingston's voice reaffirms the American poetic tradition of the poet as a public voice with a social dimension and a compromise with a society which is multicultural. Therefore, she embraces William Carlos Williams' law of poetry and makes it part of her poetic dictum: "The American poet must stay put on the ground of the Americas, and hear and be her voice" (52). This canonical reference connects Kingston's poetics with the genealogy of American poetry. But what is more important, it explains her commitment to society, as she has been working to create a writing group of war veterans for the past decade. Needless to say, for Kingston poetry entails a healing power that she describes as "feeling, seeing, noting seeing, noting feeling" (26). Her activism is reflected in her compromise with this particular social group that needs support to cure the physical and psychological wounds of war's traumatic experience:

> The greengold leaves of the birch at the window
> shoot shadows of arrowheads onto the kitchen walls
> and stove,
> and upon the bowed heads of war veterans.
> My skin and my heart awake and shiver
> in corresponding delight. (29)

Maxine Hong Kingston's prose work and poetry is a mode of writing that crosses national and cultural borders. Her writing challenges us to reconsider the assumptions and meanings of identity, nation, place, home and memory in a broad cross-cultural context. So in my view, the negotiation of cultures appears to be one of the most important themes not only in her poetry but in Asian American poetry as well, and its representation is manifested through various tropological constructions. There is clearly a need to map out the origins, ancestors and voices of a historical past that are consistently displaced—sometimes by the assimilationist ethics. As I have argued: "Asian American poets celebrate the spirit of their ethnic ethos not by representing the most obvious and colorful external signs of difference, but by disclosing what constitutes the spiritual vision any culture has on transcendence of life" (Piñero Gil 123).

Kingston's poetry displays moments of this permanent sense of negotiation of cultures in the last section of the book, "Spring Harvest." Her dialogical poem "May 29 Memorial Day" is an excellent example of her ability to articulate voices from different cultural contexts:

> Nhu, a Vietnamese American friend, has returned
> From Cuba,
> And advises me to go. My father lived in Cuba.
> 'You should go.
> Everything you('ll) love is there.
> And they will love you.
> They love las Chinitas.
> But more than Chinitas—
> they love Vietnamitas.
> Listen to the songs.
> They sing, "La Chinita, la Chinita."
> I walk down the street, and they say, "La Chinita."
> I say, "No, no, yo soy Vietnamita."
> And they say, "Oooooo, Vietnamita."
> Every little village has a street named after a
> Vietnamese freedom fighter.
> Some I never heard of.
> You're going to love Cuba.' (95)

In these lines, Kingston transcends the political implications of an obviously difficult situation and explores the cultural dimensions of Cuban people. She offers an alternative vision of the island related to the idea that there is always more to discover beyond appearances. In addition, the poem shows Kingston's remarkable assets as a storytelling poet: a narrative gift, an original oral imagination, an easy relation to other cultural realms and a flexible and musical talking voice. She is a storyteller who communicates her experiences as well as the ones she gathers from her community. Her use of direct American speech entails essentially the communication of an experience that passes from mouth to mouth and remains in our memory.

The last pages of *To Be the Poet* are devoted to the recreation of the mythic woman warrior Fa Mu Lan. But why does Kingston end her "longbook" with an alternative war story?[3] In my view, it is more than obvious that Kingston has tried to promote peace through her literary works. Indeed, she is an antiwar activist in her public acts though in spite of her radical pacifism, she considers Fa Mu Lan a powerful and positive role model for women. Naoko Sugiyama sheds light on this issue and suggests that the narrator of *The Woman Warrior* "extends and tries to transform the definition of 'warrior' by comparing her own pacifist activities to Fa Mu Lan's achievements" (145). Likewise, I interpret the Chinese woman warrior as a very constructive force that transforms the community with her radical change and the assumption of an active leadership. Kingston uses the Chinese heroine again in her last novel, *The Fifth Book of Peace* (2004), and on this occasion, as she does in *To Be the Poet*, she emphasizes that Fa Mu Lan was originally "a weaver. 'Jik jik jik' is the sound of the shuttle going back and forth across the loom. 'Jik' means 'to weave,' 'to knit,' 'to heal'" (390).

I would like to stress that Kingston revisits once more the powerful image of the woman warrior, this time in a different context, and for this reason the myth acquires other meanings related to this concrete poetic discourse. Among other connotations, I propose that the essence of the myth entails the idea that, in some way, we all become warriors when we fight injustice and the ideologies that promote racism, sexism, violence, systematically ignoring basic human rights. Therefore our symbolic metamorphosis can be compared to that of Fa Mu Lan's cross-dressing as a male general and assuming her father's role. In this way, the Chinese heroine represents her commitment to the community, and the assumption of values such as courage, independence and self-assertion. Kingston's poetic harvest re-affirms with Fa Mu Lan's re-contextualization that she is above all a poet, a weaver of words, who aspires to heal the wounds of society with her chants of transformation:

---

3. The poet refers to her book *To Be the Poet* as the "longbook" in the following lines: "At the end of Spring / the ending of the longbook" (108). Kingston probably uses this term with a certain irony as this is her shortest book.

Now, go home. By her voice,
The men recognize their general—
a beautiful woman.
You were our general?! A woman.
A woman led us though the war.
A woman has led us home.
Fa Mook Lan disbands the army.
Return home. Farewell.
Beholding—and becoming—Yin, the Feminine,
Come home from war. (110)

To Be the Poet is a metapoetic journey which has no intellectual or elitist purposes. On the contrary, we can sense the need to release freshness and a new mature vision of the complexity and simplicity of life and meaning. But for Kingston new meanings generate new forms and she revises poetry by experimenting with an original genre-bending art between poetry, prose poem, essay, diary and images, all juxtaposed and commenting on each other. As a result, this poetry collection can be considered a turning point in her literary career, as she focuses on a quest for an authentic poetic voice that encompasses and revises her most challenging topoi. In order to achieve this, Kingston meditates on a literary past that resonates throughout her flowing verse lines. As I have previously argued, there is at the same time a deep sense of transformation that is oriented towards a promising creative future: "I have a miracle—not a metaphor but a miracle. I actually felt diamonds of light touch me. / Try for poetry day and night. / Try in various places" (38).

Finally, Maxine Hong Kingston's poetry occupies a relevant position in the complex and innovative field of contemporary Asian American poetry. It is important to note that her contribution to this literary genre transcends the assumed expectations and challenges of critics and poets in the sense that she moves freely from the ethnic to the universal, from the sacred to the profane, from the aesthetic to the ethic concerns, from the Asian to the American, from the private to the public spheres and from the mainstream to the margins and vice-versa.[4] This creative fluidity is the result of a poetic journey devoid of any kind of prejudices or preconceptions. Moreover, Kingston's strategy becomes her own original way to learn and investigate on the spontaneous self-

4. Shirley Geok-lin Lim makes a distinction between Asian-American poetry and Modern American poetry based on connections to the ethno-specific origins and to the T.S. Eliot's tradition: "Modern American poetry takes its aesthetic values from T. S. Eliot's theory of the impersonality of poetry, while many Asian-American poets localize values in family and immigrant narrative and in ethno-specific social, political and highly personal themes. These themes rouse varying attitudes ranging from reverence, nostalgia, satire, humour, anger to historical urgency" (60).

expression. As she has confessed in an interview: "I try to be as free as possible from categories, constraints, traditions [...]. I do not want any tradition to hamper me" (Simal González 169).

It remains to be said that *To Be the Poet* is a lucid and honest poetic manifesto that will decisively clear out the way for more poetry books that will deepen our understanding of the writer's creative life and the contemporary world.[5]

Works Cited

Baldick, Chris. *The Concise Oxford Dictionary of Literary Terms*. Oxford: Oxford UP, 1991.

Chang, Juliana. "Reading Asian American Poetry." *MELUS* 21.1 (Spring 1996): 81-98.

Hongo, Garrett, ed. *The Open Boat. Poems from Asian America*. New York: Anchor Books, 1993.

Kingston, Maxine Hong. "Absorption of Rock." *The Open Boat. Poems from Asian America*. Ed. Garrett Hongo. New York: Anchor Books, 1993. 138.

—. *To Be the Poet*. Cambridge: Harvard UP, 2002.

—. *The Fifth Book of Peace*. New York: Vintage, 2004.

—. *I Love a Broad Margin to My Life*. London: Harvill Secker/Random House, 2011.

—. *The Woman Warrior. Memoirs of a Girlhood Among Ghosts*. 1976. New York: Vintage Books, 1977.

Lim, Shirley Geok-lin. "Reconstructing Asian-American Poetry." *MELUS* 14.2 (Summer 1987): 51-63.

Milstead, Claudia. "Li-Young Lee." *The Greenwood Encyclopedia of Asian American Literature*. Ed. Guiyou Huang. Vol. 2. Westport, CT: Greenwood Press, 2009. 607-13.

Sugiyama, Naoko. "From the Woman Warrior to Veterans of Peace. Maxine Hong Kingston's Pacifist Textual Strategies." *The Japanese Journal of American Studies* 20 (2009): 131-45.

Pinero Gil, Eulalia. "The Anxiety of Origins: Asian American Poets as Cultural Warriors." *Hitting Critical Mass. A Journal of Asian American Cultural Criticism* 4.1 (1996): 121-34.

—. "Ceremonies of Dialogism in Asian American Poetry." *Asian American Literature in the International Contex. Readings on Fiction, Poetry, and Performance*. Eds. Rocío G. Davis & Sämi Ludwig. Münster: LIT Verlag, 2002. 97-107.

5. From my point of view, Kingston's latest memoir poem book, *I Love a Broad Margin to My Life* (2011) expands on these intriguing matters.

Simal González, Begoña. "Interview with Maxine Hong Kingston." *REDEN* 14 (1997): 167-77.

Whitman, Walt. *Leaves of Grass*. 1893. New York: Norton Critical Editions, 1973.

Maxine Hong Kingston as Counterculture Writer

Agniezska Soltysik Monnet (Université de Lausanne, Switzerland)

Early in Maxine Hong Kingston's most recent book, *I Love a Broad Margin to My Life* (2011), her fictional avatar Wittman Ah Sing comes upon a group of women sitting in front of a hotel in Hong Kong. They are laughing and appear carefree, "free of husband, free of kids," buying candy from a street vendor, reminding Wittman of hippies. "Oh, let me be hippie with you," he longs silently, using the Whitmanian "Oh" that reminds us of his namesake (53). Then he notices that some are holding signs and realizes that what he is seeing is a labor demonstration by hotel cleaning women on their day off. Kingston now prods her character to speak to the women: "Tell them, Wittman: 'In San Francisco, we have immigrante workers too. We want los derechos too" (54). This anecdote is only one of many in Kingston's recent work that offers a sense of how firmly she remains rooted in the values and vision of the radical movements of the 1960s that she experienced in Berkeley as a young woman. Forty years later, while traveling halfway across the world, Kingston finds labor demonstrations, anti-war activities, and the state of mind evoked in the word "hippie," used here playfully as an adjective, wherever she goes. Although *I Love a Broad Margin to My Life* is about the author's trip to China, revisiting some of the stories and sources for *The Woman Warrior* (1975), the book reveals how far Kingston has moved as a writer from the Chinese-American material that characterized that early work. Instead, her latest (and possibly last, if we take her at her word) book focuses broadly on the pacifism that has defined Kingston's writing since the early 1990s, and returns in many ways to the counterculture sensibilities that formed Kingston in 1960s Berkeley.

Although Kingston's counterculture background has occasionally been acknowledged, it has never been seriously explored. In a 1990 interview, Kingston explains that *Tripmaster Monkey* (1989) is set in the early 60s because the "Monkey King" (an iconoclastic character from a Chinese epic novel, *Journey to the West*) was "here, in the Sixties. Abby Hoffman, Allen Ginsberg, you know? They were monkey spirits, trying to change the world with costumes and street theater" (Chin, "A MELUS Interview" 61). Similarly, during an interview in 1993, Neila C. Seshachari tells Kingston that she considers *Tripmaster Monkey* "a quintessential novel of the 1960s," and Kingston agrees, explaining that she set the novel during this time because she admired the many new words that it had spawned, such as "Be-In," "love-in," "flower power" and "tripmaster" itself (Seshachari, "Reinventing Peace " 203). Deborah Madsen's biographical textbook on Maxine Kingston for the "Literary Masters" series devotes several pages to the place of the Civil Rights movement and feminism and a paragraph on the counterculture, but no scholarly article has ever been devoted to the subject (Madsen, *Maxine Hong Kingston* 54-61).

I would like to argue that a serious look at this question is important not only for the sake of a more accurate and nuanced appreciation of Kingston's formative experiences as a writer, but also as a step towards breaking down the barriers within the discipline that keep "ethnic writers" lumped together and critics focused only on their ethnic or gender identity. While these issues are important to Kingston's work, there are other issues that have become perhaps even more important to her, such as, most notably, pacifism. At the very least, a look at the place of the 1960s in Kingston's life may help to break up the binary racial schema that the term "Chinese-American" has inevitably invited. For years, the debates about Kingston's work focused on how much was influenced by her "Chinese" origins and how much by her "American" childhood. Although Kingston warns readers from the very first pages of *The Woman Warrior* not to over-determine and simplify cultural identity, asking her Chinese-American readers how they can distinguish between what is "Chinese" and what is particular to their own family, she is less vigilant about making sure we do not ignore the complexities of her American background as well. She may well have assumed that it was not necessary, given the way the novel *Tripmaster Monkey* makes it clear that her experience of California was not limited to Stockton. And yet, the deep stamp left on Kingston's world-view and work by the Berkeley counterculture during her college years and early adulthood there has been largely overlooked.

I will be arguing that the counterculture of the 1960s, by which I refer to both the political and the lifestyle movements, is indispensable to understanding Kingston's core values, such as pacifism, as well as her signature aesthetic choices, including generic hybridity, informal tone, rhetorical playfulness and structural non-linearity. The counterculture left Kingston with a lifelong fascination with consciousness-expansion, consciousness-raising and the power of the mind and imagination to influence reality. Finally, it provided her with a model of community that goes beyond kinship-based family, village or national units to affinity-based "sanghas" created with friends and like-minded strangers and a model of the entire world as an interconnected human family. For all these reasons, I maintain that no assessment of Kingston's work and influences can make sense without taking into account the world of bohemian Berkeley in the early 60s.

Like Wittman Ah Sing from *Tripmaster Monkey,* Maxine Kingston graduated from UC Berkeley in 1962 after having majored in English literature, and continued to live in or near San Francisco until 1967. In all respects, the period 1958 to 1967, the years that Kingston lived in Berkeley, were the most important to the Bay Area counterculture. On the political side, student activism began on the UC Berkeley campus the year she enrolled, in 1958, with the organization SLATE, a precursor to the Free Speech movement. In 1960 a protest against HUAC activities led to student activists being forced down the steps of the San Francisco City Hall with fire hoses, an event that was filmed and led to the politicization of many people on the New Left. The highly visible Berkeley Free Speech movement began in 1964 with several dramatic acts of civil disobedience, including the prevention of the arrest of a CORE activist by students surrounding a police car for 32 hours and using it as a platform for speeches.

At the same time, the Haight-Ashbury scene had been coalescing since the early 60s, marijuana was abundant and LSD was legal until October of 1966. The following year, 1967, the year of the so-called "Summer of Love," was a key turning point in the history of the counterculture as well as in Kingston's own life. The year began with an event organized initially as a protest against the recent criminalization of LSD: the Human Be-In at the Golden Gate Park, also advertised as a Gathering of the Tribes. This would turn out to be a historic "coming out" party for the huge alternative community of "tribes" and people in San Francisco at this time. Sources differ, but between 20,000 and 30,000 people came to the park that January day, including Timothy Leary, Allen Ginsberg and Stanley Owsley (who distributed free samples of his famous homemade "Owsley acid").

Ironically, this celebration of the San Francisco bohemia was also the beginning of its end, largely due to the media obsession with the "hippies" that it sparked and which resulted in tens of thousands of young people, including many runaways, descending on the city for the "Summer of Love" and overwhelming its infrastructure and public services. The overcrowding, homelessness, health problems and hard drugs that flooded into San Frabcisco that summer spelled the end of the original counterculture scene. The Diggers, a group of radical community activists, who had staged happenings such as the "Death of Money" parade in the spring, organized a mock funeral happening called "Death of Hippie" at the end of the summer to announce that the "Summer of Love" was over and that visitors should go home and take what they learned to their own communities. This is not to imply that the counterculture scene itself was over, but that summer tourists were invited to take what they had learned back to their own communities. Many local residents also decided to leave. Among them, Maxine Hong Kingston moved to Hawai'i with her husband and young son, carrying her counterculture values with her.

Since "counterculture" is a broad term, and an allusion to its "values" may sound impressionistic, I will borrow and adapt the five values that Timothy Miller, in his book *The Hippies and American Values* (1991), identifies as key sites of the counterculture's ethics. These are, in his words: dope, sex, rock music, community, and cultural opposition. This last principle is in fact a conflation of the two branches of the cultural left in the 1960s, the political activists and the hippies. Theodor Roszak, in his 1969 *The Making of a Counterculture,* was the first to argue that these two groups were actually two faces of the same phenomenon, though they often seemed quite distinct, especially to each other (264-265). The two groups may have had roughly the same goals but often disagreed sharply about how to achieve them. Activists believed in organized protest and putting pressure on lawmakers and institutions, while hippies tended to prefer putting their energies into creating an alternative society by living it themselves. In practice, the line separating hippies and activists was porous, and many people found themselves charting a middle ground that included political demonstrations and activity with various degrees of hippie-ness and involvement with alternative communities. Kingston is a perfect example of this in many ways, a devoted participant of anti-war demonstrations though wary of conventional politics. In *The Fifth Book of Peace* (2003) she writes that "ideology is what got us into trouble [in the Vietnam War] in the first place ... We don't want ideology" (331). Similarly, in the recent *I Love a Broad Margin* she says that she wants to "change the world" (209), but her methods are mainly the "do-it-yourself" strategies of the counterculture: art-creation and community-formation. In the Veteran Writers Workshop, for example, the writing workshop she has run for veterans since 1991, she combines both.

This brings me to the second of Miller's principles, the ethics of community. Anyone familiar with Kingston's work would immediately recognize the centrality of this ethic to Kingston's work. Just as in the counterculture, where founding alternative communities was the most radical and important form of engaging in cultural opposition, so in Kingston's work, creating communities of readers, of writers, and of friends, constitutes a central drive. In *Tripmaster Monkey*, Wittman's peregrinations around San Francisco in the novel culminate in the staging of a play that brings together nearly everyone that he has met over the course of the narrative. The play lasts several days and creates a kind of ephemeral community of players and spectators that is no less important for being impermanent. The counterculture of the 60s put a strong accent on community, solidarity and breaking out of the mold of American individualism as well as the isolated nuclear family. The Victorian mansions of the Haight-Ashbury area housed groups of roommates that saw themselves as extended families or as small tribes. In addition to "tribe," the word "sangha" figured prominently in the consciousness of the counterculture, as it does in Kingston's work. Alongside these more structured and permanent communities, the counterculture placed great value on social interactions in the public domain such as happenings and parties. Kingston captures this spirit better than any other living American writer. In *Tripmaster Monkey*, she devotes three long chapters to a single party. In a 1989 interview, she connects her ideas about the radical potential of parties explicitly to the 1960s: "All those love-ins and

Woodstock—all that is the monkey. The monkey loves to go to parties, and if you have a wonderful enough party, you can change life" (Blauvelt, "Talking" 79).

Miller's third counterculture value is the "ethics of rock," which may be the least obvious notion to connect to Kingston's work. Yet, it is important to keep in mind the larger context of what rock music meant to the counterculture, namely, the principle that art and pleasure are an integral part of an ethical and political participation in the world. In the music of the 1960s, this engagement involved both the verbal and the performative dimensions of music. On the one hand, rock and folk music articulated the disappointments, longings and joys of the counterculture through its lyrics: Bob Dylan, Country Joe and the Fish, Joan Baez and other artists were the spokespeople for a generation, translating its political and personal aspirations into words that were sung (often collectively). On the other hand, music provided an occasion for bringing people together and creating a sense of community, solidarity, and intense connection, much as Wittman's play in *Tripmaster Monkey* creates bonds among disparate people through its performance.

In short, the spirit of the "ethics of rock" can be perceived in Kingston's lifelong commitment to artistic creativity. It is no accident that *The Woman Warrior* ends with a "song" that conveys the "sadness and anger" of the Chinese poetess captured by barbarians during her captivity. After being ransomed, she brings her songs back to China and they are passed along to her descendants. Although an ambivalent and enigmatic tale of captivity, cultural alienation and displacement, "A Song for a Barbarian Reed Pipe" closes the novel with the words "It translated well," suggesting that through music the two cultures, i.e., Chinese and "barbarian," could find a point of common ground: a shared understanding of "forever wandering" (209). This dual function of music—communicating aspirations and creating bonds between people—is the heart of the countercultural ethic of rock.

The fourth principle, the ethics of sex, Miller defines in terms of freedom to enjoy physical pleasure and one's body. Like music, sexuality does not seem at first glance to be a significant aspect of Kingston's work, and yet it appears in key moments and in key functions. For example, the first story of *The Woman Warrior* is about the suicide of the aunt who becomes pregnant while her husband was away, and serves as a powerful and cruel introduction to femininity for the narrator. Signaling that *The Woman Warrior* will be a feminist text, this story establishes Kingston's concern with the constraints and punishments that have historically defined female sexuality and defiantly displays her willingness to break taboos enforcing those restrictions.

In *China Men*, there is an equally striking and memorable description of sexuality, this time male, when Ah Goong masturbates and says that he is "fucking the world" (*China Men* 133). The word is crude but the intent is neither crudeness nor contempt for the world. Instead, Ah Goong is overwhelmed by sexual excitement as a reaction to the "beauty" of the day. The effect of the passage is to retrieve the word "fucking" from a register connoting vulgarity and domination and to instead recode it as neutral or even joyful. By doing so Kingston furthers one of the counterculture's main objectives concerning sex, that is, to strip it of aggression, mystification and shame. By "fucking the world," that is, masturbating in the open air, Ah Goong is expressing a vital personal connection with the valley far from his home where he has been brought to build the railroad. Though admittedly comic, the episode refigures "fucking" as a natural and primal connection rather than an act of aggression.

Sexuality assumes an even more important place in *Tripmaster Monkey*. First of all, in a small-scale form of early culture jamming, Wittman puts Barbie dolls into sexual positions with other toys while working at a toy shop. The loss of his job as a result of these activities sets the story of the novel into motion. Also early in the novel, Wittman imagines himself as Joang Fu, a storyteller and singer, telling a story of a scientist who invents addictive sperm. Finally, in the scene when Wittman makes love with his future wife Taña, the word "fuck" is again used synonymously with "making love," neutral and friendly: "So they got it on, and they were graceful, just so much foreplay, just so much fervor and abandon and sweat, positions normal. Classic moves. Silently went at it...Mouths against parts of the body, he did not make her blurt out, 'I love you.' Well, it was a fuck where they were hardly acquainted, after all, and one didn't want to turn off the other by seeming overly weirded out" (154). A few moments after this unsentimental and "classic" lovemaking, Wittman and Taña get more playful and he sucks her toes and licks the spaces in between. She tells him she has had an orgasm between her toes, and they are pleased to have "invented a new sex act" (157). In the spirit of sexual equality, Kingston has Wittman hope that "someday he would get to know her well enough to ask her to make love to and with his toes...Find out whether men can have orgasms down there too" (157). In keeping with Miller's definition of the ethics of sex, Kingston's polite, egalitarian and playful sex scenes assume that pleasure in one's body is a natural right and that "fucking" should be a friendly act.

Finally, the principle that Miller calls the "ethics of dope," and which will be the focus of the remainder of this essay, refers to the conscientious use of marijuana and hallucinogens (as opposed to drugs like speed or heroin, which were also used by some but which were not central to the counterculture ethos).[1] The point of taking drugs for the counterculture community was often as a means to become more aware of the worlds both inside and outside, not as an escape from lucidity. Peter Braunstein and Michael William Doyle call it a means of "deconditioning" that people used to help them perceive and critically

1. For a scholarly article on the meaning and use of marijuana and LSD in the 1960s, see David Farber, "The Intoxicated State/Illegal Nation: Drugs in the Sixties Counterculture" (2002).

distance themselves from learned forms of aggression, racism, sexism and intolerance (*Imagine Nation* 15). Drugs were thus regarded as both fun and enlightening, bringing insights to users about the interconnectedness between people and between the material and spiritual world. For some, smoking marijuana or dropping acid was mainly a harmless good time, a way to share a moment of complicity and pleasure with other people. For others, it was a life-altering experience, even a holy one, an experience that could lead to significant changes in the world if enough people shared it. In the PBS documentary *Summer of Love* (2007), Mary Kaspar, who lived in the Haight-Ashbury area in the early 60s, explains that she and her friends believed that LSD could change the world because they had been changed so profoundly by it themselves. While high on acid, she had experienced "cosmic oneness, where I truly felt I was no different than you, I was no different from my black friends; I was no different than anyone who lived in any other part of the world."[2] Kaspar describes a radical dissolution of perceived boundaries between herself and any other human being, boundaries erected by the social categories of race, class and nationality. This faculty of altering one's perception of social reality and social schemas, and for becoming aware of them as such, is at the heart of the counterculture's use of hallucinogens: as consciousness-raising and consciousness-expanding tools.

At first glance, the counterculture's ethic of "dope" may also seem remote from Kingston's main concerns, even more so than music and sex. I intend to demonstrate in what follows that psychedelic experiences are in fact the secret core of Kingston's work, the cosmic laugh at the heart of her literary world. This is not to make any concrete claims about Kingston's personal experiences with marijuana or hallucinogens. Instead, my argument is about her writing and her use of psychedelic experiences as tropes for the acquisition of a specific kind of knowledge. To put it simply, the passages that focus on drug-induced experiences are the points of articulation of many of Kingston's most important personal and political values.

I would like to begin with the story that gives Kingston's first book its name and which has been one of the most taught and most discussed sections of her writing, "White Tigers" in *The Woman Warrior*. This chapter consists of an extensively elaborated retelling of the Mulan ballad, about a young woman who disguises herself as a man to replace her father when he is conscripted into the emperor's army. Unlike Kingston's version, the original ballad and its many Chinese retellings all begin with Mulan's distraught brooding about her old father's conscription as she weaves: "You can't tell the sound of the loom/ From the sighs of the girl" (Ting 77). None of these versions includes any account of a preparation for her career as warrior. This long section of "White Tigers," which describes the narrator's imagined apprenticeship with the mysterious couple who

---

2. A complete transcript of this film is available online at the PBS website: http://www.pbs.org/wgbh/amex/love/

teaches her martial arts and puts her through a series of tests, is entirely Kingston's own, weaving together elements of counterculture psychedelia with Chinese folklore and allusions to Native American initiation rites (much in vogue in the 1960s).[3]

Kington's version begins with a bird leading the narrator away as a little girl to the mountains, in a manner that recalls Alice following the rabbit down the rabbit hole in Lewis Carroll's *Alice in Wonderland*. The drug allusions begin with her getting lost in a cloud she calls "dragon's breath" (possibly evoking "Puff the Magic Dragon," the 1960s hymn to marijuana smoking sung by the group Peter, Paul and Mary[4]), and include distortions in temporal perception ("I would not know how many hours or days passed") and a heightened sensitivity to color: she emerges from the cloud into a "yellow" world where she meets an old couple with seemingly bottomless pots and a floor that stirs up "new blends of earth colors" when she walks on it (20). After some time, she is taken to the mountains of the white tigers and left alone, as in a Native American rite of passage. Following deer tracks, she is led to the "fungus of immortality," possibly an allusion to hallucinogenic mushrooms, which she eats.[5] Soon after, she meets a white rabbit that jumps into her campfire to feed her and then sees two people made of gold dancing the earth's dances, melting from Chinese lion dances to African lion dances to Hindu Indian and American Indian dances, the lion's manes growing tall into feathers that shine, then the man and woman growing bigger and bigger, becoming tall angels.

Although there are rabbits (hares, actually) at the end of the original Mulan ballad, and Kingston's version also alludes to the story of Buddha, for whom a rabbit sacrifices itself by jumping in a fire, I would like to suggest yet another source for this fantastic fictional voyage: the white rabbit presiding over San

---

3. Sau-Ling Cynthia Wong attributes elements such as the prolonged training and the hermit's retreat on misty mountains to Chinese folk traditions, but the hallucinatory transformations of objects and the intense and colorful distortions perceived by the narrator are of Kingston's invention (Wong, "Autobiography" 48, n. 7).
4. In suggesting a local drug-linked resonance to the image of "dragon's breath," I do not mean to deny or diminish the enormous symbolic weight of the dragon in Chinese culture, which Kingston is also certainly evoking in this passage.
5. This passage seems to allude not only to hallucinogenic mushrooms, but possibly even to the McKenna's theory, published a year earlier, that human consciousness was the result of an evolutionary leap triggered by the ingestion of psilocybin-containing mushrooms growing near the droppings of ungulate herds (in Terence and Dennis McKenna, *The Invisible Landscape: Mind, Hallucinogens, and the I Ching*, 1975). The book became very popular in the 1970s, especially among counterculture readers.

Francisco culture in the 1960s (that is, the white rabbit of the Jefferson Airplane album of that name released in 1967). This song is itself a retelling of Lewis Carroll's original novel, not unlike Kingston's rewriting of the Chinese legend. Carroll's version and Grace Slick's both mention substances that upon being eaten make people smaller or bigger and provoke seemingly magical transformations of consciousness and perception.

The description of her narrator's training and experiences in this long embedded section of the chapter has been called magical realism, but I would argue that these passages could also be understood as psychedelic writing.[6] The ever-shifting fantasy of warrior apprenticeship is like a drug-enhanced daydream, which the narrator contrasts to the reality of her life as a young woman in California, in which she does not like armies and thinks martial arts are "for unsure little boys kicking away under fluorescent lights" (52). The woman warrior fantasy stands outside of the narrator's ordinary existence, something like a reverie but with elaborate and hallucinatory details, where the tripper's imagination takes priority over the original ballad that serves as point of departure. A comparison could be made to Hunter S. Thompson's work (e.g. *Fear and Loathing in Las Vegas*), which often mixed journalism, autobiographical sketch and complete fantasy (much of it drug-inspired). Nevertheless, Kingston's account of the woman warrior narrator's shamanic experience is rooted firmly in the mysticism of the West Coast Beats. Like the poetry of Lenore Kandel and Joanne Kyger, "White Tigers" reflects a counterculture engagement with Buddhist concepts of *anitya* and *anātman*, impermanence and no-self, which translate into a consciousness of the way the material world is in a state of constant, unending transformation and mutation of one thing into another, as the passage in which the dancers become lions illustrates.

China Men has even more explicit drug experiences. First of all, there is Uncle I Fu who is drugged into giving away all his money to thieves. Feeling "a surge of chemicals or light rushing through him," he goes to the bank to withdraw his life savings. Anyone familiar with drug literature would recognize the following description of his experience: "The walk he took was magical: inanimate objects glowed, but oh, the animate – the trees and the flowers and bugs and dogs were spraying colors. Human beings flared haloes around their heads and the rest of their bodies. Bands of light connected couples" (212).

---

6. Critics who identify *The Woman Warrior* as "magical realism" include Maggie Ann Bowers, *Magic(al) Realism* 58; Lois Parkinson Zamora, "Magical Romance/Magical Realism" *Magical Realism: Theory, History, Community* 542; and Theo D'haen, "Postmodernisms: From Fantastic to Magic Realist," 287. For "psychedelic writing," see Scott McCulloch's online article at the Literary Culture website: http://www.suite101.com/content/psychedelia-in-writing-a14044

Compare this to Timothy Leary's transcription of people's "first reactions to the psychedelic experience": "Why, colors are so bright! The world seems alive! I'm seeing for the first time! It's alive! It's alive!" ("The Molecular Revolution" 128). Besides enhanced visual perception, Uncle I Fu experiences a sense of connection to the ontological essence of material objects and physical properties: "He later explained how he understood the stopping quality of red light and the go of green" (212). Yet Kingston is also making fun of the altered state of the Uncle in this passage. While he may feel that "Time and fate were his invention and under the control of his will," in fact he has been duped into giving away his money to con men. Kingston's account of this scam is decidedly tongue in cheek, poking gentle fun at the anti-capitalist mantra of the counterculture, as she has the robbed Uncle rejoice to find himself "free of money ... free of burden" until his wife and employees make him "crash" down to the reality of his situation (213).

A far more positive encounter with drugs in *China Men* occurs to Great Grandfather, Bak Goong, who smokes opium on the ship to America and has an intense religious epiphany:

> the meaning of life and time and what he was doing on this ship became clear to him... His thoughts branched and flowed and branched again and connected like rivers, veins, roads, ships' lanes. New ideas sparked and he caught his breath when he saw their connection to old ideas (95).

In addition to bringing him existential insight, Bak Goong's opium trip introduces two of Kingston's own preoccupations, i.e. pacifism and interconnectedness. In the same passage, Bak Goong thinksto himself: "Wars were laughable; how could a human being remember which side he was on? ... He loved the strangers around him as much as he loved his family" (95). Compare this passage to another Kingston writes in her own voice in *The Fifth Book of Peace*: "Every time we go to war, we're in schizophrenic agony. Whoever the enemy is, they're related to us" (361). The drug experience also permits Bak Goong to think in terms of paradox, to escape the limited logic of ordinary consciousness, a theme that is important to American philosophy, especially the tradition of Emerson and Whitman that Kingston claims for herself. As Whitman says in "Song of Myself," "Do I contradict myself?/Very well then I contradict myself/(I am large, I contain multitudes)" and Emerson claimed that "consistency is the hobgoblin of little minds," so Bak Goong sees how "Everything was true ... He was Lao Tse's great thinker, who can embrace opposing thoughts at the same moment" (95). Although opium is not actually a hallucinogen, Kingston attributes the characteristics of an LSD, peyote or ayahuasca trip to Great Grandfather, these all being substances that fascinated the counterculture for their consciousness-expanding qualities. In this instance, the drug allows Bak Goong to see the many connections between people and things that normally are invisible, an idea that becomes the centerpiece of Kingston's later work.

While Bak Goong's opium experience is possibly one of the most positive accounts of a drug trip ever written, Kingston's novel *Tripmaster Monkey* is an even more explicit treatment of the countercultural scene that formed her adult values. Nevertheless, it is far from being a simple homage to that time and place. For one thing, Wittman Ah Sing is not exactly a hippie. His affinities are to the Beats, urban and nocturnal and literary, but he is well aware that he has arrived on the scene a bit late and that his Chinese background would complicate his ability to belong to that milieu just as it complicates his sense of belonging to any American institution or group.[7] During the course of the novel, which follows Wittman around for a period of around two months in 1963, much of the narrative is concentrated on two key events: a party where he meets his future wife and the play that he puts on with the help of many people he's met. Both are sprawling affairs that offer Kingston the opportunity to riff on the complex joys of the social events that defined the bohemian branch of the counterculture: parties and performances. At the party Wittman encounters a group of stoned people who are calmly watching a fire, "swimming in hallucinogen, ripped but appearing as ordinary as pie" (87). Wittman is fascinated to see "how the psychedelic state looks from the outside, that is, through the vantage eyes of a head straight from ear to ear at the moment" (87-8). Although not high himself, Wittman infers from their calm "breathing in unison" what kind of experience they are having, one that sounds very much like Bak Goong's: "that trip where the margins between human beings, and between human beings and other creatures, disappear, so that if one gets hurt, we all hurt, so that to stop war, all we have to do is drop lysergic acid into the water supply" (88). In this slightly tongue-in-cheek manner, Kingston evokes the counterculture myth or fantasy of the revolutionary potential of exposing large numbers of people to LSD. Like Mary Kaspar from the PBS documentary, Wittman attibutes to LSD the ability to make users perceive their radical interconnectedness.

What makes this notion even more subversive (as well as faithful to the counterculture understanding of how LSD works) is that it is perceived to be an insight facilitated by LSD, not an illusion caused by it. Just as for Mary Kaspar LSD was a springboard to a political consciousness based on the assumption that the connections she had perceived during her trips were real and not imagined, so Wittman corrects himself after raising the idea of LSD in the water supply by saying "but we don't even need to do that—because human beings of all time are in connection—the margins don't disappear—there aren't any margins—psychedelics only make you know about things, and do not cause a thing to be—

7. Wittman is resentfully aware that Kerouac was often racist and might well have seen him merely as a "Twinkling little Chinese," *Tripmaster Monkey* 69.

it is—it already is ... the pleasure of acid was in knowing ideas as real as one's body and the physical universe" (88). In other words, psychedelics could be considered as a short-cut to certain kinds of knowledge, but they were not necessary once the knowledge had been acquired. *Tripmaster Monkey* is thus the story of a "head" (drug user) now "straight from ear to ear" (no longer using LSD) bringing psychedelic wisdom to uninitiated readers.

Thus, even if *Tripmaster Monkey* presents LSD as a means of gaining important insights about community and the place of the self in the larger scheme of things, the book is also a kind of guide to acquiring those insights without needing to take any drugs at all. Instead, the novel seems to suggest, art itself is a kind of trip that can take you outside of yourself and show you a more complex portrait of reality. This is the first figurative leap staged by the novel around the trope of "tripmaster," which figures Wittman as a guide for the altered-consciousness experience he offers to spectators and players through his play. The play is so effective a trip that it changes even him, transforming him into a pacifist after having seen that the three brothers and warriors in the story all end up losing the war (340). Another level of meaning for the tripmaster trope is the way the novel's omniscient but not entirely neutral narrator guides Wittman on his journey through the novel, making sure that he stays out of harm's way. Finally, we can conceive behind these different layers of tripmasters the author herself, shaping and guiding the reader's trip into her fictional universe. In an interview with Neila Seshachari in 1993, Kingston affirmed that she was "very good" at being a tripmaster back in the 1960s, making sure that people went to "beautiful places" rather than "dangerous" ones (Seshachari 205). It is clear that Kingston's understanding of her work as a writer is connected to this guiding function.

The next book that Kingston published, *The Fifth Book of Peace* (2003), is a generic hybrid—part memoir, part fiction—that grows directly out of *Tripmaster Monkey* rather than Kingston's two earlier books on Chinese-American experience, though also drawing on the little-known *Hawai'i One Summer* (1987). The textual fusion between fiction and autobiography is especially visible in the chapter titled "Water," which is written as an extension of *Tripmaster Monkey*, with Wittman and his wife Taña moving to Hawai'i, but also as a lightly fictionalized memoir of the Kingstons' move to Hawai'i in 1967. The link between the Ah Sings and the Kingstons is provided by *Hawai'i One Summer*, which is a collection of sketches describing Maxine Kingston's life in Hawai'i and which provides much of the raw material for the contents of "Water."

Near the beginning of the "Water" chapter, Kingston describes the Ah Sings' first night in their new home. Although they have rented it, they tell their young son a bedtime story that rewrites their own arrival to the house as a Digger fairy tale. They tell him of a Prince and Princess who meet in an empty house and occupy it together in a counterculture tactic called squatting and end up living happily ever after with their little boy, whom their son recognizes as himself (91-91). Wittman and Taña also celebrate their new life by some smoking marijuana given to them by friends as a going-away present. Wittman is initially reluctant because he has given up drugs in general as a "political action," explained in *Tripmaster Monkey* as a gesture of commemoration of the way the British American Tobacco Company forced many Chinese into opium addiction in the nineteenth century.

Nevertheless, putting politics momentarily aside, Wittman smokes a joint with his wife and has a trip every bit as enlightening and grandiose as Bak Goong's opium dream on his passage to America. Wittman feels himself floating out of his house and across the ocean and around the world and back in time. He sees a rainbow across the North Pole and fires burning in Vietnam and he sees himself in previous lives with his wife, including one in the "Wild West." Fully alert on this journey, Wittman has "a sense of knowing the truth, aware of everything, even his doubts and having smoked dope ... He was not making this up, and not controlling the story" (92). Just like Bak Goong, Wittman realizes that "All is connected to all, and I am conscious of that, and I am conscious that I am conscious" (92).

Here again we have the essence of the value that the counterculture attributed to marijuana and psychedelics, that is, the ability to induce perception of the connections that are normally obscured by our social schemas and hierarchies. Also like Bak Goong, Wittman's drug experience is one of intense self-awareness, including the awareness that he has taken drugs. This state of heightened lucidity can be compared to the "mindfulness" that Kingston advocates through this book and her last one, a mindfulness that she associates with meditation but which clearly has some origins in the chemical experiences that came before meditation for many people who passed through the 60s counterculture. (In fact, meditation was for many an attempt to find a more natural alternative to the experience of tripping that had tacitly set the standard for mind-altering experiences.)

Perhaps because the whole book is structured around the theme of peace, the "Water" section of *The Fifth Book of Peace* claims its counterculture origins and values in a far more assertive and explicit way than even *Tripmaster Monkey* did. Shortly after arriving on the island, and tired of waiting to be formally welcomed by their neighbors, the Ah Sings decide to throw a welcome party themselves. With her signature combination of gentle irony and moral seriousness, Kingston suggests that her bohemian values have something to teach America about its own values and history:

> the nation that came together through gift-giving has broken down, or never was. It's up to us, the ones who know about potlatches, karasses, love-ins, and be-ins, to give a party. How to change society? Give it a party ... How to civilize kids? Give a party. How to radicalize Kahalu'u? [their new neighborhood] Give a party (162).

In this passage, Kingston claims for Wittman an identity rooted in the practices of the Berkeley counterculture and specifically its social events. For the Diggers, organizing free parties was actually a political tool meant to change the world, shifting its values playfully and gradually towards a more communal and less commercial and competitive register. In the same spirit, the Ah Sings hope to teach their neighbors to be friendlier, more open and welcoming, by welcoming *them* and teaching them neighborliness by example.

The Fifth Book of Peace is also full of nostalgia for the passing of those halcyon days. There are numerous references to the "good high days" of "free grass and legal LSD" when "a stranger walking by on Telegraph Avenue or in the Haight would have handed you a tab or a cookie for free" (90). While visiting another house nearby, where "hippie haoles [non-Hawaiian hippies]" party all night long, looking like "zombies and vampires," the Ah Sings can only regret that "the times and places of good trips are over" (165). Their standard of reference are the parties "back home in California" where "trippers had been such good talkers that they tape recorded themselves. Stoned, they rapped all night. Playing back the tape, they were still brilliant. Times have changed, drugs have changed" (165). The Ah Sings left Berkeley when the Summer of Love had turned dark, when overcrowding, under-aged runaways and hard drugs like amphetamines and heroine had changed the nature of the Haight-Ashbury scene into something much tougher and less wholesome. The specificity of this transformation and disappointment is visible in the passage above, where the silent stoned hippies next door fill the Ah Sings with regret for the sparkling psychedelic parties of their past.

The acuteness and clarity of the book's recognition that the drug experiences that partially formed the Ah Sings' vision and values are no longer possible (not for them nor for anyone, since those experiences were linked to a particular social context that was gone) is directly connected to the way *The Fifth Book of Peace* searches for alternatives to those experiences. These alternatives include meditation, "mindful living," reading and, above all, writing. All of these practices are tacitly offered as alternative tools for both tripping, taking meaningful mental voyages, and for creating communities or sanghas of mindful trippers and fellow-travelers. The most concrete example of this process is the phenomenally successful Veteran Writers Workshop. Since 1991, Kingston has run a workshop for veterans who want to write, and in 2006, she edited a collection of their stories and poems titled *Veterans of War, Veterans of Peace*. In the introduction, she wrote that humans "tell stories and we listen to stories in order to live. To stay conscious. To connect one with another. To understand consequences. To keep history. To rebuild civilization" (1).[8] In these six short

8. The echo of Joan Didion's *The White Album* (1979) is instructive here. While Didion also begins her book with the words "We tell ourselves stories in order to live" (11), and her book is also about the 1960s and Hawaii, her narra-

sentences, one can see the counterculture values that have informed Kingston's writing from the start: mindful living, self-awareness, community, spiritual connectedness, cultural memory and artistic production. All of these principles are basic to the counterculture, and while Timothy Leary would have argued in the 1960s that they are essentially linked to the conscientious use of psychedelics, for Kingston in *The Fifth Book of Peace* they are linked to the conscientious use of creative writing.

In her most recent book, *I Love a Broad Margin To My Life*, Kingston revisits many of the counterculture themes established in *The Fifth Book of Peace*. The drug references have receded into the background but the insights they produce and mind-altering experiences they assume are still present. Wittman Ah Sing is also back, this time explicitly as Kingston's alter-ego, who tells the story of her own return to China through Wittman's perspective. Kingston often explains her decision to use a male protagonist for *Tripmaster Monkey* in terms of the freedoms and dangers that defined men's lives in the early sixties, referring to the draft, among other things, as making men more "hip" and interesting than women, in her view. One thing for certain is that men had more freedom of movement than women in the early sixties. Her decision to fictionally travel to China in Wittman's body in *I Love a Broad Margin* seems to have a similar motive. At one point in the book, Kingston explains that Wittman, "a fiction, is free to befriend anyone" and can "enter the many places/in this world where a man is able and a lady/is not" (104). For instance, in Hong Kong, she has backpacker Wittman lie down in a public park and sleep. It would be harder to imagine a lone woman sleeping in a public space like this.

Interestingly, the dream that Wittman has during this nap recalls the drug trip he takes in *The Fifth Book of Peace* and to Bak Goong in *China Men*:

> On the grass in a city park, our male traveller
> feeling his lone hobo self, laid
> his body down with backpack for pillow.
> In San Francisco, it was 2 o'clock the night
> before. Going west from California's
> shores, jumping forward in time, he'd arrived
> at the house of maternity, the land of migrations.
> Sleeping in public, jet-lagged, soul
> not caught up with body, body
> loose from the soul, body trusted itself to
> the grass, the ground, the earth, the good earth,
> and rested in that state where dream is wake,
> wake is dream. Conscious you are conscious.
> Climb—fly—high and higher, and know:
> Now/Always, all connects to all. (60)

---

tive stance is so distanced and mediated by irony that Kingston's participatory engagement with the era stands out in stark relief.

Among other things, the passage above immediately reveals to what extent San Francisco remains Kingston/Wittman's center of reference, literally and figuratively speaking. If Wittman keeps track of the time in San Francisco while in another time zone, he also keeps those bohemian consciousness-expanding experiences as the Greenwich of his values and sense of self even when far from home. Accordingly, the passage includes references to the intense self-awareness described previously in drug trips ("conscious that you are conscious"), as well as a description of flight in which "high" is a literal perspective on the world (from above, like an omniscient narrator) as well as a state of mind. Finally the passage returns to the notion of universal interconnectedness ("all connects all") that defines Kingston's cosmology and has served as a refrain in her work since Great Grandfather in *China Men* realizes that every human being is "related" (*China Men* 95).

Another key counterculture principle that is reprieved in the book is the belief in the importance of perception and consciousness. At the heart of this principle is the notion that these are not passive but are active faculties that can shape and alter reality. Concretely, the counterculture viewed problems such as the Vietnam War and racism as products of ignorance and a dysfunctional mind-set which could be addressed through education and dialogue. Consciousness raising, teach-ins and psychedelic experience could all lead to major social changes because people would begin to perceive the world without the ideological blinkers that kept them in thrall to what Leary called the "fake-prop TV studio stage set that is called American reality" (Leary 3). A more radical version of this idea held that individual and collective acts of faith or will could influence empirical reality. Thus, Wittman's personal project after arriving in Hawai'i is not to write poems or plays but to "work on perception" (143). The stakes were high: "the way of seeing the world—even one person's seeing of it—could cause it, could change it ... End the war by knowing it to be over ... It's all connected, all related to all" (143).

This conviction, whether in its more esoteric or more moderate form, was the beating heart of the optimism of counterculture politics in all its forms. Accordingly, in *I Love a Broad Margin to My Life,* Kingston, who merges freely into Wittman's voice and body, writes: "I ended the war in Vietnam. I am determined, we shall stop warring in Iraq and Afghanistan" (117-8). Although Kingston is tongue in check here, the faith in the power of demonstrations and the agency of the individual to counter despair, quietism, and helplessness before political and historical events is very serious. Civil disobedience occupies such an important place in this book because it is a concrete example of individual actions combining into collective social agency. Mass social demonstrations are a precious legacy of the 1960s, along with street theater, culture jamming, and other forms of thoughtful, creative and playful protest. Kingston's book tacitly calls for a stop to the relentless trivialization of the 1960s and for an appreciation of the courage and achievements of a generation that refused—if only for a moment—the politics of acquisition and consumption that have increasingly shaped American culture since World War II.

A final value that Kingston's latest book tacitly rehabilitates is universalism, a concept that was crucial for 1960s political activism, but which lost favor in the wake of poststructuralist theory and multiculturalism (and the concern with "difference" central to both). Although Kingston's career has been defined by her identity as a "Chinese-American" writer, she has stressed from the beginning that she is not writing only as an Asian-American writer. The Chinese dimension of her life is a complex affair of family rituals, stories and history, acquired knowledge, and cultural practices, but her Chinese-ness is not some essential or defining quality. In an early essay, "Cultural Mis-readings by American Reviewers," Kingston insisted that she is an American writer and that *The Woman Warrior* is an American book. However, this insistence on her American identity is not a flag-waving nationalism but a reaction to the ignorant assumption on the part of critics that she is *not* American because of her Chinese parents and appearance. What is at stake for Kingston is not American identity per se but an objection to stereotyping and exclusion by exoticization. Instead of asking "Is this work typical of Chinese Americans?," Kingston suggests that we should ask, "Is this work typical of human beings?" (62). This question cuts to the core of Kinsgton's humanism, which is not based on traditional humanist notions of an essentialist subject so much as on her counterculture-informed commitment to the idea of human beings connected by relation and affinity, like a recombined family (as opposed to a blood-defined family). Universalism fell out of favor in the late 1970s, critiqued as Euro-centric and insensitive to real differences, but over-attention to cultural and racial differences can also inadvertently lead to their reification and essentialization. Kingston asks us to look beyond cultural and racial difference to perceive the inherent connectedness (not the same thing as sameness or "identity") between people.

In conclusion, Maxine Hong Kingston has been hitherto studied as a feminist and as a multicultural writer, but a recognition of her contribution to counterculture literature is long overdue. Hers is an authentic voice of the period, rapping out brilliant and unconventional prose firmly anchored in the culture and ethos of Bay Area bohemia. In addition to the usual comparisons to Leslie Marmon Silko and Toni Morrison, Kingston should be studied alongside Allen Ginsberg, Lawrence Ferlinghetti and Hunter S. Thompson. Precisely because the so-called hippie movement produced relatively little memorable literature, Kingston cannot be overlooked. Counterculture literature needs its female Chinese Beatnik as much as Asian-American literature needs its hippies and radicals. American literary studies can only become richer from relaxing some of its sub-disciplinary borders and remembering that "all is connected to all."

Works Cited

Blauvelt, William Satake. "Talking with the Woman Warrior." *Conversations with Maxine Hong Kingston*. Eds. Paul Skenazy and Tera Martin. Jackson: UP of Mississippi, 1998: 77-85.

Bonetti, Kay. "An Interview with Maxine Hong Kingston." *Conversations with Maxine Hong Kingston*. Eds. Paul Skenazy and Tera Martin. Jackson: UP of Mississippi, 1998: 33-46.

Bowers, Maggie Ann. *Magic(al) Realism*. New York: Routledge, 2004.

Braunstein, Peter, and Michael William Doyle. *Imagine Nation: The American Counterculture of the 1960s and 70s*. New York: Routledge, 2002.

Chin, Marilyn, and Maxine Hong Kingston. "A MELUS Interview: Maxine Hong Kingston." *MELUS* 16.4 "Toward the Multiculture" (Winter 1989-1990): 57-74.

D'haen, Theo. "Postmodernisms: From Fantastic to Magic Realist," *International Postmodernism: Theory and Literary Practice*. Eds. Hans Bertens and Douwe Fokkema. Amsterdam: John Benjamins Publishing Company, 1997: 283-293.

Didion, Joan. *The White Album*. New York: Farar, Straus, and Giroux, 1990.

Farber, David. "The Intoxicated State/Illegal Nation: Drugs in the Sixties Counterculture." *Imagine Nation: The American Counterculture of the 1960s and 70s*. Eds. Peter Braunstein and Michael William Doyle. New York: Routledge, 2002: 17-40.

Kingston, Maxine Hong. *I Love a Broad Margin to My Life*. London: Harvill Secher, 2011.

—. *The Fifth Book of Peace*. New York: Vintage, 2003.

—. *Tripmaster Monkey*. New York: Vintage, 1989.

—. *Hawai'i One Summer*. San Francisco: Meadow Press, 1987.

—. "Cultural Mis-readings by American Reviewers." *Asian and Western Writers in Dialogue*. Ed. Guy Amirthanaygam. London: Macmillan Press, 1982.

—. *China Men*. New York: Vintage, 1977.

—. *The Woman Warrior*. New York: Vintage, 1975.

Leary, Timothy. "The Molecular Revolution." *Turn On, Tune In, Drop Out*. Oakland: Ronin Publishing, 1965:112-141.

Lott, Eric. *The Disappearing Liberal Intellectual*. New York: Basic Books, 2006. PAGES

Madsen, Deborah. *Maxine Hong Kingston*, Literary Masters Vol. 9. Detroit, MI: The Gale Group, 2000.

Marcuse, Herbert. *One-Dimensional Man: Studies in the Ideology of Advanced Industrial Society*. Boston: Beacon Press, 1964.

McCulloch, Scott. "Psychedelic Writing: Is a Literary Genre Based on Psychedelia Possible?" Online article at the Literary Culture website:

http://www.suite101.com/content/psychedelia-in-writing-a14044. Written February 17, 2007. Accessed on June 5, 2011.

McKenna, Terence and Dennis. *The Invisible Landscape: Mind, Hallucinogens, and the I Ching*. San Francisco: Harper, 1975.

Roszak, Theodore. *The Making of a Counter Culture*. Garden City: Anchor Books, 1969.

Savio, Mario. Transcript of "Gears Speech" of December 2, 1964. Available online at: http://jasondylan.wordpress.com/2010/04/20/mario-savios-1964-berkley-gears-speech-and-its-2009-remembrance-and-reaffirmation/ (accessed July 24, 2012).

Seshachari, Neila C. "Reinventing Peace: Conversations with Tripmaster Maxine Hong Kingston." *Conversations with Maxine Hong Kingston*. Eds. Paul Skenazy and Tera Martin. Jackson: U of Mississippi P, 1998: 192-214.

Shan, Te-Hsing. "Life, Writing, and Peace: Reading Maxine Hong Kingston's *The Fifth Book of Peace*." *Journal of Transnational American Studies* 1.1 (2009): online journal.

Summer of Love. Dir. Gail Dolgin and Vicente Franco. Produced by PBS (Public Broadcasting Service). 2007.

Ting, PP. "The Ballad of Mulan." Trans. William H. Nienhauser. *Sunflower Splendor: Three Thousand Years of Chinese Poetry*. Eds. Wu-chi Liu and Irving Yucheng Lo (Bloomington: Indiana UP, 1975): 77-80.

Wong, Sau-Ling Cynthia. "Autobiography as Guided Chinatown Tour?: Maxine Hong Kingston's *The Woman Warrior* and the Chinese American Autobiography Controversy." *Maxine Hong Kingston's* The Woman Warrior*: A Casebook*. Ed. Sau-Ling Cynthia Wong. New York: Oxford UP, 1999: 29-56.

Zamora, Lois Parkinson, and Wendy B. Farris. "Magical Romance/Magical Realism." *Magical Realism: Theory, History, Community*. Durham, NC: Duke UP, 1995: 497-550.

Maxine Hong Kingston's Peace Activism: Taking Stock

Christine Lorre-Johnston (Université Sorbonne Nouvelle—Paris 3, France)

In her latest two books, Maxine Hong Kingston's personal voice is more present than in her earlier work, which had a clearer fictional bent. In *The Woman Warrior* (1976), *China Men* (1980) and *Tripmaster Monkey* (1989), she explored her heritage as a Chinese-American, starting from autobiography or family history to launch into fiction. In *The Fifth Book of Peace* (2003), she relates her quest for peace at a time when the United States, which was still dealing with the inheritance of the Vietnam War, became involved in war in Iraq. The Vietnam veterans' writing workshop that she conducts is one of the forms the quest takes, and the book is dedicated "to veterans of war, veterans of peace." Obstacles and failure are part of the search undertaken by Kingston, who lost the manuscript of the book of peace she was writing when a fire destroyed her house in 1991. The tone of *I Love a Broad Margin to My Life* (2011), which takes the form of an epic poem, is largely meditative: Kingston looks back at her ancestors, at her parents' legacy and her links to China (where she travelled), and takes stock of her life and writing, facing her mortality.[1] Both these later works can be read as books of maturity that celebrate and reflect on the author's lifelong quest for speech, origins and peace. They signal a significant shift in perspective.

This shift is explicitly stated in an article that appeared originally in *Mother Jones* in 1989, just after *Tripmaster Monkey* was published and Kingston had the first inkling of the book of peace. In *Tripmaster Monkey*, Wittman Ah Sing, Kingston's fictitious alter ego and Walt Whitman's namesake, appears for the first time, playfully alluding to the writer's formative years and the predicament of Chinese-Americans, and humorously envisioning a new form of national American epic. Writing about what her next book might be after *Tripmaster Monkey*, Kingston observes that "[w]e need a sequel to adolescence" ("Novel's next Step" 13), further arguing that "[t]he dream of the great American novel is past. We need to write the global novel. Its setting will be the United States, destination of journeys from everywhere" (16). How can this global novel be written? Kingston explains: "Wittman has to break open the Chinese-American consciousness that he built with such difficulty and be a world citizen. And Taña has to use the freedom the feminists have won. These struggles have got to result

1. I am setting apart *Hawai'i One Summer* (1978) and *To Be the Poet* (2002), which are composed of shorter collected pieces.

in happy endings for all" (17). Kingston thus proposes to move beyond the feminist and ethnic struggle of the 1970s, both of which obtained major advances, to work across established categories such as gender and race, and advocate peace. This shift in Kingston's perspective on American society mirrors the country's general evolution in the way it sees itself, from preoccupation with internal strife linked to the civil rights movement and the ethnic movement of the 1960s and 1970s, to a renewed, broader approach of issues of democracy, justice and peace. It corresponds to a time when the United States has been assimilating the inheritance of the years of protest, and seeking to redefine its international role after the end of the Cold War.

These intimate links between Kingston's writing and the history of the United States appear in particular in the way she plays on autobiography and fiction: *The Woman Warrior* is subtitled "*Memoirs* of a Girlhood Among Ghosts" (emphasis mine)[2]; *China Men* is a fictitious reconstruction of her father's and other forefathers' story to fill in details about their lives that she never heard; in *The Fifth Book of Peace*, fiction is interspersed with sections that read like journal or memoir; and the narrative voice in *I Love a Broad Margin to My Life* shifts from Wittman Ah Sing, her fictive hero and male alter ego, to Maxine, the implied author. The critic Robert Sayre has made some essential comments on American autobiography; specifically, he has observed that "American autobiographers have generally connected their own lives to the national life or to national ideas" (149), and that to some of them, "citizenship, in the broadest sense, is a major issue in their total development" (168). These remarks seem especially relevant to Kingston's works and illuminate how her holistic approach to issues of peace and war, and of democracy, is inseparable both from her personal history and from American history. Her perspective inscribes itself in an American intellectual tradition of protest that strives for peace—as opposed to conquest—and whose titular figures, both in American intellectual history and in Kingston's own development and writing, are Henry David Thoreau and Walt Whitman. It is also influenced by Buddhism and its philosophy of nonviolence.

How much can be achieved through protest, civil disobedience and peace activism? In her last two books Kingston, taking stock of the protest against the war in Iraq, has to acknowledge that protest failed to stop the war. The emblematic episode of the 2003 International Women's Day, which is related in both books, is proof of that. Yet, by continuing to argue in favour of peace, she maintains her belief in the educational and prophetic role of the artist. Focusing on *The Fifth Book of Peace*, I will analyse the development, achievements and limits of Kingston's peace activism, by examining the notions of family and

---

2. In response to a question regarding the ambiguous autobiographical status of *The Woman Warrior*, Kingston suggests reading it as autobiographical "in some ways" (Kubota 2).

sisterhood as analogies of nation and feminism, the notions of community and civil religion as forms of integration in American society, and the enduring value—and limits—of America as utopia.

Family and sisterhood

Kingston's mother reminds her in her dreams that her role as a teacher is to "go teach the big family. Teach the nation family" (*Fifth Book* 241-42). The mother's imagined words thus pave the way for a renewal of the classical analogy between nation and family, in yet another instance of Kingston's remembering the wisdom of her elders and adapting it to her time and place. The "big family" is implicitly opposed to the smaller one, which may be understood as the Chinese-American community. This leap from ethnic community to nation signals a development in the conception of community activism and, more than a change of scale, a change of perspective. For American society to be united, it is necessary to work with all the various groups that make up that society. This is different from the 1960s, when the focus was on various ethnic groups whose rights and place in American society needed to be defended—separately together. The perspective implicit in the mother's words is a national one in which ethnicity takes second row, the uniting focus being on peace, at home and abroad.

The notion of intersectionality is relevant to our reading of Kingston's quest for peace here. Patricia Hill Collins recalls how the term was coined when, "[i]n the early 1980s, several African-American women scholar-activists called for a new approach to analyzing Black women's lives. They claimed that African-American women's experiences were shaped not just by race but also by gender, social class, and sexuality" (79).[3] Intersectionality thus examines how gender, race, class and nation mutually construct one another. More specifically, Collins points out that "the family functions as a privileged exemplar of intersectionality in structuring hierarchy" (77), through various related notions such as natural equality, racial unity and solidarity (also referred to as "blood ties"), home and gender roles, neighbourhoods, nation and nationalism, rights and responsibilities. Having reviewed a complex system of multiple, linked forms of oppression, Collins concludes positively that "[b]ecause the family functions as a privileged exemplar of intersectionality in structuring hierarchy, it potentially can serve a similar function in challenging that hierarchy [...], reclaiming notions of family that reject hierarchical thinking may provide an intriguing and important site of resistance" (77). Consequently, she suggests "reclaiming the language of family for democratic ends and transforming the very conception of family itself" (78). I would like to argue that Kingston, through her work and

3. Many thanks to Hélène Quanquin for bringing my attention to this article.

especially in *The Fifth Book*, participates in the broad enterprise of challenging the established order and existing categories that Collins mentions.

In *The Fifth Book of Peace*, prompted by her dream of her mother, Kingston endeavours to "teach the nation family." Family is not a particularly prominent motif throughout the rest of the autobiographical sections of the book, but the mention of the author's "sister writers" in the epilogue is significant. Kingston and other women activists are demonstrating for peace in front of the White House on International Women's Day in 1991: "The spirit of Yin—a feeling of peace and love—suffused everyone, including counterdemonstrators and police officers. [...]. The police carefully arrested two dozen women, including me and my sister writers—Rachel Bagby, Susan Griffin, Alice Walker, and Terry Tempest Williams" (402). "Sister writers" implies fellowship in trade, but also in ideas. "Sister" suggests feminist (and feminine) sisterhood, a notion which itself originated amongst the black community—"sisters" and "brothers" referring to all the members of the black community, regardless of blood ties. Yet the term has no racial connotation here, quite the opposite: Rachel Bagby and Alice Walker are African-American, and Susan Griffin and Terry Tempest Williams are white. There is no racial divide in this feminist sisterhood. But there is a gender line, as all the protesters are women—and the police are male.[4] However, these women are protesting, not for women's rights specifically, but for the benefit of men and women together. For as Kingston explains in a 2003 interview, she believes that women who joined the military during the war in Iraq, and women senators who defend their right to join, have the wrong idea: "We should work for men to have equal rights—not to join the military or go to war" (Jaggi). Such pacifist ideas, which involve a reversal of gender perspective, have not yet been imposed as a predominant view.

Kingston's phrase, "the spirit of Yin—a feeling of peace and love," reads like a translation into American cultural language, with its reference to the 1960s hippie movement, of a concept originally Chinese, but by now familiar in its broad lines to most readers. Kingston is thus importing and adapting to American culture a foreign concept, stirring it into the melting pot of moral values. The mention of the counterdemonstrators and the police officers being taken over by the warmth of the moment, even though the women get arrested for trespassing in the White House area, suggests that this was a mild confrontation, almost a soft replay of more aggressive and dramatic ones during the Vietnam War. Susan Griffin's testimony of that day is revealing:

> I felt calm [...], despite the fact that I could no longer bend my 60-year-old arthritic knees [...]. It was only after we moved still further, right in front of

4. See Kingston's BBC interview with Mishal Husain, 8 March 2011. Warm thanks to Sämi Ludwig for signaling the two BBC interviews referred to in this paper.

> the fence, to the zone that has been illegal since 9-11, that without fanfare and with the greatest politeness and consideration, the arrests finally began. In the annals of resistance, we were not especially heroic. (Griffin)

Civil disobedience, always first a symbolic gesture of protest against one's government, is being performed, and there is insistence on the protesters' part on performing it to its conclusion, that is to say, arrest. It is by then a well-rehearsed protocol, and the protagonists each play their part. This is not where passionate confrontation is to be found—it crops up instead in Kingston's workshop, where the old and venomous wounds of the Vietnam War resurface, and sisterhood is challenged.

As a feminist, Kingston is convinced that women have a special role in creating or repairing community and promoting peace. The workshop proves that this ancient idea, that women can bring relief to men in war times, largely corresponds to the way the Vietnam War was experienced by men and women. Kingston reports that "one Anonymous Veteran wrote explaining to me why veterans need to report to women. Yes, women are sanctuary; women bring soldiers home. But also women need to hear the war stories" (*Fifth Book* 247-48). Lily Adams, a participant in the workshop, played this role during and after the war: she "identifies herself as a triage nurse in Viet Nam, now a readjustment counselor at the San Francisco Vet Center" (263). Jean Watson, another participant, reads about

> working as a nurse in a burned-out village. [...]. Women pick up the pieces. Waist, hip in blood. It was our job to fix the wounded. Help them return to battle to kill again. Women follow the soldiers and the war. I was sisters with the Vietnamese women selling sex to the soldiers... Now, working for peace is my obsession... Women transmute war. (345)

Jean's experience crosses racial and moral barriers, and her sense of sisterhood includes Vietnamese prostitutes. Like other women veterans, she became reluctantly involved in the war, and has been doing her best since to bring relief to the soldiers. Many spouses of soldiers in Vietnam, though not veterans themselves, played a similar role through letter writing; Edie Heineman is one of them. She "speaks about writing letters to her husband every day when he was in Viet Nam. [...]. She wrote him the details of life back home, the daily events, the ordinary activities of family and friends, school. 'Nothing important, not about the war.' She wrote him safe; she wrote him home" (291). All these testimonies reinforce a well-established pattern of gender roles in times of war, with women alleviating the pain of it, and "transmuting" it into peace.

This potentially essentialist-sounding position is quickly challenged and put in perspective during the sessions of the Veterans Writing Workshop, when Kingston also hears a lot of "women warrior stories" (304)—stories from women who are ready to fight for what they believe in. She reports two very different cases. Woman Vet, one of the workshop participants, feels insulted when she is mistaken for a Doughnut Dolly—that is to say a Red Cross Vietnam girl: "We women went to Viet Nam for many of the same reasons you men did—out of a sense of duty, loyalty, adventure, or patriotism" (318). Woman Vet lashes out at Grace Paley and "hippies from Berserkeley, ... cowardly stay-at-homes, ... hypocrites, ... partying while servicemen and servicewomen were risking their lives. ... I was against the war, and I went to Viet Nam. Responsibility and patriotism moved me" (345). This woman reveals how deep the gap is, still, within American society, between veterans and pacifists. Kingston's greatest challenge in the workshop is to get American Vietnam War veterans, who are able to reconcile themselves with North Vietnamese veterans, to do the same with American peaceniks. This is achieved by a hugging meditation which turned participants to the workshop into a "mass of loving humanity" (396). In contrast to Woman Vet, Lee Minh Khue, a North Vietnamese guest participant in one of the sessions, remembers the war as "the most wonderful time. I felt love. I felt romance" (355). Kingston is dismayed by her lack of awareness: "Khue is not the woman warrior I wished for" (355).

In the same way as she revisits family ties and sisterhood, Kingston revisits the notion of home. She considers *The Woman Warrior* "a women's liberation story, and [...] a war story," and sees it now as "a homecoming story. Fa Mook Lan leads her army home from war. She shows the troops herself changing back from a man to a woman, and gives them a vision of the Feminine. It is possible for a soldier to become feminine. Veterans can return to civil society; they do not have to be homeless" (390). In Kingston's vision of home, women play a crucial part, but they are not necessarily related as spouses or mothers. The symbolic family that welcomes the veterans home is made up of various people, in fact as varied a group as is possible. What matters is for communication to be (re)established. Family and home are thus reconfigured, and through the redefinition of these tropes, a new vision of the community emerges, the smaller community reflecting the larger one.

Community and civil religion

In "Fire," the first of the four sections of *The Fifth Book of Peace*, which tells the story of the fire that devastated the Oakland-Berkeley hills in October 1991 and destroyed Kingston's house, she laments the community that was lost to the fire, and describes it with great fondness—a range of neighbours from various ethnic and socio-economic backgrounds, and quite different histories:

> We had blind-chosen one another at random, and were not trying for it, but we'd gathered a community. [...]. We were integrated in a way that I've not seen in other places: rich people and not-so-rich people lived side by side. Big houses were hodgepodged with little houses, a villa next to a cottage, a mansion next to a bungalow. Some of us were owners, and some were renters.

> We did have a go-around once with a petition to zone out renters, but few people signed it. (18, 20)

The community that Kingston evokes is symbolic of a rare form of social integration. It could be said to embody the ideal community wished for by civil rights fighters in the 1960s and, more generally, by advocates of social change and equality. The symbolic associations that Kingston establishes between the destruction of this community by fire and the destruction brought to Iraq by the United States suggest that the consequences of the 1991 Iraq war are to be felt in the United States, too: the social fabric is deteriorating, is being destroyed again. There is a sense of the repetition of history, of lessons from the Vietnam War not having been heeded, and of a need to rebuild the community after destruction—that is, not simply Kingston's local neighbourhood, but the community of the American nation at large. This is what Kingston feels she can do as a teacher, and a moment of revelation comes when the jade heart that her mother gave her a long time ago is found again amongst the ashes of her house. "Jade for a peaceful heart. Jade, a sign of being Chinese. [...]. My jade heart has returned to me; I have to pacify the world" (32). She then starts the Vietnam veterans' writing workshop, and comes to realize that her own project for a Book of Peace, the manuscript of which was lost in the fire, is tightly linked to the workshop: "[T]he fire's aftermath [...] gave me the method of how to write it—with others, in community" (40). Her memoir about the workshop eventually makes up "Earth," the fourth part of *The Fifth Book of Peace*. In the genealogy of the book, Kingston's experience of social integration and her Chinese heritage work together towards defining her vision of America, and the book she needs to write.

Kingston's vision of community is manifold. Talking to a BBC documentary-maker about community, she tells him about

> Sangha. The Buddhist word for the community that lives in peace and harmony is "sangha". [...]. Build the community with resources at hand, whatever's, whoever's here, whoever shows up, whoever happens by. Make community, *communitas*, sangha of those people in your apartment building, on your street, at your job, wherever you are. (364)

Even though Kingston's sense of the importance of renewing community bonds is influenced by Buddhism, it cannot be said to be strictly religious, but appears as a civil version of Buddhist religious principles. Kingston turned to Buddhism in the 1960s, after reading the Beat poets who went to Asia and brought Buddhism back to the West and to young Americans (see Kingston, "Buddhism," 177-78).[5] But the way she suggests adopting and adapting these principles is also democratic, so that her definition of community can be

5. I am grateful to Nicoleta Alexoae Zagni for having pointed out this interview.

interpreted as a new form of civil religion that mixes Buddhism and democracy. She thus manages to redefine a core American value, by relying on the practice of civil religion, renewing at the same time the functioning of the melting pot by mixing in an Asian element.

It is worth noting that Kingston's injunction to "make community" is in keeping with a concept of democracy held forth by left-wing activists and social change advocates which came back to the forefront in the context of the Iraq war, when tension within American society started to grow again and conflicting understandings of patriotism were defended. To some, patriotism meant supporting the war in Iraq; to others who were opposed to the war, it meant making extra efforts to communicate and not let division poison American society again. Todd Gitlin, also a veteran of the Civil Rights movement of the 1960s, defines democratic patriotism, in a 2006 book entitled *The Intellectuals and the Flag*:

> The work of civic engagement is the living out of the democratic commitment to govern ourselves. [...]. Actual patriotic experience in a democracy is more demanding—far more so—than the profession of sentiments; [...] far more demanding than signifying loyalty to the regime. [...]. It may well require that we curb our individual freedoms—the indulgences that normally we count as the highest of values. [...]. These citizenly relationships are not ones we choose. To the contrary. (139)

Gitlin and Kingston share a certain idea of civic commitment; in Kingston's case, it consists in conducting workshops for Vietnam veterans. In doing so, she emphasizes the need to redefine American democracy along the lines of more understanding and community, against the grain of individualism and the hardening of viewpoints.

To come back to Buddhism, not only does it influence Kingston's vision of America, but she also brings Buddhism to the Vietnam veterans' writing workshop participants. The sessions are punctuated by moments of meditation, and at one point, one of the women participants in the workshop hands out copies of Buddhist moral precepts to other participants. Kingston remarks that "[t]he Precepts are not too different from the Bill of Rights. You could just as well put the First Amendment into practice. Speak. Write. Assemble. Practice a religion, or not" (336). There is confluence, rather than conflict, between Buddhist principles and the fundamental principles of the American Constitution. Again, in the limited sphere of the workshop, ethnic culture harmoniously contributes to democratic life. Can this process be repeated on a larger scale?

America as utopia

The better nation, or community, or "family" that Kingston envisages is based on a number of fundamental principles, such as education, activism, democracy, peace and social bonding. Kingston evokes a temple she saw in China that was built according to the idea that "EDUCATION HAS NO CLASS. Meaning that education is classless; anyone can learn" (*Fifth Book* 242, original capitals). What is presented as a Chinese precept that Kingston's mother keeps reminding her of as her personal duty, is also based on a certain idea—which she calls her "Idea" (capital I)—of American democracy, citizenship, and community. This idea is the belief that education can cross class borders, and that it is the basis of healthy social relations. It goes against greed and individualism, which Kingston ties to America's war-mongering spirit. Having lost all her possessions in the fire, she playfully responds to William Carlos Williams's famous statement, "No ideas but in things," with "No things but in ideas": "Things—red wheelbarrows, white chickens, rainwater—all gone, Idea remains" (21). Material possessions do not matter; ideals and the life of hearts and minds do.

Kingston believes her role is to foster reconciliation, and claims Walt Whitman as a literary and intellectual ancestor through the fictional character of Wittman Ah Sing in "Water," the third section of the book. A 1960s peace activist, Wittman Ah Sing is an ironic masculine avatar of Kingston who also enables her to establish a distance between herself and the idealism of her search for peace—in the same way as it enabled her to look back ironically at her younger self in *Tripmaster Monkey*, through the traditional Chinese character of the Monkey King. In "Water," Wittman, his wife Taña and son Mario leave the United States in protest against the government's Vietnam policy to go to Hawai'i where they try to live in agreement with their moral beliefs. A fictionalization of Kingston's own move to Hawai'i with her family in the 1960s,[6] "Water" is often comical, but nonetheless reinforces the notion of commitment to peace.

Irony in "Water" derives mainly from the fact that Hawai'i, which first appears as paradise on earth to the protagonist, was a crucial point for the United States on the way to Vietnam, as Wittman realizes once there. The natural beauty of the land, sunrise on the Pacific, are taken over by American military maneuvers: "The full sun came up out of the sea—roseate, golden ocean. And shooting stars made meteoric lines that streaked the sky, and lasted. They're jet trails caused by the planes taking off from the Kaneohe Marine Corps Air Station" (99). This realization forces Wittman to renewed anti-war activism, which he thought he had performed by leaving the American mainland and coming to Hawai'i. Everywhere are signs of the intrusion of the American military; walking around, Wittman sees a sign that reads: "KAPU / KEEP OUT /

---

6. See Kingston's memoir, *Hawai'i one Summer* (1987).

PROPERTY OF U.S. GOVERNMENT." His response is dictated by his resistance to the military: "PROPERTY OF U.S. GOVERNMENT means it's my property, my territory, my valley, my mountain. This land is my land. I am an American taxpayer walking on my land. Nobody kapu my 'aina. Nobody kapu me" (118). The form of Wittman's response is shaped by the tradition and rhetoric of civil disobedience. By removing himself from the United States, Wittman thought he would be able to live in retreat, as a sign of protest against the government's policy, a modern-day Thoreau retiring to the natural beauty of Walden Pond in protest against slavery and the Mexican War, refusing to pay his tax. The allusion in this passage to "This Land is Your Land," one of the stock protest songs of the 1960s, clearly ties Wittman to his times.[7]

Shortly after Wittman's arrival in Hawai'i, early forms of civil disobedience, relatively mild and symbolic, are used to express a refusal to be part of an economy and industry that support the military. When welcome by generous Hawaiians who urge him to take food with him, Wittman remains war-conscious: "He accepted paper plates full of meat except for pig, wrapped with Saran Wrap (made by Dow Chemical, who makes napalm)" (116). Even though his act of protest seems trivial, Wittman's analysis of the war situation in Marxist terms of how one relates to the means of production is revealing of a class awareness in the protest movement, in Noam Chomsky fashion, that examines the superstructure of American society for its ideological and political implications. But Wittman's main means of action lies elsewhere.

Wittman Ah Sing participates in the Sanctuary that is set up by the Church of the Crossroads, helping with writing Statements of Conscience, listening to soldiers tell their stories and find peace. The parallels between Wittman Ah Sing and Walt Whitman, "the healing poet of the American Civil War" (236), are explicit: "Wittman's namesake had spent the Civil War in hospitals, reading to the wounded, giving them nickels to buy milk, writing to their mothers, holding the dying in his arms, and kissing them goodbye" (234). Like Wittman, Whitman acted and wrote about war and democracy, advocating reconciliation after the Civil War, and celebrating the potential greatness of America.[8] In

---

7. A song originally written by Woodie Guthrie and published in 1945 in response to the Depression, "This Land Is Your Land" has since been associated with the left-wing's claims for more democracy. It was taken up in the 1960s by folksingers like Pete Seeger who defended international disarmament, civil rights and environmental causes altogether. More recently, it was sung in front of the Lincoln memorial by Pete Seeger and Bruce Springsteen at President Obama's January 2009 inauguration, following an election that raised huge hopes for yet more racial and social justice.
8. The poem entitled "Reconciliation," in *Leaves of Grass*, captures Whitman's spirit of national reconciliation: "For my enemy is dead, a man divine as myself is dead, / I look where he lies white-faced and still in the coffin—I draw

"Water," AWOL GIs can join the Sanctuary and become public about their opposition to the war—until after about a month the Sanctuary is busted by the forces of the American government. The Sanctuary plays an important role in enabling soldiers to "reveal themselves as being for peace in Viet Nam" (199). It is about free speech and civil disobedience as a means to protest, but it is also already about reconciliation.

As in *Tripmaster Monkey*, Wittman Ah Sing in "Water" is a fictitious projection of Kingston. Wittman listening to soldiers at the Sanctuary tell others about their war experience, or "talk story," resonates with Kingston's work with the participants in the veterans writing workshop. The sense that peace is a utopia is present in both parts of the book. Wittman, a more naive version of a pacifist, goes to Hawai'i in the hope that it will be removed from the war context, a haven from the violence of it, but such place seems not to exist: the U.S. military is everywhere, and peace is nowhere, a utopia, a no-place. Kingston knows that peace is utopian, but treasures symbolic experiments in peace such as Plum Village, the Buddhist community headed by Thich Nhat Hanh near Sainte-Foy-la-Grande in France. Talking to a BBC documentary maker, she observes "that Plum Village was a successful experiment in international community. Crossing, erasing, broadening boundaries, people had come here from all over the world [...]. And they were of various religious traditions" (389-90). These small-scale experiments have the value of moral statements about the possibility of international peace, which depends on the crossing of the various types of boundaries that separate people and prevent them from communicating constructively.

But Kingston's workshop, which brings her and the participants to meet in various parts of the United States, also has a deterritorialised dimension to it, even though it is rooted in American history. For Kingston, criss-crossing the country to help alleviate the pain of Vietnam veterans and help them find internal peace is a way to erase boundaries, to make people meet on different grounds, literally and figuratively. The fact that her memoir about the workshop is entitled "Earth" suggests both that it is a down-to-earth kind of job for a writer, but conversely, also refers to the fact that men should strive to find peace on earth, in particular by appreciating its natural beauties—the way Wittman admires the sunrise in Hawai'i, or Hawai'ians' sense of aloha, which is usually translated as love. There is a certain ecological dimension to Kingston's holistic approach, which is also found in the work of most of the sister writers she mentions in the epilogue, as well as in many of the folksongs of the 1960s, a search for personal development in harmony with one's environment, in one's community. As a 21st-century autobiographer, Kingston wants to cross or erase

---

near, / Bend down and touch lightly with my lips the white face in the coffin" (Whitman 321). See also "Ashes of Soldiers" (1865) and "Old War-Dreams" (1865-66) as examples.

regional and other borders that may yet separate Americans, and bridge them through communication and reconciliation, in order to unite a divided nation, and to repair a damaged national fabric.

This search for peace is not a state, but a process that happens in the present moment. It constantly needs to be created, and is only found in moments when communication can be achieved. Communication is what enables people to cross the borders that separate them from one another. Watching veterans talking to one another, Kingston is grateful for such moments, speaking in overtones of thanksgiving and prayer.

> Oh, I am so happy; I am happy watching over people in communication. [...]. This communication is what I live for. I am accomplishing the purpose of my life: to get each to communicate with each, and all with all. [...]. Oh, most wonderful world. For this day, I have made some of the world as I like it. May it last. (340)

Kingston's writing of *The Fifth Book of Peace* starts with a dream that prompts her vain quest for the Book of Peace, which supposedly originated with Chinese civilization, but quickly takes on a symbolic and universal dimension. She ends up writing the book of peace herself, concluding from her quest that "[t]he reasons for peace, the definitions of peace, the very idea of peace have to be invented, and invented again" (402). Peace is nowhere to be found, and in that sense, it is a utopia, but it is also to be created, always, and can be made real in small ways. This is how one can help create the state wished for by Thoreau: "I please myself with imagining a State at last which can afford to be just to all men, and to treat the individual with respect as a neighbor [... Such a state] would prepare the way for a still more perfect and glorious State, which also I have imagined, but not yet anywhere seen" (Thoreau 304).

At the end of *I Love a Broad Margin to My Life*, Kingston declares that she will stop writing. Bearing in mind the sections of the book that deal with the Iraq War and especially Operation Shock and Awe, which peace demonstrators couldn't stop from happening, this wish to stop writing may be read as an indirect avowal of defeat in the face of the persistence of war. This is also when Kingston takes leave of Wittman, the Monkey King, her travelling companion, by dissociating her narrative voice from his. Her perspective then becomes graver and slightly somber, as she is facing her own mortality, as if the degree of the merging of her voice with that of Wittman were a barometer of her faith in the possibility to change the course of things. By referring to Thoreau's taste for meditation in the title of the book, Kingston shifts to a more reflective mode.

Times of war are when the sense of nation—or community, to use Kingston's preferred word—comes under renewed scrutiny. The conflict in Iraq acted as such a catalyst for Kingston, and she returned to Thoreau's idea of civil disobedience, to Whitman's vision of reconciliation, reflecting on how to play her part in trying to bring America back together, through her work as a teacher and peace activist. She keeps challenging what American founding values, which have universal reach, are about in a global context, condemning the consequences of war. Although the action of American peace demonstrators like herself failed to stop the Iraq war, she believes in the impact of the role of the artist in the long term.[9] Ultimately, by inscribing herself as a writer in the American tradition of protest and peace activism, Kingston becomes part of that tradition and renews it, which is a way to invest in peacemaking for future generations.

Works Cited

Collins, Patricia Hill. "It's All in the Family: Intersections of Gender, Race, and Nation." *Hypatia* 13.3, "Border Crossings: Multicultural and Postcolonial Feminist Challenges to Philosophy" (part 2) (Summer 1998): 62-82.

Gitlin, Todd. *The Intellectuals and the Flag*. New York: Columbia UP, 2006.

Griffin, Susan. "Fearlessness." *Yes!* Summer 2003. http://www.yesmagazine.org/article.asp?ID=604, consulted 15 November 2008.

Husain, Mishal. "Is Gender Still an Issue?" BBC interview broadcast 8 March 2011. http://news.bbc.co.uk/2/hi/programmes/impact_asia/9419059.stm. Accessed 15 October 2011.

Jaggi, Maya. "The Warrior Skylark." *The Guardian*, 11 December 2003.

Kingston, Maxine Hong. *China Men*. New York: Knopf, 1980.

—. *The Fifth Book of Peace*. New York: Knopf, 2003.

—. *Hawai'i One Summer*. San Francisco: Meadow Press, 1987.

—. *I Love a Broad Margin to My Life*. London: Harvill Secker, 2011.

—. "The Novel's Next Step: From the Novel of the Americas to the Global Novel." 1989. Reprinted in *The Novel in the Americas*. Ed. Raymond Leslie Williams. Niwot, CO: UP of Colorado, 1992. 13-18.

—. *Tripmaster Monkey: His Fake Book*. New York: Knopf, 1989.

—. *The Woman Warrior: Memoirs of a Girlhood Among Ghosts*. New York: Knopf, 1976.

Lang, Kirsty. "Front Row. *Fair Game* Review and Author Maxine Hong Kingston". BBC interview by Kirsty Lang. Broadcast 9 March 2011 on BBC Radio 4. http://www.bbc.co.uk/programmes/b00z6dxj#p00fktr4. Accessed 15 October 2011.

Sayre, Robert. "Autobiography and the Making of America." *Autobiography: Essays Theoretical and Critical*. Ed. James Olney. Princeton, NJ: Princeton UP, 1980. 146-68.

9. See Kingston, BBC interview by Kirsty Lang.

Kubota, Gary. "Maxine Hong Kingston: Something Comes from Outside Onto the Paper." *Conversations with Maxine Hong Kingston*. Eds. Paul Skenazy and Tera Martin. Jackson: UP of Mississippi, 1998. 1-4.

Thoreau, Henry David. *Walden. On the Duty of Civil Disobedience*. 1849, 1854. New York: Rinehart, 1948.

Whalen-Bridge, John. "Buddhism, the Chinese Religion, and the Ceremony of Writing. An Interview with Maxine Hong Kingston." *The Emergence of Buddhist American Literature*. Eds. John Whalen-Bridge and Gary Storhof. Albany: State U of New York P, 2009. 177-88.

Whitman, Walt. *Leaves of Grass*. "Deathbed edition" 1892. New York: Norton, 1973.

The 'Engaged Aesthetics' of Maxine Hong Kingston's *Fifth Book of Peace*

John Whalen-Bridge (National University of Singapore)

With reference to Engaged Buddhism pioneers such as Thich Nhat Hanh and Sulak Sivaraksa, I will discuss some of Maxine Hong Kingston's recent writing and consider it as the 'aesthetic front' of this worldwide political-spiritual movement. Specifically, I wish to show that her 2003 book *The Fifth Book of Peace* can be considered as a form of 'Engaged Buddhism.' It is one thing to say that the book describes the practice of Engaged Buddhism, but I wish to go a bit further and argue that the book, both in terms of the author's composition and the reader's reception, is itself a form of Engaged Buddhism. My discussion will have three parts. First, in "Quietism, Modernity, and Engaged Buddhism," I will distinguish Engaged Buddhism from other kinds of Buddhism. Second, I will discuss Maxine Hong Kingston's *Fifth Book of Peace* to explore the degree to which we can make connections between literature and Engaged Buddhism. I will close with a brief consideration of "Art and Engaged Buddhism Engaged" to ask whether artistic practice can or should be considered a form of Engaged Buddhism.

Quietism, Modernity, and Engaged Buddhism

Engaged Buddhism is a modern trend primarily known for the integration of political activism with the cultivation of mindfulness, but it is not a mindfulness of the lone individual. Stressing the importance of understanding our mutual co-existence and interdependence, Thich Nhat Hanh writes in his book *Being Peace* that "[w]e are imprisoned in our small selves, thinking only of the comfortable conditions for the small self, while we destroy our large self" (68). Thich Nhat Hanh is saying that a self is much more than what is bound within our human skins: "One day I suddenly saw that the sun is my heart, my heart outside my body" (68). Thich Nhat Hanh calls this notion of interdependence "interbeing" (87), a formulation which can to some degree be considered a reaction to quietism. Ken Jones, a proponent of Buddhist-inflected political activism, notes that quietism—the complete or predominant withdrawal of the individual from worldly concerns—is a problem for many contemplative traditions, not just Buddhism. In *The Social Face of Buddhism*, a manual of sorts for Buddhist activists, he notes "an inherent danger of sinking into other-worldly quietism [that exists] in any meditative tradition" (Jones 99).

Jones notes, however, that Buddhism is commonly associated with quietism, since there "is the popular association of Buddhism with an other-worldly nirvana that lies beyond the sufferings of this illusory world" (203). Western scholars such as Max Weber have singled out Buddhism among religious for the separation of the individual from social responsibility: "Salvation is an absolutely personal performance of the self-reliant individual. No one, and particularly no social community, can help him. The specific asocial character of genuine mysticism is here [in Buddhism] carried to its maximum" (quoted in Jones 203). To some degree, we can say that this reduction of Buddhism to navel-gazing is an Orientalist fantasy-construction of the West, and the French scholar Roger-Pol Droit demonstrates how this portrait of Buddhism was assembled in his book *The Cult of Nothingness: The Philosophers and the Buddha.* Many Buddhist writers and scholars of Buddhism have refuted this charge, noting, for example, that Buddha presented a rather direct challenge to the caste system and that his decision to allow the ordination of women also challenged social morals of his time.

The consensus is that Engaged Buddhism is more or less a modern trend, although its exponents argue for a continuity between Buddha's earliest teachings and the practices of Engaged Buddhism. David L. McMahan in *Buddhist Modernism* notes the "explosion of socially engaged Buddhism onto the international scene," adding that the "transnational movement combines the traditional language of Buddhism on suffering, compassion, and liberation with that of emancipatory strains of modern western thought"—by which he means assertions on behalf of "human rights, social justice, equality, and women's rights" (251). Engaged Buddhists also participate in peace activism, advocacy for homeless and disenfranchised people, and calls for greater responsibility for the natural environment.

Sulak Sivaraksha acknowledges Thich Nhat Hanh as the one who coined the term "engaged Buddhism," and Sivaraksha finds especially useful the idea that people must do more than cultivate personal peace; it is necessary to work towards a healthy social structure, as well. In *Conflict, Culture, and Change* he writes that we must, to create a culture of peace, "begin by making society more just" (9). Sivaraksha emphasizes that peacemaking and non-harming (*ahimsa*) are *actions* rather than withdrawals from activity. He quotes the Prime Minister of Tibet's Government in Exile, Samdhong Rinpoche, to support this point. According to Samdhong Rinpoche, "Nonviolence is an action, not merely the absence of violence" (Sivaraksha, *Conflict* 3). Engaged Buddhism calls our attention to the gap between Buddhist practices such as meditation and devotion, on the one hand, and social and ethical responsibilities on the other. First and foremost, we see it as a movement that updates or renews Buddhism. Thich Nhat Hanh has said that terms like "engaged Buddhism" came out of essays and books he started writing in Vietnamese in 1954, books with titles (when translated into English) such as "A Fresh Look at Buddhism," "Buddhism Today," "Engaged Buddhism," and "Buddhism Renewed." These books were all written between 1954 and 1964, with the Vietnamese civil war as the primary backdrop. In 1964 he was exiled from Vietnam (Nhat Hanh, "History" 5-6). As important as war has been as a background to Engaged Buddhism, it is nonetheless important to stress that Engaged Buddhism does not focus on politics to the exclusion of all else—that would be completely beside the point. Engaged Buddhism, writes Thich Nhat Hanh in his history of the term, "is the kind of wisdom that responds to anything that happens in the here and the now—global warming, climate change, the destruction of the ecosystem, the lack of communication, war, conflict, suicide, divorce"—and so on (6). This approach to Buddhism foregrounds the importance of dependent co-arising, and Thich Nhat Hanh insists that Buddhist practice in not to be limited to the temple or the meditation cushion; rather, it should be part of one's whole life. In *Being Peace*—perhaps his most famous book—he is explicit about this point: "Engaged Buddhism does not only mean to use Buddhism to solve social and political problems, protesting against the bombs, and protesting against social injustice. First of all we have to bring Buddhism into our daily lives" (53).

Buddhism in Kingston's *Fifth Book of Peace*

Maxine Hong Kingston recounts Thich Nhat Hanh's explanation of interdependence and nonduality in a workshop for veterans of war:

> I remember Thich Nhat Hanh picking up a sheet of white paper, tearing it in half, and tearing it again, showing that there is no such thing as duality: the left cannot be rid of the right, and the right cannot be rid of the left. In paper, a poet is able to see a tree, and a cloud, and water, earth, and the sun. (266)

The lesson in Thich Nhat Hanh's paper-tearing is that it is a mistake, when resisting a social pattern that is conducive to suffering such a pro-war government, to consider others as one's opposite or enemy, and this lesson is especially important to those traumatized by war such as veterans.

There are five sections of this book. The first is "Fire," in which Kingston tells the story of how she came home from her father's funeral to find Oakland, California burning. Her house burned to the ground, and in it were the only copies of her long-awaited novel, *The Fourth Book of Peace*, the title of which is explained in her second section, "Paper." As a young girl, Kingston heard, or *thinks* she heard, stories about the mythical-or-real lost "Three Books of Peace." But no one she spoke to in her adult life could identify these books with any certainty, even though Kingston brought this question with her wherever she went, including Europe, the Far East, and Southeast Asia. When I was teaching in Okinawa, I had the good fortune to see Kingston electrify an audience with her account of her lost book, her search for the mysterious books of peace, and her utterly disarming and charming way of involving *any* audience in her quest: each listener was given the homework assignment of trying to find out where such books have existed—or how they *might* exist. Pieces of story began to find their way home, and Kingston has woven the quest for a peace-book into her own book, the *Fifth Book of Peace*.

When the Oakland fire destroys her neighborhood and her novel-in-progress, Kingston herself feels traumatized and reports being unable to continue her book. For Kingston, interdependence of a sort became her salvation as an author, in her practice of what we might call "communal writing." Several times, she mentions the American writer Ralph Ellison, who was not able to write his second novel because the anxiety of thinking about the lost novel was too great. Rather than suffer this isolation along, Kingston involved her readers in her literary composition, collecting their stories and working them into what would become *The Fifth Book of Peace*. At the end of the second section she presents three ideas that clearly link literary creation with the life-entering approach to Buddhism of Engaged Buddhism. First, she identifies the work of literature with compassion itself, writing that "Fiction cares for others; it is compassion, and gives others voice. It time-travels the past and the future, and pulls the non-now, not-yet into existence" (62). She says the narrator of her lost book, which should have been entitled *The Fourth Book of Peace*, was to have been Kuan Yin, "who has mercy on all characters."

Second, she commits to a writing process that embraces interdependence rather than individual self-assertion. Speaking of the writing study she lost in the fire, she says: "The garret where I wrote, which was just my height, burned. A sign. I do not want the aloneness of the writer's life. No more solitary. I need a community of like minds. The Book of Peace, to be reconstructed, needs community" (62) The third idea is that the struggle for peace will fail again and again, and then peace-makers must reconstruct peace out of ruin.

The third section is called "Water," and it is fiction rather than non-fiction; it continues the fictional storyline of Kingston's only completely fictional work, *Tripmaster Monkey*, but it takes the characters Wittman Ah Sing and his now-wife Tania to Hawai'i, where they are in flight from the militarized culture of America during the Vietnam War: "Don't think about it anymore. Quit reading the news about it. Curiosity also makes it grow. Let it go. Leave it behind" (65). Kingston finds new ways to help readers ask themselves why we put reality and fiction on different shelves. What are we doing when we make this distinction? "Water" will not stand alone as a novel or a novella, but that is an inadequate way to approach this beautiful and gentle variation of Kingston's signature "talk-story." This section of *The Fifth Book of Peace* is Kingston's attempt to reconstruct her lost novel, and it is clearly an incomplete fragment. But the fiction is the story of the frustrated attempt to create a sanctuary for veterans during the Vietnam War, and the inclusion of the frustrated fragment within the larger work of nonfiction is a demonstration of another important idea—also a literary correlative to Engaged Buddhism: the writer cannot settle for a tragic denouement but must keep writing until she finds a happy ending. To Kingston, the separation of fiction and non-fiction is itself a fiction. As she will demonstrate in a later section, the despair of readers and writers cannot be a final resting place. A powerful but desperate tragic ending would be an expression of the First Noble Truth, the truth of suffering or "dukkha," but it would not be a proper expression of the Four Noble Truths, which also include the Third Truth asserting the possibility of cessation and the Fourth Truth offering a set of approaches for achieving this cessation.

In short, the third section, "Water," is the story of a failed attempt to protect soldiers from war in the form of a failed work of fiction, but this literary expression of failure is not the end of *The Fifth Book of Peace*. Kingston will tell veterans of war who want to express their suffering in literary form that they must not stop until they find a happy ending, and the inclusion of failure—which is not failed conclusion—expresses her insistence that we can mindfully face failure without submitting to it.

The fourth section, "Earth," continues the theme of reconstruction. Kingston and her husband Earll must rebuild their house. American veterans of the Vietnam War must rebuild themselves. Kingston must continue to work and develop even after the catastrophic loss of her novel. She forms writing workshops to teach writing to veterans who wish to rebuild their minds and lives. This section of *The Fifth Book of Peace* applies mindfulness trainings of the sort described by Thich Nhat Hanh to her new work in which she develops writing workshops for veterans. Kingston specifically asks members of "the Community of Mindful Living, Buddhists, to help" her organize the workshops (248). In some of these workshops a meditation instructor connects the sort of walking meditation associated with Thich Nhat Hanh to the act of writing. The meditation instructor who participates, Kingston writes,

> connects the walking to the writing! 'There's no destination that we have to get to. We're walking to be walking.' The writer doesn't have to know where the story leads or ends. Build the road as you go. Step by step. You are mindful of every step and of inhaling and exhaling ... (268)

She finds various ways to integrate mindfulness practice with the work of literature, the work of remembrance, which is an acute problem especially for combat veterans who experience Post Traumatic Stress Disorder, who suffer from depression, and who must resist suicidal impulses and other manifestations of despair:

> The point is not to avoid these memories or to withdraw from the forms of social life that create such suffering. Thich Nhat Hanh writes: "Meditation is not to get out of society, to escape from society, but to prepare for a re-entry into society. We call this 'engaged Buddhism'" (*Being Peace* 45).

In the "Epilogue," in which Kingston discusses her own resistance to America's avoidable war in Iraq, she connects the peace-work she had practiced with the veterans, the imagination of a sanctuary in the fictional section, the concern about loss of the first section, and the dream of peace in the second section to America's current adventure in Iraq. She mentions many responses to 9/11, including a demonstration in San Francisco in which she and her husband Earll protested through Buddhist meditation: "Earll and I mustered with the Buddhists, who sat meditation in three or four rows on the grassy hill overlooking the excitement. We made an area of peace" (401).

Kingston very clearly ends her book with an event, a peaceful protest, that in no way stops the war in Iraq from developing, but there is a lesson in this activity as well. The mysterious "three books of peace" were never found, and her "Fourth Book of Peace" was destroyed in a fire, but *The Fifth Book of Peace* has come into existence. She writes: "The images of peace are ephemeral. The language of peace is subtle. The reasons for peace, the definitions of peace, the very idea of peace have to be invented, and invented again" (402). Every word of *The Fifth Book of Peace* is conditioned by the author's first sentence: "If a woman is going to write a Book of Peace, it is given her to know devastation" (3). Knowing peace is not escaping war and pain, but is rather an acknowledgement of the non-dual world in which we really live. But, as Thich Nhat Hanh often says, "Suffering is not enough."

Works Cited

Aitken, Robert. "Precepts and Responsible Practice," in *Engaged Buddhist Reader: Ten Years of Engaged Buddhist Publishing*, ed. Arnold Kotler. Berkeley: Parallax Press, 1996

Chin, Frank, Jeffery Paul Chan, Lawson Fusao Inada, and Shawn Wong, eds. *Aiiieeeee!: An Anthology of Asian American Writers*. Washington, DC: Howard UP, 1974.

Droit, Roger-Pol. *The Cult of Nothingness: The Philosophers and the Buddha*, translated by David Streight and Pamela Vohnson. Chapel Hill: U of North Carolina P, 2003.

Harris, Sam. "Killing the Buddha," in McLeod, ed. 293-99.

Jones, Ken, ed. *The Social Face of Buddhism: an Approach to Political and Social Activism*. London: Wisdom Publications, 1989.

Kingston, Maxine Hong. "Buddhism, the Chinese Religion, and the Ceremony of Writing: An Interview with Maxine Hong Kingston." Interview by John Whalen-Bridge, in *The Emergence of Buddhist American Literature*, eds. John Whalen-Bridge and Gary Storhoff. Albany: SUNY P, 2009. 177-87.

—. *The Fifth Book of Peace*. New York: Alfred A. Knopf, 2003.

—. *Hawai'i One Summer*. Honolulu: U of Hawai'i P, 1987.

—. "Home Again," in Nhat Hanh, ed., *For a Future*. Pp. 90-92.
—. *The Woman Warrior: Memoirs of a Girlhood Among Ghosts*. New York: Random House, 1976.
—, ed. *Veterans of War, Veterans of Peace*. Kihei, Hawai'i: Koa Books, 2006.
McLeod, Melvin, ed. *Mindful Politics: A Buddhist Guide to Making the World a Better Place*. Boston: Wisdom Publications, 2006.
McMahan, David L. *The Making of Modernist Buddhism*. Oxford: Oxford UP, 2008.
Nhat Hanh, Thich. *Being Peace*. Ed. Arnold Kotler, with illustrations by Mayumi Oda. Berkeley, CA: Parallax P, 1987.
—. "History of Engaged Buddhism." *The Mindfulness Bell: a Publication of Plum Village* 49 (August 2008): 4-9.
—, ed. *For a Future to Be Possible: Commentaries on the Five Mindfulness Trainings*. Rev. ed. Berkeley, CA: Parallax P, 1998.
Sivaraksa, Sulak. "Buddhism Is More than Meditation: A Conversation with Sulak Sivaraksa," interviewed by Katherine Marshall. http://networkedblogs.com/aMzkU [accessed 20 November 2010].
—. "A Buddhist Response to Globalization." Jones 285-90.
—. *Conflict, Culture, Change: Engaged Buddhism in a Globalizing World*, foreword by Donald Swearer. Boston: Wisdom Publications, 2005.
Tanahashi, Kazuaki. "Four Truths and Ten Laws." McLeod 301-2.

Out of the 'Chinese' Box: 'Literary' Life Writing in Maxine Hong Kingston's *Tripmaster Monkey* and *The Fifth Book of Peace*

Manuela Vastolo (University of Naples "L'Orientale," Italy)

Published in 2003, *The Fifth Book of Peace* is the latest prose text by Maxine Hong Kingston. Unlike her earlier books—*The Woman Warrior* and *China Men*, which are still at the center of the Asian American canon, and similarly to the latter works, *Tripmaster Monkey* and *To Be the Poet*, *The Fifth Book of Peace* has received many reviews but little attention by critics and readers at large. As reviews attest, one of the initial difficulties when confronted with *The Fifth Book of Peace* concerns the generic classification of the book: Clausen considers it a "long writing-out of peace logic" worth critical treatment as an autobiography, an anti-militarist tract, a memoir, and an Emersonian essay (5); Eastman calls it a "ghost" book on war (51); Hood sees it as a "hybrid book"; and, last but not least, in *The New York Times*, Shulman defines it as "a strange, scarred thing, pieced together from fragments" (8). To add a further twist, this generic blurring is employed to focus on the central themes of the novel—the active 'quest' for peace and the multiple methods utilized by human beings to cope with the physical and spiritual effects of war—which are uneasily included in the generic framework of traditional Asian American literature, thus defying the readers' horizons of expectation.[1]

This paper explores Maxine Hong Kingston's challenge to fixed genre definitions in order to draw out the arbitrary and ideologically grounded nature of generic classifications by examining the strategies she utilizes to 'literary-fy' her factual experiences and at the way the referential data are constantly de-realized and fictionalized.[2] More particularly, it aims to investigate her conscious use of the conventions of fictional narratives and her challenge to the conventional idea of a fictional plot as a well-built structure leading from a problem to a climax and then to a resolution and a happy ending, as well as the idea of character as a fully-fledged 'human being.'

This paper analyses the plot by drawing some comparisons with her first two books, *The Woman Warrior* and *China Men,* whose generic categorization, as is

---

1. I would like to thank Prof. Donatella Izzo for providing generous advice and reading several drafts of this essay.
2. For another perspective on Kingston's uses of genre, see Schultermandl.

widely known, has undergone a very long and heated debate.[3] (The use of the word "book" is deliberate: I am aware of its inaccuracy, but it is the most neutral word available for the purpose of this essay).

Conventionally, the novel in the traditional definition has a precise architecture and conveys clear meanings, even while they are layered.[4] Both *The Woman Warrior* and *China Men*, which have been labeled as non-fiction, are cleverly structured as traditional novels. There are balanced recurrences, leading metaphors, and a sophisticated use of ancient Chinese mythology intertwined with women's stories in *The Woman Warrior*, whereas Chinese and Western myths are juxtaposed to men's stories in *China Men*, which also has a completely symmetrical structure with the chapter "The Laws" in the center of the book.

The Fifth Book of Peace is well structured too: it is made up of four sections titled "Fire," "Paper," "Water," "Earth" and a short "Epilogue." As Gérard Genette (4) states, the paratext is a threshold between the world and the text, the textual area where an authorial strategy addressed to the readers is played out. The "Contents" page at the beginning of the book is extremely significant from this point of view: "Fire" and "Paper" are respectively defined as "A *true* story" and "The *history* of lost Books of Peace"; "Water" is defined as a "*fiction*"; and "Earth" as a "*nonfiction*"; while the "Epilogue" receives no definition. The programmatic juxtaposition of texts having a variety of reality statuses is stated from the very beginning of the book. As this paper shall demonstrate, Maxine Hong Kingston builds the non-fiction sections of the *Fifth Book of Peace* as if they were parts of a novel (as she did in her first two published books). Not only does she recreate recurrent patterns in the text, but she also weaves a complex intertextual connection with the previous texts.

In the "Fire" section, Kingston narrates her experience of the Oakland fire that took place in 1991 and in which she lost both her house and the manuscript of her book-in-progress: "I have lost my book—156 good pages" (3). It happened, as she says in the opening page of *The Fifth Book of Peace*, while she was participating in the full-month ceremony for her father's death: "I have lost my father" (3). The loss of her father, the loss of the house (which she constantly describes as a living thing, for example, "The house was prey, wholly swallowed by an orange translucent python" [21]), the loss of the manuscript (which she compares to the loss of a child), as well as the deaths of twenty-five other people in the fire, are conveyed through descriptions of dead nature, such as the recurrent image of burnt trees and black-and-white scenery. And black refers to mourning in the Western tradition just as white refers to mourning in the Chinese tradition.

---

3. For a synthesis of the debate, see Wong and Cheung.
4. Interestingly ethnic literature is often seen as lacking layers of meanings.

The fourth section, "Earth," focuses on the scars left by the Vietnam War in the minds of the veterans and draws a parallel with the first section, between her experience of the Oakland Fire and the Vietnam War: not only in the loss of many human lives, the images of explosions and fire, but also through some other elements such as colors: she quotes James Jones's description of the war: "The first thing you noticed was the color. There wasn't any. It was a black-and-white movie" (330). The Oakland fire and the personal losses of the first section become directly related to the social damage created by the imperialistic war in Vietnam.

On the other hand, the loss evoked in the first chapter is balanced by images of reconstruction and rebirth in the "Earth" section, where on a personal level, we find Maxine physically sowing the land, and we witness the regeneration of nature and the return of colors (255) as well as, on a community level, the "rebirth" of the veterans through the telling of their stories. The figure of the Phoenix, woven by Brave Orchid on a quilt brought from China, which is lost in the fire but which Brave Orchid promptly promises to sew again, becomes a perfect mise-en-abyme of the whole process (29). And mise-en-abyme is a figure of authorial control on the structure of a text. Moreover, the death of Maxine's father at the beginning of the first section is balanced by Brave Orchid's death at the end of the "Earth" section, again conveying the image of a perfectly structured text.

On an intratextual and intertextual level, female myths frame the novel: the story of Ming Hong, the new woman warrior, told by Brave Orchid to an adult Maxine in the "Paper" section, is balanced by the return of Fa Mu Lan in the "Earth" section, recalling Maxine Hong Kingston's celebrated first book (58; 391).[5] Furthermore, as an intertextual point, the image of fire and of burnt paper recurs in Maxine Hong Kingston's books on many occasions. It is not only her own books that get lost in a fire but also her father's book (28) and, significantly, her father's draft card too (4). Hence it could be argued that the author is creating a parallel between the Oakland fire and the San Francisco Fire and Earthquake in 1906. She describes that event in *China Men*, in the story of Ah Goong: he dies (probably) during the earthquake, swallowed by the cracking earth and what Maxine Hong Kingston describes as a "miraculous fire" (*China*

5. While the chapter "White Tigers" in *The Woman Warrior* contains a post-modern retelling of the Chinese legend, in *The Fifth Book of Peace* Kingston states that she is translating the version of the story she learned from Brave Orchid. If on the one hand this seems a jump back to the past, and it clearly evokes the first book, on the other hand it is a move forward: this version of the legend actually appears here for the first time. In relation to Kingston's whole oeuvre, the ideologically loaded question of the "original" version, as problematically conceived as the "first" version, undergoes another significant turn of the screw which would be worth analysing.

Men 149-50). The miracle that takes place on that occasion is the chance to claim American citizenship because all the papers that allowed citizenship to immigrants from China were lost in the fire. After the event, anybody could claim to be a legal citizen, stating that his/her papers had been burnt. So the material loss of the papers, which in this case on a representational level is the loss of a life, becomes in *China Men* the opportunity to gain and invent a new life. Similarly, in the *Fifth Book of Peace* the veterans' rebuilding of their lives through "new paper" on which they write their stories and sublimate their feelings in words, finds its equivalent in Maxine's own rebuilding of her book and her house.[6]

Tripmaster Monkey and the third section of *The Fifth Book of Peace*, "Water"—both featuring the same character, Wittman Ah Sing, in 1963 and then in 1969—present a systematic lack of any unifying structural device: the stories of almost a hundred characters are juxtaposed and there is only a loose chronological sequence in the events. To make short but significant examples, the lack of a closely knit structure can be epitomized by Wittman Ah Sing's long pointless stroll which takes place at the beginning of *Tripmaster Monkey*. Similarly, in the "Water" section of *The Fifth Book of Peace*, the long driving trip that he undertakes to return the car is constantly interrupted by digressions: the phenomenological reality surrounding Wittman keeps modifying his journey and leads him into a variety of adventures: he meets a Hawaiian community which asks him to join them, he becomes the target of a shooting person, he joins a Vietnam War protest (101-41). Moreover, everything is highly unlikely and far from any verisimilitude if we consider that these events concentrate in a single day with no premeditation.[7]

Some years ago in "The Novel's Next Step" Maxine Hong Kingston said: "There is a creative writing adage that the loaded gun in an early chapter has to go off later on. How to break that rule?" (37). In the *incipit* of *Tripmaster Monkey* there is a loaded gun: "There slid beside his right eye a black gun. He looked side-eyed for it. Here it comes. He actually crooked his trigger finger and—bang!—his head breaks into pieces that fly far apart in the scattered universe. [...]. He groaned. [...]. He was aware of the run of his mind, that's all. He was not making plans to do himself in" (3). That is all and no loaded guns will ever shoot in the whole book, at least not on the 'reality level' of the book. The generic principle underlying the novel—the linearity and the internal consequentiality according to a principle of logical causality—is unquestionably challenged.

6. These are Maxine's intent and desire, but we are confronted with the material difficulties of achieving them when veterans are unable to forgive the draft resisters.
7. Similarly, in *Tripmaster Monkey*, the marriage between Wittman and Taña happens suddenly and almost 'casually' (163).

The 'rule of the novel' is also explicitly put into question in *The Fifth Book of Peace*. In the first paragraph of the "Earth" section Maxine reflects upon her lost book, just reconstructed in the "Water" section, and says, "I wrote past the place where the burned book left off. But found no happy ending. The War in Vietnam won't come to a happy ending" (241): no resolution, no escapism is allowed in fiction; that is, on a formal level, a balanced structure by no way means the sine qua non condition for a novel.

Another founding category of the novel that is destabilized in both *Tripmaster Monkey* and *The Fifth Book of Peace* is the traditional notion of character. The complexity of this category, as Roland Barthes argues, lies in its intermingling of formalistic features—the character seen as a selection of differential traits—and an ideological surplus—the character as a living human being (74). Its connection to all the other categories of a novel, such as plot and point of view, and to the readers' continuous projection of a "person" on it, makes it central and worth exploring in Kingston's texts. What this paper will argue is that the way Wittman Ah Sing is constructed disrupts any concept of the well-rounded, realistic character, so as to convey a strong disorienting effect.

According to Barthes, it is the name that transforms a semiotic combination into an ideological effect; it is the name that directs us to an extratextual reality that is our reference frame; it is the name that "allows" a character to become a "person." The possible meaningful layers of the protagonist's name therefore are well worth analyzing, all the more so if we bear in mind the meaningfulness of all written characters in the Chinese language, which always literally convey a meaning. Thus a name like Wittman Ah Sing implies numerous references. First of all, as James Tanner has shown, it refers to the American 'revolutionary' bard Walt Whitman, who wrote poems in search of an American identity and an American language, exalting self-definition and self-representation, ready to speak to and for his people, willing to 'use' his poetry as a political tool. All these traits are projected through the name on Kingston's character. Wittman's surname, "Ah Sing," because of its resemblance to "I Sing," a recurrent phrase in *Song of Myself*, only reinforces this literary reference, upholding a new Chinese American version of self in *Tripmaster Monkey*. A second literary reference enmeshed in the protagonist's name is Bret Harte's poem "The Heathen Chinee," in which the name of the main character is Ah Sin, as well as Bret Harte and Mark Twain's play entitled "Ah Sin."

In *Tripmaster Monkey*, and to some extent also in *The Fifth Book of Peace*, the interweaving of literary allusions multiplies if we consider the numerous similes between Wittman and literary characters and authors, such as Rainer Maria Rilke, Malte Laurids Brigge, Jack Kerouac, the Chinese Monkey King, James Joyce, Ernest Hemingway, Billy Budd, just to name a few.

Moreover, in the "Water" section of *The Fifth Book of Peace*, the constant turning of Wittman's thoughts into generic descriptions of Hawaiian nature, history, surroundings, characters, which gradually increases towards the end of the section, does not allow any psychological depth in which readers could follow him. The overall effect is that of a character almost 'performing on a stage' rather than a 'living being,' a character that is built and explained in language rather than shown in action, whose cultural milieu is composed of myriad strands, which offer so many multiple, fragmentary hints to the readers as to ultimately leave them disoriented. Both in *Tripmaster Monkey* and in the "Water" section of *The Fifth Book of Peace*, Wittman is constructed as a trickster figure taken to a sort of absurd conclusion through the verbal profusion pervading both narrative textures.

Even an analysis of the sources used by Maxine Hong Kingston in each of her books demonstrates her more than complex relation to fiction and nonfiction and the impossibility of any easy categorization. In *The Woman Warrior* and in *China Men*, a great part of the material cannot but be fictional, either because it is mythical or because it is the result of Brave Orchid's talk-story in the first place, and consequently already narrative, while in *Tripmaster Monkey* and in *The Fifth Book of Peace*, Kingston processes her experiences in Berkeley as well as her life in Hawaii with her husband and son in the fictional mode. Furthermore, in the last two books the correspondences between Wittman's life and her own are numerous: same age, same place of study (Berkeley), same interests (literature), both are writers and each married a white artist. Finally, Wittman's last monologue contains long quotations from a well-known article that Maxine Hong Kingston published in response to the reviews of *The Woman Warrior*, entitled "Cultural Mis-readings by American Reviewers."

In *The Fifth Book of Peace* the fictionalization of the author's own life is explicitly acknowledged in the two non-fiction sections framing the fictional one: at the end of the "Paper" section she says: "I should be able to write again about the time during war when Earll and I took our son, Joseph, and left to live in Hawaii" (62), while at the beginning of the fourth section we read: "Fiction won't tell me what's happened to 'Eddie' and 'Sam' and 'Sheraton' [these are the fictional characters in the previous chapter], people Earll and I knew in our real Hawaii years" (241). Thus in one of her interviews Maxine Hong Kingston herself goes back to the question of genre and says: "There ought to be a genre called 'nonfiction-and-fiction.' Or 'fiction/nonfiction.' 'Novel' is a good word, simply meaning 'new.' Strange that it's been co-opted to mean 'fiction.' There are fiction novels and nonfiction novels. The working name that I made up for the form that I was writing is: 'A fiction-nonfiction sandwich'" (WaterBridge Review 84).

What is the intended function of this continuous destabilization of generic boundaries? To try to provide an answer to this question, I will start from this novel's effect on its readers and critics. Kingston's earlier texts are still at the center of the Asian American canon and are still widely read and discussed at major universities, yet the latest books have not received much attention either by critics or by readers. On the one hand, this might be ascribed to the fact that

Maxine Hong Kingston is forcing the categories through which we read a novel: her last two novels create an objective difficulty, a zero degree of readability (what Roland Barthes calls "lisibilité") because they fail to match the expectations of the readers. On the other hand, Maxine Hong Kingston seems to be forcing the categories through which we read an Asian American novel. Racial identity is no longer the central issue in *The Fifth Book of Peace*, nor is the author interested in other issues on which critical attention has been increasingly focused over the last few years, such as diaspora. It is very difficult to place this book within the existing academic and editorial frameworks for the Asian American novel and it is difficult to identify the audience that Kingston is currently addressing.

In a 2004 interview Kingston said: "I think that having two categories—fiction and nonfiction—is too small. I picture a border between fiction and nonfiction, and I am making that border very wide; fiction is a narrow place on one side and nonfiction is a narrow place on another side, and there's this great big border in the middle, in which real life is taking place and also fantasies and dreams and visions" (Schroeder 216). Could it be that, through her systematic destabilization of generic boundaries, Maxine Hong Kingston is reversing the novel and life, fiction and non-fiction? "Things that fiction can't solve must be worked out in life" (241), she writes at the beginning of the "Earth" section.

The "Epilogue" of *The Fifth Book of Peace* is a very short section that differs extremely from the others for its content and the way it is written.[8] The events narrated take place right after 9/11 and then in March 2003. Maxine tells the experience of her arrest, together with other women, during a protest against the war in Iraq, and denounces the silencing and censorship the government enacts against the journalists and the photographers that are present and willing to record the event (402). In many ways this is a transgression of all the categories of fiction: it forces open the literary grid in order to reflect metafictionally on the reality and the function of the writer, not only the ethnic artist (as she does to some extent in *Tripmaster Monkey*), but on the artist *tout court*, as well as on the core issues of literature—its relation to life, the relationship between representation, truth, literature and life, and the social function of art. After all, according to Brave Orchid, Maxine's task is the education of America: "Educate America. Teach everybody" (60). Once more, Kingston suggests the coexistence of many paradoxical positions, the coexistence of many stances and leaves it to the reader to disentangle them in his or her own life.

---

8. For a similar analysis of this section, see E. San Juan's review in *Amerasia Journal*.

Works Cited

Barthes, Roland. *S/Z*. Paris: Seuil, 1970.

Cheung, King-kok. "*The Woman Warrior* versus *The Chinaman Pacific*: Must a Chinese American Critic Choose Between Feminism and Heroism?" *Conflicts in Feminism*. Eds. Marianne Hirsch and Evelyn Fox Keller. New York: Routledge, 1990. 234-51.

Clausen, Jan. "Narrative Without a Bang." *The Women's Review of Books* (Nov. 2003): 5+.

Eastman, Dale. "Peace to the Max." *Far Eastern Economic Review* (March 2004): 50+.

Genette, Gérard. *Seuils*. Paris: Seuil, 1987.

Harte, Bret, and Mark Twain. *Ah Sin, a Play in Four Acts*. 1877. University of Virginia. http://etext.virginia.edu/railton/onstage/playscripts/ahsinhp.html. Consulted 20 May 2011.

Harte, Bret. "Plain Language from Truthful James (The Heathen Chinee)." *The Complete Poetical Works*. Charleston, S.C.: Nabu Press, 2012. 135-37.

Hood, Alison. "Kingston's Triumphant Return." *Bookpage review*. http://bookpage.com/review/the-fifth-book-of-peace/kingston's-triumphant-return. Consulted 24 May 2011.

Kingston, Maxine Hong. *China Men*. New York: Knopf, 1980.

—. "Cultural Mis-readings by American Reviewers." *Asian American Writers in Dialogue: New Cultural Identities*. Ed. Guy Amirthanayagam. London: Macmillan, 1982. 55-65.

—. *The Fifth Book of Peace*. New York: Knopf, 2003.

—. "The Novel's Next Step." *Mother Jones* (Dec. 1989): 37-41.

—. *Tripmaster Monkey: His Fake Book*. New York: Knopf, 1989.

—. *The Woman Warrior: Memoirs of a Girlhood Among Ghosts*. New York: Knopf, 1976.

San Juan, Epifanio. Rev. of *The Fifth Book of Peace*. *Amerasia Journal* 31.3 (2005): 197-206.

Schroeder, Eric J. "As Truthful As Possible: An Interview with Maxine Hong Kingston." *Conversations with Maxine Hong Kingston*. Eds. Paul Skenazy and Tera Martin. Jackson: UP of Mississippi, 1998. 215-28.

Schultermandl, Silvia. "Writing Against the Grain: the Cross-Over Genres of Maxine Hong Kingston's *The Woman Warrior*, *China Men*, and *The Fifth Book of Peace*." *Interactions* 16.2 (Fall 2007): 111-22.

Shulman, Polly. "Out of the Ashes." *The New York Times* 28 Sept. 2003, final ed.: 8.

Tanner, James T.F. "Walt Whitman's Presence in Maxine Hong Kingston's *Tripmaster Monkey: His Fake Book*." *MELUS* 20.4 (Winter 1995): 61-74.

WaterBridge Review. "Conversations: Maxine Hong Kingston." *WaterBridge review*. May 2004. http://www.waterbridgereview.org/052004/cnv_kingston_p1.php 22 June 2009.

Wong, Sau-ling Cynthia. "Autobiography as Guided Chinatown Tour? Maxine Hong Kingston's *The Woman Warrior* and the Chinese-American Autobiographical Controversy." *Multicultural Autobiography: American Lives*. Ed. James Robert Payne. Knoxville: U of Tennessee P, 1992. 248-79.

"How does a writer write something true and permanent when events are happening all over the place, and destruction is happening?": Sanctuary in Hawai'i: a dramatic reading of three—plus Q&A

with *Maxine Hong Kingston, Earll Kingston*, and *Buff Parry* (USA, Canada)

In the closing session of our conference, Maxine Hong Kingston decided to organize a dramatic reading of certain passages from *The Fifth Book of Peace* by the main protagonists involved, namely herself, her husband Earll, and Buff Parry, the 'character' from "Water," the fictional part of her book, who had contacted us and decided to come to Mulhouse as a real person after not having seen the Kingstons for more than 40 years (!).[1]

MHK: This truly is a reunion. In 1969 the Vietnam War was at its worst and suddenly an idea was coming through. There were people coming to Hawai'i for R&R. There were also some going to Hawai'i to be mustered out to Vietnam. So there were some servicemen, who thought, "Wait a minute, I'm not going to go; I'm not going to participate in this war anymore. And then one day everything was catalyzed around Buff Parry here, who led a walk into Sanctuary. And the Church of the Crossroads received these men who kept coming and held Sanctuary there. This was the longest sanctuary in American history (and the largest!).

Another thing that was very important about this peace movement: most of us think that the peace movement came from college students, but this was a blue-collar Sanctuary. A lot of the men had dropped out of high school—they did not even have a high school diploma! They instinctively wanted peace—they wanted to stop that war; they worked out a way to have non-violent protest, and most importantly: they wrote their statements of conscience. They existentially built their conscience. Sanctuary was not a place where you just hide. This was not draft evading. The AWOL G.I.s made a public stand, sending their Statements of Conscience to the world press. They said: "We are making a stand. Holding Sanctuary is way we are making peace."

Sanctuary was big, even though the physical plan of the Church of the Crossroads wasn't that big. But there was so much going on, everywhere. One of

---

1. At the beginning of the session, John Whalen-Bridge announced the intention of starting the organization of a Maxine Hong Kingston Society. For more information, email jwb@nus.edu.sg.

my happiest memories is: at night there be campfires all over and something was going on at every campfire. There was the American Servicemen's Union coffee shop, and that was a wonderful hangout. One day Earll came and put on a show. So there was theater. Since so much was happening and I couldn't be everywhere at once, although I wanted to be everywhere at once, I decided I would write it as fiction, and thereby I could be everywhere at once. I could write about places where I didn't go—but I just wrote it as closely as I could, as if the narrator were actually witnessing for herself.

So in the *Fifth Book of Peace*, I would like us to dramatically read from the section about Sanctuary. [They read from *Peace* (193-203).]

MHK: I read it as if it were Wittman—actually I am Wittman [laughter] but, you know …

Earll Kingston: Just a prefatory note. The theater in Hawai'i in those days was the most wonderful thing because it was paradise and you were doing the job you loved. To be in the place you loved and to do the job you loved was just wonderful. Even if it really was not too remunerative. And so we had a theater company, but sometimes there was no work. Somebody came to us and said: "Would you mind doing a play with High School students? You choose it and choose where you want to put it on. So Sherry Topp and I (we were both working on our Masters at the university) said: "How about *Viet Rock*?" Because another wonderful thing that was happening at the time was that the theater was exploring all new forms: there was Peter Brook; there was Grotowski, the Americans' Megan Terry, *Hair* … all this stuff was happening and all the forms were up for grabs. So this play was … it was singing, it was dancing, it was political theater … it was right at the Nixon administration's throat. I didn't want to direct and so I said to my friend: "You'll direct it and I'll play the role of the sergeant"—which was the big role. And the High School kids were wonderful. Because High School kids have no fear and they have no sense of ego preservation so they'll just throw themselves into anything. We had trouble finding a stage because a lot of people didn't want to do such a political play, but the Church of the Crossroads, which had a long history of political activism, said: "Sure, come on, and do the play here." And it was this: [They read from *Peace* (204-9).]

EK: There's a parallel with reality. What we did and what she's writing are just kind of working side by side but not quite the same. Wittman's play and our play are kind of the same thing. But she's jumping across realities.

Buff Parry reads his part: "The walk for Peace went …" (195 fol.) [laughter when he reads his own description: "Buffy shone. He was blond, a leader, an officer." He comments:] And by the way, this is exactly accurate. I mean I know the thing. The fiction stuff keeps coming up. And this is exactly what happened—it's on film. So, talk to me afterwards if you want to bear a fight. This part of me is word for word accurate. "Buffy Perry was our Billy Budd, the handsome sailor …" [laughter] The photos, if you want to see them later! It's been a slight change … just four decades and a couple of days. [He reads on and comments on Kingston's rendering of his Statement of Conscience:] And I'll have to repeat this again: She did this word for word after the fire. I'll show you! I have the original speech hand-written here—what I am about to read to you. And as I said before: she corrected some of my grammar, but you know, that's ok.

MHK: Now we're going to get back into chronological order. And this is where we begin the Marathon … so you may want to say something about Marathon!

BP: A lot of the young men who joined me were really in bad shape. Some of them were on R &R. Some were definitely psychologically wounded, severely. We would have these sessions, throw a ball at each other, and then whoever caught the ball or whoever it was thrown at and caught it would have to speak, like the speaking stick the indigenous community is used to this day; and this went on for a very long period of time.

But I do want to tell you a little episode that happened just before this Marathon started. I came late because there was an interview on the Huntley Brinkley, I think it was. Most of you will not remember who Huntley and Brinkley are, but they were a great television news duo who conducted interviews and helped the evening news, and so forth. And this very good friend of mine, Jay Wallrabinstein, an albino Jew—very interesting looking character—was taking my place while I was on the phone during this interview, and someone had come along with a 2 by 4. There were people who were very opposed to this Sanctuary. It was intended for me. A little-known story, but it's like yesterday! And he reminded me of this account, so that had happened just before this Mid-Marathon that I'm about to read to you. [They finish the reading (*Peace* 218-19)].

Comments and discussion:

BP: I recently sent Maxine two poems that arose out of the horrors happening in Japan right now [2011 Tsunami, Fukushima] and they seemed so oddly coincidental considering this book and this symposium, and that the Sanctuary started on Hiroshima Day, and the linkages between nuclear energy and nuclear weapons. I wrote two poems and they're dated to specific dates, so they are already a little bit out of sync with what we now know what's happened in Japan. If you would pay attention just to one little point here: I've compared the Hindu goddess Kali to a Chinese goddess and there is a difference of opinion about which one came from which and whether Kali is even in the picture. But it's Kali's characteristics. She is depicted in statuary, holding a knife with blood, but a newborn baby in the other hand. And that's always a depiction of killing, an age stopping, or coming to the end of a cycle, so that they knew you got a good start.

OF DROUGHTS AND DOLPHINS

February-March, 2011
Written on the occasion when a Janus-faced plexus of news reached me at one and the same time. The good news was about the symposium honoring Maxine Hong Kingston; the bad news was about the scores of baby dolphins, conceived during the BP oil gusher, victims of infanticide that, with their mothers, are washing up dead along the coast of the Gulf of Mexico. Dedicated to my friends Wittman Ah Sing, his great-mother-creator Maxine Hong Kingston, and to all cited Chinese and Indian Goddesses to which I pay tribute.

Walt Whitman, O bard of my transcendence,
this is not a Song of Myself
as I hear America Singing once again,
from the lungs of Wittman Ah Sing,

from the lungs of dieing dolphins far away
from the Mexican Gulf Stream.
America Ah Sing this song of freedom
as the walls come tumbling down 'round Kingston Town

and Kali rises up from the Gulf Stream waters.
To the Max - ine Hong a Kingston song Ah Sing:
Would that the dolphins have stayed
in Kingston's Dolphin's Cove

as Kali sank beneath the Gulf Stream blackened waters.
Of Great Pi-Hsia Yuan Chin incarnate,
this ode bodes well.
Ah Sing to you Kuan Yin

China's own *thesbian* Kali, and to you
Nu Kua, mother of mankind;
but with the dolphins I too know
there is no stopping the drought of Pa, Ah *Noh*

The next poem, which really is intimately bound up with this one, is called

THE REACTORS OF SENDAI, OF FUKUSHIMA, AND THE ICONOCLAST FATHER OF ALL MISBEHAVING NUCLEAR REACTORS

Friday, March 11, 2011
Written while preparing for Maxine Hong Kingston's Mulhouse celebration, six months before the tenth anniversary of September 11, 2011

Remembering Hiroshima and Nagasaki, August 6 and 9, 1945
Remembering my Church of the Crossroads Sanctuary for Hiroshima, August 6, 1969
Remembering the Fukushima Reactors of Sendai, March 11, 2011
Remembering the Sun God for tomorrow, when we can finally forget today
The Sun God of Chernobyl's Reactor, Ukrainian Dazh Boh,
was thrown into the Dnepr River by Prince Vladimir
to be replaced by a man on a cross.
The Sun God of America's Three Mile Island Reactor,
the Munsi Lenape Delaware kittatinny Mountain's Manitou,
was moved to Oklahoma and Ontario by those who put that man on a cross.
But the Sun God of Fukushima Reactors One and Two,
still quaking, maybe melting, in aftershock,
is *a woman* named Amaterasu, daughter of Izanagi,
more recently replaced by Sol Invictus, who still hangs
on the cross of Constantine
in the clouds of Hiroshima and Nagasaki;
in the radioactive steaming clouds of the Fukushima Reactors of Sendai.
[applause]

EK: Just being here takes me back to the Vietnam War years. Between midnight and two in the morning, I'm yelling and screaming at my father and he's screaming at me the War the War, and finally my mother grabbing my father and Maxine grabbing me would separate us. Those years were such a cloud over the country for so long that I'm not sure our country has come out from under it even now. But the fact is that we did something; we demonstrated and Berkeley erupted, then, going to Hawai'i, perhaps on our way to Japan, finding ourselves in this place that Joan Didion called "the sugar-coated fortress" was just another call to keep working for peace, to keep doing it. Being here, today, with Maxine and Buff, is just a reminder to keep working for peace and justice. A kind of a tiredness sets in when you see the rush to war happen again and happen again more quickly than it seemed to have happened before, but that you do have to keep working. And then there's nothing else than that, as Maxine says so eloquently: the peace movement is not a fire department, and it's not sent in to put out the fire right now. That's not how time works and that's simply not how human nature is. You just know that what you're doing now will have effect eventually. I look at a child in front of me when I'm on stage and what we're doing is for that child. I know what I'm saying is going to change that child because the child is still open. Imagination is still open. The heart is open. It's important that what we say and do is truthful.

Questions from the floor:

Agnieszka Soltysik: I have a great factual question, really: since the publication of this book [*The Fifth Book of Peace*] coincided with the Iraq War, when did you actually write the section "Water"?

MHK: Let's see. First, 1991 was the fire in the Berkeley-Oakland Hills and then I gathered the Veteran Writers' Workshop. I am very bad with years! In 2003 I finished the book and sent it to the publisher—they were ready to go to press, and then 9/11 happened. When that happened, it seemed to make all kinds of things irrelevant or trivial. I remember magazines coming out—and it was too late for them to have an article about 9/11 because magazines are put together months ahead of time. So everybody had an American flag on the covers, and everybody was saying ... whatever we're doing, it doesn't match the enormity of what just happened. And so my book is at the publisher's and it's about ready to come out. So I wrote an epilogue, which I got to the publisher's on time. In the "Epilogue" I told about what happened to some of the people in the book and I was able to talk about my going to the White House to protest and prevent Shock and Awe, and the consequences of that. [...]. The last page of this book has to do with using all our best art and nonviolent tactics, and failing to stop war from beginning. [MHK reads the "Epilogue" and comments on the International Women's Day White House demonstration:] It was maybe the only truly non-violent demonstration I've ever been in. Other times, there was something violent that spoiled it, a fight at the edge of the crowd, somebody hit somebody with a board, tear gas ... But this time, there was this great feeling of love. [...]. I don't say here that the War started. It was March. I might've sent the Epilogue to the publisher before the war began just 9 days after our peace demonstration. We protested and we did our best art, and it didn't work. Although I don't say that here—but you know it.

This is very interesting, this discussion right now: How does a writer write something true and permanent when events are happening all over the place, and destruction is happening? So maybe the strongest thing that you have to say is the moral principle. To state non-violence—to tell the peace story—very strongly so that even though conditions change, the ideals do not. The current situation cannot change and destroy ideals.

Jennifer Dick: How do you feel those conditions have affected you in relationship to your sense of hope?

MHK: What happened was that women came there, not just women. Poets for peace, hundreds of poets gathered their peace poems and brought it on this day to present to the White House. Dancers, the best dancers came and they did dance to their best ability. The musicians, the puppeteers, the actors—everybody did their best art. But we could not prevent the bombing. So at first, we are put into despair. I felt terrible despair: this making peace through art doesn't work. I felt very unhappy. And then the resilience or the hope comes back. I can feel it bodily coming back, I have that kind of physiology. There seems to be a return of energy, and it comes along with ideas about non-violence—which is that we are working in and for the long term. Of course, when war is going to start, you can't prevent it in two weeks. We have actually been working for peace all along, ever since Sanctuary. Even before that. There is a constant work for peace and I feel that we are changing the atmosphere, that we are stopping a war a hundred years from now, a thousand years from now. All our peace actions have consequences—just as war actions also have consequences. So that's how I keep my peace hope up. How do you keep your hope up?

EK: Listening to you! [laughs]

BP: Writing really depressing poetry. On that note: a few months after you did what you did, I had a … you know, it's hard to make anything pleasant out of war, except peace. That doesn't come so quickly. But I wrote this poem. It's very short. It's called

IRAQ T.V., ON NOVEMBER 13, 2003

See the world so very dark
by the light of an empty box;
another child blown to bits,
a soldier with a bullet in his eye
for piercing vision to see the mother
who couldn't find all her son's pieces.

See the world growing darker still
with the ever-dimming light of that empty box;
nerve gas wafting inside
the soldiers' uniform shells
closed like tanks around one last heartbeat.
No one dies when there's no one left to live.

MHK: I just thought of another answer to your question. When I am in despair and the hope is gone and I feel dark and alone, I remember that I need to get out there among my fellow good people. And though I feel tired I will go to a peace demonstration. It's just to be with the other people. I can feel their energy. Just having the other people around me, I could feel their community. I could feel *sangha* and the hope, which is returned. I think to be with other people is to love them and to have their love come to me. And that makes me happy and strong and able to continue peace work.

Jennifer Dick: Have you ever been told what it was like in France when this war broke out? There were very active and creative, but also angry and outspoken protests. The night when the war broke out and we all felt that same feeling: that we have protested, we have spoken, we have gone around. For those also that are American that were in Paris, we've gone around and made sure that other people also know that we were part of that, that we were Americans who did not support what was taking place. The night of the actual war breaking out, the Place de la Concorde filled up. It had a bid tank, blocking the Embassy. But all the people milling about were very quiet. Nobody was rallying. People just wandered in the dark and passed each other. It was a very strange feeling. But when you just said, that you go out and you go to be together with other people, it was an oddly moving moment. My best friend in Paris, who is American as well, and I: many people were surprised that we would be there as Americans, and it seemed very important to come together with people from all over the world. Even though there was an overall sense that we wanted to stop this and that we as a group felt incapable of that. I wanted to share that with you—you remind me of that.

BP: To top if off: in Edmonton, Alberta, Canada, per capita, we had the largest anti-war march and rally—in the world. Of all places the oil and gas capital of the world now, to have more people per capita coming out, tens and tens of thousand—we really felt like we worked out a deal to stop this Iraq War. When we could get that many right wingers, who were really pro war, redneck people, joining us. And then that energy that Maxine's talking about: everybody really felt it. ... it happened there. It can be done with enough work in mobilization; and I do think the Vietnam War ultimately was ended because of the antiwar movement.

MHK: I believe that too! And now there is a lot of evidence coming out—even a film made—in which the idea is that the peace movement was strongest within the military. There were something like 500 peace newsletters throughout the military forces. While the peace movement is strong outside the military, it's also very strong within the military. [noise]

John Whalen-Bridge: A literary question about *Veterans of War, Veterans of Peace*. I was talking to Earll before. When the book first was about to come out, I expected a very good introduction from yourself and a few interesting pieces and a lot of, well, just a great deal of evidence. But this is such a wonderful book. I mean, when you read it: imagine this anthology of analyzing certain issues. This thing is about 95% excellent, and I was asking Earll: how the hell did she do that? Because it doesn't just happen and this was just gripping from one end to the other. So I think you just had to monumentalize this sentiment, and people who don't know will have to catch up.

Also along those lines, a question I wanted to ask you: You've been saying sometimes: "Oh, you are Wittman!" I wanted to ask you about parallels you have drawn from you and Earll and crossed things over between Wittmann and Taña because I don't believe there is this one-to-one correspondence. I think perhaps you're commodifying and doing a curio takeover ... [laughter]

MHK: Ok. So I am going to answer the one about how *Veterans of War, Veterans of Peace* became such a fine book. And then Earll can answer the other question!

A lot of time went into its making. Before the book was published, we'd been writing for fifteen years. Fifteen years of meditation and of writing. And fifteen years of reading our stories aloud and hearing the feedback, and going over it, editing it. The other reason I think it's fine is that here are people who have important stories to tell. They've just been through hell and survived it. And it behooves them to tell the rest of us what went on. So here's the stored up stories, and living with these stories for twenty years, for thirty years, and not writing, and not expressing it. And then finally we find a place where we are saying: "Come on, tell it." And the stories and poems burst forth. I am amazed at how sometimes even the first draft is already perfect. And this is because maybe thirty years of gestating went into it. The subconscious had been finding the words. So there is this fire of the story bursting forth whole.

Now it's been almost twenty years of workshops in which we will spend all day together. It's not just a creative writing class that's for one hour and then you'll meet later. We will meet all day! Sometimes be together for all weekend, for a week. We came to France to Thich Nhat Hanh's village. We were there for about ten days, days and nights meditating together, being silent together, and also communing with one another. Establishing sangha, having a community of people who want to hear your story, *those* listeners will draw the story forth. For these reasons—the years of living with the story, the years writing it, the growing and honing of it with the support of the sangha, writing-in-community—every story is at a professional level. Writers become authors, authorities. I refuse to call this process writing therapy. This was not therapy. Nobody should think that there was anything wrong with them that had to be fixed therapeutically. This is art. We are making art, and we will wait until we find a publisher who recognizes how well we're doing. We're not going to self-publish. We're gonna wait for someone who says, "Yes, we're going to publish on a professional level, the same standards as other literary work." And so people were writing at a high level. Earll can answer the other question—which we forgot what it is! [laughs]

EK: It's hard not to make it complicated. I'll try. Maxine is and is not Wittman. Maxine has said on past occasions: In Wittman comes out the great desire to do all the things in the sixties that the guys were allowed to do and the women weren't. See, that's a writer's evasion 'cause she did a lot of things. And we all did a lot of stuff. ... I remember, she started to really get my attention when we would all sit down—all of us, friends, on Sunday afternoon, all sit and read our writing. She was the only woman in there. And then she'd read her things and all the guys, who were really good writers, published short story writers, but they would just, I think because she was a woman, hang on and say, "ok, aha, ok," you know. [laughs]

But it was amazing to me when the campus stopped during the free speech movement, 1964. And we were so close to getting our teaching credentials; we would have jobs and we would be high school teachers. But department by department we started to walk out. And Maxine was in one class, and I was in another, and we both walked out. And to say, yes, that was really important, that we were married to each other. And she *was* Wittman; she *was* active. But I think it's also important that she feels that the guys were doing everything and she wasn't. Because that's the impulse of the writing, and that's part of her drive as the writer: a kind of anger—a kind of creative anger: "I wanna be in there too, I wanna do that stuff too. Well, I'm gonna write about it—this is what I would have done, if I could have done it." But she really was doing it. It is not too complicated. As you say, she's a terrific observer. She *is* Wittman. She doesn't miss a trick. She is that person on whom nothing is lost. So there she creates a character that everybody could say, "That's me!" And so Frank Chin's friend said, "Oh, that's you, Frank!" Got it? [laughter]

MHK: Frank Chin says that I stole his personality. [more laughs] Another small answer: during this time I felt that men had a better language. They spoke slang and the women I moved among did not. And also men were in danger. I mean, they were drafted—whether they liked it or not. And danger is so dramatic. And women were just not in that danger. And … women were not hip, you know. Men were hip! And that beautiful language coming out of the sixties. That was such a psychedelic language. There was spiritual language. The music of men was just so much more interesting to write about than women. And so this is why I write Wittman. So I could use this masculine hip language.

Kuwahara Kuldip: Can we still use it to modify our government's policies as activist?

MHK: Martin Luther King, Jr. and Ghandi—they gave us tools that are still useful. They are the best tools that we have. Let me tell you something that just happened: I just gave an interview at the BBC and I am being interviewed by this person sitting in front of me. He has on headphones and there is another guy who is giving him pointers. He has a second, as in a duel. I could hear through his headphone, the two of them. They were ganging up on me. I have nobody to help me, no second. I'm just there all by myself. They kept coming at me with this question: "Surely you feel that non-violence is outdated now in this new time? And the techniques that you used during the Vietnam War are irrelevant. Isn't that so?" [laughter] And so I gotta answer it again and again, trying ways to argue for nonviolence. I am answering that those non-violent, peaceful men taught us eternal truths about how to live. And we will use them under every circumstance. We're not even going to worry whether nonviolence has any effect … it *does* have effect! Timelessly. As I am saying this—they weren't listening to me! They were sharpening up the next question. While I am talking, this other guy, the director or producer, goes, "Go, tell her this, give it to her!" They're arguing hard against non-violence. I think what they were doing is typical of what the world does. There are just a few of us quiet people. We talk about peace peacefully. And these people … they wanted to destroy this delicate beautiful thing. Earll was in the other booth—so he could hear them, saying,

"Sock it to her!" [noise, laughter, PB: "Were you tempted to … smack the guy?"] Coming down the stairs, I think, Oh my God, I should've … I don't care whether it's BBC live radio or whatever. I should have stopped and said, "This is unacceptable! There are two of you against one. You aren't listening to me. Let's do this right. This is a dialogue! You talk and listen, and then I talk. We do it that way."

KK: In England there is a large portion of the population which wants to justify why they went into the war! So he was probably talking to these people. It's very important in England.

EK: There was one magazine. It just dismissed the *Fifth Book of Peace* in one sentence. It said: "The death rattle of West Coast utopianism."

MHK: This was British, too, wasn't it?

KK: They forget it was Tony Blair. They have a problem reconciling the fact it was first the left who has gone into the war! So they are in two minds about that.

Philipp Schweighauser: Still, talking of Civil disobedience … you mentioned Gandhi, you mentioned Martin Luther King. One may miss Thoreau. Of course he has written his "Resistance to Civil Government," called "Civil Disobedience." But he has also written a plea for Captain Brown, and that's violent resistance to slavery. So there is this doubleness in Thoreau. He also condones some political violence, which is quite an interesting mixed legacy there.

MHK: And when he was in jail for not paying his taxes, he was protesting the war against Mexico.

AS: My question before was actually about the first Gulf War and to what extent that book of peace grew out of that war—which was not protested enough when it happened. It was a kind of formative moment in my life. I was in my early twenties and I couldn't read the kind of mass psychosis that took over the country, that universal sense of support and patriotism. I had students who had family members stationed in Iraq, and they were saying to me: "If you protest the war, you are killing my brother." And that was so crazy to me, then! So I was wondering to what extent is it the first Gulf War that you write about it in the "Fire" section.

MHK: When I look back on my oeuvre, I see that I'm always concerned about war! Permeating every single book is war! Even writing about being a child in *The Woman Warrior*, in the background … my mother takes me to a war movie, and I am screaming and crying, and I have to be taken out. When the family goes to wait for the aunt to come from China, there are soldiers all over the airport. And also in *China Men*, the children remember: when the bombs were dropped in Hiroshima and Nagasaki, you went to the movies and they gave you a picture of the bomb. That was our souvenir—beautiful picture with orange flames burning. Throughout all my books, there's always a reminder, and sometimes there's overt war stories, like "The Brother in Vietnam."

We've been in constant war. It's a constant human condition. I used to think that each one of us gets just one war and that's our war of the lifetime. And Vietnam seemed to be it, mine, enough, because it lasted so long and was so terrible. And yet here comes another one. We get more than one. It's constant. So many of the stories that my mother told were war stories, all the way back to the Sung dynasty!

[Answering to a final question about future projects, MHK reads from her new book:] Right at the end, I start thinking about what else do I need to do ... [She reads *Margin* 218-19]. So that's one idea I have: to translate my father's poetry! But here is the way to end this book. [She ends the session by reading the end of the book (*Margin* 221). Applause]

III. Parallel readings

... Because Violence Is Real: Ishmael Reed, Maxine Kingston and the Case of Postmodern Referentiality

Sämi Ludwig (Université de Haute Alsace, Mulhouse, France)

> I enjoy writing fiction, but I write non-fiction out of anger. [...]. I'm frustrated at the ignorance and stupidity in public life.
> —Ishmael Reed (Tayyar 190)

> A lot of people say that my writing is a lot of mumbo jumbo but I'll tell you I'm a hell of a lot clearer than Marx.
> —Ishmael Reed, *Shrovetide* (57)

> Wittman has to find a way. / And I have to find my own way.
> —Maxine Hong Kingston, *Margin* (127)

> What I am trying to say is that our work is not abstract, that we effect and affect the real world! And that real life goes into our writing and real life comes out of the writing!
> —Maxine Hong Kingston, "Opening Speech" (Mulhouse conference)

A long time ago I wrote a study on intercultural communication in Maxine Hong Kingston and Ishmael Reed,[1] and though I found much fascinating material in both, many of my colleagues were surprised that I combined these two authors in the same study. The traditional African Americanists thought that Kingston didn't have enough 'soul,' that her writing was too constructed, while many of the women critics thought Ishmael Reed was a misogynist and simply didn't read him. How could I fit two authors who were so different in the same framework? What both Kingston and Reed did have in common was their reputation as 'postmodern' artists. Reed was the first black author grouped together with the famous white "fabulators," as Robert Scholes labeled them. Critics were impressed by the crazy developments of his plots that parodied clichés and wrecked havoc on any notion of stable representation. In a somewhat different vein, Kingston was also associated with nonreferentiality in discussions of 'postmodern autobiography,' a mode that mingled fiction and personal history.[2] My point in this article is that maybe these two UC Berkeley authors of about the same age were possibly not that different when they were figureheads of postmodern American literature, and that they are still astonishingly

1. See Ludwig, *CONCRETE LANGUAGE*.
2. See, e.g., Melchior, Eakin, or the Olney collection.

comparable in their aims and intentions nowadays, though for a different reason, namely insofar as they are both very explicitly involved in the political real. I see this commitment as an aesthetic reorientation that forces us to rethink the nature of ethnic postmodernism and to reintroduce an element of historical referentiality into our assessments.

Let us remember that both, Reed and Kingston, were praised for their radical opposition to any kind of simple referential realism based on 'facts.' Writing dealt with all kinds of linguistic and conceptual issues that were theorized as more complicated than simplistic positivism. Reed was praised for his postmodern unrealities, for threatening to "put da HooDoo on America"[3] and constructing an alternative system of representation in his Neo-HooDoo Aesthetic. In the "Neo-HooDoo Manifesto," he explained his interest in animistic religion as follows: "Neo-HooDoos are detectives of the metaphysical about to make a pinch. We have issued warrants for a god arrest" (*Conjure* 24). In his novels, allegorical figures were chasing one another in a world of conceptual crime. Reed set himself explicitly against any existentialist authenticity or ghetto realism. His early review of Claude Brown's *The Children of Ham* is a case in point. Reprinted in his first collection of essays, it makes clear that such direct but selective, reality TV-like descriptions miss the point:

> Mr. Brown meant for his book to be an earnest illustrated sermon directed at arousing the American conscience, but the book will be read as a peep show.
>
> For four hundred years Americans have made entertainment from Blacks squirming, biting each other's ears off, roasting, and hanging. Crowds used to witness these affairs in a picnic atmosphere. Placing Blacks in lurid situations, despising them, dehumanizing them, has always been a national sport. [...].
>
> The book will be read for the wrong reasons. A peep show under the guise of sociology... (*Shrovetide* 251)

As Steven Carter explains: "Reed regards the mystery novel as a vehicle for getting at other mysteries, such as 'the mystery of American civilization.' [...]. Obviously Reed is after bigger game than individual evildoers" (266). Reed would use the force of fiction to expose imbalances in racial representation and 'deconstruct' fake master narratives. His postmodernism promoted antirealism to fight false realities, 'parodies' that would replace the old conventions. As he explains: "I mean, when the parody is better than the original a mutation occurs which renders the original obsolete. Reed's Law" (*Shrovetide* 248). It was understood that this was about the comparison of "better" representations.

Maxine Hong Kingston's writing also went beyond reality. In her autobiographies she commented on the fact that there were not enough facts about her Chinese ancestors and on her need to use "imagination" to make sense

3. See McConnell.

of their lives and her own.[4] *The Woman Warrior* became one of the classics of the new autobiography studies and its theories, which made clear that *every* life is invented, constructed from our understanding in hindsight. In short, all biography is fiction. Reality and invention cannot be separated, and Kingston was a strong case that proved this intermingling. The labeling of the Vintage International paperback edition of her first autobiography is a good illustration of this. On the front cover, we read that it was "Winner of the National Book Critics Circle Award for Nonfiction" and on the back cover, at the top, we find it categorized as "FICTON/LITERATURE." Such blatant contradictions have usually been solved through the label 'postmodern' and its celebration of invention over the world of facts. What was emphasized was the freedom gained, the liberating gesture of going beyond the facts.

On the theoretical side, going one step beyond this, postmodern philosophers made it clear that such 'constructedness' was more than a literary trend or a strategic position—for the theorists this mode had to do with reality as such and its being constituted through discourse in what was called the "linguistic turn."[5] My own position as a critic is that this preoccupation with nonreferentiality went too far, losing touch and hence relevance. In that sense, I believe, much of postmodern philosophizing does not do justice to the intentions of the literary writers. Realism has become a simplified concept and the whipping boy of these theorists. Thus George Levine writes, in the introduction to his benchmark collection on the big Rutgers conference on "Realism and Representation," about the "forms of antirealism in much poststructuralist thought" (11) and observes in a footnote that many of the "Get Real" T-shirts remained unsold while the "alternative" slogan, "No Reality Without Representation" "sold out immediately" (21). To be sure, nobody believes in simplistic, so-called 'correspondence theories' nowadays, but I believe that many postmodern philosophers have been too radical about the primacy of representation when they proposed new modes of understanding reality as "simulacra" in ways that smack of what Karl Popper would call the totalitarian stance of a "historicist" world view.[6]

Postmodernity has been described as nothing less than a watershed in the history of humanity, as a moment after which things were no longer real and could no longer be real. Thus according to Jean Baudrillard:

---

4. See in particular Kingston's "Imagined Lives."
5. Also see my discussion in *Pragmatist Realism* (84).
6. See Popper: "They [...] believe that they have discovered laws of history which enable them to prophecy the course of historical events. The various social philosophies which raise claims of this kind, I have grouped together under the name *historicism*" (xix, original italics).

> The real [....] is no longer anything but operational. [...]. It is a question of substituting the signs of the real for the real, that is to say of an operation of deterring every real process via its operational double, a programmatic, metastable, perfectly descriptive machine that offers all the signs of the real and short-circuits all its vicissitudes. (2)

Reality has turned into a mechanical "machine" we can no longer influence. He writes that "it is *now impossible to isolate the process of the real*, or to prove the real" (21, original italics). And then, prophetically: "For power it is a question of life and death. But it is too late" (22). Baudrillard talks of "irreversible apparatuses of control" (33), concluding: "For us, the trick has been played" (39). My main criticism of this philosophical view is that it denies the possibility of agency and at the same time flirts with violence, with a kind of radicalism that knows no empathy because real empathy is no longer possible in a world of simulation. Since reality can no longer be grasped and all experience is now simulation—reality and representation have collapsed into a single system—that false representation has to be done away with.

This is the point where, I would claim, French critics such as Baudrillard and Debord start promoting an irresponsible discourse of violence. Thus for Baudrillard, "[t]errorism is always of the real" (47) and "explosion is always a promise" (55).[7] In a sense of baroque Babylonian disgust, he sees this world as rotten:

> It is necessary to transform this rotting into a violent process, into violent death, through mockery and defiance, through a multiplied simulation that would offer the ritual of the death of the university as the model of decomposition to the whole of society, a contagious model of the disaffection of the whole social structure, where death would finally make its ravages ... (150)

Hence he wants to "revive something of the violence necessary to live—whether suffered or inflicted. The violence of ritual, the violence of work, the violence of power and the political is good! It is clear, luminous, the relations of force, contradictions, exploitation, repression! This is lacking today, and the need for it makes itself felt" (156). The radical simulation is paired with a radical counterbalancing existentialist luminosity of force.

A similar advocacy of violence can be found in Guy Debord, who expects

> a new spontaneous struggle emerging under the sign of *criminality* [...] a second proletarian onslaught on class society. When the *enfants perdus* of this as yet immobile horde enter once again upon the battlefield, which has

---

7. See also later, when Baudrillard describes "The Beaubourg Effect": "Simulation of an imminent, increasingly dense, irreversible order, one that is potentially saturated and that will never again witness the liberating explosion" (71).

> changed yet stayed the same, a new General Ludd will be at their head—leading them this time in an onslaught on the *machinery of permitted consumption*. (86, original italics)

Since there is no reality, you are allowed to destroy the simulation, the meaningless spectacle. What is ignored in such a view is that even this 'wrong' world is alive and that the advocated violence will backfire, will at some point be experienced by somebody and thus create victims. This is why I plead for a new theory of referentiality, for a more sophisticated kind of 'realism' that does not merely phenomenally collapse sign and thing, representation and object, but tries to navigate this tenuous relationship in more humane ways.

My point about Reed and Kingston, who are both of the postmodern generation and figureheads of its literature, is that their fictional creativity cannot be simplified to the doctrinaire tenets of a continental postmodernism strongly influenced by the formalist 'critique' and logic of poststructuralism and deconstruction. Thus we have to differentiate between the writers and the philosophers. While some of the philosophers have cavalierly abolished reality as such ("Il n'y a pas de hors-texte"), the writers, the creative explorers, never subscribed to such radicalism. They never limited themselves to a linguistic universe. For them, fiction has remained a means rather than an end. As I will show in the exemplary cases of Reed and Kingston, they have never lost sight of reality but instead fought for it. Though much of their discourse is powerfully 'fictional,' its intentional target has always been reality. This 'reality' is not something easy to refer to yet it is ultimately what 'matters' in the most tangible sense. The task at hand is now for us to understand how exactly such postmodern authors approach reality. Instead of celebrating nonreferentiality, we should try to redefine the particular qualities of such a committed postmodern approach to reality.

The case of Ishmael Reed is particularly interesting because he has explicitly reacted to referential issues in his work. Not only has he constantly been writing essays, which have been collected in six books so far, but he has a reputation as an opinionator in his fiction as well, arguing his thinly disguised views in particular on issues of race, gender, and media representation. At one point in a private conversation, he even called the quality of his fiction "essel," a mixture of essay and novel.[8] We get plenty of straight talk from Ishmael Reed, which is why he has the reputation of a crank among certain critics who would rather praise his esoteric Voodoo references than recognize his political points. As Thomas Pynchon himself advertised in *Gravity's Rainbow*: "Check out Ishmael Reed. He knows more about [Masonic Mysteries] than you'll ever find here"

---

8. Another symptom of this is the fact that the *New York Times* no longer reviews his fiction—yet they still hire him as an op-ed contributor (see bibliography)!

(588). Over the years it has been hard for Reed to rid himself of this postmodern reputation of metaphysics and downright antirealism, and one wonders whether this love of incomprehensible complexity on the part of the critics is not a leftover of the new criticism and its love of ambiguity merely revived as poststructuralist 'undecidability.' Though postmodernism comes after modernism, and though it is in many crucial ways different, it still thrives on formal issues.

However, in Ishmael Reed's work referentiality matters, and his mixture of fact and fiction has more and more tended towards the side of facts. Already his first novels have been read as *romans à clé*, with types sometimes very close to historical individuals, e.g., *Yellow Back Radio Broke-Down*'s neo-realist Marxist gangster Bo Shmo as Irving Howe, or Minnie of *The Last Days of Louisiana Red* as Angela Davis.[9] In *The Terrible Threes* Reed punishes *The New York Times*'s Michiko Kakutani for a bad review of his *Reckless Eyeballing* in an appearance as the character "Beechiko," who finds herself imprisoned in the body of a blonde (100). Such stabs clearly point *hors-texte* and engage in the historical world!

Furthermore, for Reed, fiction is supposed to impact on reality and be prophetic; he tells Peter Nazareth that "writing can often be prescient: you write these events and they happen in the real world" (120). Thus Reed claims that the picture on page 61 in *Mumbo Jumbo*, of Nixon officials on a balcony of the Watergate hotel, was prophetic:

> I began *Mumbo Jumbo* long before the Watergate scandal, although it's interesting that in the book I have a photograph that includes, from right to left, John Mitchell, Richard Kleindienst, and behind, if you look closely enough, John Dean. I had no idea that the Watergate thing was about to break when I used this picture. The book was submitted to Doubleday in April, 1971. [...]. I think I was right on target. (quoted in O'Brien 134)

He states that he "wanted to use the past to prophecy about the future—a process our ancestors called necromancy" (*Shrovetide* 130). Let us note here that this most foreign and exotically bewitching activity of "necromancy" may refer to all kinds of unexplainable things, but it clearly has a "target" that is supposed to be historically real. We may be questioning whether witchcraft really works—but there is no question that it is *intended* to work in practice! This is not a "historicist" prophecy of the Popperian kind, based on 'laws' beyond individual agency, but rather the opposite—it thrives on agency!

In Reed's most recent fiction we find even more explicit remarks in which the author tries to regain control over his text. The new critical Wimsatt and Beardsley fallacies are explicitly rejected; meaning is not merely in the "verbal

9. See Ludwig (*CONCRETE LANGUAGE* 393).

icon," but with the originator of the words and his intentions.[10] Thus Reed makes himself appear in *Japanese by Spring* to provide straight talk and refute any misunderstandings: "Ringleader Ishmael Reed never called anybody a traitor to anybody's race and not only hasn't opposed black women writing about black male misogyny but published some of it" (24). This appearance in character and as a character brings in a new dimension of performance and metalepsis. As a strategy it is confirmed in his latest novel *JUICE!*, in which the protagonist, the cartoonist Bear, explains to his wife and daughter:

> You have these self-reflexive novels where the novelist interjects himself as a character. Novels like those written by that Ishmael Reed. He's probably out in some obscure hole in California right now, thinking of another way by which he can badger himself into his work having been criticized for introducing himself as a character in his novel *Japanese by Spring*. (321)

And Bear, by the way, though a draughtsman and not a writer, has many characteristics of Reed himself: his age, point of view and attitudes, diabetes, Jewish wife[11] and daughter ... and of course he speaks Reed's language! Metafiction, furthermore, as Linda Hutcheon already observed long ago, often involves a referential dimension that involves the "problematizing of history" (87). This is a rooted or grounded kind of postmodernism that is not merely negotiating in the clouds like the deconstructive neo-formalisms.

Another curious angle on this issue is displayed in the disclaimer that appears on the copyright page of *Japanese by Spring*: "This is a work of fiction. Names, characters, places and incidents either are the product of the author's imagination or are used fictitiously. Any resemblance to actual events or persons, living or dead, is entirely coincidental." It is of course precisely *because* the "names, characters, places and incidents" are so referential that this disclaimer was legally necessary—who is the "Colin Powell" in that book anyway? No such disclaimer appears in *JUICE!*—probably because the smaller press that published it, Dalkey Archive, is less afraid of being sued than powerful Macmillan (which is in itself a comment on the nature of the American legal system). The very fact that "names, characters, places and incidents either are the product of the author's imagination or are used fictitiously" forces us to reassess the quality of this kind of fiction. The old modernist subtext—in itself a conceptual entity—yields to a referential co-text of journalism and forces the

---

10. Reed similarly contradicts the "affective fallacy"; see my observations in "Sentimental Heathen."
11. Carla Blank is also referred to by name in *JUICE!*, "discussing early Judson" (158). And so is Reed's old-time friend Gerald Vizenor—in a character called Jerry "Bearheart" (named after Vizenor's novel) who writes about a "Gerald Vizenor" (183). Thus the fiction metaleptically refers to the world of its origin.

publisher to be cautious. This is no longer a matter of meaning contained in forms or fragmented grammars, of grand narratives or even deconstructed little narratives, but it concerns stories of experience.

Of course these books are still 'text' or what the French would call *littérature*, but that essential quality of 'letteredness' is only part of the phenomenon, an ancillary function of the intentionality of the text connected to the referentiality it projects. Though the words are mere discourse and 'discourse' can conveniently be reduced to semiological issues where no outside interferes, Reed signals that the function of *his* writing is intended for the real world. It does not retreat into itself or deconstruct itself by its own intrinsic inconsistencies (it is anyway naturally inconsistent in its representational partiality), but it has a target outside itself. I see in this a function of 'realism' and I think that hemeneuticists ignore this fact a their own risk when they refuse to look beyond words.[12]

If I suggest that we can trace the development of a more and more direct 'realistic' stance in Reed's fiction, it must be understood that this is a different kind of realism from the simplistic, directly referential stance rightly rejected by 20th century aesthetics (including modern and postmodern approaches, even elements of the new historicism[13]). Clearly, in our case the reality is not in the text but in its reference, and thus it must be a complex intended function of the narrative construction. This is probably where magic, conjuring and all of these complicated things in Reed's early fiction and his Neo-HooDoo Aesthetic come in. Let us recall that Reed's central concept of 'possession' is a performative element in which the *loas*, the Voodoo gods, manifest themselves in the trance behavior of believers, and allegorical meaning becomes real.[14] Such referentiality is not an external negotiation of signs and things but it involves the

---

12. See the differentiation between "cybernetic circularity" (or feedback) and merely intertextual "hermeneutic circularity" in my introduction to *Pragmatist Realism* (3-4).
13. I am here referring to the famous chiasmic equation proposed by Louis Montrose: "The post-structuralist orientation to history now emerging in literary studies may be characterized chiastically, as a reciprocal concern with the history of texts and the textuality of history" (20). And then he explains that "such chiastic formulations [...] figure forth from within discourse itself the model of a dynamic, unstable, and reciprocal relationship between the discursive and material domains" (23). The formalist nature of this connection (the chiasmus) indicates that these new historicists see their notion of history as yet another version of "textuality" figuring "forth from within discourse."
14. See my discussion of possession in *CONCRETE LANGUAGE* (252 fol., and 278 fol.).

self, consciousness, and behavior. In Reed the intended function is not as a text of a book but rather like the performance on a stage.

Once we are aware of this, we see that this referential kind of realism already appears in Reed's earliest work. His postmodernism is not a mere celebration of representation, of simulacra grafting upon simulacra, but a tracing of crimes, of outrageous social conditions and representations that are grossly distorting the experience of people. The positioning is not inside the discourse *per se*, not inside the Nietzschean moving army of unattached metaphors. Instead, representation is *treated as fiction*, exposed in its 'constructed' quality of being made—not by aleatory de- or reconstruction, or historicist mechanical dialectics, or fissures and gaps in the discourse, but by the signifying monkeys themselves and their experience, i.e., by the people who make signs in order to explain the world. This fictionalizing attitude of 'as if' places a *caveat* on all textualist meanings and in its ironic stance[15] is deeply committed to a pragmatist attitude and a sense of realism, or rather acknowledgement, of the circumference of thought in reality (to invert Emerson's spiritualist theory of Nature). The text discusses reality, questions it, negotiates it, but it cannot replace it or stand as reality like a postmodern simulacrum. Individual people and whole societies can be possessed by untruths—but this will not mean that reality as such does not exist.

These issues are complicated and they lead us to a new kind of aesthetics. They impose new rules about the appreciation of fiction. In my view they point to the end of a long tradition of formalist aesthetics *cum* semiotics, begun with modernism and extended throughout the 20th century in its many 'post' movements, which come after but follow the same textualist premises.[16] What, then, is the crucial quality of such writing? If Reed's prose is not simply bad, odd, out of place, excentric, etc., how can we appreciate it? Cleary, it does not provide a consistent realism; nor does it provide any consistent semiological plot grammar. What we find instead are new interlacings. For example, it is very useful to teach Reed's books with the help of the internet and YouTube clips, to verify in the first place what is referential about his text and then to understand some of the issues that may not be merely 'fictitious.' We may look up a picture of the cathedral of Strasbourg when we read Goethe's *Wilhelm Meister* in order to better understand what he was so impressed with, but in Reed we have dozens of TV personages to verify (in particular in the intercultural context, when the readers are not Americans) in order to find out what exactly is real and what is invented, made-up and thus symptomatic of a will to change reality and provide alternative visions. The fictional ingredient stands for the hope to see new possibilities, change things, to offer alternatives and bend the course of history

---

15. See Vaihinger.
16. ... and his modern textualist formalism does of course build upon the older spiritual formalism of German Romanticism.

in and by the imagination. This is a realistic function of writing intended to go far beyond mimesis.

We also find these realistic intentions in Maxine Hong Kingston. Though her career was powerfully launched with *The Woman Warrior* as a 'fictional' autobiography and most critics emphasize the postmodern constructedness in her work, in view of her later writings, the point in this paper is that we turn this binary association around, i.e., that the fictional nature of Kingston's prose is not its essence but an ancillary function used in order to elucidate a target of historical reality in the writing. To be sure in *The Woman Warrior* Kingston's training as an English teacher familiar with new critical notions shows in the careful formalistic elaborations of motifs that combine into a highly sophisticated argument explaining why things happen, i.e., motivation. I have traced how these metaphorical elaborations determine the understanding of the protagonist in my study *CONCRETE LANGUAGE*, focusing on black vs. white imagery, roundness, food imagery, aural vs. visual notions, inside-out midwifery, etc. Nevertheless, the referential target of the writing is Kingston's biography, i.e., her family; and whenever she talks about her work, she treats these figures as real people. My most recent experience of this kind was at the conference in Mulhouse, when she discussed her relationship with the "quiet girl," clearly a finely crafted doppelganger figure in the book, described in semiotically loaded imagery. Kingston talked about meeting the girl's sister again and what she'd learned about their later lives. Such direct information makes it clear that these protagonists are not merely literary characters but real people of autobiographical relevance.

Again the question is posed in this association of fiction and history: which is the stronger referent? Which device is at the service of the other? If this relationship may have been truly 'ambiguous' in a new critical sense in the early postmodern biographies (remember the newspaper clipping in *China Men*, or the story of "Lo Bun Sun"), it turns into something very different in *The Fifth Book of Peace* (2003). After a third book that was officially labeled "a novel" (*Tripmaster Monkey*, 1989), Kingston went back to a mixed genre in her fourth book, which is in a sense her fifth because it is about her recovery of the book lost in the Oakland Hills fire. The publisher, Knopf, was very careful not to advertise the book in any particular category. An explanation for this may be the information on the bibliographical page: "1. Kingston, Maxine Hong. 2. Vietnamese Conflict, 1961-1975—Veterans—Interviews. 3. Authors, American—20th century—Biography. 4. Draft resisters—Fiction. 5. Hawaii—Fiction. 6. Peace." We find here a solid mix of categories, personal, historical, biographical and also fictional (though referring to history and geography), moving from "Kingston" to "Peace" (which is qualified neither as biography nor as fiction).

A basic separation of categories is also what we find in the table of contents. The first part, "Fire," is described as follows: "*The author tells about herself running through the Oakland-Berkeley Hills, which are on fire. All her material goods, including her novel-in-progress, are burned. A true story.*" There is a claim of historical veracity for this first part. It is not novel but at best *about* a novel. It is true in the referential sense. We can verify the historical facts about the Oakland Hills fire, that Kingston lived there, lost her house, etc. The second part, "Paper," stands for a phase of reflection about this traumatic experience: "*The history of lost Books of Peace, and the quests for them.*" The status of this quest is still historical, but it moves from experience to conceptual preoccupations. This part may in its quality be closest to Kingston's earlier autobiographies, and it leads to a third part, "Water," which introduces itself explicitly as a different category: "*A re-creation of the burned book. A fiction set in Hawai'i, where Wittman Ah Sing and his family seek sanctuary during the War in Viet Nam.*" We are to understand that this is a "*fiction*" and not a "*true story.*" Somehow Kingston seems to worry about the correct status of her discourse, announcing that this time, the made-up and the real will be sorted out in a particular effort. Thus the last part, "Earth," is introduced as follows: "*A nonfiction during which the author and her husband live in temporary homes while their new house is being built. She sends out a call to war veterans to help write literature of peace.*" Clearly, this is again supposed to be straight biography dealing with real "*war veterans.*" The aim of this project is, however, to "*help write literature of peace.*" I think that this setup is revealing. Kingston separates categories and she decides to contextualize the part labeled "*fiction*" between "*true*" and "*nonfiction*" parts. Clearly, these are not categories to be confused, but they are connected and lead one to the other. Kingston's calling is ultimately for a "*literature of peace.*" This is a writing of imagination and ultimately even utopia, but it grows out of experience—the "veterans of peace" she works with are called "veterans" because they have been 'veterans of war."

As in the case of Reed, the association of fact and fiction is not a mere matter of one dominating at the expense of the other (e.g., fabulation as opposed to hard facts) but subjected to complex relationships. The disentangling of these connections seems a very useful project for the future. Thus when Kingston prepares her central, 'fictional' chapter, she is very careful to specify the precise nature of this mental experiment, providing a precise rationale for her strategy:

> Peace begins in thought. Thoughts enworded go from mind to mind, and mind makes the world. Peace, illusive, abstract, negative Yin, would take a long writing out to make real. Its book has to be longer than war books—longer than a bumper sticker, longer than a sound bite. As we read, neuropeptides in the brain grow longer, longer than in non-readers. Thought becomes body. Sudden fast change is a method of war. The logic of peace has to be spoken out at length. (54)

We learn that the whole notion of peace writing or peace fiction in itself requires specific approaches that may be different from our traditional notions of a good read: "The Fourth Book of Peace, the book I was working on—156 good, rewritten pages that burned in the fire—was fiction. I was making up characters who use peace tactics. It had to be fiction because Peace has to be supposed, imagined, divined, dreamed" (61). Hence the need for fiction, but it would be a fiction of a different kind, the "happy ending was to be reached with no violent action, no violent conflict, no apocalyptic climax." Kingston worries that Buddhist peacefulness is "a bore?" (54), but then questions that belief and gives counterexamples, e.g., that "China adores nonvictorious warriors—they are honored so well that we forget they lost" (60). … her approach is obviously very different from the postmodern French philosophers!

All of this suggests new, non-standard elements of supposedly 'good' writing that will force us to reorient ourselves in our assessment of what we should praise or criticize—almost in the sense of a paradigm change. Think, for example, about the element of empathy: "Fiction cares for others; it is compassion, and gives others voices. It time-travels the past and the future, and pulls the not-now, not-yet into existence" (62). Fiction thus is a natural part of understanding our existence in time (past tense, future tense)—as real as our understanding of our past and the planning of our future behavior. It is an integrated part of human psychology, nothing radically separate. Kingston mourns the loss of the burned book in the second part, called "Paper"—significantly, it is named after the material stuff that records the thoughts. But she ends with hope: "I should be able to write again about the time during the war when Earll and I took our son, Joseph, and left to live in Hawai'i …." (62). This introduction of the third, fictional part with her own family triangle (Maxine, Earll, Joseph) makes it clear that there is knowledge transfer from biography to fiction, to the new family triangle of "Wittman and Taña, and their son, Mario" (65). Like the real Kingstons, who left the continental United States for Hawaii because of the Vietnam War, here we have a mixed-race couple and their son, artists with views and attitudes that obviously coincide with the ones of their maker, although gender and race are now inverted. There seems to be a point where the analogy has to be loosened in order to work, where you seem to need a certain distance to get the imagination going. The third part is called "Water," a labeling that emphasizes its fluidity. Fiction is not 'solid,' it allows for all kinds of processing, yet at the same time it is not categorically different from the real.

Kingston includes many elements that have little to do with a traditional suspension of disbelief. She does not want to create an illusory fiction that seems real in the sense of Roland Barthes's "reality effect." Little details show that there is no absolute consistency in her imagined world. Thus when Wittman rents a new house for his family, we read that "Mr. Tong lent or gave him mattresses" (145). Why "or"? This is a deliberate undermining of fictionalization; the author could easily decide on one or the other, on lending or giving the mattresses. The "or" thus signals a refusal of authorial responsibility, playing the game of imperfect memory with the omniscient narrator as if this were some kind of journalistic recording. Moreover, "giving" and "lending" are of course also important issues in Kingston's ethos of peaceful interaction. The blurring of the lines leads to possibilities.

A particularly glaring referentiality glitch that goes in a different direction is Kingston's introduction in this "fiction" of "Louis D. 'Buffy' Perry, the air-force lieutenant, [who] had left the protection of the church today to invite his fellow military to go AWOL and join him in Sanctuary" (195). This character is a clear role model:

> Buffy shone. He was tall, blond, a leader, an officer. [...]. Answering arguers, Buffy kept walking, and as they talked and talked, they became part of the parade. He accepted a lei, and wore it over his uniform, probably against the rules. He did not have the frantic air of those who'd been to Viet Nam. Speaking calmly, he explained Sanctuary to his fellows one by one. 'This isn't the kind of AWOL where you get stoned and miss the ship, a roll call. I'm taking full responsibility, and deliberately not showing up at the base. I'm taking political action in Sanctuary.' [...]. He was building the Sanctuary as he walked. (195)

Buffy is an idealized figure. Kingston calls him "our Billy Budd, the handsome sailor," and she follows up this characterization with multiple quotes from Melville. The reader can imagine my surprise when I was organizing an international conference on Maxine Hong Kingston in Mulhouse, France, and a month before the event received an email from a man who claimed to be this fictional character, no less:

> Dear Samuel Ludwig,
> I have only recently found in Maxine Hong Kingston's book, The Fifth Book of Peace, some 50 pages about me. She copyrighted this book in 2003. My account begins on page 194 of the 2004 First Vintage International Edition. She biographed something I did in late 1969, in this book. I am very interested in discussing this with her, particularly at the symposium in her honor March 18-20, 2011, at U of Mulhouse in Alsace, France. Could you do two things for me? First, forward this email to her so I can communicate with her directly; and second, send me info on the symposium. Since my life is detailed throughout over 15% of her book, I think it time for she and I to meet, wouldn't you say? My name, as she gave it in the book, is Louis D. Buffy Perry. Today I am simply Buff Parry (she spelled my last name incorrectly). I know she will be pleased that I found her and wish to share more of the story
> Thank you for your attention to these questions.
> With the best,
> Louis Buff Parry

This contact radically changed my perception of the fictionality in the third part of *The Fifth Book of Peace*! I found Mr. Parry's web site and we have been in contact ever since (http://louisbuffparry.com/). I was able to get him in touch with Maxine Kingston and invited him to our conference, which he gleefully attended. The reunion of Maxine, Earll, and Buffy culminated in a dramatic reading of relevant sections from *The Fifth Book of Peace*. Imagine: here we had a fictional character out of Kingston's book among all of these committed Kingstonians! Buff Parry attested that Kingston had a tape-recorder ear in describing the events at the 1969 Church of the Crossroads Sanctuary in Honolulu, which he compared to his own notes. He claimed that he knew "who that Wittman character is!" and pointed at Kingston herself (laughs).

Once we are aware of this referential dimension, we should reassess the rest of the fictionality of Kingston's 'fictional' part as well. As in Reed's later fiction, we can start googling people and events, and we find Buff Parry on YouTube, or the Church of the Crossroads web site,[17] etc. Somehow the clear-cut division of the parts into 'true story' or 'fiction' falls apart. There is no neat theory to figure the quality of this new kind of hybrid textuality and the increased referentiality and political commitment that we find in this experienced generation of American writers who started out as celebrated postmodernists. But it is clear that such a basic change of orientation needs closer analysis and that it signals a renewed interest in some kind of 'realism.' My own hunch is that this new kind of referentiality is relational and cognitive in the sense of our understanding of human interaction—as my earlier reference to empathy indicates. It is like the projective commitment to be found in the theater performance staged as the high point of the Sanctuary in *The Fifth Book of Peace*, a performance of the 1922 children's book, *The Velveteen Rabbit, or How Toys Become Real* by Margery Williams. There Skin Horse teaches the rabbit "what it means to be REAL: 'Real isn't how you are made, [....] It's a thing that happens to you. When a child loves you for a long, long time, not just to lay with, but REALLY loves you, then you become Real'" (212). And the narrator continues: "It hurts to become real. All feelings—even good feelings—shake the body. The children and the soljers [sic?] learned: becoming real takes a long time. It's ok to take a long time coming alive." Love is physical, is experience and thus involves bodily existence. But it does so as a projective inside force beyond the material nature of things (e.g., inanimate toys) and beyond conceptual abstractions, words, or mere semiotics.

Another aspect of this new realism is Kingston's informed approach to utopia as realistic utopia. This is well exemplified in her tracing the hospitality of 'aloha' in Hawaii: though sharing is wonderful, it should happen with consent, and Taña is rightly upset when she finds girls whom she let walk in and out of her house stealing her clothes: "Yolanda, I want my dress back. I did not give this dress to you" (158). There is covetousness in paradise. Similarly, when the

17. See: "... our church has continually been in the forefront of social issues—in early years assisting in the formation of labor unions, declaring itself a sanctuary during the Vietnam War."

newcomers are not invited, they take the initiative: "How to civilize the children? Give a party. How to radicalize Kahalu'u? Give a party. [...]. They've had their chance; we'll give ourselves our own housewarming party. We'll show them, we know reciprocal aloha. *We* welcome *them*" (160, original italics). Or, more formally: "And it behooves us newcomers to invite feuders to party" (161). Unfortunately this ceremony turns out to be difficult and ends in violence, just as peaceful Woodstock became violent Altamont.[18] Kingston here clearly denies the existence of any simplistic kind of exotic utopian Otherness. Rival parties are set on the same date, six altogether, and the drunken feast turns into a big brawl, a bad trip: "They're stopping a big load of dope coming through tonight" (185). The Ah Sing family hides in their house and Wittman finds himself even grab "a rifle that someone had left standing in the corner. He held it against his shoulder the way he had seen the man at Kaena Point hold the rifle, and stood in front of his wife and child, and pointed it at the door" (185-86). When he recognizes his mistaken gesture, the lesson is again psychological: "To not shoot, to not kill, he would have to rehearse, rehearse against instinct" (186). They are trying to raise their boy "practicing non-violence." Kingston's utopia thus is always in reaction to experience, based on the real. It is not merely negativity of discourse but negativity of experience, hence grounded in the real.

Utopia is not easy. The Sanctuary at the Church of the Crossroads was real, but it was busted—to be remembered by the extravagant theatricals performed and thus bodily experienced. Moreover, the private sanctuary the Ah Sing's continue at their home is not a shining success either. Their two refugees are hopeless soldiers, uneducated, who don't know Sweden from Switzerland (232). Their lives are without perspective. A good example of their state of mind is Sam's "Statement of Consciousness," written in a "handwriting [...] like a kid's": "I cannot bear the military INjustice. I did not join the U.S Army to be under The Military Code of INjustice. It is everywhere throughout the Service. Whereas, I resign. The INjustice would shock you. Hypercritical perverts took over The Army, including the officers, many of whom are homosexuals" (231). Sam's motives are illogical and full of prejudice. The section ends with a powerful teaching lesson when Wittman explains: "There's only a few life tasks you, we have to do. [...]. Create one good human being—yourself. And you don't have to love everybody. Just love one other human being" (235). The project is one of self-control, of self-education, local and personal, 'each on teach one,' and a bit like the self-making of little Maxine's metamorphosis in the *Woman Warrior* after eighteen months of mysterious illness.[19] Wittman here gives advice that is individual and local, yes, but it is also part of a larger scheme of responsibility and global peace. The "love" of "one other human being" also

18. Altamont Pass is mentioned on the first pages of the book: "... the stabbing happened at the Rolling Stones concert, after Woodstock" (3-4).
19. See my discussion in *CONCRETE LANGUAGE* (pp. 177-79).

hints at procreation beyond the self, in the sense of raising his son or other children in a humane way. If the modernist William Faulkner suggested a refusal to breed in the face of the violent legacy in his own Southern experience and has his main characters stay childless,[20] Kingston the utopian tackles this responsibility of parenting in a pedagogical sense: "Many men talked about their fathers" in the Sanctuary (217)—another comment which picks up the issue of parental responsibility. Her assessment is fairly realistic but she opts for a positive solution nevertheless, in spite of such difficulties.

Such a realist mix of experience and fictionality continues in Kingston's latest book, *I Love a Broad Margin to My Life* (2011). Maybe the fictional part in the discourse is precisely this "margin." It is not an alien simulation that is totally separate from life, a linguistic Otherness that is separate from reality as much recent theory has claimed, but a natural extension; it is not an imposed cyborgian, 'posthuman' and in that sense nonhuman artificiality, but a kind of cognitive bodily extension or "prosthetic device" as Jerome Bruner would have it (*Actual Minds* 13).[21] Treating time not as an artificial framing, Kingston dedicates her long poem to "the Ancestors and / my contemporaries and / our children." Note the principled capitalization of "Ancestors" as such, the personal "my" of the contemporary contacts, and the inclusive and responsible parental "our" of the future. Inspired by Walt Whitman and his song, Kingston here presents her own version of a mixed voice that talks about herself and the others at the same time, a voice of fusion but not necessarily appropriation.

The long poem is formed as a journey from home through different villages of reality and the imagination. It starts anchored at "HOME": "I am turning 65 years of age. / In 2 weeks I will be 65 years old. / I can accumulate time and lose / time?" (3). Also the American bard mused about his age: "I, now thirty-seven years old in perfect health begin ..." ("Song of Myself," line 8). Kingston likens time to Whitman's intake and output of space as air: "My respiration and inspiration, the beating of my heart, / the passing of blood and air through my

---

20. See Irwin: "What Quentin [Compson] realizes is that the solution he seeks must be one that frees him alike from time and generation, from fate and revenge: he must die childless, he must free himself from time without having passed on the self-perpetuating affront of sonship" (66-67). Another example is of course Faulkner's hero "Ike" McCaslin, an Isaac who refuses to continue the Abrahamic patriarchal tradition.
21. For Bruner, any theory or science "that permits intelligence to be used in certain ways, but not in others" is such a "prosthetic device" ("Narrative Construction" 2). Prosthetic devices are concepts that help human beings to better understand their environment and operate in it.

lungs" (line 23). But her version, because it is focusing on time, is closer to causality, committed to questions about why things happen.[22]

Kingston first has to face her own vanity in her interaction with a photographer, "I mind that I be good-looking. / I don't want to look like Grandmother, / Ah Po" (*Margin* 6), before leaving on her journey, a song through time and space, starting at "HOME" and moving on to "RICE VILLAGE," "BAD VILLAGE," "SPIRIT VILLAGE," "VIET NAM VILLAGE," and then "FATHER'S VILLAGE," "MOTHER'S VILLAGE," the "CITY," and finally "HOME AGAIN." Her journey connects America and China, her family's history and her personal history, like being arrested in an anti-Iraq War demonstration in front of the White House—an episode described in the "Viet Nam Village" chapter, which shows the obvious cultural connection across time of wars *and* peace demonstrations: "Crows joy. Happiness-in-people. / I am reliving peace demonstrations. / In San Francisco we were a peace dragon ..." (135). Times and places connect, and so does Kingston's voice, focalizing with the policeman, even helping him to formulate his point of view: "'Quit Smiling. What are you smiling for? / This is an arrest.' This is your mug shot, / not your prom photo" (142). Following the quote, she elaborates his words with her own. It is this sense of empathy, of overlapping consciousnesses that is inspired by the Whitmanesque singing. It is a fictional element that is naturally human and even necessary for peaceful togetherness and the understanding of others. I see Kingston's epic poetry as a writing strategy that continues her earlier efforts of understanding others in other genres of biography and fiction. In a sense, her writing comes full circle from imagining a life for the "No Name Woman" to this cosmic poetic merging with other places, times, people.

In "LEAVING HOME" Kingston treats such a journey of the imagination like a divorce, a release of attachment: "I'll watch over Wittman Ah Sing / go through the leaving of his wife" (*Margin* 30). She starts her trip traveling through her fictional character. Wittman tells his son Mario that he is "going to China": "I'm curious to know / who I am alone among a billion three / hundred

---

22. Also Ishmael Reed wrote a poem about aging that opened a collection of songs, his second *CONJURE* album *Cab Calloway Stands up For the Moon*. In "The Author Reflects on His 35th Birthday" he writes: "35? I have been looking forward / To you for many years now" (track 1). Reed's poem is earlier, harder. He no longer wants to "Try to bring out the / Best in folks." "Make me as hard as a rock." As a means of defense, he wants to become "mean": "And 35? / Don't let me trust anybody / Over Reed but / Just in case / Put a tail on that / Negro too." Vulnerability is an issue here in the sense of identification, of "Reed" with "Negro." But so is the question of efficiency—time is connected to change: what are you achieving? What have you learned?

million strangers who look like me. / I am a monkey of changes" (40). Yet he is still "infinitely" connected through the chi (31). Then we read, "My leaving is not exile" (41), and find out in hindsight that this was not really his voice: "China / begins at the Consulate, where you get your visa. / The last couple of times I, Maxine, / went, members of Falun Gong were protesting / against China persecuting them and their way of / kung fu" (42). The voice of this singer merges; she writes her "Chinese name": "Hong Ting Ting" (47). And then: "Now Wittman writes his Chinese name: / Chung Fu. Center Truth. When I first / imagined him, I gave him that name / as a brother name to my son's" (46). Kingston makes it clear that she travels with her alter ego, shifting ambiguously from he-narrator to I-narrator, when arriving at "RICE VILLAGE": "At the next station Wittman, nobody else, / got off" (76). He falls on his knees to kiss the Chinese earth: "Gravity is love force. It bends / light and time and us." And then: "I have felt Great Spirit / before: Touching the green wood door / of Canterbury Cathedral." This is probably a commentary by the narrator, and registers as an analogy, an empathetic sharing of feelings.[23] Through the character of Wittman, Kingston can explore possibilities beyond her own proper biography—like that proposed divorce and new attachments. Thus Wittman almost gets seduced: "Mr. American Teacher, will you marry me, and get me out / of the countryside?" (86). The imagination of Rice Village allows for total global communion: "All, all related. / This planting food together is heart / center" (94). Kingston insists on a principled fusion that is, however, not saturnine or appropriative. It stays enabling and leaves the individual free. Hence Wittman doesn't stay but moves on.

Making Wittman experience fear and panic ("I can understand them; they're plotting to steal / my money" [*Margin* 102]) in "BAD VILLAGE," Kingston recovers "the pilgrim" (103) from his Slough of Despond. Through Wittman, she can explore more complex dimensions of her journey: "Why I need a companion, Monkey, along: / He's unafraid and unembarrassed to butt / and nose into other people's business" (104). She explains:

> And he's able to enter the many places
> in this world that a man is allowed and a lady
> is not. And Wittman, a fiction, is free to befriend
> anyone, and tell about them; he has no relatives
> to be held hostage. (104)

We have here Kingston's clearest statement on the purpose of fiction. Wittman is her "companion." There is fellowship between them. He helps her enter new

---

23. There is actually a very similar fluid narratology in much of Ishmael Reed's work, where such a Whitmanesque, inclusive voice can be found in the phenomenon of lacking quotation marks and "free" voices (see my discussion in *CONCRETE LANGUAGE*, pp. 337 fol.).

domains of experience and knowledge. One of the parameters involved is clearly the gender category. In Wittman, the short Chinese American writer can be a big lanky bigmouth male performer and "enter" new places. Important is also the relative safety of such fictional exploration. Because of the metaleptic categorial separation no "hostage"-taking is possible. You can do speech acts under very particular felicity conditions that trace the margins of reality and possibility. In an extreme simplification, we could simply call this a strategy of 'thinking,' in the sense of trying to understand and better organize one's behavior, one's 'doing.'[24]

Kingston has been connecting her writing to older models (Whitman, Bunyan, the Monkey King), and she connects all of them to her own purposes. "Wittman has to find a way. / And I have to find my own way" (*Margin* 127). Fictional possibilities are one thing; personal attachment is another! Thus fiction also leaves you the possibility of distancing yourself. Traveling first through the "ART VILLAGE" of representations and then through the "SPIRIT VILLAGE" of "silence," as a moment of absolute communion, she takes us from abundance to nothing: "Under the vow of silence, we / can know we are all equally human. / Can't tell who's smarter than who" (119). Kingston and her character explore emptiness: "No way. No thought. No / doing. No willing. Dwell no- / where. Rest in nothing. How did no / bang the universe to life? No answer" (124). Not even an original big bang. Yet there is no retreat to this nirvana. Kingston also writes about when "I, Maxine, am worried and can't sleep" (123). Feeling the "*Dok dok. Dok dok dok*" inside, like her pulse, she stands and tries to "root in the earth, / root like a tree" (124), trying to "feel chi, imagine chi / rise up through the soles of your feet" (125) and make basic contact—which then immediately associates "police in Tiananmen Square" arresting Falun Gong members. Kingston also learns from the monks that her heroine Fa Mook Lan committed suicide; she refused to yield to power and become the Emperor's wife (127). We can see this meditation culminating in political awareness as a good example of what John Whalen-Bridge has called Kingston's "engaged Buddhism." The silence, the nothing, is not the end, but it provides the "joy" or monk's "ecstasy" to get involved. Splitting with her fictional alter ego ("Wittman has to find a way. / I have to find my own way."), the author Kingston now ends up in "VIETNAM VILLAGE" and a confusion of geography and order, citing Columbus and Kafka (129), which leads to the already mentioned demonstration against the Iraq War in front of the White House and her arrest in gestures of civil disobedience still fully compatible with the transcendentalist spirit of the age of Whitman and its foundational American philosophical beliefs.

---

24. To understand the significance of this it may be helpful to quote the title of a basic textbook on cognitive psychology, Aebli's *Denken, das Ordnen des Tuns* (trl. *Thinking: The Organizing of Our Doing*).

Kingston now can get personal and moves on to her "FATHER'S VILLAGE," where the no name aunt from *The Woman Warrior* committed the famous "spite suicide" in the family well (*Margin* 168-69). Conflict has to end:

> My husband by my side blessing himself as if
> with the holy water of his youth was stand-in
> for the rapist/lover. Forgiven. Curse lifted.
> War over. (171)

You sort out your personal history to end "war." The private experience provides allegorical power to think beyond. Kingston's journey continues to "MOTHER'S VILLAGE" and the story of poetess Wen-chi and her bicultural experience (known from the "Barbarian Reed Pipe" section in *The Woman Warrior*) and a trip home on the airplane; there she meets a "village girl" who speaks Kingston's dialect, Say Yup, on her way to New York, where the girl is going to meet her husband (197-98). Through this girl, Kingston re-experiences her own family history in a metaleptic circle: "I know your future. / I'm your child from the future. Your husband / will certainly meet you" (199). Imagination is real, like the "Chi is real" (209). In a similar déjà vu, in the "CITY" Kingston finds the "nock-whistle / that I'd invented" in a museum, and marvels: "The poet's imagination / flies true" (210). She has an experience of prophecy, of having been able to predict reality, like her Berkeley colleague Ishmael Reed. These are very particular kinds of speech acts that are very complicated, difficult to prove, but they ultimately target the real. Wittman is Kingston's 'tripmaster' on her imaginative traveling in *Margin*, which she closes with an association of the Silk Road bridging continents, mourning her dead, and a list of "reasons why live on" (218 ff.). She decides to "become reader of the world, / no more writer of it" (221). Whatever this statement means, it is a retreat into "the world."

I hope to have shown in my short analysis of the later writings of Ishmael Reed and Maxine Hong Kingston that both of these icons of postmodern writing do engage in complex fictional imaginations but ultimately find the target of their writing in the historical reality in which they live. Rather than claiming nonreferentiality like many of the postmodern philosophers, who find no way out of this except violating "simulation," or the movie-makers, who add more and more realistic surface to these illusions, our two authors anchor their artistic productions. In both cases one of the main reasons for this is their struggle against violence; in Reed his indefatigable fight against the media *because* these false representations lie and cause all kinds of active and passive violence, and in Kingston her ongoing peace work. In both cases we find a global dimension (media, peace) as well as a local one (Reed's naming names and cases,[25]

25. Also consider Reed declaration of love to his hometown Oakland in *Blues City: A Walk In Oakland*.

Kingston's workshops with war veterans[26]). To be sure, both writers use fiction. But they don't use it in an escapist way or in the sense of the 'linguistic turn' that has dominated literary criticism for almost a century now, in its formalistic imagination of a phenomenological discourse of signs that can stand by itself—a project that is much older than poststructuralism. Reed and Kingston have no illusions about such fantasy.[27] Although they play with language, fabulate, deconstruct it, and play the whole narratological gamut of tricks, the intention of their respective enterprises is realistic.

To repeat, this is not a simple realism of mimesis or an artful illusion of reality—clearly its purpose goes beyond Roland Barthes's "reality effect"! Nor does it merely suck in reality through a rhetorical device, like the New Historicism, which negotiates the rhetorical business between text and history by mixing them in chiasmic formulas. Here reality is not a phenomenal part of the writing but part of its intention, a target for its impact. Where postmodern philosophers have been and opting for violence as a solution to combat discursive falsities, the postmodern writers Reed and Kingston both abhor it and write against it. Through their new ways of writing they force us to come to grips with more indirect approaches to reality, with a realism without one-to-one correspondence in the signs themselves but an overarching concern about reality being expressed in complex metaleptical referentialities. This new kind of realism manifests itself beyond the collapsing strategy of semiotics, which focuses on the representamen in reductionist ways; instead we find a model of dynamic interaction, a step beyond narratological hierarchies that may better be explained with performative metaphors of script-writing, possession, or the cognitive organization of behavior. This double-leveled model signals a basic paradigm change from the single-level logic of formalist grammars within which much of 20th century criticism has been trying to contain writing. Further discussions must follow in order to complete this project and sort out what exactly of the past aesthetic discussions has been useful and which approaches are 'really' meaningless and should be abandoned.

Works Cited

Aebli, Hans. *Denken: Das Ordnen des Tuns*. 2 vols. Stuttgart: Ernst Klett, 1981.

Barthes, Roland. "L'Effet de Réel." *Communications* 11 (1968): 84-89.

Baudrillard, Jean. *Simulacra and Simulation*. 1981. Trans. Sheila Faria Glaser. Ann Arbor: U of Michigan P, 1994.

---

26. See Veterans of War, Veterans of Peace.
27. On Kingston's differentiation between "imagination" and "fantasy," see my discussion in *CONCRETE LANGUAGE* (77 fol.).

Bruner, Jerome. *Actual Minds, Possible Worlds*. Cambridge, MA: Harvard UP, 1986.

—. "The Narrative Construction of Reality." *Critical Inquiry* 18 (1991): 1-21.

Carter, Steven R. "Ishmael Reed's Neo-HooDoo Detection." *Dimensions of Detective Fiction*. Eds. Larry Landrum et al. Bowling Green, OH: Popular P, 1976. 265-74.

Church of the Crossroads / United Church of Christ. Official web site. http://www.churchofthecrossroadshawaii.org/index.html. Accessed 14/09/2012.

Conjure. *Cab Calloway Stands Up for the Moon*. American Clavé, 1987. Recording.

Debord, Guy. *The Society of the Spectacle*. 1967. Trans. Donald Nicholson-Smith. New York: Zone Books, 1995.

Eakin, Paul John. *Fictions in Autobiography: Studies in the Art of Self-Invention*. Princeton: Princeton UP, 1985.

Emerson, Ralph Waldo. *Nature*. 1836. http://transcendentalism.tamu.edu/authors/emerson/nature.html. Accessed 14/09/2012.

Howe, Irving. "New Black Writers." *Harpers* (December 1969): 141.

Hutcheon, Linda. *A Poetics of Postmodernism. History, Theory, Fiction*. London: Routledge, 1988.

Irwin, John T. "Repetition and Revenge." 1996. *William Faulkner's Absalom, Absalom! A Casebook*. Ed. Fred Hobson. Oxford: Oxford UP, 2003. 47-67.

Kakutani, Michiko. Rev. of *Reckless Eyeballing*, by Ishmael Reed. *The New York Times* 5 April 1986: Y13.

Kingston, Maxine Hong. *The Fifth Book of Peace*. New York: Alfred A. Knopf, 2003.

—. *I Love a Broad Margin to My Life*. London: Random House, 2011.

—. "Imagined Life." *Michigan Quarterly Review* 22 (1983): 561-70.

—. *Tripmaster Monkey: His Fake Book*. New York: Knopf, 1989.

—. *The Woman Warrior: Memoirs of a Girlhood Among Ghosts*. 1975. New York: Vintage International Edition, 1989.

—, ed. *Veterans of War, Veterans of Peace*. Kihei, Hawai'i: Koa Books, 2006.

Levine, George, ed. *Realism and Representation: Essays in the Problem of Realism in Relation to Science, Literature, and Culture*. Madison: U of Wisconsin P, 1993.

Ludwig, Sämi. *CONCRETE LANGUAGE: Intercultural Communication in Maxine Hong Kingston's* The Woman Warrior *and Ishmael Reed's* Mumbo Jumbo. Frankfurt: Peter Lang, 1996.

—. *Pragmatist Realism: The Cognitive Paradigm in American Realist Texts*. Madison: U of Wisconsin P, 2002.

—. "Ishmael Reed, the Sentimental Heathen; or: Why humans are more important than the gods." *On the Aesthetic Legacy of Ishmael Reed:*

Contemporary Assessments. Ed. Sämi Ludwig. Huntington Beach: World Parade Books, 2012. 138-60.
McConnell, Frank. "Ishmael Reed's Fiction: Da Hoodoo is Put on America." *Black Fiction*. Ed. Robert Lee. London: Vision P, 1980. 136-48.
Melchior, Bonnie. "A Marginal 'I': The Autobiographical Self Deconstructed in Maxine Hong Kingston's *The Woman Warrior*." *Biography* 17.3 (1994): 281-95.
Montrose, Louis A. "Professing the Renaissance: The Poetics and Politics of Culture." Aram Veeser, ed. *The New Historicism*. New York and London: Routledge, 1989. 15-36.
Nazareth, Peter. "An Interview with Ishmael Reed." *Iowa Review* 13.2 (1982): 117-31.
Nietzsche, Friedrich. "Über Wahrheit und Lüge im aussermoralischen Sinn." 1873. *http://gutenberg.spiegel.de/buch/3243/1*. Accessed 14/09/2012.
O'Brien, John. *Interviews with Black Writers*. New York: Liveright, 1973.
Olney, James, ed. *Autobiography: Essays Theoretical and Critical*. Princeton: Princeton UP, 1980.
Parry, Buff Louis. Personal email. 14 Feb 2011.
—. "Louis Buff Parry: Artist, scientist, inventor, international scholar and diplomat." http://louisbuffparry.com/. Accessed 14/09/2012.
Popper, Karl. *The Open Society and Its Enemies. Volume One: The Spell of Plato*. 1945. Abingdon and New York: Routledge, 1995.
Pynchon, Thomas. *Gravitiy's Rainbow*. New York: Viking Penguin, 1973.
Reed, Ishmael. *Blues City: A Walk In Oakland*. New York: Crown Publishers, 2003.
—. *Conjure: Selected Poems, 1963-1970*. Amherst: U of Massachusetts P, 1972.
—. "Fade to White." Op-ed. *New York Times*, February 4, 2010, http://www.nytimes.com/2010/02/05/opinion/05reed.html.
—. *Japanese by Spring*. New York: Atheneum, 1993.
—. *JUICE!* Champaign and London: Dalkey Archive Press, 2011.
—. *Mumbo Jumbo*. Garden City, NY: Doubleday, 1972.
—. "Neo-Classical Republicanism." Op-ed. *New York Times*, February 13, 2013, http://www.nytimes.com/2013/02/14/opinion/how-the-gop-can-win-black-voters.html.
—. *Shrovetide in Old New Orleans*. Garden City, NY: Doubleday, 1978.
—. *The Terrible Threes*. New York: Atheneum, 1989.
—. "Trouble Beside the Bay." Op-ed. *New York Times*, November 8, 2011, http://www.nytimes.com/2011/11/09/opinion/trouble-beside-the-bay.html?_r=0.
—. "What Progressives Don't Understand About Obama." Op-ed. *New York Times*, December 11, 2010, http://www.nytimes.com/2010/12/12/opinion/12reed.html.

Scholes, Robert. *Fabulation and Metafiction*. Urbana, Chicago, London: U of Illinois P, 1979.

Tayyar, Paul. "'I Enjoy Writing Fiction,But I Write Non-Fiction Out of Anger': An Interview with Ishmael Reed." *On the Aesthetic Legacy of Ishmael Reed: Contemporary Assessments*. Ed. Sämi Ludwig. Huntington Beach: World Parade Books, 2012. 183-90.

Vaihinger, Hans. *The Philosophy of 'As If': A System of the Theoretical, Practical, and Religious Fictions of Mankind*. 1935. Trans. C.K. Ogden. London: Routledge & Kegan Paul, 1965.

Whalen-Bridge, John. "Engaged Buddhism and Engaged Aesthetics in Maxine Hong Kingston's *Fifth Book of Peace*." Mulhouse, 18th March 2011. Paper.

Whitman, Walt. *Leaves of Grass*. Philadelphia: Rees Welsh and Co., 1882. http://www.whitmanarchive.org/archive1/works/leaves/1882/text/81soms.html. Accessed 14/09/2012.

Wimsatt, William K., and Monroe C. Beardsley. "The Intentional Fallacy." 1954. *The Critical Tradition: Classic Texts and Contemporary Trends*. Ed. David H. Richter. Boston: Bedford, 1998. 748-56.

Surviving the Loss: Abjection and Hypochondria in Maxine Hong Kingston's *The Woman Warrior* and Fae Myenne Ng's *Bone*

Anna Pehkoranta (University of Jyväskylä, Finland)

Loss and survival from loss are common issues in a large body of Asian American writing. Balancing at the edge between ethnic, gender, and sexual identities, Asian American women's texts are often predisposed to addressing questions associated with loss. In *The Inheritance of Loss* (2006), Kiran Desai poignantly examines the legacy of colonialism and its collision with the modern, neocolonial world from a South Asian and South Asian American perspective. My aim, in this essay, is to explore a somewhat different kind of inheritance of loss; one that, while not entirely detached from the colonial legacy and its material consequences, builds largely upon the symbolic and the affective, as they manifest in two landmark texts of Chinese American literature, Maxine Hong Kingston's *The Woman Warrior* (1976) and Fae Myenne Ng's *Bone* (1993). Loss is present in the lives of Kingston's and Ng's characters in numerous ways: as the loss of a love-object or a family member, as a sense of not belonging and as the lack of an integrated sense of self, and in the more abstract form of racial abjection, to name a few. Kingston's *The Woman Warrior* and Ng's *Bone* both address loss as a complex set of issues that resonates with the cultural past and the manifold tribulations of the immigrant generation. Even when loss and grief have a manifest reference point in the present, such as the suicide of a family member, the losses of earlier generations and the trauma of the second and third generation are immanent in both texts.

In *The Woman Warrior* and *Bone*, racial abjection and emotional displacement experienced by the protagonists result in severe cases of hypochondria. Of all the characters in the two novels, Kingston's narrator suffers from the most severe case of hypochondria, yet less obvious cases of hypochondriacal response and abjection—the cause of such "melancholic self-allergy" (Cheng 65)—inflict several other characters in *The Woman Warrior* and *Bone*. Anne Anlin Cheng notes in *The Melancholy of Race* (2001) that metaphorical manifestations of hypochondria and hypochondria as a medical condition are frequent in Asian American literature, "where assimilation foregrounds itself as a repetitive trauma" (67). To treat hypochondria as "a form of melancholic self-allergy," as Cheng (65) does, is to acknowledge that hypochondria and melancholia are symptomatically interconnected. "The Freudian melancholic" thus appears to us "as someone hypochondriacally *aware of* and *allergic to* the abjection lodged within" (65, emphasis mine). This combination of awareness and allergy is particularly interesting, because it brings to mind Freud's own notion of the "uncanny" as something that "lies within the field of frightening" without being synonymous to it; while it "arouses dread and horror," there is something disturbingly vague about it (Freud, "The 'Uncanny'" 219). In a similar way, hypochondria is a vague illness that may inflict very frightening symptoms which nevertheless often escape clear definition or a diagnosis that would entail a cure for them.

This essay discusses abjection and hypochondria as manifestations of a specifically Chinese American inheritance of loss characterized by racial melancholia in *The Woman Warrior* and *Bone*. In "Melancholia in the Late Twentieth Century," David L. Eng argues that at the turn of the twenty-first century, melancholia has become the guiding principle in defining our self-perception (1275). He also remarks that like hysteria, which largely defined the self-perception of the Western subject at the turn of the previous century, the Freudian notion of melancholia renders itself as a characteristically female condition. In both novels under analysis in this essay, melancholia can be said to dominate the ways in which their protagonists think about their subjectivities and the surrounding world. However, these novels effectively challenge the Freudian conception of melancholia as a condition that may be pathological for men, but is characteristic of normative female subjectivity. Rather, Kingston's and Ng's works seem to suggest that melancholia might function as a "necessary, perhaps even continuous, stage of mourning" in socioracial dynamics, as Cheng argues (98), and that rather than signaling permanent damage, melancholia may translate as conflict, therefore entailing psychic and emotional healing (Eng and Han 363). But while racial melancholia, in particular, may be a process leading toward psychological healing, racial abjection and hypochondria are the price that racialized subjects pay for their part as perpetual Others in American society. Maxine Hong Kingston's and Fae Myenne Ng's first novels beautifully reflect upon this fragile balance: how to find and keep inner stability, while balancing on a thin line between loss and recovery, health and pathology, submission and agency.

Melancholic Responses: Abjection and the Asian American Subject

Freud presents his thoughts on melancholia in his 1917 essay named "Mourning and Melancholia," in which he describes melancholia as a pathological response to loss, and separates it from mourning as a healthy response to loss. Central to Freud's argumentation is the opposition between healthy relinquishment and unhealthy retention; while mourning allows for the relinquishment and eventual substitution of the lost object, melancholia does not accept substitution of what is lost and is therefore indefinite in character. Freud captures the difference by stressing that in mourning, the surrounding world becomes "poor and empty" for the person who has suffered a significant loss, whereas what loses its value in melancholia is not just the world but "the ego itself" ("Mourning and Melancholia" 246). Germane to the condition of Asian immigrants to the United States and their descendants, Cheng argues that for racialized subjects, melancholia exists "both as a *sign* of rejection and as a psychic *strategy* in response to that rejection" (20, emphasis original). Cheng's articulation of racial melancholia is inextricably linked to racial abjection, which characterizes the hypochondriacal condition inflicting Kingston's and Ng's narrators. In *Powers of Horror* (1982), Julia Kristeva describes the abject as a stage in the development of individual subjectivity, in which a child rejects the mother's love because it seems to threaten the child's nascent perception of self. This rejection of the mother extends to the mother's body, which now seems utterly repulsive to the child. Consumed by an insurmountable disgust toward the mother's body, yet unable to tell the difference between subject and object, the child is left with the anxiety and horror of the abject. In accordance with Kristeva's psychoanalytical account of abjection, David Li contends that the abject is simultaneously necessary for the formation of the self and what is rejected in the process; it is "the part of ourselves that we willfully discard" (Li 6). In other words, the birth of the self necessitates the constitution of what is considered as "not-self" but what cannot be simply deemed the object or the Other. In a similar vein, Karen Shimakawa defines abjection as "an attempt to circumscribe and radically differentiate something that, although deemed repulsively *other* is, paradoxically, at some fundamental level, an undifferentiable part of the whole" (2). Furthermore, Li (6, 10) and Shimakawa (3) both argue that 'Asian American' functions as abject in relation to 'American.' This is the dynamics underlying the Asian American hypochondria and racial melancholia manifest in Kingston's and Ng's writing.

Although, as Shimakawa (3) writes, "Asian Americanness" understood as abject thus plays a key role in national subject formation, it does not signify the birth of an Asian American subject, or even the formation of an Asian American object. For Kristeva, the abject "is simply a frontier," and therefore does not constitute an object (*Powers of Horror* 9). Rather paradoxically, as Sara Ahmed remarks, it is the border itself that becomes an object in Kristeva's theory, while the 'I' who speaks is being expelled (86). The abject is "the other side of the border, the place where I am not and which permits me to be" (Kristeva, *Powers of Horror* 3) and "something rejected from which one does not part, from which one does not protect oneself as from an object" (4). The abject can therefore be perceived as ghostly, something necessarily present but unwanted; or, as Kristeva writes, as "imaginary uncanniness and real threat" that "beckons to us and ends up engulfing us" (4). What causes much of the terror inherent in abjection lies in the fact that it is threatening, as it threatens the borders of the self. As in haunting, the threat within the abject is not an external threat as much as it is internal, for "what threatens from the outside only threatens insofar as it is already within" (Ahmed 86). This is the condition that inflicts Maxine, Kingston's narrator in *The Woman Warrior*, and several members of the Leong family in Ng's *Bone*.[1] It is the threat that already lies within, not an external threat as such that drives Kingston's and Ng's characters to their desperate acts and displays of cruelty toward themselves and others. Even the suicide of Maxine's No Name Aunt, which I will soon discuss in more detail, does not simply result from the villagers' violent raid against her and her family's property; without a threat that is "already within"—a threat internalized so thoroughly it has become her own—there might have been another ending to her emotional and, unquestionably very material, impasse.

While several critics have read *The Woman Warrior* and *Bone* as narratives of haunting, it is significant that the structural mechanism in haunting resembles the dynamics at play not only in abjection, but also in melancholia, as both haunting and melancholia are conditioned by the inability to let go of the past.[2] The pull of the past becomes especially evident in the narrative structure of *Bone*, as each chapter unfolds the story by taking a chronological step back until in the final chapter—where the chronological story begins—Leila's burning need to keep reliving the past seems to dissolve as she drives away from her childhood home and leaves everything "backdaire" (Ng 191). The interplay of the temporal and the spatial is organized in the narrative structure of *Bone* in a manner that Seymour Chatman calls "sustained episodic reversal" (33-34), with the exception that in this case, an episode equals an entire chapter. With no obvious return to the narrative present, the novel ends where the story begins, and by doing so, it leaves the future of its characters open, displaced, and as disassembled as the cars in Mason's garage. Haunting, more precisely, can be regarded as an effect of a constant search for the presence of somebody who is beyond one's reach. *Bone* lays an entire web of longings before the reader, as the remaining members of the Leong family try their best to come to terms with the

1. In the following, I refer to the narrator of *The Woman Warrior* by the name Maxine "for critical convenience," when necessary, in the same fashion as King-Kok Cheung does in *Articulate Silences* (5, n8). As Cheung remarks, Kingston herself leaves the narrator unnamed throughout the text, thereby suggesting a symbolic connection between the narrator and her silenced aunt and foregrounding the indeterminacy of the young narrator's identity.
2. Haunting and the presence of ghosts is not unusual in Chinese American writing; particularly Maxine Hong Kingston's and Amy Tan's works have inspired critical readings that focus on haunting and spectrality. Recent readings of haunting and spectrality in *Bone* and *The Woman Warrior* include Lynn Ta's "Haunting the Nation: Global Labor and Grief in *Bone*" (2007), Walter Lim's "Under Eastern Eyes: Ghosts and Cultural Haunting in Maxine Hong Kingston's *The Woman Warrior* and *China Men*" (2004), and Janna Odabas' article on Kingston in the present collection.

most acute loss in their life: the self-inflicted death of Ona, the middle daughter, who jumps off the roof of a Chinatown housing project after being forced to leave Osvaldo, whom she desperately loves. But as it turns out, Ona is not the only one in the family who is unable to accept her loss and escapes. Nina, the youngest sister, leaves San Francisco's Chinatown in search of her independence to become a flight-attendant, and Leon, the girls' father, takes up a job at sea, whereas Leila, the oldest one of the three Leong daughters and the novel's narrator, spends a considerable amount of time either searching for her stepfather around Chinatown or waiting for him to return from the sea. Through the narrative of Leila's futile but unrelenting attempts to survive her life's great loss, her sister's tragic death by suicide, *Bone* addresses issues relevant to both personal and collective quest for identity and survival, thus echoing some of the thematic concerns articulated in *The Woman Warrior* nearly two decades earlier.

One of the issues raised by Kingston in *The Woman Warrior* and later rearticulated by Ng in *Bone* centers around suicide. Yoonmee Chang (2010), Deborah Madsen (2008), and Donald C. Goellnicht (2000) all discuss Ona's suicide in *Bone*, viewing it against its racially determined political and historical context. Goellnicht examines Ona's suicide as an adaptation of the trope of female suicide articulated before by Kingston in the character of the aunt called No Name Woman, whose story begins the first chapter of *The Woman Warrior* and is told to Kingston's narrator by her mother, Brave Orchid, as a warning to her daughter against the dangers of promiscuous sexual behavior. Back in China, Maxine's father had a sister who drowned herself in the family well after giving birth to an illegitimate child and after the villagers violently raid her family house, thus pressuring her to commit suicide. Whether the aunt's so-called adultery was committed willingly or not remains unclear from Brave Orchid's narrative, yet the ultimate punishment for her assumed crime is not the fact that she must take her own life and that of her newborn child, but the fact that her name is never to be mentioned again, not even by her own family (Kingston 16). Brave Orchid's version of the story and her depiction of No Name Aunt as a silenced victim of her own recklessness does not, however, satisfy Maxine, Kingston's American-born and feminist narrator. Defying her mother's adamant decision to "add nothing unless powered by Necessity" (6), Maxine re-imagines the story of No Name Aunt, recasting her in one version of the story as a feminist heroine who sacrifices herself by rebelling against the Confucian social norms, which allow little room for individuality and sexual autonomy for women. As Goellnicht notes, No Name Aunt becomes "the first symbolic female immigrant to America" (302), for "in America, it is possible [...] to recover from symbolic suicide, from denial of identity" (303). Re-imagining No Name Aunt's death as "a spite suicide—drowning herself in the drinking water" (Kingston 16), Kingston's narrator returns her aunt her subjectivity stolen by the family's long silence, and thus symbolically gives her back her name. In return, she finds in No Name Aunt a predecessor and a feminist role model, whose personal sacrifice allows her niece to discover her own feminist and narrative agency some fifty years later.

That Thing Inside My Head

> What was there in the beginning: want, deprivation, original fear, or the violence of rejection, aggressivity, the deadly death drive?
> —Julia Kristeva, *Powers of Horror* (38)

In *The Woman Warrior*, violent impulses torment Kingston's young narrator, driving her to verbally and physically abuse a quiet and withdrawn classmate. Such violent actions do not remain without punishment, and the narrator soon falls ill out of guilt. Guilt, again, is all too familiar to the surviving members of the Leong family in *Bone*. Interestingly, both novels display a similar scene, in which a school lavatory sets the stage for cruelty, guilt, and self-rejection. In *The Woman Warrior*, this scene takes up several pages and ends in poetic justice, as the novel's narrator falls mysteriously ill and stays confined to bed for eighteen months after having tortured her classmate in the lavatory. During the traumatic chain of events, the protagonist repeatedly uses physical and verbal violence in an attempt to force her quiet classmate into speaking and uttering her name. What drives Kingston's narrator to these acts of cruelty is very much a hypochondriacal response to the pressures and "intrasubjective threats" of being a racially differentiated subject in a world that is both racist and sexist, as Anne Anlin Cheng concludes (68, 73). The pressure for young Chinese American girls is to invent "an American-feminine speaking personality," as Kingston's narrator puts it, which usually means whispering and often leads to whispering "even more softly than the Americans" (172), and occasionally, to complete muteness, as in the case of her silent victim. But more than that, the narrator feels uncontrollable repugnance toward the other girl's appearance: she hates her soft features, her "pink and white" (176) cheeks, her "China doll haircut" (173), and she hates the weakness of her neck, "the way it did not support her head but let it droop" (176). It becomes evident, however, that with her actions Kingston's narrator does not only repudiate her victim, but while hating her for her silence and for her entire physical being, she also rejects herself and her own racialized body. Her dilemma arises from racial abjection and is not easily resolved, given the pressures of assimiliation and the fact that her subjectivity in American society is largely constituted by racial difference. Relevant to the condition of Kingston's narrator, Cheng asks a compelling question: "How is one to love oneself and the other when the very movement toward love is conditioned by the anticipation of denial and failure?" (74).

Disowning a fundamentally inalienable part of oneself is also at the heart of Sau-ling Wong's (1993) account of the "torture incident" (86) in *The Woman Warrior*. Wong approaches the episode through the concept of the double, the alter ego, or the "racial shadow" (86), as she terms it for the context at issue.

According to her definition, "the double is symptomatic of a crisis in self-acceptance and self-knowledge: part of the self, denied recognition by the conscious ego, emerges as an external figure exerting a hold over the protagonist that seems disproportionate to provocation or inexplicable by everyday logic" (82). In other words, the disowned part of oneself—that is, the abject—is projected onto the double. In a manner of speaking, the double (or the racial shadow) thus becomes a container for the first self's psychological dirt. For the present discussion, torture and suicide can be considered as two extremes of a hypochondriacal response to loss and abjection. While Kingston's narrator seems to succeed in projecting the disowned part of herself onto the girl she tortures in the school lavatory, Ona tragically fails to project her emotional debris onto an external figure. Internalizing her loss, she eventually resorts to suicide. Of course, the issue is more complex than it might seem on the surface. The fact that Kingston's narrator ends up bedridden with a vague illness supports the notion that as a hypochondriacal response to loss and abjection, melancholia is a bodily experience as much as it is psychological.

The corresponding episode in *Bone* is part of a two-fold temporal structure, in which the narrative present alternates with palimpsest-like traces from the past. Seamlessly weaved into the chain of events that follows when Leila first learns the news about Ona's death, the scene, an unexpectedly surfaced recollection from her childhood, takes place at a crucial point in the novel's narration. In a haze of disbelief and anguish, Leila leaves the school office and walks downstairs and into the girls' bathroom. There, in the quiet solitude of the restroom stall, she lets the horror of what has happened to Ona take over. Paradoxically, at the moment of greatest despair, her mind seizes upon any familiar sense of safety it can find: "Inside, I felt refrigerator-safe. I wanted to sink into the coolness, to freeze time" (Ng 133). It is in the stall, curled up in terror, that Leila remembers how she once found Ona hiding in the same bathroom, devastated by some unknown loss, crying and her new dress ruined. As the two temporally distinct scenes set in the school bathroom unravel by turns, time seems to be stripped off of its meaning. Leila's guilt and self-accusations for not asking Ona the reason for her devastation and for scolding her instead take turns with a detailed account of the white dress Ona wore that day. The white dress that Leila has helped their mother sew for her sister the night before becomes the symbol of Ona's innocence, and its perfection becomes the measure of Leila's guilt and self-rejection: "Mah hung the perfect and pressed white dress right above Ona's bed so that it would be the first thing she saw. / I should have asked Ona, Why are you crying? What are you sad about?" (134).

Loss and abjection knit together like bone in this episode, and the unbearable, numbing quality of the pain induced by that is set against the image of time losing its substance, as happens when Miss Lagomarsino first brings Leila the tragic news about her sister: "Time rushed ahead, swelling, and then snapped still, stopping. [...]. It felt like I'd drifted to the slow edge of the world, where time froze, then became liquid and then vapor" (132-33). The chapter ends on a similar note, as Leila picks Nina up at the airport for Ona's memorial gathering and the two enter an elevator, significantly heading to the fourth floor—phonetically, the number 'four' resembles the word for 'death' in Cantonese: "I pressed the number 4 and the big doors shut. Inside the elevator, the smooth descending momentum made me feel as if I was going way deep down into the vacuum-safe depths of an ocean liner, that we were sailing away" (152). The episode expresses Leila's persistent desire to escape the traumatic events, to stop time from running, and to avert the unbearable reality of her sister's suicide. Again, an image of sinking, sliding deep down into a stillness where time has no resonance and all movement has stopped, represents safety. But at the same time, the image also seems to suggest that there is some certainty, however fragile, in allowing oneself to face the grief in all its vastness. The ocean liner sailing away compares with sorrow moving through the heart, as the image resonates against Leon's words: "Ships are massive, but the ocean has simple superiority" (142). In another passage, Leila verbalizes her wish to detain the inevitable with remarkable candor: "What I wanted was to hold everything still. Soon, I knew, the sorrow about Ona's death would come on like jet lag" (98). The abundance of images conveying temporal and spatial stagnation—images of falling, sinking, freezing, or "holding still"—can be attributed to the inability of the characters to let go of the past, indeed to let go of the lost object of love. Despite the initial false safety of not having to face the reality, the stagnation and immobility portrayed by these images create a sense of being thrown into an abyss or a black hole that pulls you in—a melancholic state par excellence, and analogous to the "mysterious illness" (182) Kingston's narrator suffers from after the torture incident.

It is clear that Maxine's severe case of hypochondria and Leila's melancholic stagnation both arise from a deep sense of guilt. Guilt this overwhelming cannot set in without inducing bodily symptoms, even though they may be extremely vague in character, as they are in Maxine's case. Leila, too, discovers odd symptoms that she at first believes to have resulted from a physical injury: "For months, I'd had these pains. When they first came, I thought I'd strained my back at school lifting something or chasing kids on yard duty. / But it wasn't that. It was more like in my head" (Ng 46-47). Leila is not the only one in her family to be consumed by guilt over Ona's suicide. Rather, guilt inflicts all family members collectively, often manifesting in the form of anger and resentment. Despite the fact that the guilt felt by the Leong family is a shared and collective burden, it divides more than it unifies. Aside from the guilt and grief over losing her sister, Leila is faced with a growing worry over the newly surfaced rift in her mother's and stepfather's marriage; in the wake of Ona's death, "Leon and Mah fought all the time, about everything, everywhere" (87).

In their grief, each member of the family is left to overcome their loss alone because with Ona, each of them has lost something different.

In Leon's mind, guilt equals bad luck, for bad luck as well as good luck must be earned, and if someone feels guilty, he must have done something to induce bad luck. Although Leila keeps a narrative distance to Leon's conviction that his failure to bring Grandpa Leong's bones back to China after his death is what has caused such misfortune to settle into Leon's family, his words have a way of "getting under [her] skin, too" (87). She, too, feels haunted by Ona's self-inflicted death: "That's the thing that was in my head. Everything went back to Ona. And beyond Ona there was the bad luck that Leon kept talking about. What made Ona do it. Like she had no choice" (47).

Kingston's narrator, Maxine, is equally haunted by the past—not only by her personal past and her own actions, but also by the cultural past that her mother keeps alive in her talk-stories, and even more significantly, by what she remains silent about: "My aunt haunts me—her ghost drawn to me because now, after fifty years of neglect, I alone devote pages of paper to her" (Kingston 16). The silence surrounding her No Name Aunt's fate bothers her pronouncedly, not least because she feels in part responsible for her unfair treatment: "[T]here is more to this silence: they want me to participate in her punishment. And I have" (16). Beyond the feminist incentive to rewrite No Name Aunt's story in an empowering way that acknowledges her as not only a sovereign but also as an unusually courageous subject, Maxine has participated in her silencing by doing precisely what she could not stand in her defenseless classmate: withholding her name. By abusing the little girl in the school lavatory, she has become one of the raged villagers raiding her aunt's house, torn by the destructive forces within. Knowing that such a crime does not remain without consequences, she recognizes how "one human being flaring up into violence could open up a black hole, a maelstrom that pulled in the sky" (12).

Broken Bodies: The Chinese American Inheritance of Loss

In the beginning of this essay, I set out to explore *The Woman Warrior* and *Bone* from the perspective of a specifically Chinese American inheritance of loss, deeply rooted in the symbolic and the affective but equally defined by an acute awareness of the differences in material histories and in the material consequences of historical injustice. The most striking expression of this melancholic legacy, in both novels, lies in the act of suicide. In Kingston's *The Woman Warrior*, Brave Orchid's cautionary tale of the suicide of Maxine's No Name Aunt begins the novel and sets the tone for the rest of the narrative; in Ng's *Bone*, Ona's fatal jump from the rooftop of the Nam Ping Yuen, the last of the four local housing projects, motivates her sister's narration and functions as a structuring principle for the novel. In both texts, the dead and broken body becomes a metaphorical and at the same time very literal image of the brokenness that inflicts their first and second generation Chinese American characters. In *Bone*, as Donald C. Goellnicht suggests, Ona's broken body functions as a metaphorical expression to the novel's first generation immigrant parents of their "failure to claim 'America' [and] to be incorporated into the national body" (317). The failure to be incorporated into the national body refers not to assimilation but to the denial of access to the national self-image from those who are deemed perpetual Others, "depicted often as a type of disease that poses a threat to the national body and so must be controlled, at times even eradicated" (Goellnicht 327, n17). The American national body, however, is also a 'broken body' insofar as it fails to incorporate into itself its ethnic minorities and racialized Others. As Kristeva writes in *Strangers to Ourselves*: "The foreigner is within us. And when we flee from or struggle against the foreigner, we are fighting our unconscious—that 'improper' facet of our impossible 'own and proper'" (191). In this sense, 'Asian American' understood as abject in relation to 'American' is a constant rem(a)inder of the brokenness of the American national body with regard to its self-image. The Chinese American legacy of loss, then, is not simply a negative inheritance, but its expressions, such as Kingston's and Ng's works, contain transformative power that actively seeks to point out some of the fractures and fissures within the national body that need to be addressed if healing is to be possible.

At times it may seem that a melancholic response to the losses burdening the protagonists' families is more likely to inflict the female characters of the novels than the male ones, because the relationships between the female characters—sisters, mothers, and daughters—are at the center of both works. But perhaps the most striking example of a melancholic response that is less a pathological reaction to loss than it is a continuous mode of existence lies in fact in Leon Leong's character in *Bone*. Of all the characters in *Bone*, the 'foreigner within' is perhaps most acutely present in Leon's character, for he has arrived in America under a false name as Grandpa Leong's son, leaving his true identity, birth family, and Chinese past behind him for good. He has paid five thousand dollars to his paper father for his entry into the United States, but as his stepdaughter testifies, "of more consequence was the promise to send Grandpa Leong's bones back to China" (Ng 47). Not only has Leon failed to return Grandpa Leong's remains to his native country, but more significantly, he has lost track of Grandpa Leong's bones altogether, thus missing the opportunity to ever correct his mistake and earn back the good fortune. Leon evidently suffers from the condition that Anthony Sze-Fai Shiu has described as a "racialized loss or lack" characterizing the Asian American subject: a loss or a lack "of citizenhip rights, legal protections, economic opportunities, and an unfettered 'self'" (4). This racially based loss or lack is also a crucial aspect in what Jeffrey J. Santa Ana calls an "affect-identity" emerging from the dialectical process of "articulating and resolving the contradictions between historically painful emotions and the euphoria of commercialized human feeling in consumer postmodernism" (25).

Maxine Hong Kingston's *The Woman Warrior* and Fae Myenne Ng's *Bone* are both characterized by a pronounced polarity between a language defined by loss, abjection, and melancholia, on one hand, and a narrative inclined toward self-reflection, active ethical agency, and a relentless quest for personal emancipation, on the other. Melancholia, for one thing, often means "holding still," as Leila Leong would put it. Pathological or not, it can also provide a necessary opportunity for active self-reflecting, of which longing and remembrance are an essential part. Remembering and longing for places, times, and affects of the past are equally constitutive of the sense of emotional exile that resonates through these two narratives. While loss and abjection are by no means synonymous and should not be treated as such, there are certain affinities between the two concepts. One of those affinities is that loss and abjection both sometimes result in hypochondria, itself a condition of internalized grief, as happens to the narrators in both of the novels under analysis in this essay. However, these two texts also suggest that feeling grief—and even melancholia—*to the bone* does in fact entail a prospect for agency and survival instead of a melancholic resignation in the face of a continuous flow of losses and the legacy of a racialized loss or lack. While Maxine attempts to see beyond the taboo, to voice the unspeakable by rewriting No Name Aunt's story, Leila finds strength needed for survival in stillness and in words left unspoken: "I believe in holding still. I believe that the secrets we hold in our hearts are our anchors, that even the unspoken between us is a measure of our every promise to the living and to the dead" (Ng 190). Like Maxine's rewriting of the story surrounding her aunt's suicide, Leila's wish "to remember Ona alive, whole" and not "to see her broken" (149) resonates against her immigrant parents' wish to succeed in their efforts to claim America, "to be incorporated into the national body" (Goellnicht 317) of their new homeland.

Works Cited

Ahmed, Sara. *The Cultural Politics of Emotion*. Edinburgh: Edinburgh UP, 2004.

Chang, Yoonmee. "Chinese Suicide: Political Desire and Queer Exogamy in Fae Myenne Ng's *Bone*." *Modern Fiction Studies* 56.1 (2010): 90-112.

Chatman, Seymour. "Backwards." *Narrative* 17.1 (2009): 31-55.

Cheng, Anne Anlin. *The Melancholy of Race: Psychoanalysis, Assimilation, and Hidden Grief*. Oxford: Oxford UP, 2001.

Cheung, King-Kok. *Articulate Silences: Hisaye Yamamoto, Maxine Hong Kingston, Joy Kogawa*. Ithaca & London: Cornell UP, 1993.

Eng, David L. "Melancholia in the Late Twentieth Century." *Signs* 25.4 (2000): 1275-81.

Eng, David L., and Shinhee Han. "A Dialogue on Racial Melancholia." *Loss: The Politics of Mourning*. Eds. David L. Eng and David Kazanjian. Berkeley: U of California P, 2003. 343-71.

Freud, Sigmund. "Mourning and Melancholia." 1917. *The Standard Edition of the Complete Psychological Works of Sigmund Freud, 14*. Trans. James Strachey. London: Hogarth P, 1957. 237-60.

—. "The 'Uncanny.'" 1919. *The Standard Edition of the Complete Psychological Works of Sigmund Freud, 17*. Trans. James Strachey. London: Hogarth P, 1955. 217-56.

Goellnicht, Donald C. "Of Bones and Suicide: Sky Lee's *Disappearing Moon Café* and Fae Myenne Ng's *Bone*." *Modern Fiction Studies* 46.2 (2000): 300-30.

Kingston, Maxine Hong. *The Woman Warrior: Memoirs of a Girlhood among Ghosts*. 1976. New York: Vintage International, 1989.

Kristeva, Julia. *Powers of Horror: As Essay on Abjection*. Trans. Leon S. Roudiez. New York: Columbia UP, 1982.

—. *Strangers to Ourselves*. Trans. Leon S. Roudiez. New York: Harvester Wheatsheaf, 1991.

Li, David Leiwei. *Imagining the Nation: Asian American Literature and Cultural Consent*. Stanford: Stanford UP, 1998.

Lim, Walter S. H. "Under Eastern Eyes: Ghosts and Cultural Haunting in Maxine Hong Kingston's *The Woman Warrior* and *China Men*." *Crossing Oceans: Reconfiguring American Literary Studies in the Pacific Rim*. Eds. Noelle Brada-Williams and Karen Chow. Hong Kong: Hong Kong UP, 2004. 155-63.

Madsen, Deborah L. "Bearing the Diasporic Burden: Representations of Suicide in Sky Lee's *Disappearing Moon Café*, Fae Myenne Ng's *Bone*, and Hsu-Ming Teo's *Love and Vertigo*." *China Fictions/English Language: Literary Essays in Diaspora*. Ed. Robert A. Lee. Amsterdam: Rodopi, 2008. 101-17.

Ng, Fae Myenne. *Bone*. 1993. New York: Hyperion, 2008.

Shimakawa, Karen. *National Abjection: the Asian American Body Onstage*. Durham, NC: Duke UP, 2002.

Santa Ana, Jeffrey J. "Affect-Identity: The Emotions of Assimilation, Multiculturality, and Asian American Subjectivity." *Asian North American Identities: Beyond the Hyphen*. Eds. Eleanor Ty and Donald C. Goellnicht. Bloomington: Indiana UP, 2004. 15-42.

Shiu, Anthony Sze-Fai. "On Loss: Anticipating a Future for Asian American Studies." *MELUS* 31.1 (2006): 3-33.

Ta, Lynn. "Haunting the Nation: Global Labor and Grief in *Bone*." *Ghosts, Stories, Histories: Ghost Stories and Alternative Histories*. Ed. Sladja

Blazan. Newcastle upon Tyne: Cambridge Scholars Publishing, 2007. 142-58.

Wong, Sau-ling Cynthia. *Reading Asian American Literature: From Necessity to Extravagance*. Princeton: Princeton UP, 1993.

Maxine Hong Kingston's *The Woman Warrior* and Fatima Mernissi's *Dreams of Trespass*: A Legacy of Genre/Gender Transgression

Sihem Arfaoui Abidi (ISSHJ, University of Jendouba, Tunisia)

> "If I had lived in China, I would have been an outlaw knotmaker."
> —Maxine Hong Kingston, *Woman Warrior* (163)

> "I was born in the midst of chaos, since neither Christians nor women accepted the frontiers."
> —Fatima Mernissi, *Dreams* (1)

1. A Prepositional Re-orientation from *On* to *Of*

Phenomenal is the number of critical essays exploring the textual and aesthetic influences on Maxine Hong Kingston on the basis of the affinities of her texts with Western literature and Asian literature. A case in point is Sämi Ludwig's "Celebrating Ourselves in the Other," pointing out the abundant use of Western traditions, ideas and images which Kingston makes by relying on T. S. Eliot's *The Wasteland*, Herman Melville's *Moby Dick*, Sherwood Anderson's *Winesburg, Ohio*, William Carlos Williams's *In the American Grain*, Nathanial Hawthorne's *The Scarlet Letter* ... and so on. Other scholars rather turn towards comparisons of Kingston with multicultural American literature, such as Karen Chow's "Stories to Pass On: Pedagogically Dialoguing Maxine Hong Kingston and Toni Morrison," or Judith Oster's *Creating Identity in Chinese and Jewish American Literature*.[1]

But, none to my knowledge materialize the interest in possible trans-connections between Kingston and writers beyond the Western canon and/or outside the orbit of ethnically-oriented literatures. As a matter of fact, even the effort to re-orient the issue from the influences *on* Kingston to the influence *of* Kingston's literature, mainly of her best-seller *The Woman Warrior: Memoirs of a Girlhood among Ghosts* (1975), on other writers might bring to mind only primary examples comprising Amy Tan's *The Joy Luck Club*. Indeed, both texts have much in common, ranging from the mother/daughter relationship to the preference for Americanization and assimilation, and even Frank Chin's denouncing both. Yet we should be aware that it is too reductive to speak of

---

1. For a different type of comparison, one should also mention Yiorgos Kalogeros, "Producing History and Telling Stories: Maxine Hong Kingston's *China Men* and Zeese Papanikolas's *Buried Unsung*."

Kingston's legacy just in Asian American literary studies, since that shuts down and silences other ways of influencing inside this ethnic orbit or in terms of world literature.

To fill this gap in terms of literary studies, the present piece proposes a shift from the dialogue between Kingston and her European/ethnic heritage to an emphasis on the legacy of Kingston in the context of so-called third world literature, mainly North African Anglophone texts.[2] It shows a particular interest in Kingston's legacy of genre and gender transgression and its embedding in Dreams of Trespass: Tales of a Harem Girlhood, a memoir published in 1994 by Moroccan writer Fatima Mernissi set in the background of national activism during the Spanish/French colonization of Morocco.[3] I argue that Kingston's influence transcends the Chinese/Asian American literary scope to garner a global dimension in the specific veins of a counter-culture of transgression, mainly in reference to individual and collective endeavors to go beyond existing aesthetic and social norms and extend them.

From the perspective that Kingston's heritage consciously or unconsciously envelopes such North African writings as Mernissi's English memoir, the present work endeavors to prove that it owes its staying power to the legacy of transgression (in the sense of rebellion and insurrection) which we see best transferred through Mernissi's title in its struggle with aesthetic and cultural frontiers. Somehow following on the heels of Kingston's text as being informative of and informed by the concept of transgression in both senses of the term as aberration and emancipation or innovation, *Dreams of Trespass* manifests transgression in terms of deviating from artistic norms, space boundaries and social codes. Through all this, I adopt Shari Benstock's observation that genre and gender are two etymologically linked terms, thus, re-affirming that "genre itself raises questions about gender" (152).

---

2. Used for the first time in 1952 by the French demographer Alfred Sauvy as Barbara Harlow quotes him in her book, *Resistance Literature*—"this Third World, ignored, scorned, exploited, as was the Third Estate, also wants to say something" (5), the expression "Third World" is a rather pejorative way to refer to the postcolonial world.
3. Mernissi's text gives different explanations of the term harem, which Nawar Al-Hassan Golley defines as follows: "The word 'harem' (in Arabic hareem) can be used to mean simply women. Hareem is derived from the word haraam meaning 'sacred', 'forbidden' 'inviolable' and 'holy'. Hence the section of the house where women and children dwell is figuratively referred to as the 'harem'. Even today, however, for a Westerner the mere utterance of the word conjures up a whole set of exotic and erotic images, because of a long history of representing the 'harem' through the eyes of the colonizer" (523).

Before developing these issues in detail, it is essential to indicate that the use and understanding of the concept of transgression lends itself to a few ideas generated by two major theorists. The references to transgression call to mind the English sociologist Chris Jenks' definition of the term as "that conduct which breaks rules or exceeds boundaries" (3). Placing transgression within the frames of modernity and postmodernity, Jenks states: "A feature of modernity, accelerating into postmodernity, is the desire to transcend limits—limits that are physical, racial, aesthetic, sexual, national, legal and moral [...]. Modernity has unintentionally generated an ungoverned desire to extend, exceed, or go beyond the margins of acceptability or normal performance" (8). Thus, generically speaking, destabilization is equivalent to any transgression of the law of genre which asserts that "genres are not to be mixed" (Derrida 203). Adding that "as soon as genre announces itself, one must respect a norm, one must not cross a line of demarcation," Jacques Derrida indicates that impurity, anomaly or monstrosity arise as the major aftermath of such a transgression (203).

In parallel, from a gender point of view, the variegated references to transgression—especially in the discussion of Mernissi's text—are theoretically shaped by Masserat Amir-Ebrahimi's article "Transgression in Narration: The Lives of Iranian Women in Cyberspace" and its elaborate examination of narrative transgression in connection to meanings, values and gestures of Iranian women's resistance to *urf* and *sharia* as two forms of Islamic law which regulate the Islamization of the Iranian society (89). For many Muslim women, this particular critic explains, "transgression does not mean breaking the law, but rather trespassing the red lines of *urf* or *sharia* which confine them not only behind walls and veils but also in their words and expressions" (98). As in the Mernissi harem, transgression becomes a regaining of power wherein the political and the religious become enmeshed targets of this counter-action.

Despite their different contexts, both Kingston's and Mernissi's theoretical frameworks have the advantage of offering up an array of complementary meanings which refer the reader to transgression in the sense of any trespass of rules, a protest toward modernity, and resistance to traditional and canonical boundaries in whatever form, such as the opposition to or the subversion of what is dominant and/or he/she who has the upper-hand in the game of power.

It is crucial to state that this essay does not claim to argue for thorough intertextuality between the involved titles and writers, but proposes to study the ways in which Kingston's approach to transgression at the levels of genre and gender resonates in Mernissi's text. Its objective is to establish and develop the argument that *The Woman Warrior* almost sets a kind of a literary and cultural counter tradition which crosses over to offer one cogent *fil-conducteur* for *Dreams of Trespass*.

A major focus will be placed on Mernissi's indirect conversation with Kingston at the level of their interlocking defying strategies in abiding by a culture of transgression that affects generic and gendered hierarchies. To accomplish this, I shall first ground the staying power of *The Woman Warrior* in an unprecedented mingling of genres which shall, in turn, be related to Mernissi's similar dismantling agenda. At a later stage, I shall affiliate the rebellious Mernissi harem with the transgressing tribe formed of figures such as Fa Mu Lan and Maxine the narrator on the basis of their will to break codes and endeavor to assert their voices. Here, issues to be considered revolve around the stark connection between hearkening back towards the figure of female heroism and Mernissi's debunking of women's seclusion by challenging the imposition of the harem and the veil.

2. Generic Transgressions

At the level of genre as a range of features making one literary form or mode stand as being particular and different from other writings, Kingston's resistant legacy lends itself to the concomitant openness of her *Woman Warrior* on myriad modes of literary and non-literary writings.[4] As an explicit rejection of the tradition of generic purity and symmetry, the inspiration from an array of generic types, canonical and popular, oral and written, aligns *The Woman Warrior* with generic transgression.

A key feature of this generic transgression includes the deviation from the memoir genre that Kingston's title announces on the cover and its front pages. Due to the amount of fragmentation on which the controversial re-writing of the narrator-protagonist's family history and legendary lore is based, the presupposed omniscience of the I-memoirist gets deflected. Besides, the memoirist gives up most of the dominant space in her life writing to her female kin. Indeed, "No Name Woman," "White Tigers," and "At the Western Palace" are pervasively inhabited by various female characters other than Maxine, such as historical heroines, and the narrator's maternal and paternal aunts in addition to her own mother. Thus, of all *The Woman Warrior*'s chapters, only "A Song for a Barbarian Reed Pipe" does unravel the I-memoirist as the central subject in a deliberately incoherent autobiography and move away from female models in the distant past to the writer's own recent experience. As a result of this deliberate inclination to mingle many and various references, we end up with a memoir that is far from representing the convention wherein the narrator-protagonist occupies a central role.

Throughout *The Woman Warrior*, generic indecisiveness blurs the dividing-lines between literature, history and myth, interconnecting disconnected forms of writings. The text veers towards an incessant fusion of the oral and the written and of inter/dis-connected forms of writings. Indeed, even if we uphold its

4. On *The Woman Warrior*'s generic un-decidability, see the different contributions in the MLA's *Approaches to Teaching Kingston's The Woman Warrior*.

reading as an autobiography, presupposing truth and imitation, what is at stake is the stated amount of fiction which is at work in every piece of this presumed authentically-personal narrative. At best, one ends up vacillating between truth and invention, especially, in the folds of the memoir's opening tale. "No Name Woman" swiftly slides from fiction to non-fiction and vice versa through the relentless endeavor to retell the ostracism and the oblivion of the sinful aunt. To a certain degree, deciphering possibility from probability in the considered narrative becomes intractable in the sense that the narrative is not merely insufficiently grounded in reliability, but, more importantly, it is keen on trying out one version of events only to eventually replace it by another.

Following the same principle of generic amalgamation of fiction and non-fiction, the narrator spends time spinning the pitiful yarn of Moon Orchid's trip to Los Angeles to confront a disloyal, prodigal husband only to begin deconstructing it. Even more, she vows that she has not been present during the wife-husband confrontation and that her aunt's story has actually been transmitted via one of the narrator's sisters who, originally, heard it from her brother (*Woman* 163). Not only leading the reader to be at least three times removed from what really occurred, such fluidity brings out the (un)reliability of a self ever positioned at the periphery of two cultures. It results in a certain form of generic un-decidability which lends itself to a range of silences and gaps out of which *The Woman Warrior* originally took shape. In the midst of this disarray, Kingston cannot help but try out a variety of interpretations and make up her own hypotheses for what was going on. She leaves the reader with a narrative at best "twisted into designs" (163), a figure denoting the imaginary inventions coming into play at each stage of the narrator's supposedly personal story and opening windows into the consequent fissures and indeterminacy which should accompany any discussion of genre in Kingston.

Perhaps, what articulates best Kingston's stark inclination to disruption as a resistant politics to shake the dominant generic conventions is the cogent symbol of the forbidden stitch. The latter can be re-interpreted as a metaphor for the transcendence of asymmetries involving generic divisions and as a strategic resistance against the law of authenticity. The narrator relates: "There was one knot so complicated that it blinded the knot-maker. Finally an emperor outlawed this cruel knot, and the nobles could not order it anymore. If I had lived in China, I would have been an outlaw knotmaker" (*Woman* 163). According to Margaret Miller, here Kingston boasts of her ability "to 'make it all up,' to embroider the stories she hears from her mother, darning the holes in the fabric and making out of the fragments a crazy-quilt whole" (25). Indeed, in the process of training herself to dissect the knots which engulfed her girlhood, she chooses to embrace the forbidden by dismantling the dominant genre types and turning the norms of life-writing as well as the oral/written hierarchy upside down via a mere fusion of multifaceted narrative modes. At its simplest, Kingston's narrative is meandering between fiction and non-fiction, particularly, in view of the term memoir figuring in its subtitle and the obvious inspirations from the author's real experiences as opposed to the iconic instance of the myriad inventions and re-inventions driving the deceased aunt's imagined punishment for sinning.

In brief, the whole issue of generic transgression is undecipherable outside the postmodernist indeterminacy running through *The Woman Warrior*. In this regard, Kingston's design has much in common with the aesthetics of pluralism, incoherence, and diffusion. It treasures an impulse for iconoclastic openness and un-expected combinations, and, above all, purposeful ambiguity in narration. All this gives legitimacy to the prominent comparison of Kingston to "a literary trickster" *sine qua non* (TuSmith 51). To appreciate similar twists, we have to "learn to make [our] mind, as large as the universe is large, so that there is room for paradoxes" (*Woman* 19).

In view of this postmodern mixture of modes, reading *Dreams of Trespass* strongly reminisces of *The Woman Warrior*. From a glimpse at the former's structure, we can already see a palimpsest of modes ranging from tales to musical and theatrical performances and/or from prose to verse. The book's major bulk and imagery undercut any aesthetic value of elitist exclusion of one particular mode in favour of another. It adapts some features of picture books, given the inclusion of pictures of the Mernissi harem, courtyard, threshold, terrace and gate, possibly, for illustration and to create some sense of separation of the chapters inside the memoir. The embedding of the visual in the memoir is likely to introduce the latter as a pictorial self-referential story.[5] Mernissi equally draws on theatricality by enacting scenes from the lives of Egyptian and Lebanese feminists and the Muslim mystic Rabea al-Adaouiya, with Fatima's Aunt Habiba as a stage-director (*Dreams* 127-28). In the meantime, theatre co-exists with some sort of film-making, considering the various performances of history-based films such as the film *Dananir*, based on the reigning era of Caliph Harun al-Rashid (*Dreams* 116).

In the same context, the memoirist slides from a pictorial/prosaic narrative to poetic interludes in free verse (*Dreams* 214-17). Scattered here and there in the middle of the narration, these interludes articulate the aspirations of the anti-conformist women figures for modernity and liberation, including the memoirist's mother and her Aunt Chama. This feature is also related to the thirst of the Mernissi harem for Egyptian divas singing for love and romance, such as Oum Kalthoum or Farid Elatrash. In addition to music, Mernissi's book not only

---

5. Sidonie Smith interestingly notes that "[p]hotographs never simply illustrate a written narrative. Each photo tells a separate story and, taken together, they form a separate system of meaning. And the stories in photographs may support, or be in tension with or conduct the claims of the verbal text. To read these multimedia texts we need to develop familiarity with the narrative and generic conventions of visual compositions" (76).

cites passages from Scheherazade's story in *A Thousand and One Nights* but, is also inspired by popular fairy tales such as Habiba's favorite, entitled "The Woman's with Wings" (22), which is narrated only on special occasions and reminiscent of Brave Orchid as she funnels stories of unconventional women into Maxine's ears. Here, blending genres seems to create a palimpsest, challenging the preference and/or legitimacy of one genre over another, in addition to resisting the prerequisite of abiding by a well-defined mode. As such, Mernissi is in no way writing within a merely (auto)biographical genre.

By hybridizing the mentioned forms and modes into a compact personal-political narrative, *Dreams of Trespass* brings to the reader's mind a guiding metaphor that keeps re-emerging in order to reinforce an embrace of generic and/or aesthetic transgression. It consists in the figure of the Moroccan caftan emblematic of the traditional/modern or constricting/liberating chasm in the Mernissi harem. It mirrors a locus of negotiation between embracing a standard authentic representation of art and other deviant creations.

The resistance of the women rebels to knit their caftan following one single pattern as they are traditionally trained to do triggers a direct challenge to the representative mouthpieces of artistic conventionalism who defend the need to conform to *taqlid,* i.e., tradition. The traditionalist view of art is undermined in the defying embroidery by the rebel figures in the Mernissi harem who keep inventing a patchwork of patterns. These significantly hearken back to Kingston's forbidden stitch in the sense that they opt for multiplicity and innovation and are more associated with the value of pleasure and personal identification:

> *Taqlidi* (traditional) embroidery was an ostentatious and time-consuming endeavour, while *'asri* (modern) designs were pure fun, meant for personal enjoyment. *Taqlidi* embroidery was tedious; you had to make very tight stitches with thin thread for hours, just to cover a few inches of material [...]. The stitches had to look identical on both sides, and the connections between the threads had to be woven in so the knots never showed on the back [...]. In contrast, the birds that Chama and Mother designed did not take much time to embroider at all. Their stitches were looser, they used doubled thread, and the careless, prominent knots that showed on the backside of their cloths were to be expected. Still, the effect was just as lovely as *taqlidi* embroidery, or maybe even more so, thanks to the excitement of the unexpected designs and strange color combinations. (*Dreams* 209)

This passage points to the amount of artistic fancy involved in the modern designs of the caftan, an asset centred on breaking with the strict rules of knitting. Because the latter require plenty of precision and consistence, the Mernissi harem prefer a genuine play on the old and the new, loose and double knots, the imaginative and the unexpected. Such diversity plays out an endeavour to transgress generic purity, unity and authenticity.

3. Challenging Gender boundaries

Since the time-span separating the publication of *The Woman Warrior* from *Dreams of Trespass* is roughly two decades, it is possible arguing that Kingston sets out a tradition of gender transgression after which Mernissi seems to shape out her portrait of the harem. For both writers, the enactment of transgression stands out as a counter strategy that blurs gender hierarchies and at the same time, additionally, turns regulatory conventions of femininity upside down. From such a perspective, reviewing the main aspects of the transgressive legacy in *The Woman Warrior* is essential in order to identify the gender disruptions in *Dreams of Trespass* and explain their meanings. In fact, the significance of *The Woman Warrior*'s heritage is intrinsically related to its contesting the very clear-cut defining of such gender dichotomies as active/passive, rational/emotional and its disclosure of the arbitrariness and unfairness of these cultural definitions.

Essentially, Kingston tacitly filters her counteraction against the masculinist essence of culture through the mimesis of the eminent swordswoman model Fa Mu Lan. The narrator asserts that "[w]e could be heroines, swordswomen," commenting that she failed if she grew up to be but a wife or a slave (*Woman* 19). Besides her resistance to conventional womanly work and in the endeavor to regenerate the legendary woman warrior, the narrator spurs a tough desire to attain male privileges, by bringing home straight A's and voicing the intention to become a lumberjack in Oregon (48-49). This way, the book's transgressive kernel remains embedded in Fa Mu Lan's chant which embodies a pacifist struggle for equality by affirming that "the reporting is the vengeance—not the beheading, not the gutting, but *the words*" (53, my italics). Since reporting refers to telling the stories of the wrongs committed against women in the name of male favoritism, it turns into an empowering means to counteract the stereotype of feminine submission and effacement.

Fa Mu Lan's story best triggers issues of gender transgression also by occasioning performances which shake up the accepted norms of femininity and undermine the rigid split that has long defined its oppositional, inferior subordination to masculinity. It incites the narrator to transform the non-heroic reality of her life mainly through refraining from participating in such traditional female occupations as feeding her family and intending to be a "bad girl," which—in her eyes—is almost a boy (*Woman* 47). Even as a college student in Berkeley in the sixties, she maintains her quest for the phallic woman by rejecting passivity and marching for political causes including protest against the Vietnam War. She even becomes adamant on sabotaging her family's attempts to marry her to a mentally retarded boy (47). Such gestures cast the narrator's quest for becoming a trespasser by excellence within the metaphorical image of the legendary warrior woman.

On the whole, Kingston's gender disruptions amount to a tradition which repeats itself with some variation in Mernissi's *Dreams of Trespass*, as the latter harks back to *The Woman Warrior* mainly by counteracting feminine conventions. In keeping with a Kingstonian spirit, Mernissi overtly challenges male-made boundaries, mirroring "women intent on questioning and subverting the boundaries placed around them" (Jefferey 765). These women's ultimate endeavor consists in changing the laws and codes of their oppression and repression. As Mernissi puts it, the only way to get out is "to change the rules and turn the whole planet upside down" (*Dreams* 63). Only strategic rebellion could ensure a room of one's own in Virginia Woolf's manner and give meaning to an exercise of "all kinds of rights, from the right to move to the right to create, compete, and challenge" (80).

In parallel with *The Woman Warrior* but in a fresh new way, *Dreams of Trespass* is replete with reminiscences of gender transgression, most of which take as a muse the embedded tale of "The Woman's with Wings who could fly away from the courtyard whenever she wanted to" (*Dreams* 22). Hence, much like a rebel mother who dreams of roaming freely in Fez—referred to as "every woman's dream" (22), Fatima tries her chances to become "harem-free" (62) by visiting the forbidden terrace (145) while other women search for love songs in the men's radio after unlocking it with an illegal key (103).[6] This way, nurturing the dream of freedom becomes a spark of liberation, similar to Maxine's total merging with the personality of the Amazonian woman in search of empowerment.

Although similar manifestoes of transgression might sound devoid of courage, none of them are pointless nor can we undermine their dismantling potential, since they still represent a direct defiance against the laws of female seclusion and demureness. On the one hand, these seditious practices remain both clandestine as well as temporally and spatially confined to late afternoons in the courtyard or evenings on the deserted terraces (*Dreams* 81). On the other, they define vigorous gestures of challenge against the *status quo*, hence, resonating with Maxine's anti-marriage schemes or her intention to become a lumberjack in Oregon.

These instances lead us to comment on Mernissi's announced negotiation of the nature of actions that fall under gender transgression. In fact, she points out that the dream to dismantle the private/public dividing line as the only weapon of the dis-empowered against despair does not have the same potential of transgression as the act itself. Moreover, she indicates that such gestures as escaping to the outside streets through the clandestine, covert terrace route can be considered "repulsive to those who were fighting for the principle of a woman's right to free movement" in the sense that it "did not carry with it that inspiring, subversive flame of liberation" (*Dreams* 60). On these grounds, true transgression should rather be associated with more defying counteractions that

6. See appendices 1 and 2 below.

range from a confrontation with the harem gate-keeper (60) to a tactful staging of sedition. Referring to her mother, Fatima relates:

> Often she encouraged me to rebel, and kept repeating that relying on Samir to be aggressive for the both of us would not do. But whenever I threw myself on the floor and started screaming at her, she would stop me on the spot. 'I did not say you ought to rebel against me! You should rebel against all the others, but you still have to obey your mother. Otherwise, it will lead to chaos. And in any case, you shouldn't rebel stupidly. You ought to carefully consider the situation, and analyze everything. Rebel when you know there is some chance you may win.' (117)

As a variation of transgression, sedition needs to be rationalized rather than a pretext for mere anarchy. Strongly reminiscent of Maxine's memorable outbursts toward the closure of *The Woman Warrior*, Fatima's sedition is rather a skill which requires learning and forging.

In a further transgression, Mernissi targets the veil as a significant symbol of female isolation.[7] Thus Fatima's mother is adamant on deterring her nine-year-old daughter from wearing the veil (*Dreams* 100). Instead, she encourages her face the world with her "hair uncovered," since hiding behind the veil "does not solve a woman's problems. It just identifies her as an easy victim" (100). The mother in turn wears a transparent, provocative *litham*, "a tiny triangular black veil made of sheer silk chiffon," but not the traditional veil, "a rectangular piece of white cotton so heavy that it made the simple act of breathing a real accomplishment" (118).[8] In the manner of the nationalists' wives, she explicitly undermines the mouthpieces which treasure conformism in Moroccan embroidery. This points out the rebels' innovative stamina and re-affirms the double interruption of gender and genre boundaries *à la Kingston*.

Eventually, noteworthy about Mernissi's stature as a trespasser comparable to Kingston is the tendency to ground her transgressive tendency in its legitimate context. As a matter of fact, in order to make the frontier worth transgressing, Mernissi takes care to underpin its illogicality, inconsistence and contradictions.

---

7. In explaining the etymology and development of the veil, Golley states: "The veil, in Arabic *hijab*, which linguistically means anything that hides, separates and makes forbidden, was introduced to Islam but went through different stages of meaning [...]. The first refers to a curtain that separates the Prophet from other men, and the last means the veil that covers the women's bodies and faces. The first women to be advised to wear a veil were the women in the family of the Prophet in order to distinguish them from other women, for in those days women especially slaves, were sexually harassed and abused by men in the streets. Eventually, most Muslim women whatever their class, were required to wear the veil" (524).
8. See appendix 3 below.

For one thing, she observes that the male/female boundaries that confine women to a harem life violate "the *hudud* protecting women" by deviating from a fundamental Islamic law which affirms that "[w]hen you hurt a woman, you are violating Allah's sacred frontier. It is unlawful to hurt the weak" (*Dreams* 3). For another thing, from the perspective that "Allah made us all equal," Mernissi surmises that women's seclusion is inhuman as well as irreligious, since it distorts the Islamic *shariya* (9).[9] Further on, she relies on a counter argument provided by the local women in the countryside of Fez and the heroic role they fulfilled, especially, in times of war when they unconventionally joined their male fellows in the battle against colonization (*Dreams* 51). All these examples provide lively examples of how the Moroccan society sows the seeds of its own transgression from within.

4. The Transgressor as Feminist

Such interactive elements between Kingston and Mernissi embody the staying power of *The Woman Warrior* and its international influence on the transnational feminist agenda. Indeed, they attest to the ever-lasting legacy of Kingston as a feminist icon for third world Anglophone writers. This iconic significance emanates essentially from questioning the father's symbolic role as "a limit-setter" or a teacher about laws and taboos (Benstock 148).

However, the argument that the feminist thrust running along *Dreams of Trespass* hinges back to Kingston's transgressions as a feminist writer is no claim that Mernissi's form of Moroccan feminism is western in origin.[10] At least theoretically, colonization is likely to make the modernization of Moroccan women, including their feminism, natural in the sense that the trespassing of conventional gender roles might grow into a legitimate politics of resistance and self-fashioning. Nonetheless, it is important to indicate that "[t]he rise of the women's movement in the Arab world has indeed been affected by women's movements from other parts of the world, but that does not make it alien to Arab culture as such" (Golley 521). What is at stake is that Arab feminism is not a purely imported discourse.

As a matter of fact, arguing for dismantling the existent and dominant norms, aesthetically as well socially speaking, as a *fil-conducteur* between Kingston and Mernissi does not imply sheer imitation, for the mere reason that "Arab

---

9. For an interesting reading of Fatima Mernissi as a re-interpreter of the Islamic texts about the status of women, see Makani.
10. Moroccan feminism is used here "as a general rubric including everything from women in legend and myth, the active roles that women played in social and economic life throughout Moroccan history, to the emancipation of Moroccan women in the context of the nationalist movement, to the situation of young women in Morocco today" (Baker 16).

feminism was not imported from the West. It was an inevitable result of the changes that took place in the area, which encompassed all aspects of life. Arab feminism was born out of the struggle between the dying, traditional, religious feudal Ottoman way of life and the rising, modern, secular, capitalist European ways of life" (Golley 529). Consequently, the present paper does in no way aim to perpetuate Orientalist discourses according to which "the movement for women's liberation is [...] not indigenous to Arab countries" and even "described as mere imitation of similar movements in Europe and the USA" (Golley 522).

Essentially, the transgression of traditional repressive gender rules in favor of modernization and emancipation in *Dreams of Trespass* brings out Kingston's transgressive power as a strategy and a legacy, but this would not have been possible without a range of cultural factors and historical circumstances in colonized Morocco. One major force pushing towards this condition includes the agenda of the nationalist movement about the creation of a New Morocco "with equality for all. Every woman was to have the same right to education as a man, as well as the right to enjoy monogamy—a privileged, exclusive relationship with her husband" (*Dreams* 35). Religious authorities in Morocco played an equally important role in turning gender hierarchies upside down, at least to the extent that they "supported women's rights to go to school" and "encouraged the nationalists to open up institutions of learning for girls" (196). Another factor that paved the way for the modernization of the Moroccan woman lies in the exposure of the Mernissi harem to Egyptian and Lebanese feminists who Fatima's mother, albeit illiterate, remains a fan of (121).

5. Conclusion

In establishing a dialogue between Kingston and Mernissi, I have attempted to demonstrate the ways in which reading the latter's transgressive discourse directly suggests the former's. Nonetheless, it is crucial to add that the circumstances of this transgressive heritage vary from Kingston's context to Mernissi's. In fact, while Kingston's inclination to transgression has much to do with the writer's ethnic status, Mernissi traces back the harem's seditious imagination to the women's identity as Postcolonial Muslim Arabs. With respect to Kingston, transgression is grounded in her Chinese roots and experience of U.S. multiculturalism. Mernissi's negotiation of transgression is broadly interrelated with Western influences (colonization and the writer's college education in the U.S.), but it would not have been possible irrespective of the writer's Islamic/Arab feminism, let alone the chaotic condition of postcolonialism. Thus, it should be noted that both writers keep on straddling boundaries in terms of genre and gender, underpinning their equal status as writers of the in-between. As Mernissi puts it: "To live in a combination of two worlds was much more appealing than living in just one. The idea of being able to swing between two cultures, two personalities, two codes, and two languages enchanted everyone! Mother wanted me to be like Princess Aisha (the teenage daughter of our King Mohammed V who made public speeches in both Arabic and French) who wore both long caftans and short French dresses" (*Dreams* 180).

I have at the same time tried to show that the development of genre and gender transgression in *Dreams of Trespass* leans a great deal on *The Woman Warrior*—mainly in terms of metaphors, strategies, and meanings. From this vantage point, I have pointed out strong indications that Mernissi shapes her counter strategy, at least indirectly, after Kingston in the spirit of challenging voices and spheres seeking to re-assert aesthetic and social conventionalism as a phallocentric commandment. Yet, I should indicate that tracing the reverberating myriad features of transgression in both texts does not aim in any way to perpetuate a stereotype of Kingston's and Mernissi's women characters as being merely submissive and oppressed. On the contrary, if the depicted gestures of genre and gender transgression prove something, it is these characters' stamina of power and their continuous struggle for a voice and independent personalities. Indeed, much like the emphasis in Kingston on the inspirational potential of transgression inherent in the characters' matrilineal legacy, *Dreams of Trespass* equally places the major role of the Mernissi harem as rebel figures within a matrilineal realm perseverant in fighting back silencing and looking for articulation as well as a religious tradition sowing the initial seeds of human rights.[11]

In a strong affinity with Kingston, Mernissi shows a keen interest in interrogating the seclusion of the Mernissi harem and looking for possibilities to treasure their innovative artistic and political expressions. As a result, *The Woman Warrior: Memoirs of a Girlhood* crosses national borders to serve as a kind of a subliminal muse to *Dreams of Trespass: Tales of a Harem Girlhood* at the level of passing on its will to transgress whatever constricting boundaries in favor of delimitation. More importantly, from *The Woman Warrior* to *Dreams of Trespass*, the transgression of genre and gender hierarchies keeps renovating its manifestoes and emerges as a gradual agenda. This renovation re-affirms the continuity between both writers and books without missing out on the multifaceted array through which the straddling of gender and genre boundaries, recasting its indeterminate poetics. In certain ways, Mernissi's *Dreams of Trespass* picks up Kingston's same defying strategy, but also recasts its intention

11. In the Preface to *Women and Islam: A Historical and Theological Enquiry*, Mernissi states that "Muslim women can walk into the modern world with pride, knowing that the quest for dignity, democracy, and human rights, for full participation in the political and social affairs of our country, stems from no imported western values, but is a true part of the Muslim tradition" (viii).

as a non-final process, open to recreation and endlessness. In the meantime, the parameters of this straddling emerge and re-emerge in interconnections.

Appendices:

1. The street outside the harem (photo by Ruth Ward, Mernissi, *Dreams* 19)

2. The Mernissi harem spreading their arms wide as if they were about to fly (photo by Ruth Ward, Mernissi, *Dreams* 19)

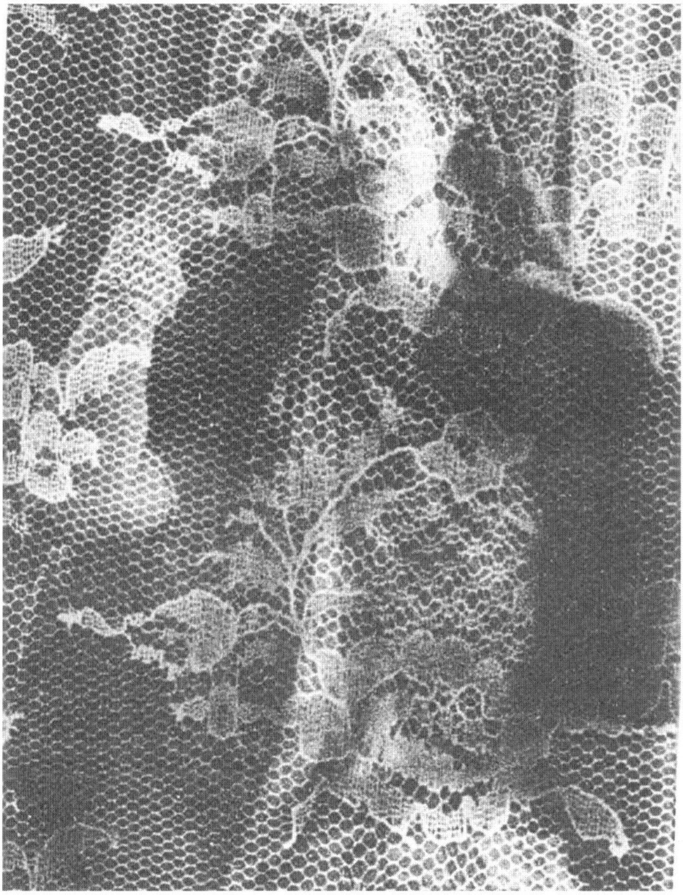

3. The modern veil (photo by Ruth Ward, Mernissi, *Dreams* 20)

Works Cited:

Amir-Ebrahimi, Masserat. "Transgression in Narration: The Lives of Iranian Women in Cyberspace." *Journal of Middle East Women's Studies* 4.3. (Fall 2008): 89-118.

Baker, Alison. *Voices of Resistance and Histories of Moroccan Women*. State U of New York P: New York, 1998.

Benstock, Shari. "Authorizing the Autobiographical." Smith and Watson. 145-55.

Chow, Karen. "Stories to Pass On: Pedagogically Dialoguing Maxine Hong Kingston and Toni Morrison." *Reconfiguring American Literary Studies in the Pacific Rim*. Eds. Noelle Brada Williams and Karen Chow. Hong Kong: Hong Kong UP, 2004. 99-106.

Derrida, Jacques. "The Law of Genre." Trans. Avital Ronell. *Glyph* 7 (1980): 203-4.

Golley, Nawar Al-Hassan. "Is Feminism Relevant to Arab Women?" *Third World Quarterly* 25.3 (2004): 521-36.

Harlow, Barbara. *Resistance Literature*. New York: Methuen, 1987.

Jefferey, Patricia. Review of *Dreams of Trespass: Tales of a Harem Girlhood*, by Fatima Mernissi. New York: Addison-Wesley, 1994. *Social Hierarchies* 24.6 (1995): 764-65.

Jenks, Chris. *Transgression*. London: Routledge, 2003.

Kalogeros, Yiorgos. "Producing History and Telling Stories: Maxine Hong Kingston's *China Men* and Zeese Papanikolas's *Buried Unsung*." *Memory and Cultural Politics*. Eds. Amritjit Singh, Joseph T. Skerrett Jr. and Robert E. Hogan. Boston: Northeastern UP, 1996. 227-44.

Kingston, Maxine Hong. *The Woman Warrior: Memoirs of a Girlhood Among Ghosts*. 1975. New York: Vintage, 1989.

Lim, Shirley Geok-lin, ed. *Approaches to Teaching Kingston's The Woman Warrior*. New York: MLA, 1991.

Ludwig, Sämi. "Celebrating Ourselves in the Other, Or: Who Controls the Conceptual Allusions in Kingston?" *Asian American Literature in the International Context: Readings on Fiction, Poetry, and Performance*. Eds. Rocío G. Davis and Sämi Ludwig. Münster: Lit Verlag, 2002. 37-55.

Makani, Shabana "Islam and Women's Rights." Review of *Women and Islam: A Historical and Theological Enquiry*, by Fatima Mernissi. Trl. Mary Jo Lakeland. New Delhi: Kali Publications, 1993. *Economic and Political Weekly* (July 31, 1993): 1583-84.

Mernissi, Fatima. *Dreams of Trespass: Tales of a Harem Girlhood*. New York: Addison-Wesley, 1994.

—. Preface. *Women and Islam: A Historical and Theological Enquiry*. Trl. Mary Jo Lakeland. New Delhi: Kali Publications, 1993.

Miller, Margaret. "Threads of Identity in Maxine Hong Kingston's *The Woman Warrior*." *Biography* 6.1 (1983): 13-33.

Oster, Judith. *Creating Identity in Chinese and Jewish American Literature*. Columbia and London: U of Missouri P, 2003.

Smith, Sidonie. *Reading Autobiography: A Guide for Interpretive Life Narratives*. Minneapolis: U of Minnesota P, 2001.

Smith, Sidonie and Julia Watson, eds. *Women, Autobiography, Theory: A Reader*. Wisconsin: Wisconsin UP, 1998.

TuSmith, Bonnie. *All My Relatives: Community in Contemporary Ethnic American Literatures*. Ann Arbor: The U of Michigan P, 1996.

IV. Kingston's influence—between paying homage and experiencing an 'anxiety of influence'

Self-Referential Narrative and Creative Filiation in Chinese American Writing: Maxine Hong Kingston and Shirley Geok-lin Lim

Nicoleta Alexoae-Zagni (ISTOM and Université Paris Ouest, Nanterre, France)

This article is a continuation of the analyses undertaken in my doctoral thesis,[1] which interrogated the discursive condition of the contemporary Chinese American location and positioning by discussing three literary works inscribed, from their peritext,[2] in the horizon of expectation of self-referential writing. More precisely, published at an interval of twenty years, the diptych *The Woman Warrior: Memoirs of a Girlhood among Ghosts* (1976) / *China Men* (1980) by Maxine Hong Kingston, on the one hand, and *Among the White Moon Faces: An Asian-American Memoir of Homelands* by Shirley Geok-lin Lim (1996), on the other, testify to creative appropriations of this genre. In dwelling on representatives of different generations, itineraries and ethnic affiliations, my choice also aimed at limning the heteroglossia of the Chinese American writing field. I would like to extend this work here by exploring several facets of a relationship towards heritage conceived otherwise than (only) on a biological mode. For if the question of the identity of the writing subject is examined, in the case of both authors, within a family context and inescapably implies a detour—through one's parents and forebears and their stories—as well as reveals itself as necessarily declined in the light of family, collective and national history, the question of one's filiation is also intimately related to an attitude towards cultural heritage. Interestingly enough, when this question is examined from a literary perspective and focuses on different possible relations to writers and works belonging to a different generation, it mobilizes notions of

1. De l'écriture de soi et ses évolutions dans les œuvres de deux écrivaines sino-américaines : Maxine Hong Kingston et Shirley Geok-lin Lim (On Self-Writing and its Evolutions in the Works of Two Chinese American Writers: Maxine Hong Kingston and Shirley Geok-lin Lim), successfully defended at Paris Diderot University in June 2011 (to be published).
2. As a reminder, the peritext refers to textual and iconographic elements surrounding the text as such, i.e. the title and the subtitle, the name of the author and of the publishing house, the preface, the epigraph, the illustrations and so on. For more see Gérard Genette's masterful analysis of the paratext in *Palimpsestes* (1982).

intertextuality, *mise en abyme* and critical engagement with the memory of literature and its dynamic.

This articulation between biological and literary filiation is forefronted from the opening of *Among the White Moon Faces*, where a paginal juxtaposition of lyrical and narrative sections introduces what I would identify as the structuring motif of the memoir:

> Midlife stalled, I look for women.
> Where are they my mothers and sisters?
> I listen for their voices in poems.
> Help me, I have fallen asleep, fallen
> With sleepers. These women have murdered
> Themselves, violent, wrenched from home.
>
> Grandmother was barren. She died,
> Tubes in nose and green shaky arm,
> Hair yellow, a dirty dye, patches
> Like fungus on a stricken pine.
>
> I read terrible stories—
> Hate, rage, futility of will—
> And look for women, the small
> Sufficient swans, showers of stars (*Moon Faces* 5th inside front cover)

The question of the existence of feminine referential figures is openly addressed from the threshold of the book by means of a first line that the punctuation marks as self-sufficient. This reinforces its revealing force of positing key (self-) referential and thematic aspects: an enunciative instance halfway through her life, in search of a community of women. The quest is outlined as one for a familial as well as for an artistic community, a quest for figures of transmission in a broad sense of the term, and it seems marked by sterility and stasis. The notion of filiation, in a biological acceptation—that locates the body in relation to an origin—or in a symbolic one—that informs and sustains one's existence and hence provides directions to and through its possibles—is highlighted here; the text is placed under the sign of the quest for protective and inspiring tutelary figures, the identity and the subjectivity of the woman writer being compelled to shape and imagine themselves from and despite this shriveling, ill blossomed, discontinuous and uncertain genealogy.

Along these lines, it seems potentially enriching to read Lim's musing on cultural lineage according to a principle of active intertextuality, regarding, more particularly, Maxine Hong Kingston's *The Woman Warrior. Memoirs of a Girlhood among Ghosts*. My basic postulation is that references to this seminal and uniquely innovative work in (Chinese) American letters are visible on a double level, diegetic and extradiegetic, and weave a fruitful relationship not only with the conceptualizations of self-representation that emerge in Kingston's first *opus*, but also with the narrative and discursive configurations that sustain them. These are, to a certain extent, expected and legitimate references if one keeps in mind Lim's work on, as well as appreciation of this book—Lim the academic, the literature scholar and theoretician. For that matter, if a lifelong commitment to the defense and study of literature in general and to the field of Asian American letters in particular were not sufficient an indicator, the Chinese Malaysian explicitly dwells on it in an interview:

> Kingston is a writer I admire tremendously. She has a great deal of integrity. She is my model. Although she is not much older than I, she has achieved more, in a much more profound way in terms of writing. [...]. She is a writer whom I deeply appreciate and admire. But my 'memoir,' perhaps deliberately, has not sought to model on *The Woman Warrior* or *China Men*. [...]. I don't want to be a second-rate Kingston, I want to be myself. (Wang 158)

Lim's assertions and especially the comment following the adversative conjunction "but" invite the idea of the necessity of coming to terms with a literary role figure, of acknowledging her influence without being shadowed by her achievements. This operates on a double-level: on an auctorial one, to the extent that Kingston can be seen as a symbolic, imaginary, trailblazing mother, an ideal Lim refers to but wants to distance herself from to stand out; as well as on a thematic, textual and metatexual one, traces of which I will attempt to fathom here.

This interweaving of a mental literary geography and of a cultural geology suggests that here, the notion of literary filiation takes other acceptations than the traditional pitting against one's predecessors' aesthetics to include a critical reading that turns the scrutinizing gaze back upon oneself. This reading that actually searches in the narrative of another the traces and the negotiations of one's own queries so as to confront them and take them to even greater depths evinces itself at a turning point in *Among the White Moon Faces*—when the narrator evokes her decision to change her career by leaving the community college and enroll in a summer seminar hosted by the feminist intellectual Nancy K. Miller:

> I began the seminar almost a decade after the publication of Maxine Hong Kingston's *The Woman Warrior*. Many of the stories of a misogynist Chinese immigrant society in [her] fiercely imagined book were familiar to me. [...]. For years I had been writing to myself, the poems and stories in my desk drawer growing dog-eared and yellow. (*Moon Faces* 226)

To read Lim's narrative effectively, one should then be attentive to this manner in which the subject moves forward into herself and undertakes to work and build an *oeuvre* through a creative development that practices the deference in the difference, the dialogue and the critical engagement that allow for passing judgment on one's own position and negotiating its inscription by querying the real-life itinerary of another as well as her scriptural approach and mediation of it. This strategy has the advantage of accommodating a liberation from an "anxiety of influence" exerted by a predecessor's work so well established in the canon of American letters to the point of becoming a sort of procrustean standard for publishers and / or mainstream readers, as Lim didn't fail to notice:

> What I hear from a lot of writers who are now being published is that when they first go to a press, the press will say to them, 'Oh, this isn't like Maxine Hong Kingston.' What the press wants is a sure-fire success, a product. They want you to have a sequel the way that Hollywood has a sequel to a hit. (Templin 82)

This liberation is based on the lucid avowal that whatever anxiety or distancing might be, they should be understood not only as being driven by a desire of singularity, the wish to impose a unique creative vision, but also by having to deal with the stereotypes imposing upon the reading of ethnic texts:

> When Maxine Hong Kingston's first book [...] came out in 1976, a number of academic friends, inferring that my immigrant Asian background would tilt me toward the book, suggested strongly I check it out. I was so offended by their blatant stereotyping that I did not read the book until three years later... ("*The Woman Warrior*" 4)

Like other Asian American writers in the 80s and 90s,[3] Lim faced the challenge of inscribing her originality while at the same time inserting herself into a literary tradition.

For the purpose of the present discussion, I will now turn to examining some specific aspects that attest, in *Among the White Moon Faces. An Asian-American Memoir of Homelands*, to this (re)generating relationship to *The Woman Warrior. Memoirs of a Girlhood among Ghosts*, undeniably a founding book in the tradition of Chinese American self-writing, one that has run a gamut of responses, from admiration or hesitation to anxiety or rejection.

As explained earlier, with Lim we address a critical and reflexive writing that engages with other imaginings and representations in search of a dialogue that enable it to test and experience itself, and this emerges from the threshold of the narrative, from its peritext and its *incipit*. With respect to the latter, I owe a terminological and methodological clarification: its delimitation will be made following Andrea Del Lungo's pioneering analyses in *L'Incipit romanesque* (2003), where he departs from the traditional approaches that often limit the

3. The editors of the most significant collection of interviews with Maxine Hong Kingston, Paul Skenazy and Tera Martin, recall that "her voice had so stamped itself on the publishing industry as the Asian American consciousness that some young writers complained to her that they were getting 'a generic Maxine Hong Kingston rejection letter' from publishers looking for Kingston imitations," with the publishers going as far as advising them to read her work before attempting anything else ("Introduction" vii).

examination to the first sentence only, by positing the notion of an initial textual unit—formal and/or thematic—of variable length (50-54). One could thus wonder if, in the presence of, on the one hand, a title marked by the parageneric indication "memoir" and conveying a spectral theme as well as of, on the other hand, a textual icebreaker that hails the reader by means of an expression of confusion and doubts conveyed by a narrator confronted to a multiplicity of ambivalent, concealed, denied and ambiguous presences, if all these elements do not prefigure an aesthetical and ideological relation to the celebrated account of a "girlhood among ghosts." With the aim of teasing this out, I'll follow in the wake of Del Lungo's conceptualization of the incipit as a textual space which, due to its intermediate position, has a close metonymical relationship with the elements of the peritext that precede it as well as with the text that follows it (55). This understanding presents the advantage of proceeding to an examination of the inaugural sections of both narratives, before turning to the peritext.

"'You must not tell anyone,' my mother said, 'what I am about to tell you'" (*Woman Warrior* 1). The kingstonian narrative opens *in medias res*, or rather *in media verba*. The "attack phrase" (Del Lungo 55) singles out, by means of quotation marks, the speech ban while simultaneously displaying the transgressive character of the inaugural speech act. The words belong to the mother and the narrator distinguishes her voice through diacritical signs. The narration is placed from the *incipit* under the aegis of the forbidden, the highlighting of the ban finally appearing all the more ironic since the narrator chooses to break it in a radical way. The literary enunciation proceeds to reveal the fate of an adulterous aunt who humiliated and brought disgrace not only upon her family but also upon the village, now completely erased from the family lineage (1-2). Maternal speech, always delimited by quotes, seems to relay the demands and constraints of the patriarchal system—the use of the plural pronoun "us" or "we" suggesting indeed an identification of the mother with a collective voice—, the injunction to silence and exclusion imposed by the old culture bespeaking an attempt to maintain dignity and secrecy, closely linked to cultural etiquette. The necessity to conceal the shameful event is reinforced several times over the next few paragraphs which recount this embarrassing event (3-5).

What the dramatic intensity of the inaugural scene announces is without any doubt the refusal of conformism and the quest for another way and / or voice. A sudden custodian of a legacy that befuddles her, the narrator first keeps it at a distance (as evinced by the quotes) but refuses to let herself be petrified by it: the warning is perceived as disturbing rather than instructive and entails questioning at the boundaries of the forbidden as well as of one's self. The closing quotation mark that puts as abrupt a stop to Brave Orchid's words as was given to their start, allows the narrator to gradually prepare the ground for addressing a fundamentally disturbing question. Thus, within three paragraphs are tossed off a number of critical elements defining the everyday life of immigrant Asian families; they spell out the shock of the socio-cultural change and adjustment for the representatives of the first generation—"those [...] who could not reassert brute survival died young and far from home" (5)—and the strict legislative measures regulating the Asian presence in the American national space, leading to specific adaptation patterns and strategies: "The Chinese I know hide their names; sojourners take new names when their lives change and guard their real names with silence "(5). It is then no wonder that cross-generational communication is vexed or non-existent: "[The immigrants] must try to confuse their offspring as well; who, I suppose, threaten them in similar ways" (5). Having enumerated all this on a rising tone, the voicing reaches an explosion: "Chinese-Americans, when you try to understand what things in you are Chinese, how do you separate what is peculiar to childhood, to poverty, insanities, one family, your mother who marked your growing with stories, with what is Chinese? What is Chinese tradition and what is the movies?" (5-6). As noted by Sau-ling Wong, the question arising here addresses the possibility of telling the difference between Chinese traditions and their representations or distortions, or even individual peculiarities, especially in cases when one's parents were transplanted to an "isolated ethnic community" and experience themselves, often unawares, major cultural transformations—and this even more so when the dominant society systematically denies legitimacy to their existence ("Ethnic Dimensions" 276). For if one cannot even understand what is related to Chineseness in everyday life, how can that person assert herself with confidence as a "Chinese American"?

The answer is not given directly but emerges obliquely; for if the narrator knows that her mothers' silence is definitive—"My mother has told me once and for all the useful parts. She will add nothing unless powered by necessity" (6), she shifts the focus from the result on the causes and seeks to give new meanings to the story of the unnamed aunt by offering alternative readings. It is urgent to find a meaning that can be applied to her own life and create a significant connection to this ancestor—to "see her life branching into mine" (8). As this is a well-known section and has been abundantly commented upon, I will not dwell on it here, only remember, for the sake of my argument, that the recreated versions are more sympathetic towards the forerunner's figure, choosing to highlight how the expectations projected upon women were actually synonyms of restrictions, or to depict the aunt as a determined woman who chose adultery of her own will and desire. In both imagined versions the "unnamed woman" commits suicide by drowning with her newborn in the family well, refusing to disclose the name of the genitor.

With the construction of a rebellious female figure, the reader is presented, indeed, with alternative mises-en-scène of female subjectivity. But something even more transgressive takes place at the level of the enunciative act itself, namely the presence of an enunciator who is both intra- and extradiegetic, positioning herself constantly in relation to the narrative itself. This transgression of narrative levels that Gérard Genette has termed "metalepsis" inscribes a relationship between the author and the work in the making (*Métalepse* 10). The intrusion into the diegesis is indicated, in *The Woman Warrior*'s opening scene, through persuasive narrative and stylistic rebellions. What they signify is that imagining a life for the aunt and using, to that end, fictional techniques, this does not automatically imply writing a text that would be fiction in the generic or conventional sense of the term. Accordingly, the moments of discursive disobedience are advertised as deliberate transgressions. Several warnings hail the reader, suggesting that he/she take a step in the text without expecting a historical narrative or a fictional one, but rather an interplay of the two, symbolizing a search for truth through writing. Epanorthosis, already installed as a narrative strategy with the imagination of several hypotheses leading to adultery and suicide, is amplified by means of explicitly formulated speculations, conjectures, hesitations; the narration fumbles under the sign of "perhaps" or "I wonder whether" (6), trying to probe deeper into the limits of the cautionary tale in order to find useful props for self-construction. "She may have been unusually loved," assumes, for instance, the scriptural instance (10), introducing, in search of a stronger ancestral figure, the idea of parental love for girls despite the prevailing mentality that deems them of little value.

The metaleptic situation is pushed even further, as every time the narrator imagines alternative versions of the life of her forebear, the reality of her own life, extradiegetic, is woven with the imagined possibilities and the material conditions of the aunt's story or with aspects of the lives of Asian immigrants in general. These fictional constructions enable her to reflect on purely personal realities, relevant of an American context: "I used to add 'brother' silently to boys' names. It hexed the boys, who would or would not ask me to dance, and made them less scary and as familiar and deserving of benevolence as girls" (12). Through sudden bursts of humor that lighten up the seriousness of the text, digressions reveal facets of the double binds in a Chinese American woman's existence: "But, of course, I hexed myself also—no dates. I should have stood up, both arms waving, and shouted out across libraries, 'Hey, you! Love me back.' I had no idea how to make attraction selective, how to control its direction and magnitude" (12). By means of this ludic metalepsis, a more mature and adult voice ironically comments on the choice of Maxine the narrator. The blurring of narrative levels entailed by this strategy shakes the certainties of self-representation and invites the reader into a relationship of complicity.

If imagination is harnessed to fill in the gaps, this is not done at the expense of the real, authentic socio-cultural background or historical subtext. The *hic et nunc* of the story are mediated by a foregrounding of this ignored family member as a subject living in a society where, for instance, personal freedom, including that of a woman, endanger the collective survival—"The villagers punished her for acting as if she could have a private life, secret and apart from them" (12), or as experiencing historical moments pertaining not only to the native country but equally shaping the relationship between China and America at the beginning of the twentieth century—as the allusion to the "hurried wedding" and the husband who "sailed for America, the Gold Mountain" (3) prove. Accordingly, the metaleptical gesture displays the questions that torment and assail the enunciator and the narrative, as well as the formal qualms that haunt them—in the line of comments such as "[i]magining her free with sex doesn't fit. [...]. I don't know any woman like that, or man either" (8).

Ambiguity is reinstated with the last paragraph of the *incipit*: in relating the story of the unnamed woman, the enunciative instance underscores her Americanness revealed precisely by this courage to "name the unspeakable" that the parents fear (5); yet, other comments disclose paradoxically a set of strongly internalized superstitions testifying to her Chinese heritage: "My aunt haunts me—her ghost drawn to me [...]. I do not think she always means me well. [...]. I am telling on her" (16). Her mind and reason appear as if torn between two different systems of thought and worldviews, the final lines of the *incipit* inscribing an even deeper disarray.

Consequently in Kingston's case, delineating one's own memorial space with words is a process that does not tolerate solipsism or condone narcissistic complacency. The act of self-enunciation breaks with a tradition of monological and monolinear autoreferential representations[4] and exposes the very efforts towards understanding, recovering and pulling together. Self-expression can only be achieved by violating the ban—here lies the ambivalence of the maternal injunction that accompanies the entry into adulthood. The female, the feminine and the question of matrilineage are inscribed from the beginning: this is a story of women, about women, between and among women negotiating different systems of thought, modes of subjectivity and contradicting stories.

In *Among the White Moon Faces*, the section following the poem that I examined earlier is entitled "Prologue." It is not only a reverberant space of the obsessive quest for female community and lineage, but also an introduction, *ex abrupto*, to a personal and historical context marked by syncretic and eclectic cultural and linguistic configurations:

> The first time I heard Shakespeare quoted, it was as a joke. Malayans speaking pidgin English would dolefully break out into Elizabethan lines, 'Romeo, Romeo, wherefore art thou, Romeo?' before bursting into chortles and sly looks. 'Aiyah! Dia Romeo, lah!'—'He's a Romeo!'—I heard said over and over again of any number of men, including my father, Baba. (*Moon Faces* 1)

The playful subversion of traditional or canonical Western references through hybridized practices is immediately pointed out as underlying a darker reality.

---

4. For a detailed discussion of this tradition see Sau-ling Wong's essay "Immigrant Autobiography: Some Questions of Definition and Approach" (1991).

Indeed, the antonomasis is dwelt on and explicated as spelling out limiting social configurations for women, for if Romeo denotes "zany male freedom permitted under Westernization," and "there was a Romeo around every corner," there is no trace of a Malayan "Juliette" (1).

The quest for inspiring feminine figures is reiterated by a positioning in the childhood's space and time, a *lieu de mémoire* defined by the narrator through specific references and tones that convey an early awareness of the hybridity and multiplicity of her cultural environment, where Chinese, Malayan, British and American cultures blend seamlessly. Its importance is thus not only confirmed but equally increased, as it is increasingly associated with an epistemological difficulty in this context marked by omissions, subversions and double meanings: "This was Shakespeare in my tropics, and romantic love, and the English language: mashed and chewed, then served up in a pattering patois which was our very own. Our very own confusion" (1-2). The process of self-understanding and definition is faced with the difficulty of negotiating the tensions arising from contradictions and conflicts of cultures, languages, influences and desires; on this shaky ground, as if attempting to reach some confirmation and assertion of certainty, the narrator's reflections resort to a common strategy of autobiographical narratives: the reference to one's origin. The turn to a self-referential terrain is abrupt—"I didn't know about Juliet, but I knew my name" (2), and in an obvious attempt to prove that she "knows," the narrative instance dwells on the origin and meaning of the name that appears on her birth certificate. She thus enlarges on how her arrival into the world placed her directly in an ancestral line, a patrilineal and patriarchal clan, as revealed by "Geok-lin Lim," a name chosen from a list prepared in advance by the paternal grandfather. It is then Baba, her father, steeped in Western culture and particularly in Hollywood films, who names her "Shirley" in reference to the child actress Shirley Temple (2-3). Later, for her religious confirmation, she herself chooses the name of "Jennifer" after Jennifer Jones, a Hollywood actress she admires (4).

Expertly wrought as this is, it doesn't take long though for the narratorial "I" to show signs of difficulty in identifying with her full name; the "excess of belonging"[5] is encapsulated in one sentence sapping any feeling of confidence/sureness, revealing a deep identity confusion and crisis: "Too many names, too many identities, too many languages" (4). Any expectation of a retrospective story that would proceed to an affirmation of the coherence and unity of one's life is thus shattered from the very introductory paragraphs. The few remaining pages of the "Prologue" can only convey a strong sense of confusion: directly, when the narrator recollects the shock of seeing Shirley Temple for the first time and whose physical appearance, so different from hers,

5. I use here Aijaz Ahmad formulation in his study on Salman Rushdie (Ahmad 127).

triggers a true identity shock (2-3); indirectly, through statements pertaining much too frequently to a semantic field mapping different shades of distress, marked by words such as "confusion," "mystery," "uncertain," alternating with rhetorical questions such as "what would I call myself?" (3), or musings trying to grasp with the benefit of hindsight the meaning of certain gestures or actions.

The paragraphs that express this difficulty of self-designation—"what would I call myself?" (3)—are outstandingly interesting from the standpoint of the enunciation, in particular with respect to focalization. What the narrative undertakes, on several occasions, is to recount an event first as a subject who remembers it and to (re)present it afterwards again, as a critical voice examining the possible meanings of this event. To give an illustration of this, let me return to the question of the name: the narrator recalls that all her cousins were called by their Chinese ming (the "personal name")—Ah Lan, Ah Mui, Ah Pei, while she remained Shirley for everyone: "'Ah Shirley,' my aunts called me" (2). These memories, rendered in a rather light and funny tone, are followed by reflections on the reasons underlying her father's unconventional choice of a name for somebody belonging by birth to a traditional Chinese family. In placing these considerations under the sign of retrospective desire—"I'd like to think"—the enunciative instance imagines that this early westernization that she is subject to is not a mere sign of colonial imitation, but Baba's wish for her to transgress any identity attachments predestined by birth as well as any form of denial of civil liberties in the name of ancestral traditions:

> It remains a mystery to me what strange racial yearnings moved Baba to name me after a blond child. I'd like to think he was not tied to the fixities of race and class, that this presumption was less colonized mimicry than bold experiment. Looking at the dozens of nieces duplicated for a domestic future, did he rebel for me? Although, unarguably, he has written in his neat English script my Chinese name on my birth certificate, he never called me anything but Shirley, a Hollywood name for a daughter for whom he wished, despite everything his heritage dictated, a life freer than his own. (3)

As Rocío Davis has observed, the interpretation of the paternal decision clearly projects the author's own perspective on issues that have been a major concern in her academic career, issues that will also be at the heart of the unfolding text: "individuality in the context of Chinese girlhood, the choice of English as a marker of identity, and the need to escape the strictures of poverty and Malay society" (Davis 450). I would include to this metaleptic gesture the preoccupation with a more symbolic genealogy and artistic inheritance, as indicated by the reference to Virginia Woolf and artistic matrilineage in the last paragraph of this introductory section (5). This approach equally prefigures a scriptural undertaking more complex than a simple transcription or recounting of experiences, where self-writing is deployed as a gesture of analysis and evaluation. This memoir is not about asserting certainties, but rather about trying to understand the meaning of an action in the past or retrieving continuities, even by means of impossible-to-answer questions. It reveals the very attempts at apprehending and interpreting, awareness and understanding being particularly important in the economy of the work. Thus, if the structure of the memoir (the parts and the chapters) follow an advancing in life chronology, the "Prologue" introduces a multiplicity of perspectives, translated by a constant insertion of retrospective comments, musings and questions that complement the simple act of telling.

Like Maxine Hong Kingston's, these strategies, whose result is generic ambiguity, bespeak epistemological doubt. Lim's narrative is obviously in the tradition of its famous intertext, inscribing itself in a recognizable genealogy. Redrawing boundaries in scriptural and interpretative acts, Kingston has indeed set the tone in self-referential writing by formulating the impossibility of impermeable borders between facts and stories, truth and imagination. Lim adheres to this notion of self-writing that should not be understood as asserting certainties, but as trying to negotiate and reconcile meanings, even by means of questions without answers, as the excerpts analyzed above illustrate it. She shares Kingston's doubts as to the possibility of transcribing one's experience with ease and certainty, introducing the same reflective pauses cracking the linearity of the narrative. The writing instance, no longer pretending to know everything about her life, cuts sequences that will be unraveled and replayed, never fully certain or reassured as to their meaning. Along these lines, both *incipits* foreground a narrative voice rhythmed by comings and goings between the past and the present, and inscribe a quest for self-consistency which can obviously not be accomplished on a syntagmatic mode of a retrospective, teleological, totalizing account. The enunciation interweaves the two discursive registers, of the factual and of the fictive, the "I" emerging as polyphonic and dialogical, outward and community focused, encompassing and claiming other "I"s of real and/or mythical figures that haunt it. Consequently, the questions of filiation, belonging or collective memory break the referential singularity of a univocal enunciative instance, and justify a biographical focalization on other people or characters who are the inspiration and/or the skeletal structure of the *mise-en-scène* of one's own self. In both cases, the *incipits* formulate the first steps of this search and signify the importance of writing as a means of affirming one's identity, the only one able to facilitate negotiations and allow for reconciliations. Strategic locations, they impose themselves as metaphors of highly thought-out (self-)representations, directing the eye not only to the text they invest as the very instrument of the quest for self-understanding and expression itself, but also shed a retrospective signifying light on several key elements of the peritextual apparatus. With this conviction in mind, it is to some elements of the latter that I will now turn my attention, to see how this historical and critical consciousness that animates Lim's narrative also reveals a considerable inflection of the kingstonian tradition.

Let me only recall here that the Malacca native writer works with, or rather starts, from her illegitimacy, of which she herself is very clearly aware: "If American culture and the English language form the singular norm by which an Asian-American identity has been recognized, then clearly I am insufficiently American, possessing as I do a personal history of multiple cultures and languages" (THE WOMEN'S 211). In this context, my take is that when she proceeds to inscribing an itinerary of palimpsestic and multidirectional locations and affiliations, she actually blatantly advocates a reconfiguration of the boundaries of the US literary imagination by imposing the reconceptualization of "Chinese Americanness" as necessarily transcultural and transnational. With this gesture, the question of intertextuality conceived as filiation not only posits that inheritance is possible, but also shows that innovation, reformulation and displacement do not necessarily have to be matricidal. As such, Lim is a genuine disciple of Kingston's—by this, I mean that not only does she inherit from her, but equally takes her where she has not been or more precisely, where she will go much later.

This extension of the contours of previous modes of representation and paradigms is obvious on a both generic and thematic level and with the benefit of hindsight, especially when considered in the light of the cultural practice in vogue before the 1990s whereby Asian Americans preferred to omit the hyphen between the two words "Asian" and "American," as Americanization or Americanness were perceived as difficultly compatible with the expression of Asian affiliations. Kingston herself encouraged this elimination, in the same vein as her incitement to "claim America" in a context of cultural and political marginalization and exclusion of both people and cultural productions:

> [W]e ought to leave out the hyphen in 'Chinese-American,' because the hyphen gives the word on either side equal weight, as if linking two nouns. It looks as if a Chinese-American is double citizenship, which is impossible in today's world. Without the hyphen, 'Chinese' is an adjective and 'American' a noun; a Chinese American is a type of American. ("Cultural Mis-readings" 59)

This idea mattered so much to her that she chose to reintroduce it, almost word-for-word, in *Tripmaster Monkey* through Wittman Ah Sing, male character, her alter-ego (*Tripmaster Monkey* 27).

With Lim, who deliberately positions her narrative in the memorial tradition—"[I wrote] to produce a work that would 'stand' on its use of language, *a contribution to the long line of other literary productions recognized as memoirs*" (Singh 139, my emphasis)—and conspicuously proceeds to it in the vein of her illustrious predecessor by means of parageneric and thematic indications and allusions from the subtitle and the title,[6] an emancipatory evolution and renewal of interpretative frameworks is proposed. "An Asian-American Memoir of Homelands": in spelling the epithet "Asian-American" with a hyphen, Lim stakes a different "claim": that to non-hierarchical multiple belongings, echoing the plural "homelands"; that to a vision driven by this hyphen relating the Asian and the American identity, or by the search for a hyphen. This kind of dialectic between roots and routes programmatically announced from the peritext challenges from the outset any notion of a unique motherland and expresses the audacity of drawing up a mapping of the self which is not limited to a single national territory. This is strongly confirmed and illustrated in the *incipit*, through the aforementioned inscription of an itinerary of palimpsestic and multidirectional locations and affiliations. What is simultaneously disturbed are the implicit, the traditional or the newly acquired valences of memoir writing by an expansion as well as a reconfiguration of the boundaries of this self-referential genre. *Among the White Moon Faces* is thus a book undermining any impulse to generic or interpretative fixity altogether by proposing an inscription of specific forms of an intertwining of these coexistent belongings and itineraries disturbing U.S. nationalist epistemologies. For that matter, Lim has repeatedly criticized the easy antinomies as ineffective for the understanding of the other, in all of his/her multiplicity and contradictions—and the temptation to reduce a plural reality to a univocal whole: "[W]hile my memoir is chiefly read as U.S. ethnic, it is in fact transnational, threading between at least two subjectivities, a Malaysian Chinese and an Asian American" ("Academic and Other Memoirs" 36). Ultimately, even if it connects the two texts, even if it appears as the locus through which transmission operates, the title subverts the initial established meanings and recontextualizes them, using them as reflecting model of the text it precedes.

For all these reasons, *Among the White Moon Faces* appears as a narrative that inscribes the movement of its own memory, of the echoes and tensions between the return and the origin. It also evinces a treelike genealogy, with numerous branches where filiations disperse, their developments both vertical and horizontal. Texts influence one another, in a relational and transformational manner, according to a principle of redistribution of hierarchies. Testifying to this is the fact that in Kingston's latest work *I Love a Broad Margin to My Life* (2011) Wittman Ah Sing feels finally free to consider a similar two-continent spanning cartography and accounts for it as follows:

> … I'm going to China
> I regret I missed the Revolution, and ongoing

---

6. Because of space constraints, I cannot aim at exhausting the interpretative possibilities of this issue by including a discussion of the spectral theme common to both.

> Revolutions. I was kept busy claiming
> this country. 'Love it or leave it.' 'Chink,
> go back to China, Chink.' I had to
> claim my place, root down, own
> America. This land is my land (41)

The trip to China can only be envisaged after having "claimed" America. Undeniably, it was Maxine Hong Kingston who laid down an innovative framework in which Asian American literature could firmly establish a tradition and develop. Unquestionably, it was she who first vehemently denounced the predominant interpretative tendencies of categorizing Asian American writers by foregrounding their otherness:

> Another bothersome characteristic of the reviews is the ignorance of the fact that I am an American. [...]. *The Woman Warrior* is an American book. Yet many reviewers do not see the American-ness of it, nor the fact of my own American-ness. ("Cultural Mis-Readings" 57)

And undoubtedly, it is *The Woman Warrior* that stands out as not only a moment of rupture with respect to an auctorial doxa compelled to correspond to predefined criteria of ethnic literary production, but more significantly one of overcoming and redrawing of boundaries.

Nevertheless, my firm take is that only thanks to the creative and intellectual vision and investment of writers like Lim, who have been striving to impose an enlarged acceptation of "Asian American," has Wittman (and Kingston herself by the same token) managed to transcend the fissures and the fragmentation of the hyphenated subject. This character concludes, indeed, in the California native's latest book, by serenely outlining the contours of the third millennium Chinese Americanness as encompassing entity of multiple territories and imaginaries, real and/or symbolic—what he calls "Asia America" (*Broad Margin* 41).

My own conclusion to this paper would be that the negotiation of legacy and heritage in contemporary Chinese American writing reaches multiple truths by crossing the memory of a time that is not only individual and/or North American, covering topographies and chronologies of anteriority and otherness, in order to assert them freely in a space conceived as transnational and diasporic, as well as necessarily dialogic. In Lim's and Kingston's case, the questions of heritage or, for that matter, the one of transmission go beyond the simple following in someone's footsteps or unilateralism to which they are usually reduced, weaving into the literary field other connections than those established by chronology or aesthetics. These two writers' narratives put forward a notion of filiation understood and built as a legitimizing, inspiring and productive relationship with the previous or contemporary literature, where the writer extends and takes to greater depths the literary issues that 'created' her, in a permanent intersection of familial, communal, national, textual and intertextual memories, where the lines between filiation and affiliation blur in cross-fertilization.

Works Cited

Ahmad, Aijaz. *In Theory: Classes, Nations, Literatures*. Delhi: Oxford UP, 1994.

Davis, Rocío G. "Academic Autobiography and Transdisciplinary Crossings in Shirley Geok-lin Lim's *Among the White Moon Faces*." *Journal of American Studies* 43.3 (2009): 441-57.

Del Lungo, Andrea. *L'Incipit romanesque*. Paris: Éd. du Seuil, 2003.

Genette, Gérard. *Métalepse*. Paris: Éd. du Seuil, 2004.

—. *Palimpsestes. La Littérature au second degré*. Paris: Éd. du Seuil, 1982.

Kingston, Maxine Hong. "Cultural Mis-readings." *Asian and Western Writers in Dialogue: New Cultural Identities*. Ed. Guy Amirthanayagam. London: MacMillan, 1982. 55-65.

—. *I Love a Broad Margin to My Life*. London: Harvill Secker, Random House, 2011.

—. *Tripmaster Monkey: His Fake Book*. 1989. New York: Vintage Books, 1990.

—. *The Woman Warrior: Memoirs of a Girlhood among Ghosts*. 1976. New York: Vintage International, 1989.

Lim, Shirley Geok-lin. "Academic and Other Memoirs: Memory, Poetry, and the Body." *Ethnic Life Writing and Histories: Genres, Performance and Culture*. Eds. Rocío G. Davis, Jaume Aurell and Ana Beatriz Delgado. Berlin: LIT Verlag, 2007. 22-39.

—. *Among the White Moon Faces: An Asian-American Memoir of Homelands*. New York: The Feminist Press, 1996.

—. "*The Woman Warrior*: Her Planetary Asian American Imagination." *American Book Review* 31.1 (November/December 2009): 4-5.

Singh, Kirpal. "An Interview with Shirley Geok-lin Lim." *ARIEL: A Review of International English Literature* 4.4 (October 1999): 135-41.

Skenazy, Paul and Martin, Tera. "Introduction." *Conversations with Maxine Hong Kingston*. Eds. Paul Skenazy and Tera Martin. Jackson: UP of Mississippi, 1998. vii-xix.

Templin, Charlotte. "Creative Writer, Woman, Academic: Shirley Lim in Dialogue with Charlotte Templin." *Asian American Writing. The Diasporic Imagination*. Ed. Somdatta Mandal. New Delhi: Prestige Books, 2000. 71-84.

THE WOMEN'S REVIEW OF BOOKS. "Singapore on My Mind: Fiona Cheung, Lydia Kwa and Shirley Geok-lin Lim Compare Notes." *Women's Review of Books* 19.10/11 (July 2002): 24-26.

Wang, Jennie. "An Interview with Shirley Geok-lin Lim." *Speaking of the Short Story: Interviews with Contemporary Writers*. Eds. Farhat Iftekharuddin, Mary Rohrberger and Maurice Lee. Jackson: UP of Mississippi, 1997. 153-65.

Wong, Sau-ling Cynthia. "Ethnic Dimensions of Postmodern Indeterminacy: Maxine Hong Kingston's *The Woman Warrior* as Avant-garde Autobiography." *Autobiographie & Avant-garde*. Eds. Alfred Hornung and Ernstpeter Ruhe. Tübingen: Gunter Narr Verlag, 1992. 273-84.

—. "Immigrant Autobiography: Some Questions of Definition and Approach." *American Autobiography: Retrospect and Prospect*. Ed. Paul John Eakin. Madison: UP of Wisconsin, 1991. 142-70.

Staying Alive: Kingston's *Woman Warrior* Afterlife and Marilyn Chin's *Revenge of the Mooncake Vixen*

Sau-ling Cynthia Wong (University of California, Berkeley, U.S.A.)

Over three decades after it appeared on the American cultural scene, Maxine Hong Kingston's *The Woman Warrior* (1976) is arguably the only Asian American literary text securely canonized in American literature, having withstood potential challenges in popular reach from Amy Tan's *The Joy Luck Club* (1989), and in academic institutional status from Theresa Hak Kyung Cha's *Dictee* (first published in 1982 and republished in 2001 after a critic-led "revival"). With the Cold War's end and the steady growth of American Studies all over the world, of which the dissemination of the American literary canon forms a significant part, *The Woman Warrior* has also become a staple of "world literature." In a thoughtful essay published in 2008, entitled "'The Beginning Is Hers': The Political and Literary Legacies of Maxine Hong Kingston and Amy Tan," Helena Grice notes that while it is important to appreciate these writers' thematic legacies (such as mother-daughter relationships, the figure of the "woman who endures," and "China fictions" in the diasporic imagination) and formal legacies (such as genre-crossing and the short story cycle; see Davis), one must also consider the risk of ossification, that is, allowing issues about a text from one critical practice to obscure other equally valid ones, or one familiar narrative of the text's role in the larger literary tradition to overshadow other possible perspectives (Grice 34, 36-37). Grice's example is how overemphasizing the authenticity debate and the "mother-daughter nexus" obscures the fact that *The Woman Warrior*, like *The Joy Luck Club*, can also be located in a tradition of "writing about twentieth-century China," which not many critics have done (36). Taking a cue from Grice, I want to investigate the afterlife of *The Woman Warrior* in this essay; by the term *afterlife* I refer to the text's continued production of cultural activity beyond its initial appearance and fairly swift induction into the American canon. What happens when a canonized work becomes firmly ensconced in one critical tradition, one national literature, or one institutional usage, as succeeding generations of readers and teachers gradually leave behind the original circumstances of its production and dissemination? How does one keep a canonized text alive?

In material terms, a canonized text is kept alive by being kept in circulation by formal or informal instruments and institutions of cultural transmission, such as course syllabi in schools and colleges, journal articles and academic books, reading lists for degree exams, library collections, book clubs,[1] and translations into foreign languages, all of which incentivize publishers to keep the book in print. *The Woman Warrior* has benefited from all of the above mechanisms both in the U.S. and abroad; in that sense, it is alive and well. However, the substance of the text must also be deemed sufficiently relevant and compelling for cultural consumers to continue to engage it. May not a text so showered with accolades turn into a kind of cultural fixture that no longer sparks excitement? In the second decade of the twentieth-first century, what exactly is the cultural status of *The Woman Warrior*?

There is no doubt that *The Woman Warrior*'s has exerted considerable cultural impact over the last several decades, which is a most impressive form of afterlife. The book's commercial and critical success has empowered and inspired subsequent generations of Chinese and other Asian American writers, female and male, but especially female, to give voice to their experiences. Kingston has raised the visibility of and expanded the readership for Asian American writers, and enhanced publishers' willingness to take risks and publish them. In particular, Kingston's pioneering work in matrilineal narratives featuring two or three generations of strong, inspiring female ancestors has generated numerous similar stories, of which Amy Tan's bestsellers *The Joy Luck Club* (1989) and *The Kitchen God's Wife* (1991) are particularly marketable and well-known examples. Grice (39) counted about a dozen Asian American and Asian Canadian fiction and nonfiction titles with matrilineal themes which appeared since 1976, and cites one writer, Phoebe Eng, who directly pays tribute to Kingston in her title and theme: *Warrior Lessons: An Asian American Woman's Journey into Power* (1999). To this list I can add Ronyoung Kim's *Clay Walls* (1986); Rachna Mara's *Of Customs and Excise* (1991; Canadian); Denise Chong, *The Concubine's Children* (1994; Canadian); Lan Cao, *Monkey Bridge* (1997); Nora Okja Keller's *Comfort Women* (1997); Leslie Chang's *Beyond the Narrow Gate* (2000); Alice Pung's *Unpolished Gen: My Mother, My Grandmother, and Me* (2006); Kao Kalia Yang's *The Latehomecomer: A Hmong Family Memoir* (2008); Deanna Fei's *A Thread of Sky* (2010); and Jessica Hagedorn's *Toxicology* (2011).[2] Regardless of whether

---

1. Publishers have been keen to cater to the large number of female readers in book clubs—Oprah Winfrey's book club is particularly powerful—by providing an interview with the author and study questions, a practice that did not yet exist when *The Woman Warrior* first appeared. *Mooncake Vixen* is marketed with this apparatus.
2. The immensely popular *Wild Swans: Three Daughters of China* (1991) by Chinese British writer Jung Chang, comes from different traditions in English-language publications by Chinese-born authors—family sagas about historical upheavals in China and narratives about the Cultural Revolutions.

these authors directly and consciously drew upon Kingston, and regardless of any other factor that might have affected publishing, it is undeniable that the market for matrilineal stories was greatly expanded by *The Woman Warrior*. The sheer ethnic diversity in these authors' background—Cambodian, Chinese, Filipino, Hmong, Indian, Korean, Vietnamese—is partly a function of changing immigration patterns but also partly a measure of how receptive publishers have become to the mother-daughter trope. Relatedly, as a post-1965 Asian American female *Bildungsroman* par excellence (see the Kingston sections in Feng and Chu), *The Woman Warrior* has likewise re-ignited publishers' interest in Asian American women writing about their experiences growing up Asian and female (and frequently poor) in America.[3] Its influence on Chinese American women writers may be especially strong. From Fae Myenne Ng's *Bone* (1993) to Mei Ng's *Eating Chinese Food Naked* (1998) to M. Elaine Mar's *Paper Daughter* (1999), and as recently as Jean Kwok's *Girl in Translation* (2010), versions of the "leaving Chinatown" (or "not being able to leave Chinatown") narrative continue.

In addition to opening up discursive space for Asian American writers, *The Woman Warrior* broke into the American canon and occupied an assured place in college and graduate school curricula (even some high school curricula), thus ensuring generations of students will be introduced to it. One measure of the book's position in the academy is the existence of reference guides or introductory studies such as Shirley Lim's *Approaches to Teaching Kingston's* The Woman Warrior (1991); my own *Maxine Hong Kingston's* The Woman Warrior: *A Casebook* (1999); E.D. Huntley's *Maxine Hong Kingston: A Critical Companion* (2001); or Maureen Sabine's *Maxine Hong Kingston's Broken Book of Life* (2004). (And let us not forget the ever-helpful CliffsNotes—perhaps the true mark of the book's arrival in academe? And now we have SparkNotes online too!) On the scholarship front, from its secure perch, *The Woman Warrior* has provided linkages to mainstream critical discourses such as postmodernist theory; reinforced Asian American studies' foothold in the academy; challenged Western academic feminism to rethink its biases; and generated comparative scholarship on contemporaneous women of color writers like Alice Walker (*The Color Purple*, 1982); Sandra Cisneros (*The House on Mango Street,* 1984) and Louise Erdrich (*Love Medicine,* 1984). Further afield, as an integral part of the American literary canon, *The Woman Warrior* has traveled with American studies as the latter spread all over the world; in translation, it has spoken to

---

Still, the "three generations of strong Chinese women" motif might have contributed to its popularity when the book was introduced to the U.S.

3. Before the liberalization of immigration laws in 1965 led to radical transformations in the Chinese American population and in race relations, Jade Snow Wong's autobiography about growing up in San Francisco Chinatown, *Fifth Chinese Daughter* (1945), was once a bestseller in Cold War-era America.

many diverse readerships. In the Sinophone world, it has stimulated interest in Chinese American literary studies, which then broadened to Chinese diasporic and Asian American literary studies.[4]

It is fair to say that as time passes, some of the critical questions provoked by the success of *The Woman Warrior* may have gradually lost some of their urgency and acuteness. As with any other canonized text worth its salt, new critical approaches arise to take their place, giving *The Woman Warrior* a continued critical afterlife. For example, the "authenticity" and "representativeness" debates that used to rage around *The Woman Warrior*, along with the gender wars with which they were entangled (Cheung; my own "Autobiography as Guided Chinatown Tour?"), still form an obligatory item in the training of any Asian Americanist and are still productive of criticism (e.g., Madsen). However, as works published by Asian American writers of both genders and multiple ethnicities[5] increased explosively in recent years, the burden on individual writers to speak for his/her group has lessened, thus also reducing the stakes of the previous controversies.[6] Meanwhile, other critical frames came to the fore, based, for example, on form and genre (e.g., Ling; Feng; Davis); communications theory (e.g., Ludwig); psychoanalysis (e.g., Cheng; Eng); trauma studies (e.g., Griffiths), and so on. Thus one means of keeping a canonized text alive is for critics to continue their engagement with it, using ever-evolving conceptual frameworks. In this, *The Woman Warrior* is not very different from any other canonized text rich enough to be amenable to a variety of critical concepts and methods, in the same way that *The Adventures of Huckleberry Finn* has been fruitfully studied as a work of regional literature, an example of American humor, a variation on the archetypical hero's journey, an

4. In this essay I am limiting myself to English-language criticism. *The Woman Warrior*'s reception overseas is an important aspect of its afterlife that I will not have the space to address here.
5. Asian ethnicities represented in literature include not only the longest-established immigrant groups (Chinese, Filipino, Japanese, Korean, South Asian) or more recent, fast-growing ones (such as Vietnamese), but also small, previously less vocal ones (e.g., Burmese, Hmong, Laotian, Thai) as well as groups recently admitted under the Asian American rubric because of changing geopolitics and disciplinary regrouping (e.g., Afghans). The issue of whether Pacific Islanders should be included is a complex one and cannot be addressed here.
6. Kingston has expressed the hope that "some day when a great body of Chinese American writing becomes published and known, then readers will no longer have to put such a burden on each book that comes out. Readers can see the variety of ways for Chinese Americans to be" ("Cultural Misreadings" 63).

American mobility narrative; a race relations parable, a psychoanalytic tale, or a homosocial text.

And yet, while the criticism industry moves along according to its own intellectual and institutional logic, certain aspects of reader response to *The Woman Warrior* appear to be persistent: something about the "Chineseness" of the book seems to react with its lone status in the canon to facilitate certain types of readings. As far back as 1982, six years after the publication of *The Woman Warrior*, Kingston complained that critics, even authors of favorable reviews, misread her book in exasperating ways. "I expected *The Woman Warrior* to be read from the women's lib angle and the Third World angle, the *Roots* angle" (55), writes Kingston, but not the Orientalist one. From this perspective, an "inscrutable, mysterious, exotic" (56) "Chineseness" colored every image, every character, every incident—from Maxine's[7] hometown (*not* San Francisco!) to the nature of the "White Tigers" chapter, which, in Kingston's words, is "not a Chinese myth but one transformed by America, a sort of kung fu movie parody" ("Cultural Mis-readings" 57). The "Americanness" of the book, in other words, routinely got left out of consideration.

In the years since 1982, I have taught *The Woman Warrior* to undergraduates a number of times, and interestingly, virtually in every class one or two students would do exactly what Kingston's early reviewers did, ignoring words on the page in favor of preconceived notions in one's head. My students would mistakenly assert that the protagonist Maxine's hometown is San Francisco Chinatown, not Stockton (the former being much bigger and better known)—just as some of the professional critics did. A far more serious problem is to make an unthinking equation of "voice" with Americanness and "silence" with "Chineseness"—a sign of having fallen prey to the hegemonic national myth that in an immigrant family, an American-born child's ancestral culture represents nothing but passivity and irrationality, and must therefore be cast aside or transcended as she grows into "modern" American subjecthood. Such a reading completely negates a key point—if not *the* central point—in the book: namely, that Brave Orchid, though a transmitter of certain aspects of sexist, patriarchal traditional Chinese culture, *also* passes on certain *other* aspects of traditional Chinese culture, such as outspokenness, strength and bravery (expressed in different forms than their American counterparts), through "talk-story" and her own example. Maxine must disabuse herself of the stereotypes of "Chineseness" that she grew up with; her confusion is what propels her toward eventual self-integration and a viable, if uneasy, form of *Chinese American* subjecthood.

---

7. I adopt some critics' usage of using the author's first name to designate the narrator/protagonist of an autobiographical narrative, to distinguish her from the person who produces the narrative.

Though my observations on my students' partial text-blindness are strictly anecdotal, their resemblance to the earlier professional reviewers is intriguing. Is there something about *The Woman Warrior*'s "Chineseness" and lone existence in the American canon that somehow "freezes" it for certain readers? A vast body of critical scholarship and pedagogical reference guides has helped to keep *The Woman Warrior* in print and available to generations of new readers. Nevertheless, unless the research and exegeses reach the new reader *ahead of* her opening the book, would the encounter not recapitulate the frustrating reception history of *The Woman Warrior*?

Of course, one might reply that "That's what classes are for"—to help the reader sort through confusion. But even in a pedagogical setting, may not the weight of accumulating scholarship available to the teacher end up not counteracting but intensifying the tendency to see the text atomistically? Will there not be a danger that the venerated text would be lifted out of the historical context of its production and studied intensively and reverently, as a free-standing exemplum of literary significance or excellence, uncontextualized by historical time or place, or fellow writers and kindred works? In theory, all this could happen to any part of a national canon. A host of institutional factors—such as survey courses covering highly selective texts, sometimes predetermined by departmental reading lists or by anthologizers; or overworked instructors who don't conduct background research before teaching—could encourage responses detached from history. Nevertheless, the fact remains that the more a text is aligned with national ideology, and the more familiar to the majority population its narrative and descriptive details, the more one can assume some historical knowledge about it on the part of both teacher and pupil; dehistoricization might therefore be more easily forestalled. With an "ethnic" text like *The Woman Warrior*, fewer such braking mechanisms appear to be available.[8] (Thus, for example, students trained in the American school system would be much more knowledgeable about slavery in *The Adventures of Huckleberry Finn* than about the kind of slavery narrated by Brave Orchid, who tells Maxine she once purchased a "slave girl" in a market.) This problem is exacerbated by Kingston's interrogative mode of narration, putting out multiple versions of an alleged "event" (e.g., the No Name Woman's adultery); or denying something immediately after presenting it as if it actually did happen (e.g., Moon Orchid's husband-claiming trip); or the protagonist expressing self-doubt about her own past (e.g., did the retarded hulk really exist?).

---

8. One might also consider the effect of temporal distance: Whereas an obviously ancient text, or at least one far enough removed from contemporary life to seem "dated," would alert a reader to her possible ignorance, the events and conditions described in *The Woman Warrior* may be just recent enough to give readers of a certain age an inflated sense of their historical competence.

Broad cultural changes brought about by the passage of time further complicate the afterlife of *The Woman Warrior*. The figure of the woman warrior was once a bold rallying point and an inspiration for second-wave feminists and people of color seeking social justice and a voice of their own. The diversity debates and multiculturalist movement in the 1980s solidified *The Woman Warrio*r's status as representative both of Asian American and feminist concerns. However, the trickling down of feminist ideas into popular culture means that many new variations of the woman warrior figure from a variety of sources have appeared between the 1990s and today. ("Ethnic" concerns have had a harder time making similar inroads.) To name just a few: the Riot Grrrl movement in punk rock; Disney's cartoon *Mulan* (1998), whose version of Fa Mulan is known to millions more than Kingston's retelling; gun-toting Lara Croft and her sisterhood of scantily clad kick-ass fighters in video/computer games; in imported Asian film, Hayao Miyazaki's mythic Princess Mononoke (1997) and smart, gutsy and resourceful adolescent girl-heroes in *Kiki's Delivery Service* (1989); *Spirited Away* (2001); and *Howl's Moving Castle* (2004); as well as assorted female swordswomen and assassins in Hong Kong-style kung fu movies (which are technically much more sophisticated than the ones that stirred the young Maxine's fantasies in Stockton, with viewerships beyond ethnic enclaves). Most recently, we have the well pierced, well tattooed and erstwhile mohawked Lisbeth Salander, the dark avenger of the late Stieg Larsson's Millenium Trilogy, in both book and film form; and archer-princess Merida in the Disney Pixar animation *Brave* (2012), who can easily outshoot all her testosterone-poisoned suitors. A young girl growing up today will have seen more iterations of the woman warrior than Kingston's early feminist supporters who came of age in the 1960s and 1970s, could ever have imagined. All in all, it is not an exaggeration to say that since her first appearance, Kingston's woman warrior figure has lost quite a bit of its novelty, which may compromise its potential to serve as a role model for girls and women.

Last but not least, we should consider how, since *The Woman Warrior*'s publication, Chinese American communities have changed demographically, economically and culturally by new patterns of immigration and settlement (Zhou 41-90). Maxine's village-like Stockton Chinatown is a closed and inward-turning community, still suffering from decades of racist exclusion policy, cut off from "Red China" by a long embargo, and made paranoid by Cold War politics. (The ghost trope that pervades the book is thus not simply a sign of the family's dysfunction or the young girls' individual psychopathology, but an index of the Chinese American community's fraught situation in global geopolitics.) To its children, their "ancestral land," China, is remote and incomprehensible, while the mainstream American society to whose membership they are taught to aspire is less than hospitable. However, by at least the 1980s, "suburban Chinatowns" (Fong) have arisen,[9] as part of the "ethnoburbs" phenomenon (Li, "Anatomy"; see also Li, *From Urban Enclave to Ethnic Suburb*). These new Chinatowns are markedly different from the Chinatowns of old in place of origin, pre-immigration backgrounds, educational level, economic activities, cultural orientation, and so on.[10] (Of this, more later.) They also form part of a pattern of Pacific Rim "global cities," between which professional, middle-class and affluent inhabitants often shuttle. Immersed as they are in the discourses and practices of globalization, and feeling the confidence-boosting pull of a rising (or risen) China, these immigrants tend to be more open and assertive than Maxine's Stockton Chinatown relatives. The country onto which Maxine projects her imagined China—a land of shamanism, curious rural customs, and starving, suffering relatives under Communist rule—has been morphing at breakneck speed into a country more capitalistic, even futuristic, than the U.S.

In the face of all these changes, will *The Woman Warrior* remain relevant? Will Kingston's legacy endure, and if so, on what basis and in what form? If critical understanding of the text has, in a way, become ossified or frozen, how can that state of affairs be shaken up? How can one rehistoricize the icon, prompting reanimating questions appropriate to the new times, while doing justice to all that *The Woman Warrior* has done for the many constituencies it has touched over the years? Is it a contradiction in terms to say that a canonized text can be outdated? Does a canonized text ever need updating?

These questions bring me to the second part of this essay, which will focus on Marilyn Chin's *Revenge of the Mooncake Vixen*, published in 2009, 33 years after *The Woman Warrior*. In my view, among the numerous thought-provoking (sometimes just provoking) issues raised by Chin are precisely the type of questions I have posed above, and Chin appears ready to tackle them in an original, protean form of parody[11] that is at once respectful and irreverent, affectionate and pointed, hilarious and poignant. Evoking *The Woman Warrior* at numerous levels of detail, from theme, character, plot to imagery or even specific phrasing at times, Chin's exuberant extended riff on Kingston's book serves not only to pay grateful tribute to it, but also to 'update' aspects of it that

---

9. The term was apparently first used by Arax.
10. A recent "snapshot" of the Asian American community, based on a survey by Pew Research Center, "The Rise of Asian Americans," shows how Chinese Americans fit into the overall Asian American population.
11. The definition of *parody* is notorious difficult to pin down. See, for example, Bakhtin (127-28; 185-94); Genette; Hutcheon, *A Theory of Parody* (esp. 30-49). For the purposes of this paper, I will not adjudicate between various definitions of *parody* and related terms like *satire*, *irony*, *pastiche*, *travesty*, etc. I do find Hutcheon's formulations to be most relevant to my analysis of *Mooncake Vixen*. I will clarify my usage of the term as my argument unfolds.

might look out of touch with or inapplicable to today's world, thereby enhancing its continued relevance. Chin does this through preservation of certain features recognizable from *The Woman Warrior*, while altering them to reflect a new set of domestic American and global circumstances, new patterns of cultural flow, and new ideas about the meaning of womanhood.

Chin's project can be understood in terms of Linda Hutcheon's description of parody in *A Theory of Parody*. Hutcheon argues that parody presupposes "both a law and its transgression," or both "repetition and difference," and that "therein lies the key to its double potential: it can be both conservative and transformative, both 'mystificatory' [...] and critical" (101). "To parody is not to destroy the past; in fact, to parody is both to enshrine the past and to question it" ("Historiographic" 6). Furthermore, she suggests that "parody acts as a consciousness-raising device, preventing the acceptance of the narrow, doctrinaire, dogmatic views of any particular ideological group" (*Theory* 103). Parody has the "power to renew," to "revitalize" (115). It serves to "[open] the text up, rather than close it down" ("Historiographic" 7).

Without necessarily adopting Hutcheon's theorizing wholesale, we can see how her analysis serves as a useful gloss on Chin's stylistic, formal and thematic maneuvers. While reaffirming *The Woman Warrior*'s core relevance, Chin also gently points up the need to bring it up to date in order to reflect changes in the world, thereby rehistoricizing it. Hutcheon's "repetition and difference" description is particularly apt. The numerous parallels between *The Woman Warrior* and *Revenge of the Mooncake Vixen* would be virtually plagiaristic were it not for two glaring differences: the latter's self-conscious deviations from these similarities, and its complex tone combining affection and respect for the original, and inventive, exaggerated, at times simply impossible, take-offs from it. But while satire is certainly pervasive throughout Chin's text, it is essential to note that Chin never directs her teasing mockery against Kingston herself. Rather, the target is whoever is in danger, as reader, critic or scholar, of reading *The Woman Warrior* in a dehistoricized and simplistic manner and, further, taking his/her interpretations too seriously. The overall effect is, in fact, corrective—"consciousness-raising," in Hutcheon's formulation—except the term sounds too didactic and self-righteous, utterly out of character with the sheer wildness, hilarity, playfulness, and exuberance of Chin's tone and its infectiousness to the audience.

It is important to clarify that placing *The Woman Warrior* in a "hypotextual"[12] position is not meant to imply that it is so lacking in humor as to cry out for a deflationary treatment. *The Woman Warrior* is actually filled with situations and descriptions at once hilarious and poignant, such as the squid eye that keeps reappearing at meals until eaten (108); Brave Orchid's huge supply of home-brought snacks to avoid paying for food at the airport (132); or the

12. The term is Genette's; it refers to the source or previous versions of a text.

retarded "hulk" who Maxine fears she has been betrothed to: "His lumpiness was sending out germs that would lower my IQ. His leechiness was drawing IQ points out of the back of my head" (228). Clearly, a master of such comedic prose needs no reminder to lighten up.[13] Rather, it is misguided readers who take the original meaning of *canon* too literally who need their pretentiousness deflated.

We turn first to the "repetition" aspect of Chin's parody. The similarities between *The Woman Warrior* and *Revenge of the Mooncake Vixen* are impossible to enumerate in full; a few examples will suffice to support the argument that the former serves as the latter's source text. We begin with a shared theme, revenge. Revenge is a key element in Kingston's book, whether in the form of the No Name Woman's suicide that poisons the family well; the narrator's fantasized return to her home village, upon the completion of her warrior training, to kill her family's enemies; the "real life" Maxine's desire to take back her parents' properties lost to urban development; Moon Orchid's feeble attempt to punish her husband's new American wife; the characters carved on Mulan's back; or the very writing of the book to "report" (63) the many crimes against the girl-child and her family. Revenge is the first word in Chin's book title, and the first chapter, "Moon," subtitled "A Chinese American Revenge Tale" (13), depicts vengeance of biblical proportions, with many more tales of revenge to come in the later chapters: against oppressive elders, against one's sibling, against colonizers, against invaders of one's home and property, to name just a few.

For the girl-protagonists in both books—Maxine and the Wong twins Mei-Ling and Moon—their desire for revenge is fueled by the hardships and contradictions of growing up Chinese American, female, and poor. All three of them are American-born descendants of Cantonese immigrants engaged in "iconic" Chinese American occupations notorious for cheapness: running a laundry and a Chinese restaurant, respectively. Both Maxine's and the Wong twin's fathers, displaced, reduced to menial labor, and overworked, can only vent their unhappiness by spouting sexist proverbs and writing Chinese insults on the rude customers' laundry packet; or else swearing and spitting into the customers' food. The hapless fathers are seriously overshadowed by the powerful women in the family, Maxine's mother and Moon and Mei-Ling's grandmother respectively.

Yet the girls are ambivalent about the matriarchal figures who oversee their growing up, whom they perceive as lacking in understanding of their needs and feelings. The matriarchs are survivors par excellence, compelled to emigrate to the U.S. by—in a handy list provided by Chin—"a series of natural and man-made disasters: the Sino-Japanese war, famine, drought, flood, torrential rain,

13. Lowe places Kingston in the company of Ishmael Reed and Gerald Vizenor, as practitioners of "postmodern ethnic humor."

bloodthirsty warlords, the Nationalist debacle, Communist tyranny, even a long bout of the cholera epidemic" (25-26). Both Brave Orchid and Grandmother Wong are extremely hard workers, incredibly tough despite their diminutive size, not given to coddling the girls' delicate, "Americanized" sensibilities, practical and ruthless when it comes to conserving resources and feeding their charges—all characteristics of the "big eater" equipped to triumph over scarcity and pain (see my *Reading Asian American Literature* 18-76). The famous catalog of animals in the account of extreme eating in Kingston's "Shaman" chapter is paralleled in *Mooncake Vixen* by the grandmother's stealing and serving of an ornamental carp in a public garden ("Parable of the Fish"); as well as her almost-executed plan to serve the girls' pet pigeons as banquet squab in the restaurant ("Parable of Squab").[14] Brave Orchid's disdain for fine, tasty food, a symbol for assimilation (her favorite Chinese proverb being "If it tastes good, it's bad for you; if it tastes bad, it's good for you" [108]) is echoed in Grandmother Wong's warning in Chin's "Parable of the Cake." As Brave Orchid's puts it: "All heroes are bold toward food" (104).

While chafing under the matriarchs' demanding and restrictive upbringing, all three girls also derive strength from the "Chinese" wisdom—"Chinese" in quotation marks because the girls have no direct link to traditional Chinese culture and must resort to imagination and guesswork—dispensed by or embodied by their female ancestors. The matriarchs are both engaging tellers of stories, including tales of revenge, drawn from Chinese lore and their own rich store of life experience. While the girls are inspired to learn to become "women warriors," in varying guises and reaching varying degrees of success, they cannot escape humiliating and confusing assimilationist pressures from American society, having to live with rabid racists (Maxine's paint store boss who gleefully says "nigger yellow"; Moon's twin blond rapists; and others) and "normal" people who commit racism-inflected acts without awareness (Maxine's druggist who gives her candy for the wrong reasons; townsfolk who circulate gossip about Grandmother Wong's witchy occult practices).

On the social front, Maxine is self-conscious of her nerdy Chinese immigrant girl look in American eyes; is torn between the divergent ideals of Chinese and American femininity (e.g., 13; 14; 56; 200); and is driven to torture her double, the quiet Chinese girl, in the school bathroom in "A Song for Barbarian Reed Pipe." In *Mooncake Vixen*, the chubby young Moon has developed an obsessive crush on a pair of blond surfer twins, who string her along and then sexually assault her ("Moon"). Mei Ling is ashamed of her Asian single-lid eyes; in a magic realism moment, she wakes up with the round eyes but is immediately racked with ethnic and familial guilt ("Round Eyes"). In terms of academic performance, the model minority stereotype, originated and promoted by white

14. Pigeon-eating is an allusion not only to Kingston but also Fae Myenne Ng's *Bone* (30-31).

society for one set of reasons and subscribed to and enforced by Asian immigrants for another,[15] in a deadly synergy for the younger generation, hangs over the head of all three girls. To be the straight-A student growing into Ivy-League graduate, then high-earning professional, is the aspirational template held up by the matriarchs in both texts. The young Maxine does become a high achiever in American school, though she complains that her American life is still a "disappointment" (54); in adulthood, she achieves "American success," which she wraps around her "like a shawl" (62). Moon, after her initial sexual misstep, grows up to be a brilliant and famous scientist, a "genius" in her rebellious sister Mei Ling's eyes (22). In fact, both girls manage to get into Harvard.

Despite the above similarities ("repetition") between the two texts, the material world of *Mooncake Vixen* is so different that Maxine and her mother could hardly have imagined it. After the immigration reforms of 1965 took effect, "oldtimers" who brought over rural values, rituals, and proverbs have been eclipsed by Taiwan and Hong Kong immigrants, and later, beginning in the 1980s, those from mainland China. These immigrants are often from urban areas, already familiar with Western consumerism and American popular culture (especially through music and movies), as well as pan-Asian popular culture (e.g., Hong Kong kung fu movies; Japanese *manga* and *anime*; and Korean soap operas). Once in the U.S., they are enabled by technology to maintain Chinese cultural ties while navigating American society. They interact more directly with a multiethnic population. Grandmother Wong does business with not just the "white ghosts" and "black ghosts" evoked in *The Woman Warrior*, but also Samoans Hawaiians and Latinos (e.g., "Oh Lord! Here Come the Double Happiness Twins" and "Ten Views of the Flying Matriarch"). The latter part of *Mooncake Vixen* witnesses the rise of now-ultra-capitalist China, freer interchange between Chinese Americans and "Chinese Chinese." (In Moon's case, this takes the form of a hot affair with a "half-Chinese, half-Mongolian beauty" of a scientist; 181.) Globalization has ushered in a bolder, more hybrid, more wide-open, more cacophonous, and more rapidly transforming world for the Wong twins to grow up in. It presents them with new concerns, new political and social issues to contemplate, new models for womanhood; as a result, the idea of the woman warrior also needs to be revised, in sensibility and in method.

15. A common account of the function of the model minority idea is that Asian success is used to illustrate the fairness of the American economic system and show up the self-induced failures of African Americans (and later, Latinos). In other words, model minority discourse serves a disciplinary function on behalf of white society. On the part of Asian immigrant parents, creating model minority children appears to many of them to be the safest and most assured path to achieve upward mobility as well as to earn prestige in the immigrant community.

In *Mooncake Vixen*, Chin's carefully executed combination of numerous borrowings from *The Woman Warrior* with rich contemporary contextualization has the effect of at once of *updating* it and *dating* it: maintaining the ground-breaking work's continued significance today, while exposing the distance Chinese American women have traveled in the decades since Kingston wrote it. If *The Woman Warrior*'s canonization has rendered the historical circumstances of its creation and reception more or less invisible (or, if visible, confined to scholarly analyses and hardly trickling down to the general reader), thus encouraging the tendency to read statically, *Mooncake Vixen*'s parodic play lays them bare, dislodging Kingston's book gently from its discrete niche in the canon and restoring it to history.

I do not wish to imply Kingston's historical location is destined to make for a narrow mind. A diasporic consciousness is already traceable in *The Woman Warrior*, in the constant oral circulation of stories from China or a tenacious memory of the Cantonese emigrants' travails. This consciousness is to become even more pronounced and further elaborated in her later works—think of the epic journeys of the fathers in *China Men* (1980), for example, or Wittman Ah Sing's roots-seeking trip to China in *I Love a Broad Margin to My Life* (2011). Further, Kingston's sensibility may also be described as transnational in that it has been deeply marked the Vietnam War and its aftermath, and has expressed a fervent wish for world peace throughout her *oeuvre*, for example, the brother in Vietnam in *China Men*; Wittman's pacifist activities in *The Fifth Book of Peace* (2003); or the edited anthology *Veterans of War, Veterans of Peace* (2006). She is not bounded by the national borders of the U.S. However, it remains true that the monologic form of *The Woman Warrior* as a female *Bildungsroman* limits its ability to go far beyond the American-born, small town girl's subjectivity. Formal constraints conspire to facilitate the careless reader's tendency to impose familiar master narratives as a reading grid. Kingston has had to turn to other types of canvases in later works to accommodate her concerns for issues such as the traumas experienced by veterans, or world citizenship, or philosophical reflections on ethnic identity in the temporal context of aging and the spatial context of globalization.

Chin, in updating *The Woman Warrior*, has made formal choices that would throw the reader off balance whenever a reading position gets too comfortable. In structure, *Mooncake Vixen* is more similar to *China Men* than to *The Woman Warrior*, being a pastiche of first-person as well as omniscient narratives, now realist in mode, now magic realist; illusion-breaking comments from a metafictional speaker; fantasies and dreamscape; fables and parables; retellings of religious literature; quoted oral history; multiple alternative endings, and so on. The picaresque segments of *Mooncake Vixen* also recall Wittman's road trip searching for his grandmother in *Tripmaster Monkey*. The conceit of the twins driving around the San Diego area to deliver takeout food allows Chin to provide snapshots of a cross-section of multiethnic, multicultural American society. Between the sheer heteroglossic cacophony of voices in *Mooncake Vixen*, including that of a zygote ("A Zygote's Confession" 175-79), and the author's carefree, spirited jump-cuts through time, space, and genre, the reader will be dissuaded from over-relying on familiar forms such as the classic *Bildungsroman* or the American immigrant autobiography.

Three themes in *Mooncake Vixen* can be profitably analyzed from the perspective of "repetition and difference" vis-à-vis *The Woman Warrior*. First, the doubling of Kingston's protagonist into the "Double Happiness Twins," Moon and Mei Ling, is rich in parodic potential and conducive to rehistoricization. Layers of historical and cultural meaning can be teased apart in the figure of twinning. Chinese in the U.S. have long been stereotyped as faceless hordes; individual Chinese are seen as all looking the same and interchangeable. In the nineteenth century, the Siamese twins Cheng and Eng, known as the "Chinese twins" (because of their partial Chinese blood), were exhibited as freaks at one time before they became successful, naturalized U.S. citizens. (The magic theater show staged by Wittman Ah Sing at the end of *Tripmaster Monkey* mentions them.) For many impoverished Chinese American immigrants with traditional patriarchal values, as Ng notes on the first page of *Bone*, multiple daughters would mean multiple mouths to feed. Against this background, Chin boldly presents the "Double Happiness Twins," "double happiness" being a Chinese symbol made up of side-by-side characters for happiness/joy/good fortune, typically used for weddings. She defies the devaluation of women by associating girl twins with happiness. To misguided if well-meaning readers or critics eager to mine Chinese American literature for evidence of sexism against Chinese women, Chin's doubling of the protagonist throws a monkey wrench into their generalizing effort, as it is built into the novel that there cannot be one single "representative" Chinese American girl. The twins embody such vastly divergent qualities—Moon is studious and responsible, for instance, while Mei Ling is rebellious and sex-crazed—that any attempt to theorize "*the* Chinese American female subject" from them must confront this glaring heterogeneity.

Twinning may also be a rehabilitative allusion to Maxine and the voiceless Chinese girl she tortures in the bathroom; they are described as having the same haircut and demeanor, treated as interchangeable by others. Chin further confounds us by opening with "Moon," a short but packed tale about Moon's blond obsession, hunger for white acceptance, unrequited romantic love, and subsequent rude sexual awakening—which, as we read on, appear more Mei Ling-like than Moon-like. Thus even the convenient bifurcation into the obedient older child versus the rebellious younger one might be too schematic for Chin's purposes and requires some "complexification."[16] The fact that *The Woman Warrior* contains complaints against Chinese sexism that dovetail into Western feminists' dehistoricized preconceptions about "Third World Women" has, unfortunately, invited just such schematicism. That Chin deliberately uses the "double happiness" twinning to foil this tendency can be deduced when we compare it to the Tweedledee-and-Tweedledum-style comedic twinning of the blond beach boys; Julio and Coolio; Igor and Ivor; and Patsy and Ratsy, who are more or less interchangeable and static, simply serving as foils to the twins' *Bildung*.

A second repeated but different feature of *Mooncake Vixen* that allows Chin to at once pay homage to and critique, supplement and enrich *The Woman Warrior* is an unusual arrangement of the matriline in the Wong family. As suggested in the first part of this paper, *The Woman Warrior* is arguably the originator of the Asian (especially Chinese) American mother-daughter trope: it has been credited with—or blamed for, depending on one's perspective—iconizing the relationship and opening up the market for similarly themed books.[17] As one critic puts it in her review of *The Kitchen God's Wife*: "Whether by a quirk of literary fate or because it is their psychological destiny, Chinese American women seem to have won the world rights to the mother/daughter relationship" (Perrick 6). Surprisingly, although *Mooncake Vixen* fits into this tradition, Chin has chosen to show an absentee mother, demoted, as it were, from her usual place of honor as direct inspiration for the American-born daughters. The counterpart of Brave Orchid in *The Woman Warrior* is Grandmother Wong and not Mrs. Wong. Why such a shift? What could be Chin's purpose in "skipping a generation" in the matriline?

The most obvious, but not necessarily an adequate, explanation is that the author wants to avoid the mother-daughter transmission pattern that has, over the decades, become an eye-roll-inducing cliché about Asian American women. In my view, skipping a generation in the matriline has a rehistoricizing effect, much like Chin's other variations on Kingston's storytelling. As noted above, certain readers and critics of *The Woman Warrior* have the tendency to imagine a sort of faraway, mystical, timeless China filled with culture and suffering. Kingston's book does occasionally mention recent Chinese historical events that shaped the Chinese diaspora—the Japanese invasion for example, or the Communists' ascension to power in the mainland in 1949. Now such events, in another context, would be felt by mainstream American readers as exerting

---

16. Since "Moon" first appeared in 2003 in the anthology *Charlie Chan Is Dead 2*, the confusing effect may simply have been a matter of publication history. It is entirely possible that I am "overreading" here.
17. As far as I know, among current works of Asian American literature, only William Poy Lee's *The Eighth Promise* focuses on the mother-son relationship.

direct impacts on American history itself. Yet in the context of the Chinese American "talk story" in *The Woman Warrior*, this history might come across as having been time-shifted to a "timeless" (read "stagnant") realm, thanks to the protagonist's own naïveté and vague understanding as well as some readers' Orientalist propensities. With the grandmother's rare appearances, such as when she sends the whole family off to the theater in the face of a bandit raid, she becomes even more than Brave Orchid a symbol of frozen tradition. She is the source from which Brave Orchid draws her Chinese mother-essence, and Brave Orchid in turn tries to inculcate this wisdom into Maxine.

In *Mooncake* Vixen, Chin breaks the expected line of transmission and gives the day-to-day mothering role to the grandmother. Chin is thus able to preserve the notion of matrilineage without falling into the trap of reinforcing the formula, reifying East-West cultural conflict, and inadvertently replicating the American national myth of immigrant assimilation. Chin shows a grandmother exists "in time," in history, as a hardworking immigrant to the U.S. running a restaurant, interacting with workers and customers of various ethnicities, and raising two granddaughters singlehandedly. Further rehistoricizing is achieved in a thought-provoking (but sidesplittingly funny) chapter entitled "Monologue: Grandmother Wong's New Year Blessings: Or, They Can't Kill Us If They Don't Know Our Names" (39-47), in which the matriarch proves to be much more historically informed and politically aware than her well-schooled granddaughters.

At Chinese New Year, the twins are made to drive Grandmother Wong to visit three of her old friends—"old" meaning "aged"; "old" referring to long-term friendships; and "old" in the sense of having seen too much of life's sufferings. Mrs. Faith is a refugee from Sudan who has to raise her grandchildren after their parents were slaughtered by the Janjaweed; she still suffers from post-traumatic stress syndrome: "I worry, nightmare every night, can't sleep, carry big machete" (41). Grandmother Wong's gift to Mrs. Faith is a huge Chinese cleaver: "[Y]ou chop chop Janjaweed, lion, hyenas, demons—boil in big soup. Eat for New Year. Nobody bothers you" (42). (Readers familiar with *The Woman Warrior* would recognize echoes of the Sitting Ghost episode in the "Shaman" chapter.) Grandmother Wong's second friend, Mrs. Maria Gonzalez, lives in an apartment complex filled with drug addicts. Like her visitor, and like Mrs. Faith, Mrs. Gonzalez has to babysit her grandchildren—four of them. The children's mother, abandoned by her husband, is gone all day, working two jobs and studying to be an accountant. Mrs. Gonzalez has to wake up at 3 a.m. and make "one thousand Mexican dumplings [empanadas] to sell at market" (44). Grandmother Wong's gift to her is tiger-bone wine, a reputed powerful tonic. The third friend, Mrs. Goldstein, is a Holocaust survivor. She lives in a wealthy part of town, but has to take care of her grandson Benny, who plays dungeons and dragons all day. Benny's father has divorced his "good wife" for a "shiksa" and is too busy making money to care. Now Mrs. Goldstein is dying of cancer. Grandmother Wong commiserates with the Jewish woman by talking about German and Japanese atrocities. "She say, like killing cockroach, like killing lice. I say, cockroach, lice, we okay, we survived!" (45). Grandmother Wong's gift to Mrs. Goldstein is a duck dish from her restaurant, but more importantly, she promises to watch Benny—"make sure he does homework" (45)—after the old woman dies.

This short chapter has the simplicity of a folktale or fable, with its repetition of three's and the repeated motif of gift bearing. At the same time, the details are all drawn from recent history and contemporary life, faraway wars and local demographics. The grandmother's profound identification across race and class lines with the sufferings of women in diaspora is contrasted with the twins' superficial world view derived from their presumably progressive, multicultural schooling. Their education is Americentric (the girls' assignments are to memorize the Declaration of Independence—"life, liberty and hirsute happiness," in Grandmother Wong's memorable malapropism—and to write a paper on *Moby Dick*, "big fish story"); Eurocentric (they study the Holocaust and go on a field trip to a survivors' museum, but have not been taught about wars and genocides in Africa, Latin America, or Asia); preoccupied with superficial "political correctness" (they criticize Grandmother Wong's word choices: "Don't say 'black town,'" "Don't say 'Mexican town'"); and fosters short-sightedness (to the twins WWII is "ancient history"). The unlettered Grandmother Wong turns out to have a much more sophisticated picture of the U.S. not as a self-contained, exceptionalist nation superior to the rest of the world, but as just one member of a network of nations (and subnations) whose fates are bound together through war, trade, and migration in a globalized world. She understands "history from the bottom up" and, without benefit of Western feminist terminology and concepts, builds a "womanist" community of women of color through sustained acts of solidarity.

Even the twins' absentee mother serves a rehistoricizing function. The chapter "Duets," a tour de force of irony and a delightful parable of postcolonial revenge, takes place in Hong Kong and is made up entirely of a dinner conversation between the twins' mother, Mrs. Wong, and Mrs. Jones, whose son Douglas wants to marry Mei Ling. Mrs. Jones is a typical colonial: she and her husband manage to have learned not a word of Chinese after living thirty years in Hong Kong. She is racist and patronizing, insulting Mrs. Wong left and right while pretending to apologize for her insensitivity. But she proves to be no match for Mrs. Wong, a "tongue-fu" master with a keen sense of the history of Western imperialism and an impious sense of humor.

Without once overstepping her role as the perfect Chinese hostess, speaking modestly and self-deprecatingly at all times, sometimes deliberately playing into Orientalist stereotypes, Mrs. Wong manages to hide an anti-colonial barb in every civility, with the ultimate aim of driving away the white suitor. Unspoken vengeance can be decoded in seemingly innocuous factual statements. For example, when Mrs. Jones begins by complimenting Mrs. Wong for her English, the latter answers:

> No, no offense taken, Mrs. Jones. My people came from Guangzhou after the Communist takeover in '49. We're all strangers here. No, my English is quite substandard. I learned it in the orphanage in Hong Kong from an Italian nun named Sister Theresa. She had a thick Sicilian accent but purported that she spoke 'the King's English' and not 'the Queen's.' So my English is quite wretched really, but I guess it's tolerable for a Chinese housewife in Hong Kong. Most of my people refuse to even bother. (93)

This passage is really a history lesson in the Western powers' political and cultural colonization of Hong Kong, a flaunting of the Hong Kong Chinese's cosmopolitanism, and an adumbration of the locals' increasingly defiant attitude as the colony's reversion to Chinese rule in 1997 approaches. ("Look, look to the west, beyond Repulse Bay. Can you see the black clouds gathering up into a violent storm?" [99].) Through apparently random chit-chat about South African vs. Australian air conditioners, Mrs. Wong steers the conversation toward an indictment of white people beyond the British and Americans (Apartheid and the White Australia policy), until Mrs. Jones, now silenced, begins to sweat. Mrs. Wong taunts, "I am not afraid of 'the takeover,' are you?" (98). She concludes with a pointed pun: "You know what they say—in the Colonies, it's not so much the heat as it is the humility" (99)—humility which Mrs. Jones and her ilk must now develop in a hurry. While "Duets" could be considered structurally odd in that it is the only chapter in which the twins' mother plays a substantial role, the addition of this piece to the pastiche of *Mooncake Vixen* becomes understandable if we consider the rehistoricizng project that Chin is engaged in, as a part of her effort to provide a parodic alternative vision to *The Woman Warrior*, in which all the scenes set in China are either transmitted second-hand or else imagined.

Chin shares Kingston's interest in reimagining heroic ancestors and creating a usable matriline for contemporary young women. In the words of the narrator of *The Woman Warrior* contemplating her No Name aunt's suicide: "Unless I see her life branching into mine, the gives me no ancestral help" (10). The personal and cultural undertaking of extracting "ancestral help" is frankly constructivist, and as such it must contain an element of arbitrariness, even absurdity.[18] In Kingston's case, critical debates about "authenticity" and "representativenss"—about the nature of the "ancestral"—have somewhat

18. Gish Jen makes fun of this idea in *Mona in the Promised Land*. An African American young woman Naomi, newly constructivist thanks to a Harvard education, exhorts Mona's sister Callie to "forget you parents" and "choose" her own "ancestors." "Naomi herself claims for her ancestors a number of people not related to her" (129).

obscured the necessarily arbitrary nature of the effort. Chin, on the other hand, deconstructs the very process by which an image of an ancestor is made in two sections of *Mooncake Vixen*. Furthermore, as the author proceeds with her complex storytelling, elements outside of the feminist matrilineal project emerge, compelling the reader to revise the very idea of the matriline.

The chapter "Parable of Squab" is a relatively simple and benign version of a hagiographic narrative. Grandmother Wong is initially bent on slaughtering the twin's pet pigeons in order to serve them as squab at a wedding party at the restaurant. At the last minute, she experiences an attack of Buddhist conscience and trans-species identification:

> She decided that these were very wise and virtuous pigeons. And like herself they were survivors and were probably exiles from a different land. Their ancestors suffered both natural and man-made disasters. [...]. And besides, they were born hated creatures. People were prejudiced against them and despised them for no reason. It was a kind of racism! She decided after much thought that these birds deserved a long life. (37)

Grandmother Wong spares the pigeons and continues to take care of them even after the twins have left home for college; she dies on the roof "two days before her ninety-fifth birthday" in the midst of hand-feeding the birds. The twins decide to set them free.

Now the myth-making begins. As the neighborhood undergoes demographic changes, "the tale of Grandmother Wong's magnificent pigeons lives on in the children's imagination" (38). "And to this day, when young kids in the neighborhood see a group of pigeons flying high in a kindred flock, they point up and say, 'There they go, Grandmother Wong's pigeons, they're looking for her in paradise'" (38). Grandmother Wong has been beatified, in a process that is spontaneous, informal, and communal. Her legacy now belongs to the neighborhood, not just to her granddaughters (who actually have much more ambivalent feelings toward her).

Chapter 6 of *Mooncake Vixen*, entitled "Ten Views of the Flying Matriarch," further complicates our understanding of whether (and how) a heroic female ancestor can be known. The title, of course, recalls Wallace Stevens's "Thirteen Ways of Looking at a Blackbird," that classic statement of perspectivism; as well as the "Squab" chapter, with the flying matriarch replacing the flying pigeons. As expected, in this chapter we get views of Grandmother Wong from various members of her restaurant staff and of the community. The wild rumors circulating in town about Grandmother Wong are also spontaneous, informal, and communal, but they form the flip side to the "Squab" chapter: she is linked to dog-killing and dog-eating; occult powers like flying, hexing and telekinesis; superhuman martial skills; and secret vampire identity. This tiny old lady, all but four foot nine, is apparently capable of bloody deeds to repel invaders and punish assorted wrongdoers. But she is also a compassionate mother to everyone in her orbit who has been abused, who has suffered, who is lost and drifting, down and out, all regardless of gender, skin color, culture, or language. She saves the Blond Surfer Dude from a vicious attack and offers to become his grandmother when his own dies. She adopts Ming, a Chinese-Vietnamese "boat person," and sends him to college; she takes in an escaped sex slave smuggled into the U.S. from Hong Kong. In a scene that reads like a variation on "Monologue: Grandmother Wong's New Year Blessing," the old lady and the male members of the restaurant staff compare scars over drinks. This time, though, Grandmother Wong's compassion and empathy are not limited to people like her in age, gender, and circumstance. When asked about her age by the staff, she says, "I'm old enough to be your ancestor" (153). Thus, beginning with a matrilineal story, Chin has gradually built up a broader vision of Grandmother Wong's compassion.

Adopting a common postmodern technique, in this section Chin presents details about Grandmother Wong quite different from the ones she offers in earlier parts of the book. When Grandmother Wong dies in this section, she is not ninety-five but 124. She dies of a cold, not while feeding pigeons on the roof. The Wong restaurant is in Rose River (nicknamed Piss River), Oregon, not in San Diego, California. This narrative uncertainty is reminiscent of what Kingston does in *China Men*: presenting multiple accounts of male Chinese immigrants and refraining from settling on a definitive family history. Kingston's purpose might be to educate mainstream American readers by creating a composite portrait of early male Chinese immigrants; the inclusion of the chapter entitled "The Laws" is in fact deliberately pedagogical. On the other hand, Chin seems to use the proliferating and contradictory stories to shake loose any fixation on the specific attributes of one person, however remarkable, and to promote a Buddhist spiritual vision that encompasses sentient beings outside one's "own kind."

The third example of rehistoricization through "repetition and difference" concerns sexuality. Here the "repetition" is implicit: although *The Woman Warrior* opens with the onset Maxine's puberty, references to her sexuality are infrequent and oblique. Except for one mention or two of menstruation, Maxine's sexuality is out of the picture. The "difference" posited by Chin is therefore more supplementary than contrastive in nature. *Mooncake Vixen* is characterized by the assigning of excessive, out-of-control sexuality to one of the twins, Mei Ling, together with portraying her as the driven, aggressive desiring subject. The former is easy to understand as a feminist intervention to reclaim sexuality for women. Not to range too far afield, a number of Chinese and other Asian American writers before Chin have created sexually charged "bad girls" who break taboos and upset authority figures. They are "unruly women" who are "unable or unwilling to confine herself to her proper place. [...]. Her body is excessive. [...]. Her speech is excess in quantity, content, or tone" (Rowe 31; cited in Stetz 101). To name a few, Ginu Kamani's *Junglee*

Girl (1995); R. Zamora Linmark's *Rolling the Rs* (1996); Catherine Liu's *Oriental Girls Desire Romance* (1997); and Nami Mun's *Miles from Nowhere* (2009) all contain variations of this sexually transgressive figure. However, for Chinese Americans, a writer who uses this intervention risks replicating stereotypes of Suzie Wong, that childlike prostitute in the colonies, natural adorer and server of white men; or the oriental courtesan promising sexual ecstasy through secret ancient techniques. Again, some radical "complexification" is in order. Mei Ling's nymphomaniacal attacks, barely held in check by Moon's physical tackling, combined with her cartoonish martial exploits drawn from *manga*, *anime* and kung fu films (e.g., Grigsby; Ogi), define the woman as agent, not object. With hyperbolic and inventive details, Chin effectively neutralizes any unwanted associations with Asian sex kittens, mail-order brides (now internet-order brides), or geisha girls. The nympho-attacks also poke fun at the myth of the uncontrollable penis, which men routinely cite to absolve themselves of moral responsibility for sexual harassment and rape. When transposed to a woman—Moon feels a "pussy-control meter" is called for!" (58)—the idea is shown up as patently ridiculous beyond words.

The twins' wild sexuality is inextricable from their martial prowess, both expressions of female power (Saito; Arons; Cai). Moon and Mei Ling are both accomplished martial artists trained by Grandmother Wong. Kung fu being, like Asian female sexuality, burdened by exotic, stereotypical associations, Chin consciously sets about de-exoticizing it, at the same time fondly incorporating contemporary pop culture's iterations of it (Williams; Yound; Lo). Thus the twins' teacher is a real-life wise woman and kung fu master, who has to work in a restaurant to make a living. This is in distinct contrast to the fantasized old couple with traits of "immortals" (*xian*) on top of some misty mountain who trains Maxine's alter ego, the aspiring woman warrior, in the "White Tigers" chapter. The set of routines the girls are trained in from childhood, invented by their grandmother and named "the dance of the mooncake vixen" by her, freely scramble ancient *taichi* (*taiji*) and "Five Animals Play," an ancient form of *qigong*. The names of the postures and moves (71) are wicked take-offs on real terms used in Chinese martial arts. De-exoticization extends to the girls' attire. On their delivery rounds, an inebriated Mei Ling wears "a pair of three-inch platform flip-flops" (66), which, when energetically kicked off, decapitate a bystander's toupee, much like a ninja deathstar or the "stealth projectiles" (in Chinese, *anqi*; typically a small poison-tipped nail or dart) used to fatal effect in kung fu lore. Mei Ling's sexy, trendy footwear is reminiscent of "beautiful girl fighters" in Japanese *manga* and *anime*, such as Sailormoon and her fellow "guardians" in their short, short skirts and thigh-high, high-heeled boots (Grigsby). Although some knowledge of Chin's range of cultural references would allow one to fully enjoy her playfulness, without it one can still understand how her deliberate mixture of incongruities spoofs the serious image of the self-sacrificing, responsibility-laden avenger in Kingston's text.

Chan's deft handling of the twins' sexuality in the novel illustrates the precarious balancing act that the author has to maintain in order to pull off her rehistoricizing parody. How does one register outrage toward various forms of oppression and violence against Chinese (and by extension Asian) American women, how does one celebrate their strength and dignity, without becoming insufferably sanctimonious and didactic? Chin's solution is to go for broke, making everything so extreme that it would be impossible to take anything too seriously: to take offense would risk appearing obtuse or naïve. In this manner, Chin can make her pointed political critique while keeping a broad, tolerant perspective. Those who are her political allies and fellow-admirers of *The Woman Warrior*, she seems to want to remind us, are equally capable of foibles of excess. Ethnic absolutism and feminist dogmaticism come in for their share of gentle ribbing as readily as racism and sexism—exactly what Hutcheon sees as parody's salutary function: to act as "a consciousness-raising device, preventing the acceptance of the narrow, doctrinaire, dogmatic views of any particular ideological group."

An amusing example of Chin's disregard of "political correctness" is the way she uses the figure of the buff, blond white guy. Both the young Moon and the teenage Mei Ling ("Immigrant Dreams III [A Portrait of My Sister Sexing Tofu]") have lusted after specimens of this figure. At one point, Mei Ling is even engaged to Douglas, a white man ("Duets: Two Mothers, or How East and West Fought Over Hong Kong and How the Boxers Finally Won"). The white man - Asian woman pairing has been a sensitive topic of debate among Asian Americans for decades, ever since Cultural Nationalist days.[19] The "party line" among politically aware Asian Americans would be to attribute the phenomenon to Asian Americans' self-hatred and internalization of racism. Chin charges straight into the heart of this controversy by throwing political correctness to the winds, playing up and playing with the stereotype of the dumb-and-dumber surfer dude. She makes the figure of the surfer dude so laughable that the silliness of the twins' infatuation is shown up without a shot being fired, so to speak. Tongue in cheek, Chin describes the blond twins whom Moon falls for as "functionally illiterate [...] speaking in very short sentences between grunts or long, run-on sentences with ambiguous antecedent" (14). Now this could be a

19. For a recent (2011) chart showing national intermarriage rates for various ethnic groups, see "Who Is Marrying Whom" http://www.nytimes.com/interactive/2011/01/29/us/20110130mixedrace.html ?ref=us. Note that most recently (2012) the incidence of Asian-non Asian intermarriage has apparently decreased: http://www.nytimes.com/2012/04/01/fashion/more-asian-americans-marrying-within-their-race.html?pagewanted=all.

hazardous move: though part of the humor here stems from *American* gender and regional stereotypes (the Neanderthal-like macho man; and the male version of the Valley Girl who is all body and no brain), it raises the specter of Chinese cultural chauvinism (Sautman). However, Chin's wording and imagery are so outré that crying foul about reverse racism would put the protestor into the position of the dour killjoy: someone who wouldn't be able to recognize farce if it bonked him on the nose. Moreover, in the latter part of the book, in "Ten Views of the Flying Matriarch," Chin humanizes one version of the blond surfer dude, Jeremy, by giving the reader his sad back story and showing Grandmother Wong taking care of him. Thus Chin demonstrates by her action as an author that binary thinking, about race or anything else, needs to be transcended. She can give as good as she gets in stereotyping, she seems to suggest, but there is more to life than revenge, even with the best of political motivations.

Interestingly, the twins' upbringing, dominated by the immigrant philosophy of deferred gratification and repressed sexuality, is very similar to Maxine's, yet the end results are quite different. Maxine has been trained to endure pain and deprivation, to "eat bitter," and then, as soon as she hits puberty, has been sternly warned by Brave Orchid to never indulge her sexuality on pain of being obliterated from collective memory, like No Name Woman. The Wong twins too have been taught a similar code of values:

> One must not satisfy one's itch. One must sit up straight, cross one's legs, keep one's focus on one's homework and forge onward toward one's future. [...]. If you scratch an itch, that itch could turn into a wound. [...]. It could eventually mean the death of your tribe and your people. [...]. Self-control means self-abnegation [...]. In short, one must not disappoint the elders. One must sew up one's gonopore pussy for the common good. (87-88)

When Mei Ling, who "understands pleasure for its own sake," satisfies her "itch" without inhibition or shame, she is doing something "unheard of in immigrant behavioral history" (87). Yet not only does she not meet with a disastrous fate, she manages to fulfill her grandmother's and the Chinese immigrant community's model minority expectations without giving up her desires.[20] Even Moon, who once muses that she doesn't like either men or women (61), grows up to take a lesbian lover from China. Both sisters are shown to be self-determining sexual beings in adulthood. In short, they get to do with impunity what the No Name Woman is driven to suicide for doing. In this, *Mooncake Vixen* represents a marked departure from not only *The Woman Warrior* but a contrast with numerous Asian American autobiographies and fictions, in which family relationships predominate while adult love and sex are

---

20. In this she is reminiscent of a character in Linmark's *Rolling the Rs*: Orlando Domingo, who is at once a flamboyant cross-dresser and a straight-A model student the school principal and teachers don't dare to punish.

seldom shown. Chin appears to want to challenge the idea—one that *The Woman Warrior* might have inadvertently encouraged—that for the ethnic minority subject, leaving the family to enter "the larger (read 'white') world" represents the culminating moment of their growth, after which mainstream readers need no longer be interested in their lives.

Lest her feminist lesson on sexuality sounds too rigged, Chin laughs at her project at the same time that she affirms it. She can be as unsparing toward minority-generated orthodoxies as toward hegemonic national myths. In "Happiness: A Manifesto" (195-201), mindful of how Asian American and feminist academics have made much institutional hay out of *The Woman Warrior*, she makes the adult Mei Ling an Asian American feminist poet-scholar (specialty: "immigrant erotica" [166])[21] teaching ethnic studies and gender studies in a Southern California state university, much like the author herself, a professor at San Diego State University. (Indeed Mei Ling is Chin's Chinese given name.) While having raucous, mind-blowing sex with her lover, her teenage crush Donny Jesus Romero, Mei Ling is caught in an earthquake. "And suddenly, in slow motion, the giant metal shelf cradling the A through Z of major and minor female literary geniuses started toppling" (200). A roll-call of these writers, their names often intimately abbreviated and accompanied by apposite clarifications—"Chopin, Kate, not the pianist"; "Eliot (George and not Tom)"—include ancients (Li Ch'ing Chao) and contemporaries ([Trinh] Minh-ha, and yes, [Maxine] Hong Kingston); black, white, brown and yellow; gay and straight: "The shelves came tumbling down. O Mother Jericho, what a historical occasion! How appropriately synchronized with our orgasmic paroxysms!" (201). With such touches of comic genius, Chin enters the select company of funny Asian American women, a tradition surveyed in Stetz that includes writers and performers such as Margaret Cho, Sandra Tsing Loh, Gish Jen, and Lois Yamanaka (to which list I will add the Kingston of *Tripmaster Monkey*).

My analysis of Kingston and Chin above barely scratches the surface of the synergistic meanings created when the two are read against each: the non-historical spiritual[22] component in each has been left out of the discussion, in part due to constraints of length. Yet I cannot end this essay without pointing out both authors' paradoxical ability to move between "history" and a spiritual realm beyond history: a realm that much contemporary scholarship on "minority" literature lacks the vocabulary, concept or inclination to explore. While firmly embedded in sociohistorical particulars, and referencing concrete

---

21. Perhaps a playful, gender-switched allusion to Darrell Hamamoto. The professor of Asian American Studies at University of California, Davis is a scholar on male Asian sexuality in the media who produced a controversial pornographic film using Asian actors.
22. "Spiritual" is used here as an alternative to "religious," which to me refers more to organized religion.

instances of social injustices, *The Woman Warrior*'s account of self-cultivation ("White Tigers") and self-healing (the entire book) tends toward broad, Buddhism-tinged philosophical understanding of transcendence, forgiveness, compassion, and acceptance of contradictions (for example, the self-sacrificing self-immolating rabbit during Mulan's survival test [31-32] is an allusion to a well-known Buddhist tale[23]; Mulan's vision during her fast [32] is typical of vision quests): "I tried to make my mind large, as the universe is large, so that there is room for paradoxes" (35). *Mooncake Vixen* has two long chapters related to Zen (Chan in Chinese romanization) Buddhism: Chapter 4 entitled "After Enlightenment, There Is Yam Gruel [Thirteen Buddhist Tales]"; and Chapter 5, "Beasts of Burden," in which absurdist tales echo both animal folktales and fables from various cultures (especially those involving trickster figures) but also Zen *koans* that defy logic. The very last section of the book, "Three Endings," is at once postmodernist in flavor and reminiscent of ancient *koans*. Grandmother Wong emerges from rumors and gossip as the embodiment of Buddhist compassion. But her compassion is not incompatible with picking up a cleaver and fighting off attackers (or teaching others to do so). The material and the metaphysical dimensions coexist in Chin's world, in true Zen fashion.

The Woman Warrior hints at spirituality rather sporadically. Kingston's Buddhist beliefs, especially her pacifism, will become much more apparent in her later works, in particular *The Fifth Book of Peace* and *Veterans of War, Veterans of Peace*, and in her own efforts to help veterans overcome their traumas by holding writing workshops for them. Given that *The Woman Warrior* is typically the 'gateway' text into Asian American literature in the American academy, I venture to suggest two ways to sustain and enrich the afterlife of Kingston's first book. First, I highly recommend assigning *Mooncake Vixen* as an enjoyable and thought-provoking companion piece whenever *The Woman Warrior* is taught, for all the reasons I laid out earlier in this essay, but in particular, for *Mooncake Vixen*'s power to 'update' Kingston's text. Secondly, I recommend studying *The Woman Warrior* with one or more of Kingston's later, Buddhism-infused works. Grice has argued, rightly, I think, that Kingston's *oeuvre* as a whole is preoccupied with pacificism and offers her readers "a manifesto of pacifism for a contemporary era" (51). In recent years, Asian American scholars appear to express an increasing interest in spirituality (e.g., Yoon [1999]; Min and Kim [2002]; Iwamura and Spickard [2004]; Jeung [2005]). While most of these studies focus on the more tangible, externally observable (and "actionable") social phenomena, such as church or temple attendance, the institutional history of religious groups, and so on, others have

---

23. Apparently other cultures have similar legends; see http://en.wikipedia.org/wiki/Moon_rabbit.

begun to explore linkages between the spiritual and the political dimensions of Asian American life (e.g., S. Wong [2006]; Shan [2009]; D. Kim [2003]). Is every aspect of life "raced," "classed," and "gendered," or are there some areas of private psychic experience that don't lend themselves to these popular categories? What is the nature of suffering, and how is it related to political structure? What form should "right action"—understood not only in social activism terms but also in the spiritual sense—take? Perhaps one day these will be some of the questions addressed by students of Kingston?

Acknowledgments

I am most grateful to two people without whom this essay quite literally could not have been written: Sämi Ludwig, who invited me to contribute to this volume, was infinitely patient with me during its long gestation, and gave me valuable feedback on improving my draft; and Sunny Xiang, who conducted research for me with an intuitive understanding of what I needed and spoiled me with her promptness and efficiency.

My heartfelt thanks to Marilyn Chin, for supporting my project with enthusiasm and confirming that I was on the right track when I was working on it.

Works Cited

Arax, Mark. "Monterey Park: The Nation's 1st Suburban Chinatown." *Los Angeles Times* 6 April, 1987: 1.

Arons, Wendy. "'If Her Stunning Beauty Doesn't Bring You to Your Knees, Her Deadly Drop Kick Will': Violent Women in the Hong Kong Kung Fu Film." *Reel Knockouts: Violent Women in Movies*. Ed. Martha McCaughey and Neal King. Austin, TX: U of Texas P, 2001. 27-51.

Bakhtin, Mikhail. *Problems of Dostoevsky's Poetics*. Theory and History of Literture, Vol. 8. Ed. and trans. Caryl Emerson. Minneapolis: U of Minnesota P, 1984.

Cai, Rong. "Gender Imaginations in Crouching Tiger, Hidden Dragon and the Wuxia World." *Positions: east asia cultures critique* 13.2 (2005): 441-71.

Cao, Lan. *Monkey Bridge*. New York: Penguin, 1997.

Chang, Jung. *Wild Swans: Three Daughters of China*. London: Simon & Schuster, 1991.

Chang, Leslie. *Beyond the Narrow Gate: The Journey of Four Chinese Women from the Middle Kingdom to Middle America*. New York: Plume/Penguin, 1999.

Cheng, Anne Anlin. *The Melancholy of Race: Psychoanalysis, Assimilation, and Hidden Grief*. New York: Oxford UP, 2001.

Cheung, King-Kok. "The Woman Warrior vs. the Chinaman Pacific: Must a Chinese American Critic Choose Between Feminism and Heroism?" *Conflicts in Feminism*. Ed. Marianne Hirsch and Evelyn Fox Keller. New York: Routledge, 1990. 234-51.

Chin, Marilyn. *Revenge of the Mooncake Vixen*. New York: Norton, 2009.

Chu, Patricia. *Assimilating Asians: Gendered Strategies of Authorship in Asian America*. Durham, NC: Duke UP, 2000.

Cisneros, Sandra. *The House on Mango Street*. Houston, TX: Arte Publico P, 1984.

Davis, Rocio G. *Transcultural Reinventions: Asian American and Asian Canadian Short-Story Cycles*. Toronto: Tsar. 2001.

Eng, David. *Racial Castration: Managing Masculinity in Asian America*. Durham, NC: Duke UP, 2001.

Eng, Phoebe. *Warrior Lessons: An Asian American Woman's Journey into Power*. New York: Pocket Books, 1999.

Erdrich, Louise. 1984. *Love Medicine*. New York: Harper Perennial. 1993.

Fei, Deanna. *A Thread of Sky*. New York: Penguin, 2010.

Feng, Pin-chia. *The Female Bildungsroman by Toni Morrison and Maxine Hong Kingston: A Postmodern Reading*. Modern American Literature: New Approaches. New York: Peter Lang, 1997.

Fong, Timothy P. *The First Suburban Chinatown: The Remaking of Monterey Park, California*. Philadelphia: Temple UP, 1994.

Genette, Gerard. *Palimpsests: Literature in the Second Degree*. 1982. Trans. Channa Newman and Claude Doubinski. Lincoln: U of Nebraska P, 1997.

Grice, Helena. "'The Beginning Is Hers': The Political and Literary Legacies of Maxine Hong Kingston and Amy Tan." *China Fictions/English Language: Literary Essays in Diaspora, Memory, Story*. Ed. A. Robert Lee. Amsterdam: Rodopi, 2008. 33-55.

Griffiths, Jennifer. "Uncanny Spaces: Trauma, Cultural Memory, and the Female Body in Gayl Jones's *Corregidora* and Maxine Hong Kingston's *The Woman Warrior*." *Studies in the Novel* (2006) 38.3: 353-70.

Grigsby, Mary. "Sailormoon: *Manga* (Comis) and *Anima* (Cartoon) Superheroine Meets Barbie: Global Entertainment Commodity Comes to the United States." *The Journal of Popular Culture* 32 (1998): 59-80.

Hagedorn, Jessica. *Toxicology*. New York: Viking, 2011.

—, ed. *Charlie Chan Is Dead: At Home in the World*. New York: Penguin, 2003.

Huntley, E.D. *Maxine Hong Kingston: A Critical Companion*. Critical Companions to Popular Contemporary Writers. Westport, CT: Greenwood, 2001.

Hutcheon, Linda. *A Theory of Parody: The Teachings of Twentieth-Century Art Forms*. 1985. Urbana: U of Illinois P., 2000.

—. "Historiographic Metafiction: Parody and the Intertextuality of History." *Intertextuality and Contemporary American Fiction*. Ed. Patrick O'Donnell, and Robert Con Davis. Baltimore, MD: Johns Hopkins UP, 1989. 3-32.

Iwamura, Jane Naomi, and Paul Spickard, eds. *Revealing the Sacred in Asian & Pacific America*. New York: Routledge, 2003.

Jen, Gish. *Mona in the Promised Land*. New York: Knopf, 1996.

Jeung, Russell. *Faithful Generations: Race and New Asian American Churches*. New Brunswick, NY: Rutgers UP, 2005.

Kamani, Ginu. *Junglee Girl*. San Francisco: Aunt Lute Books, 1995.

Keller, Nora Okja. *Comfort Women*. New York: Penguin, 1997.

Kim, David Kyuman. "Enchanting Diasporas, Asian Americans, and the Passionate Attachment of Race." *Revealing the Sacred in Asian & Pacific America*. 327-40.

Kim, Ronyoung. *Clay Walls*. Sag Harbor, NY: Permanent P, 1986.

Kingston, Maxine Hong. *China Men*. 1980. New York: Ballantine, 1981.

—. "Cultural Mis-readings by American Reviewers." *Asian and Western Writers in Dialogue: New Cultural Identities*. Ed. Guy Amirthanayagam. London: MacMillan, 1982. 55-65.

—. *The Fifth Book of Peace*. New York: Knopf, 2003.

—. *I Love a Broad Margin to My Life*. New York: Knopf, 2011.

—. *Tripmaster Monkey: His Fake Book*. New York: Knopf, 1989.

—. *The Woman Warrior: Memoirs of a Girlhood Among Ghosts*. New York: Vintage, 1977. 1976.

—, ed. *Veterans of War, Veterans of Peace*. Kihei, HI: Koa Books, 2006.

Kwok, Jean. *Girl in Translation*. New York: Penguin, 2010.

Lee, William Poy. *The Eighth Promise: An American Son's Tribute to His Toisanese Mother*. New York: Rodale, 2007.

Li, Wei. "Anatomy of a New Ethnic Settlement: The Chinese Ethnoburb in Los Angeles." *Urban Studies* 35.3 (1998): 479-501.

—. ed. *From Urban Enclave to Ethnic Suburb: New Asian Communities in Pacific Rim Countries*. Honolulu: U of Hawaii P, 2006.

Lim, Shirley Geok-lin, ed. *Approaches to Teaching* The Woman Warrior. Approaches to Teaching World Literature. New York: Modern Language Association, 1991.

Ling, Jinqi. *Narrating Nationalisms: Ideology and Form in Asian American Literature*. NY: Oxford UP, 1998.

Linmark, R. Zamora. *Rolling the Rs*. 1996. New York: Kaya, 1997.

Liu, Catherine. *Oriental Girl Desires Romance*. New York: Kaya, 1997.

Lo, Kwai-Cheung. "Copies of Hollywood and Hong Kong Cinema: Rethinking the Woman-Warrior Figures." *Hong Kong Film, Hollywood, and the New Global Cinema*. Eds. Gina Marchetti and Tan See-Kam. London and New York: Routledge, 2007. 126-36.

Lowe, John. "Monkey King and Mojo: Postmodern Ethnic Humor in Kingston, Reed, and Vizenor." *MELUS* 2.4 (Winter 1996): 103-26.

Ludwig, Samuel M. "Concrete Language: Intercultural Communication and Identity in Maxine Hong Kingston's *The Woman Warrior* and Ishmael Reed's *Mumbo Jumbo*." Diss. Universität Bern. 1994.

Madsen, Deborah L. "Chinese American Writers of the Real and the Fake: Authenticity and the Twin Traditions of Life Writing." *Canadian Review of American Studies/Revue Canadienne d'Études Américaines* 36.3 (2006): 257-71.

Mar, M. Elaine. *Paper Daughter: A Memoir*. New York: HarperCollins, 1999.

Mara, Rachna. *Of Customs and Excise*. Toronto: Second Story P, 1991.

Min, Pyong Gap, and Jung Ha Kim, eds. *Building Faith Communities: Religions in Asian America*. Walnut Creek, CA: Altamira, 2002.

Mun, Nami. *Miles from Nowhere*. New York: Riverhead, 2009.

Ng, Fae Myenne. *Bone*. New York: Hyperion, 1993.

Ng. Mei. *Eating Chinese Food Naked*. New York: Scribner, 1998.

Ogi, Fusami. "Female Subjectivity and Shoujo (Girls) *Manga* (Japanese Comics): Shoujo in Ladies' Comics and Young Ladies' Comics." *The Journal of Popular Culture* 36 (2003): 780-803.

Perrick, Penny. "Daughters of America." Review of Amy Tan's *The Kitchen God's Wife*. *Sunday Times Book Review*. 14 July 1991:6.

Pew Research Center. "The Rise of Asian Americans." 2012. http://www.pewsocialtrends.org/2012/06/19/the-rise-of-asian-americans/

Rowe, Kathleen. *The Unruly Woman: Gender and the Genres of Laughters*. Austin: U of Texas P, 1995.

Sabine, Maureen. *Maxine Hong Kingston's Broken of Life: An Intertextual Study of* The Woman Warrior *and* China Men. Honolulu: U of Hawaii P, 2004.

Saito, Tamaki. *Beautiful Fighting Girl*. Trans. J. Keith Vincent and Dawn Lawson. Minneapolis: U of Minnesota P, 2011.

Sautman, Barry. "Theories of East Asian Intellectual and Behavioral Superiority and Discourses on "Race Differences." *positions: east asia cultures critique* 4.3 (Winter 1996): 519-67.

Shan, Te-hsing. "Life, Writing, and Peace: Reading Maxine Hong Kingston's *Fifth Book of Peace*." *Journal of Transnational American Studies* 1.1 (2009). (n.p.)

Stetz, Margaret D. "*Who's Hu*? And Where is the Asian American Women's Comic Tradition in Fiction?" *Studies in American Humor*. New Series 3.15 (2006): 101-12.

Tan, Amy. *The Kitchen God's Wife*. New York: Putnam 1991.

—. *The Joy Luck Club*. New York: Putnam, 1989.

Walker, Alice. *The Color Purple*. 1982. New York: Pocket Books, 1985.

Williams, Tony. "Hong Kong Martial Arts Women." *Asian Cinema* 17.1 (Spring/Summer 2006): 155-65.

Wong, Jade Snow. *Fifth Chinese Daughter*. New York: Harper, 1945.

Wong, Sau-ling Cynthia. "Autobiography as Guided Chinatown Tour? Maxine Hong Kingston's *The Woman Warrior* and the Chinese American Autobiographical Controversy." *Multicultural Autobiography: American Lives*. Ed. James Robert Payne. U of Tennessee P, 1992. 248-79.

—. "Circuits/Cycles of Desire: Buddhism, Diaspora Theory, and Identity Politics in Russell Leong's *Phoenix Eyes." New Asian American Writers and News from UK, Italy and Asia: Literature and the Visual Arts*. Vol. 1. Ed. with an Introduction by Lina Unali. 2006 [an ebook], pp. 7-25.

—. *Reading Asian American Literature: From Necessity to Extravagance*. Princeton, NJ: Princeton UP, 1993.

—, ed. *Maxine Hong Kingston's* The Woman Warrior*: A Casebook*. New York: Oxford UP, 1999.

Yang, Kao Kalia. *The Latehomecomer: A Hmong Memoir*. Minneapolis: Coffee House P, 2008.

Yoo, David K. Ed. *New Spiritual Homes: Religion and Asian Americans*. Honolulu: U of Hawaii P, in association with UCLA Asian American Studies Center, Los Angeles, 1999.

Yound, Suzie S.F. "How Positively Levitating! Chinese Heroines of Kung Fu and Wuxia Pian." *Killing Women: The Visual Culture of Gender and Violence*. Ed. Annette Burfoot and Susan Lord. Waterloo, ON: Wilfred Laurier UP, 2006. 219-35.

Zhou, Min. *Chinatown: The Socioeconomic Potential of an Urban Enclave*. Philadelphia: Temple UP, 1992.

Notes on Contributors

NICOLETA ALEXOAE-ZAGNI finished her PhD thesis right after the Mulhouse conference. It is one of the first dissertations in French focusing exclusively on Asian American writing. Simultaneously with her doctoral studies, she holds a tenured position of English instructor in a French *Higher Education College of International Agro-Development*, ISTOM. Within this research framework and following one year of research as visiting scholar at the *Center for the Study of Ethnicity and Race at Columbia University* (2005-2006), she has been active in the field of Asian American Literature—she has been involved in academic events, published several articles and presented papers on subjects relative to her area of scientific investigation (among which, most notably, a recent interview with Maxine Hong Kingston in *Revue Française d'Etudes Américaines* or a review of Shirley Geok-lin Lim's latest novel in *Women's Studies Quarterly*).

SIHEM ARFAOUI ABIDI, Ph.D., is a professor-assistant at the High Institute of Human Sciences of Jendouba, (Jendouba University, Tunisia), specialized in comparative studies and ethnic American writings. Her recent publications include "Reading Against African Children's Literature: Nationalist Didacticism in Fatima Mernissi's *Dreams of Trespass*," in *Writing Difference: Nationalism, Literature and Identity* (Atlantic Books, 2013); "Gish Jen and Diana Abu-Jaber as Trespassers of Cultural Homogeneity: Claiming Hyphenated Cultures," *Dynamisme des Langues, Souveraineté des Cultures* (Tunis, 2012); and "Imagining Shadows of an 'Empire in Denial': A Study of American *Imperium* in Diana Abu-Jaber's *Crescent Hyphen*" (2011).

CHENG LOK CHUA is Professor Emeritus of English (California State University, Fresno) where he has taught American Ethnic Literature and World Literature for 20 years. He has also taught at his native National University of Singapore and at Moorhead State University (Minnesota) where he chaired the English Department. He co-edits the MELA series (Multi-Ethnic Literature of the Americas) of Rutgers University Press, and has published on Asian American literature in *MELUS* and *Ethnic Groups* as well as on French literature in *Neophilologus*, *Modern Language Quarterly*, and *Revue des lêttres modernes*, having studied at the Université de Strasbourg. In 2012, he was a Fulbright Lecturer at Tribhuvan University, Kirtipur-Kathmandu, Nepal.

LAN DONG is Associate Professor of English at University of Illinois, Springfield. She is the author of *Mulan's Legend and Legacy in China and the United States* (2011), *Reading Amy Tan* (2009), and a number of journal articles and book chapters on Asian American literature and films, children's literature, and popular culture. She edited two books: *Transnationalism and the Asian American Heroine: Essays on Literature, Film, Myth and Media* (2010) and *Teaching Comics and Graphic Narratives: Essays on Theory, Strategy and Practice* (2012). Currently she is editing a two-volume *Encyclopedia of Asian American Culture*.

PIN–CHIA FENG is Distinguished Professor of the Department of Foreign Languages and Literatures at National Chiao Tung University, Research Fellow of the Institute of European and American Studies, Academia Sinica (joint appointment). She was NCTU's Provost of Academic Affairs, President of the Comparative Literature Association of ROC (2005-2008), President of the Association of English and American Literature (2009-2011), and a recipient of the 2007 and 2010 Outstanding Research Award of Taiwan's National Science Council. Feng received her Ph.D. in English from the University of Wisconsin-Madison (1994). She writes on issues of gender, race, and representation in films as well as in Asian American, African American and Afro-Caribbean literatures.

CHRISTINE LORRE-JOHNSTON is a senior lecturer at Université Sorbonne Nouvelle—Paris 3 and a member of ARIAS (UMR 7172). Her research is in postcolonial literature, Asian American literature, and postcolonial theory. She is the author of a study entitled "The Canon as Dialectical Process: A Study of Three Recent Chinese American Narratives" (*Revue Française d'Études Américaines* (RFEA), n° 110, December 2006), and of several articles and book chapters on Asian American and Asian Canadian writers, including Amy Tan, Lan Samantha Chang, Larissa Lai, Wayson Choy, Madeleine Thien, Ying Chen, and François Cheng.

SÄMI LUDWIG works at the UHA Mulhouse in Alsace, France. He received his education at the University of Berne (Switzerland) and has published a Ph.D. thesis on intercultural communication in Maxine Hong Kingston and Ishmael Reed, called *CONCRETE LANGUAGE* (published by Peter Lang in 1996), in which he outlines a theory of the metaphorical tracing of the intention constructions of the other. His second book is on the convergences of American Realism and pragmatist theory: *Cognitive Realism: The Pragmatist Paradigm in American Literary Realism* was published by Wisconsin UP (2002). Together with Rocío Davis (City University of Hong Kong) he edits *Contributions to Asian American Literary Studies*, the only European book series on Asian American cultural studies (LIT Verlag, Germany). In addition to intercultural issues and questions of cognitive and pragmatist approaches to literature, he is also interested in the big picture of literary history, in colonial American culture, and occasionally even writes on drama or poetry.

SEAN MATTIO is a graduate of the Department of English and Comparative Literature at the University of North Carolina at Chapel Hill. His research interests include the Gothic genre, the monstrous, fantastic, and macabre, as well as African American and Asian American literature. As with his work on *The*

Woman Warrior, he is particularly interested in the uncanny spaces in which these themes intersect. He ultimately hopes to return to school to pursue a PhD in English.

NELLY MOK is Assistant Professor of English at Montpellier 3 Paul Valéry University. She defended her Ph.D., *Writing Of or From the Margin in Twentieth-century Autobiographical Narratives by Chinese American Women Writers*, at Bordeaux 3 Michel de Montaigne University in 2011. She is the author of "Every path I/i take is edged with thorns: liminality in the works of Maxine Hong Kingston, Amy Tan and Kip Fulbeck," published in *Paradoxes de la réserve* (*Paradoxes of Reserve/Reservation*, CLIMAS Bordeaux 3, 2011), and of "Sabotaging the 'Cultural Bridge', Dropping the Hyphen: Love and Sexuality as Escape Routes in Gish Jen's *Mona in the Promised Land*," published in *Positioning the New: Chinese American Literature and the Changing Image of the American Literary Canon* (Cambridge Scholars Publishing, 2010).

JANNA ODABAS is a PhD student at the Graduate School of North American Studies, associated with the John-F.-Kennedy-Institute, at the Free University in Berlin. Her dissertation project focuses on ghost figures in contemporary Asian American literature. Before she started the program in Berlin in 2011, she earned her MA and BA degrees at the Leibniz University of Hannover.

From the period in which BUFF PARRY was featured in MHK's *The Fifth Book of Peace* (by way of the misspelled name Louis D. "Buffy" Perry) he went on to craft a bi-national life of research and publication in the sciences and arts including inventions in food & other industries, topology, agriculture. He has held/holds academic posts & completed two lengthy global lecture tours in India, Iran, Turkey, Libya, Europe, and N. America. Recently he has published on Leonard da Vinci under the high patronage of the President of the Republic of Italy Giorgio Napolitano; guest lectured in archaeology and Islam at Lakehead University, Thunder Bay, Ontario, and at the University of Alberta. He has designed an interdisciplinary course (linguistics, history, and theology) titled "The Unknown Holy Land"—a full credit course he teaches every fall semester in the U of Alberta's Department of Saint Stephen's College. Today he also designs fountains; write and stage musical theatre pieces; continue to invent topologues, etc. He remains the President and CEO of The Salai Project Inc; and of late has on request applied his avocation of code decipherment to a very high level profiling case involving the FBI, Homeland Security, and other specialists.

ANNA PEHKORANTA is completing her PhD dissertation entitled "Rewriting Loss: Melancholia, Ethics, and Aesthetics in Selected Works by Chuang Hua, Maxine Hong Kingston, and Fae Myenne Ng," at the Department of Art and Culture Studies, University of Jyväskylä, Finland, in 2013. Her research interests include Asian American literature, transnational and postcolonial fiction and theory, and feminist and psychoanalytical literary criticism. Her recent and upcoming articles and conference papers investigate topics related to these areas of research with an emphasis on questions of melancholia, ethics, and aesthetics in Chinese American women's fiction.

MARIE-CLAUDE PERRIN-CHENOUR is a Professor of American Literature at the University of Paris Ouest Nanterre La Défense, France. She has published several books on Women Writers (more particularly on Willa Cather, Kate Chopin and Flannery O'Connor) and many articles on American literature (including essays on Maxine Hong Kingston). She is also the editor of a volume on *Minority Literatures in the United States* in which she has contributed the chapter on Chinese American literature. She is currently writing a study of Edith Wharton's novel *The House of Mirth* for a French publishing house.

EULALIA PIÑERO-GIL is Associate Professor of American Literature at the Universidad Autónoma of Madrid, Spain. She has published numerous critical articles on Asian American and Asian Canadian women's poetry and fiction. She has co-edited *Visions of Canada Approaching the Millenium* (1999), *Voices and Images of Women in XXth Century Theater. Anglo-American Women Playwrights* (2002), and *Women and Art: Visions of Change and Social Development* (2010). She has translated and published the critical editions of Herman Melville's *Bartleby, the Scrivener* (2006) and E. A. Poe's *Short Stories* (1999). In 2012, she published the first critical edition and translation into Spanish of Kate Chopin's *The Awakening* (2012). As a result of her contribution to Kate Chopin Studies she has been appointed as a member of the *Kate Chopin International Society Website Advisory Committee*. She is currently working on Maxine Hong Kingston's poetry.

SILVIA SCHULTERMANDL is an assistant professor of American Studies at the University of Graz, where she teaches courses in American literature and culture studies. She has published widely on ethnic American literature, transnational feminism, and 9/11. She is the author of *Transnational Matrilineage: Mother-Daughter Relationships in Asian American Literature* (2009) and the (co-)editor of *Contemporary Asian American and British Asian Literatures* (2006), *A Fluid Sense of Self: The Politics of Transnational Identity* (2010), *Growing Up Transnational: Identity and Kinship in a Global Era* (2011), and *Contact Spaces of American Culture: Localizing Global Phenomena* (2012). Together with Erin Kenny (Drury University), she is the series editor of LIT Verlag's book series *Contributions to Transnational Feminism*.

BEGOÑA SIMAL GONZÁLEZ is Associate Professor at the University of Corunna, Spain. She has written extensively on ethnic literatures, particularly on Asian American authors. Her book-length publications include *Identidad étnica y género en la narrativa de escritoras chinoamericanas* (SP UDC, 2000), *Transnational, National and Personal Voices: Asian American and Asian Diasporic Women Writers* (Lit Verlag, 2004, co-edited with Elisabetta Marino), and *Uncertain Mirrors: Magic Realism in US Ethnic Literatures*, co-written with Jesús Benito and Ana Manzanas (Rodopi, 2009). Her articles have also appeared in different collections and journals (*MELUS* , *Journal of*

Transnational American Studies, Critical Mass, Revista de Estudios Norteamericanos, etc.).

AGNIESZKA SOLTYSIK MONNET is Assistant Professor of American Literature at the University of Lausanne. Her book, *Poetics and Politics of the American Gothic*, focused on the treatment of race, gender and sexuality in nineteenth-century literature. She has also published on transnational queer literature, melodrama and the war film, Edgar Allan Poe, Louisa May Alcott, and Diane Arbus. Her current research project is on representations of war and soldiers in American culture. Growing out of a lifelong interest in countercultural practices, she has recently organized a doctoral workshop on Altered States and Literature.

MANUELA VASTOLO holds a PhD in Comparative Literature from the University of Naples "L'Orientale." She has studied in China, the United States, Germany, and Canada. She is the author of several articles on Asian American and Asian Canadian writers and she is currently completing a book about the role of genres in Asian American Literature.

JOHN WHALEN-BRIDGE is Associate Professor of English at the National University of Singapore. Author of *Political Fiction and the American Self* (1998), he has co-edited (with Gary Storhoff) the SUNY series, "Buddhism and American Culture." This series includes *Emergence of Buddhist American Literature* (2009), *American Buddhism as a Way of Life* (2010), and *Writing as Enlightenment* (2010). The fourth volume, under review, is "Moving Pictures: Buddhism and American Cinema." His article "Multiple Modernities and the Tibetan Diaspora" has appeared in *South Asian Diaspora*, and he is writing a book for Palgrave's "Pivot" series on Tibetan self-immolation. While in Amherst, he will be completing a study of Engaged Buddhism and countercultural writing in postwar America, focusing on Gary Snyder, Charles Johnson, and Maxine Hong Kingston.

SAU-LING CYNTHIA WONG is Professor Emerita at the Asian American and Asian Diaspora Studies Program, Department of Ethnic Studies, University of California, Berkeley. She has published extensively on various aspects of Asian American literature, specializing in both Anglophone and Sinophone Chinese American and Chinese diaspora literatures. She is author of *Reading Asian American Literature: From Necessity to Extravagance*; editor of *Maxine Hong Kingston's* The Woman Warrior: *A Casebook*; and coeditor of *A Resource Guide to Asian American Literature* (with Stephen H. Sumida); *AsianAmerica.Net: Ethnicity, Nationalism, and Cyberspace* (with Rachel C. Lee); and two books on immigrant language education (with Sandra Lee McKay).

Contributions to Asian American Literary Studies
edited by Rocío G. Davis (City University of Hong Kong)
and Sämi Ludwig (Université de Haute-Alsace Mulhouse)

Alicia Otano
Speaking the Past
Child Perspective in the Asian American "Bildungsroman"
Child perspective is a symbolic narrative strategy that designs multilayered possibilities for meaning in ethnic writing. This book positions Asian American bildungsromane in the context of American writing about children, reading them through the lens of their narrators ,– the oftentimes dual child/adult perspe tive ,– to examine how narrative point of view nuances and shapes issues of personal, ethnic, and nation positioning. This approach privileges the authors' narrative choices and engagement with genre, revealing how these critical writerly decisions construct texts that signify on multiple levels, and dialogue productively with ofher texts. Their interpretation and creative negotiation of the key elements of narrat perspective lead us to uncover aspects which are constitutive of the successful manipulation of narrative voice.
Bd. 2, 2004, 184 S., 19,90 €, br., ISBN 3-8258-7748-5

Contributions to Asian American Literary Studies
Begoña Simal, Elisabetta Marino (eds.)
Transnational, National, and Personal Voices
New Perspectives on Asian American and Asian Diasporic Women Writers
LIT

Rocío G. Davis; Jaume Aurell; Ana Beatriz Delgado (Eds.)
Ethnic Life Writing and Histories
Genres, Performance, and Culture
This collection focuses on how literary creativity and historical inscriptions produce texts that require n anced readings of forms of life writing. These reflections support the use of life writing as an interpreta frame for historical information, validating it for historical discourse as the act of telling and writing on story affirms as it performs identity. Our approach is based on a methodology that connects genre studi and historiography, to arrive at conclusions about the writing of the history of globalization, immigratic racial and ethnic negotiation.
Bd. 4, 2007, 256 S., 24,90 €, br., ISBN 978-3-8258-0257-8

LIT Verlag Berlin – Münster – Wien – Zürich – London
Auslieferung Deutschland / Österreich / Schweiz: siehe Impressumsseite

Pin-chia Feng

Diasporic Representations

Reading Chinese American Women's Fiction

In Diasporic Representations, Feng examines the stratification of various diasporic subjectivities throug close reading fiction by Chinese American women writers of different social and class backgrounds. De ploying a strategy of "attentive reading", Feng engages the intersecting issues of historicity, spatiality, a bodily imagination from diasporic and feminist perspectives to illuminate the dynamics of deterritoriali zation and reterritorialization in Chinese American novels in this transnational age. The authors studied include Diana Chang, Edith Eaton, Yan Geling, Nieh Hualing, Gish Jen, Shirley Geok-lin Lim, Aimee Liu, Fae Myenne Ng, Sigrid Nunez, Han Suyin, and Amy Tan.

Bd. 6, 2010, 200 S., 29,90 €, br., ISBN 978-3-643-10831-9

LIT Verlag Berlin – Münster – Wien – Zürich – London

Auslieferung Deutschland / Österreich / Schweiz: siehe Impressumsseite